人文素质教育丛书

丛书主编 刘世平 王春阁

走进英国

Understanding the UK

艾蓉 朱雪梅 冯健 胡晶 编

WUHAN UNIVERSITY PRESS
武汉大学出版社

图书在版编目(CIP)数据

走进英国 = Understanding the UK/艾蓉等编. —武汉：武汉大学出版社,2017.7

人文素质教育丛书/刘世平,王春阁主编

ISBN 978-7-307-19312-3

Ⅰ.走… Ⅱ.艾… Ⅲ.英国—概况 Ⅳ.K956.1

中国版本图书馆 CIP 数据核字(2017)第 112274 号

责任编辑:顾素萍　　责任校对:李孟潇　　版式设计:马　佳

出版发行：**武汉大学出版社**　(430072　武昌　珞珈山)

(电子邮件：cbs22@whu.edu.cn　网址：www.wdp.com.cn)

印刷:湖北睿智印务有限公司

开本：720×1000　1/16　印张:19.5　字数:392 千字　插页:1

版次:2017 年 7 月第 1 版　2017 年 7 月第 1 次印刷

ISBN 978-7-307-19312-3　定价:37.00 元

序　言

根据《国家中长期教育改革和发展规划纲要(2010—2020)》和教育部《关于全面提高高等教育质量的若干意见》等文件精神，大学外语课程是高等学校人文教育的一部分，兼有工具性和人文性双重性质。就人文性而言，大学外语课程的重要任务之一是进行跨文化教育。语言是文化的载体，同时也是文化的组成部分，学习者学习和掌握外语这一交流工具，除了学习、交流先进的科学技术或专业信息之外，还要了解国外的社会与文化，增进对不同文化的理解，培养跨文化交际能力。人文性的核心是“以人为本”，弘扬人的价值，注重人的综合素质培养和全面发展。因此，高校应充分挖掘大学外语课程丰富的人文内涵，帮助学习者了解中外不同的世界观、价值观、思维方式等方面的差异，培养学习者跨文化意识，提高学习者社会语言能力和跨文化交际能力。

为了进一步提升学习者的人文修养，我们编写了人文素质教育丛书，旨在丰富学习者中外文化知识，培养学习者中外文化差异意识，帮助学习者提升文化和跨文化意识，提高跨文化交际能力。

《走进英国》(*Understanding the UK*)为人文素质教育丛书之一，是一本重点介绍英国历史与文化的中英文对照的教材，内容涵盖英国自史前到现代的各主要历史阶段(朝代)、英国的人文、自然特征、当今英国的政治体制、教育体制、宗教信仰、经济贸易、社会福利、传统习俗、生活方式、礼仪举止、休闲娱乐、文学艺术等方面。教材主要以英国历史和文化为依托，旨在提升学习者的语言技能，扩展学习者的知识面，提高学习者的语言和人文素质修养。

为了帮助学习者更好地理解，各章节的文章除了配以汉语译文以外，还对一些重点知识做了简明扼要的注释，每章节后设有一些理解性的问题和思考题。

本教材主要用做高等学校外语通识课教材，也可供其他英语和文化爱好者阅读。

编　者

2017 年 3 月

Contents

Chapter 1 Formation of the British Empire and Its Monarchies /1

1. 1 Early Settlers in Britain /1
1. 2 Roman Britain (AD 43 to AD 410) /3
1. 3 Saxon Britain (AD 450 to AD 779) /6
1. 4 Viking Britain (AD 793 to AD 1055) /8
1. 5 Norman Britain—Medieval Britain (1066-1485) /11
1. 6 Tudor Britain (1485-1603) /14
1. 7 Stuart Britain (1603-1649) (1660-1714) /17
1. 8 Georgian Britain /Hanoverian (1714-1834) /20
1. 9 Victorian Britain (1837-1901) /23
1. 10 Modern Britain (1902+) /25

Chapter 2 Facts and Figures of the United Kingdom /29

2. 1 The Countries and Names /29
2. 2 The Origin of the British Flag /32
2. 3 The Population Structure and National Identity /36
2. 4 The Landscape and Climate /39

Chapter 3 Political and Legal Systems of the United Kingdom /42

3. 1 Government System /42
3. 2 Major Political Parities and General Elections /45
3. 3 Legal System /48

Chapter 4 Religion and Beliefs /52

4. 1 History of Religion in Britain /52
4. 2 Church of England /55
4. 3 Religion and British Culture /57

Chapter 5 Economy and Social Welfare /60
5.1 Domestic Economy and Foreign Trade /60
5.2 Social Welfare /64

Chapter 6 Education System /68
6.1 Education Stages /68
6.2 Types of Schools /71
6.3 Homeschooling /74
6.4 University Degrees and Requirements /77

Chapter 7 Daily Life of the British People /81
7.1 Family and Marriage /81
7.2 Housing /83
7.3 Transport /87
7.4 Sports /89
7.5 Shopping /91
7.6 Pubs /95

Chapter 8 Famous People /98
8.1 Monarchs /98
8.2 Politicians /101
8.3 Scientists /104
8.4 Musicians /108
8.5 Film Stars /112

Chapter 9 Famous Landmarks and Top Attractions /116
9.1 Historic Sites and Landmarks /116
9.2 Castles, Palaces and Stately Home /120
9.3 Churches, Cathedrals and Abbeys /122
9.4 Museums and Galleries /125
9.5 Amusement and Theme Parks /128

Chapter 10 Etiquette and Manners in the UK /132
10.1 Courtesy Manners /132
10.2 Visiting People in Their Houses /135

10.3 Eating Utensil Etiquette /137
10.4 Business Etiquette /139

Chapter 11 Festivals and Holidays /144
11.1 Religious Festivals /144
11.2 National Holidays /147
11.3 Bank Holidays /150

Chapter 12 British Literature /153
12.1 Development of British Literature /153
12.2 Famous Writers and Their Works /162

Chapter 13 Mass Media /181
13.1 The Press (Newspapers and Magazines) /181
13.2 Television and Broadcasting /184

Chinese Version /188
第 1 章 大英帝国的形成及其历代君主 /188
第 2 章 英国概况 /204
第 3 章 英国的政治和法律体系 /210
第 4 章 宗教信仰 /215
第 5 章 经济和社会福利 /221
第 6 章 英国的教育体系 /226
第 7 章 英国人的日常生活 /232
第 8 章 英国著名人物 /243
第 9 章 英国著名景点 /256
第 10 章 英国的礼仪和礼节 /266
第 11 章 节日和假日 /274
第 12 章 英国文学 /279
第 13 章 大众传媒 /298

References /304

Chapter 1

Formation of the British Empire and Its Monarchies

British history has been a history of conquest and merger. It has experienced several dynasty changes and has been reigned by over forty Monarchies. It has undergone civil wars, international wars, occasional insurrections or rebellions, and widespread political intrigues amongst the aristocratic and monarchic elite. It has also seen a lot of destructive natural and man-made disasters. Yet it is those changes and events that contribute to the evolution and development of the country politically, militarily, diplomatically, economically, industrially, as well as linguistically and culturally.

The formation of the British Empire was the result of over 300 years' trade, immigration and the conquest by force. At the peak of its power, it was the largest empire in history. It used to be described as "the empire on which the sun never sets", because its expanse around the globe meant that the sun was always shining on at least one of its territories.

1.1 Early Settlers in Britain

Thousands of years ago, Great Britain was joined to Europe and was covered with ice. About 15,000 years ago, the weather became warmer. The ice melted and the sea level rose. Great Britain became an island about 8000 years ago.

The first known settlers of Britain were the Iberians. At about 3000 BC[1] during the New Stone Age, they came to Britain probably from the Iberian peninsula, now Spain. At about 2000 BC the Beaker Folk[2] arrived from the areas now known as Holland and Rhineland.

About 700 BC, during the Iron Age, the Celts began to arrive at Britain. The name "Iron Age" comes from the discovery of a new metal called iron. The Celts found out how to make iron tools and weapons. Before the Iron Age the only metal used in Britain to make tools was bronze, which is an alloy of copper and tin (hence the Bronze Age). The Celts lived across most of Europe, especially what are now Austria, Switzerland, southern France and Spain. The Celts came to Britain in three main waves. The Goidelic Celts (Gaels or Gaelic) were first to invade Britain in about 600 BC. They were later pushed into Ireland by their cousins the Brythonic Celts (Britons or British) who came over in 500-400 BC. The Brythonic occupied present day England and Wales. The small tribes of Brythonic Celts grew over the years into larger tribes with their own distinctive identities and living in their own special regions throughout Britain. By the time Julius Caesar Gaius[3] was ready to launch his Roman invasion of Britain, more Celts had crossed over from Gaul, and had settled in the south-east of England. These were largely the Belgic tribes—the Belgae, from what is now southern Belgium and northern France. The Celts living in Britain today stem from the two main types of Celt who invaded Britain: the Goidelic Celts—Scotland, Isle of Man and Ireland; the Brythonic Celts—roughly Wales and Cornwall.

The Iron Age Celts living in Britain were warriors and farmers who were skilled at making metal tools and weapons. There were lots of different tribes and each large tribe was ruled by a chieftain / king or queen. A chief would lead his warriors into battle in chariots pulled by horses. For defense against enemies, they built forts on hilltops. These hill-forts had earth banks and wooden walls.

In Celtic Britain there were no towns. Most people were farmers living in villages. They made round houses from wood and mud, with thatched roofs. There were no roads. People travelled by boats on rivers, or along muddy paths. Some British Celts crossed the sea to trade with other Celts in the Roman Empire.

There are still quite a lot of Celts living in the British Isles today. They live mainly in Wales, Cornwall, Scotland, the Isle of Man and Ireland.

The Celts of different tribes spoke a vaguely common language. The word Celt comes from the Greek word, Keltoi, which means barbarians and is properly pronounced as "Kelt". They were not called Celts until the 18th century. The Romans called these people Britons, not Celts. The name Celts is a "modern" name and is used to collectively describe all the many tribes of people living during the Iron Age. Celts called Gaels lived in Ireland.

The Celtic languages form a branch of the larger Indo-European family. By the time speakers of Celtic languages enter history around 400 BC, they were already split into several language groups, and spread over much of Western continental Europe, the Iberian Peninsula, Ireland and Britain.

Today, the term Celtic generally refers to the languages and respective cultures of

Ireland, Scotland, Wales, Cornwall, the Isle of Man, and Brittany, also known as the Celtic nations. These are the regions where four Celtic languages are still spoken to some extent as mother tongues. The four are Irish Gaelic, Scottish Gaelic, Welsh, and Breton; plus two recent revivals, Cornish (one of the Brythonic languages) and Manx (one of the Goidelic languages). There are also attempts to reconstruct the Cumbric language (a Brythonic language from North West England and South West Scotland).

☞ Notes

1. **BC**(Before Christ)　公元前(基督教会历法用)。BC 通常的书写形式是放在年代的后面，如 700 BC.
2. **the Beaker Folk**　宽口陶器人。公元前 2000 年左右，从荷兰和莱茵兰地区来到不列颠。宽口陶器人因他们墓穴中陪葬的宽口陶制容器而得名，他们带来了陶器制造工艺。
3. **Julius Caesar Gaius**　尤利乌斯·恺撒·盖乌斯(公元前 100—公元前 44)，罗马将军，政治家。

☞ Questions for comprehension and discussion

1. Who were early settlers in Britain?
2. What have you learnt about the Celts: what kind of people they were; where they came from? What were the Celts called by the Romans? What did the Iron Age Celts do?
3. What were the three main Celtic groups coming to Britain in the Iron Age?
4. What are the two main types of Celts in Britain today and where do they live?
5. What languages do the Celts speak? What are the characteristics of the Celtic languages?

1.2 Roman Britain (AD[1] 43 to AD 410)

British recorded history begins with the Roman invasion. The Romans came to Britain 2,000 years ago. They changed the country. The Roman Empire made its mark on Britain, and even today, the ruins of Roman buildings, forts, roads, and baths can be found all over Britain.

The Romans lived in Rome, a city in the centre of the country of Italy. In August 55 BC the Roman general, Emperor Julius Caesar invaded Britain. He took with him two Roman legions. After winning several battles against the Celtic tribes (Britons) in south-east England he returned to France.

The following summer (in 54 BC) Caesar came to Britain again landing at Walmer near Deal in Kent. This time he brought with him no fewer than five legions, 30,000 foot soldiers and 2,000 cavalrymen (horse riders). This time the Romans crossed the River Thames. After more fighting, the British tribes promised to pay tribute to Rome and were then left in peace for nearly a century.

Nearly one hundred years later, in AD 43, Emperor Claudius organised the final and successful Roman invasion of Britain. General Aulus Plautius led four legions with 25,000 men, plus an equal number of auxiliary soldiers. They crossed the Channel in three divisions, landing at Richborough, Dover, and Lympne.

The biggest battle was fought on the banks of the River Medway, close to Rochester. It went on for two days before the Celtic tribes retreated.

Many tribes tried to resist the Romans. It took about four years for the invaders to finally gain control over southern England, and another 30 years for them to conquer all of the West Countries and the mountains and valleys of Wales. The battle for Yorkshire and the remainder of northern England was still underway in AD 70.

The first Roman city was Camulodunum, which is known by the name of Colchester. It was the seat of Roman power and governance of Brittania until sacked during the Boudiccan revolt[2]. London was then established as a seat of governance, and only became important after the Camulodunum event.

The Romans called London "Londinium". The River Thames was quick way to transport goods between Britain and the Continent. The Romans saw this and built the town of Londinium around the river's main crossing point.

Why the Romans came to Britain is not quite certain. Two reasons have been suggested:

- The Romans were cross with Britain for helping the Gauls (now called the French) fight against the Roman general Julius Caesar.
- They came to Britain looking for riches — land, slaves, and most of all, iron, lead, zinc, copper, silver and gold.

Britain (not Scotland) was part of the Roman Empire for almost 400 years (AD 43 to AD 410)! The Romans divided England into four areas centred by the following towns London, Cirencester, York and Lincoln. The Romans left Britain because their homes in Italy were being attacked by fierce tribes and every soldier was needed.

The Roman Empire, even today, play an important part in the British lives. Many of the things originated from the Romans.

- The language was developed from the Romans. Many English words are derived from the Latin language of the Romans.

- The Calendar the British use today is more than 2,000 years old. It was started by Julius Caesar. It is based on the movement of the earth around the sun, and so is called the "solar calendar." The solar calendar has 365 days a year, and 366 days every leap year, or every fourth year.
- The names of the months are taken from the names of Roman gods and rulers. The month "July", in fact, is named after Julius Caesar himself.
- Laws and a legal system came originally from the Roman Empire.
- The Census. The Roman Empire was huge and included millions of people living over a large area. In order to keep track of all these people, the Roman Empire began the practice of taking a census, or a "count", of all the people within its boundaries every so often. Today, many countries like Britain take a census every 10 years.

The Romans also gave the British many other things, such as medical practice, great public buildings and straight roads, temples, central heating, baths, concrete and aqueducts (bridges for water). They made good use of Britain's natural resources. They also brought the new religion, Christianity, to Britain.

☞ Notes

1. **AD** (Anno Domini)　〈拉〉公元。AD 通常置于数字的前面，如：AD 375。但是与世纪（century）一起用时，AD 则置于 century 的后面，如：the third century AD。
2. **the Boudiccan revolt**　布狄卡起义。布狄卡的丈夫普拉苏塔古斯 Prasutagus 是不列颠一个名为爱西尼部落（Iceni tribe，凯尔特人的一个部落）的首领。普拉苏塔古斯去世后，罗马人于公元 61 年初夏并吞了爱西尼人在英格兰东部的领土。他的遗孀布狄卡领导了一场反抗罗马帝国占领军统治的起义。

☞ Questions for comprehension and discussion

1. When and why did the Romans invade Britain?
2. What do you know about Julius Caesar and his invasions? Who led the final invasion?
3. What names did Romans use for these places respectively: Britain, London and Colchester?
4. How long did the Romans stay in Britain? Why did they leave Britain?
5. What did the Romans contribute to Britain? What other things originated from the Romans?

1.3 Saxon Britain (AD 450 to AD 779)

The last Roman soldiers left Britain in AD 410, and then new people came in ships across the North Sea. The new settlers were a mixture of people from north Germany, Denmark and northern Holland. Most were Saxons, Angles and Jutes. There were some Franks and Frisians too.

The Angles and the Saxon tribes were the largest of the three attacking tribes and so they are often known as Anglo-Saxons. They were warrior-farmers, tall, fair-haired men, armed with swords and spears and round shields. They loved fighting and were very fierce.

Historians are not sure why the Anglo-Saxons came to Britain. Some sources say that the Saxon warriors were invited to come to the area now known as England, to help keep out invaders from Scotland and Ireland. Another reason for coming may have been because their land often flooded and it was difficult to grow crops, so they were looking for new places to settle down and farm.

They ruled in England for about 500 years (100 years longer than the Romans). However, unlike the Romans, the Anglo-Saxons never "went home"; many people living in Britain today have Anglo Saxon ancestors. The name England even comes from the Saxon word "Angle-Land".

Whether they settled peacefully, or drove the Britons from their lands, the Anglo-Saxons took control of most of Britain. However, they never conquered Scotland, Wales or Cornwall. The historian Bede, who lived in the 700s, wrote that Angles settled in East Anglia, the East Midlands and further north in Northumbria. Saxons moved in to Sussex (named after the "South Saxons"), Essex (East Saxons), Middlesex (Middle Saxons) and Wessex (West Saxons). Jutes settled mainly in Kent, Hampshire and the Isle of Wight. The seven principal kingdoms of Kent, Essex, Sussex, Wessex, East Anglia, Mercia and Northumbria have been given the name of Heptarchy.

Great Anglo-Saxon kings included Offa of Mercia (who built Offa's Dyke) and Edwin of Northumbria (who founded Edinburgh or "Edwin's burh"). But the most famous of all is Alfred, the only king in British history to be called "Great". He was King of Wessex from 871 to 899 and became king of all England.

The Anglo-Saxon settlers shared the same language. Each group had a leader or war-chief. A strong leader became "cyning" — Anglo-Saxon for "king". Each king ruled a kingdom and led a small army. There were many quarrels and wars between kings, to see who was the strongest.

The Roman Britons spoke Latin or local Celtic languages. The newcomers spoke their own languages, which in time became a language now known as Anglo-Saxon or Old English. The Anglo-Saxons themselves called it "Englisc". The country taken over by the new settlers became "England".

Some Britons settled down with the newcomers. Others moved west and north, taking their Latin-Celtic culture with them. Place names give clues to where the new "English" lived. A place-name ending in-ham, for instance, shows it was once a Saxon settlement. Ham in Anglo-Saxon English meant "village".

Anglo-Saxons name for towns was burh or borough. The word "borough" still appears in place names in Britain — Peterborough and Scarborough are two examples.

The first Anglo Saxon Villages were often named after the Chieftain (Leader of the village). This made it clear which tribe the village belonged to. These places often have the letters "ing" of "folk" somewhere in their name, often at the end. The first part of the name was most likely to have been the name of the local chieftain.

The people who lived in the "village" of Hastings were "Haesta's people" -Haesta was the chieftain. The people who lived in the "village" of Reading were "Redda's people" -Redda was the chieftain .

Later Anglo-Saxon villages were named after a feature in their surroundings rather than the name of the chieftain. Oxford got its name because it was a place where oxen were driven across a ford in a river.

The Anglo-Saxons laid the foundations of the English state. Firstly, they divided the country into shires, which the Normans later called counties, with shire courts and shire reeves, or sheriffs, responsible for administering law as comprehensive as any in the early medieval world. Secondly, they devised the narrow-strip, three-field farming system[1] which continued to the 18th century. Thirdly, they also established the manorial system[2]. Finally, they created the Witan[3] (council or meeting of the wisemen) to advise the king, the basis of the Privy Council which still exists today.

Anglo-Saxon identity survived beyond the Norman Conquest, and came to be known as Englishry[4] under Norman rule and ultimately developed into the modern English people.

☞ Notes

1. **the narrow-strip, three-field farming system** 窄条三圃田农耕制。这是英国中世纪的一种轮作制度，田地分成相间窄条，一条种植农作物，两条长牧草，轮换种植，以保持肥力。
2. **the manorial system** 采邑制度（封地制度）。中世纪在西欧实施的一种土地占有制度，以服骑兵役为条件，供终身享用，但是不能世袭。

3. **the Witan** 贤人会议，也称作盎格鲁-撒克逊国王的顾问团（Anglo-Saxon council, or the council of the Anglo-Saxon kings）。
4. **Englishry**（或 Englescherie） 英国血统的人。中世纪的英国对于英国人的合法的名称，特指本土的盎格鲁-撒克逊血统的平民，而非盎格鲁-诺曼精英。

☞ Questions for comprehension and discussion

1. Who were the Anglo-Saxons? Where were they from?
2. Why did the Anglo-Saxons come to Britain? How long did they stay there?
3. What are modern words for these words respectively: Anglia, Englisc, Sussex, Essex, Middlesex and Wessex? What is the word for the seven principal kingdoms?
4. In what ways were the Anglo-Saxon villages named?
5. What do the Roman Britons and the Anglo-Saxons call the languages they speak respectively?

1.4 Viking Britain (AD 793 to AD 1055)

The Viking Age in Britain began about 1,200 years ago in the 9th Century AD and lasted for just over 200 years.

About the year 800, bands of fierce raiders came across the North Sea and began to attack British coasts, just as the Anglo-Saxons had done 400 years earlier. They were the Vikings (also called the Danes although they didn't just come from Denmark). In time, like the Anglo-Saxons, the Vikings made their home here. They drove the Saxons out of part of the country and took it for themselves.

Vikings were also known as the Norsemen, which means "people from the North". They came from the three countries in Scandinavia (in Northern Europe): Denmark, Norway, and Sweden, where they were farmers, fishermen, seafarers and traders. Many Vikings were great travelers and sailed in their long ships to other parts of Europe and the Atlantic Ocean. Viking craftsmen made beautiful objects out of wood, metal and bone; Viking women were skilful weavers, produced fine, warm textiles.

Most Vikings were simply searching for better land for their farms. Their land was not very good for growing crops or rearing animals: Norway was very hilly, Sweden was covered in forests, and Denmark had a lot of sandy soil.

Some historians believe the Vikings left their homes because of over crowding. There was not enough good land for everyone to share. In a Viking family only the eldest son inherited the family farm so younger brothers had to make their living elsewhere.

The Vikings searched for treasures to make them rich. Britain was particularly a good place to raid, as there was much to steal.

The Vikings first invaded Britain in AD 793 and last invaded in 1066 when William the Conqueror[1] became King of England after the Battle of Hastings[2].

As the Vikings were attracted by the wealth of the Monasteries and the easy treasure to be found within, the first place they raided in Britain was the monastery at Lindisfarne, a small holy island located off the northeast coast of England. Some of the monks were drowned in the sea, others killed or taken away as slaves along with many treasures of the church.

The raid on Lindisfarne marks the start of the Viking migration from Scandinavia in 793.

In the years that followed, villages near the sea, monasteries and even cities found themselves besieged by these sea-based foreign intruders. Soon no region of the British Isles (Britain and nearby islands) was safe from the Vikings. They attacked villages and towns in Wales, Scotland, Ireland, the Isle of Man and England.

By 866 the Vikings had arrived in York. They made York (or Jorvik as they called it) the second biggest city in the country after London.

No matter how many times the Vikings were beaten, they always came back, and in the end all their efforts paid off. It was the Vikings of Normandy who finally conquered England in 1066 and changed British history for ever. King Alfred, Saxon king of Wessex, fought them in a great battle, but he could not drive them right away and had to let them have part of the country, called Danelaw, which covered an area roughly east of a line on a map joining London and Chester. The Saxons lived south of the line.

The Vikings settled in Islands off the coast of Scotland — Shetland, Orkney and the Hebrides, around the north and north west coast of Scotland, parts of Ireland — Dublin is a Viking city, the Isle of Man, small parts of Wales, Northumbria (which included modern Yorkshire), East Anglia, Leicester, Nottingham, Derby, Stamford and Lincoln.

The long-term linguistic effect of the Viking settlements in England was threefold: over a thousand Old Norse words eventually became part of Standard English; numerous places in the East and North-east of England have Danish names, and many English personal names are of Scandinavian origin.

Scandinavian words that entered the English language included landing, score, beck, fellow, take, busting and steersman. The vast majority of loan words did not appear in documents until the early 12th century; these included many modern words which used sksounds, such as skirt, sky, and skin; other words appearing in written sources at this time included again, awkward, birth, cake, dregs, fog, freckles, gasp, law, moss, neck, ransack, root, scowl, sister, seat, sly, smile, want, weak and window from Old Norse meaning "wind-eye". Some of the words that came into use are among the most common in English, such as to go, to come, to sit, to listen, to eat, both, same, get and give. The system of personal pronouns was affected, with they, them and their replacing the earlier forms.

There are more than 1,500 Scandinavian place names in England, mainly in Yorkshire and Lincolnshire (within the former boundaries of the Danelaw): over 600 end in -by, the Scandinavian word for "village" — for example Derby, Rugby, Whitby, Selby, Grimsby; many others ending in -thorpe (or -thorp, -throp or -trop) meant "farms", eg. Scunthorpe and Grimethorpe. Place names ending in -toft or -tofts. A -toft referred to the site of a house or a plot of land. These places mark the earliest Viking settlements.

The distribution of family names showing Scandinavian influence is still, as an analysis of names ending in -son reveals, concentrated in the north and east, corresponding to areas of former Viking settlement. Early medieval records indicate that over 60% of personal names in Yorkshire and North Lincolnshire showed Scandinavian influence.

☞ Notes

1. **William the Conqueror** 征服者威廉，英格兰诺曼王朝第一任国王(1066—1087年在位)，又名：威廉一世、征服王威廉 King William Ⅰ the Conqueror。英国国王威廉一世以"征服者"闻名于世。
2. **the Battle of Hastings** 黑斯廷斯战役，1066年10月14日，哈罗德二世国王(Harold Ⅱ)率领的盎格鲁-撒克逊军队和诺曼底公爵威廉一世(William of Normandy)的军队在黑斯廷斯(英国东萨塞克斯郡濒临加来海峡的城市)地域进行的一场交战。

☞ Questions for comprehension and discussion

1. Where did the Vikings come from? What kind of people were they?
2. Why did the Vikings come to Britain? What were their homelands like?
3. What was the first place raided by the Vikings, and why?
4. Where in Britain did the Vikings settle?
5. What was the long-term linguistic effect of the Viking settlements in England?

1.5 Norman Britain — Medieval Britain (1066-1485)

The Middle Ages in Britain cover a huge period, from the shock of the Norman Conquest, which began in 1066, to the devasting Black Death of 1348, the Hundred Years' War with France[1] and the War of the Roses[2], which finally ended in 1485.

King Edward Ⅲ of England (called "The Confessor" because he built Westminster Abbey) died on January 5, 1066, after a reign of 23 years.

William, Duke of Normandy, was a distant cousin of Edward the Confessor. It was said that King Edward had promised the English throne to William, but the Witan chose Harold Godwinson as king.

Harold was the son of Earl Godwin, the most powerful noble in England, and the brother of Edward's wife. He was born and bred in England and popular with ordinary people, but he did not have a direct blood link to the king and was not of royal birth. Harold had won a number of battles for Edward. He also said that it was Edward's dying wish that he, Harold, should have the crown (There were no witnesses to Edward saying this). The day after Edward died, Harold became King Harold Ⅱ of England.

So William led his army to invade England. In October 1066, during the important Battle of Hasting, William defeated Harold and killed him.

When William won the Battle of Hastings, he earned himself the title "Conqueror". He marched to London and was crowned King in Westminster Abbey on Christmas Day 1066.

The Norman Conquest of 1066 is perhaps the best-known event in English history. The Norman Dynasty established by William the Conqueror ruled England for over half a century before the period of succession crisis known as the Anarchy (1135-1154). It changed the course of History. It made England a closer part of Europe, and for the next three hundred years, the rulers and the nobility of England spoke French, not English.

The Norman victory changed the way in which England was ruled. Under the Saxons, the earls were often as important as the king, but now the king was firmly in control. He governed the whole country, and his rule was law. William the Conqueror replaced the weak Saxon rule with a strong Norman government and established a "Feudal System" in England. According to this system, the King owned all the land personally. He gave his Barons large estates in England in return for a promise of military service and a proportion of the land's produce. These estates were scattered far and wide over the country, so that those who held them could not easily combine to rebel the king. He increased the function of the traditional English shires (shares, autonomous administrative regions), which he brought under central control; he decreased the power of the earls by restricting them to one shire apiece. All administrative functions of his government remained fixed at specific English towns, except the court itself; they would progressively strengthen, and the English institutions became among the most in Europe. He governed the whole country, and his rule was law.

In 1085, in order to ascertain the extent of his new dominions and to improve taxation, William ordered the compilation of the Doomsday Book[3], which was published in 1086. The book is a manuscript record of the "Great Survey" of much of England and parts of Wales, similar to a modern census.

The *Doomsday Book* records all land and property, every mill and cottage, as well as every cow and pig. It also records the rights and duties of every landowner and every court. Thanks to the *Domesday Book* we know much about England in the eleventh century. It shows, for example, that by 1086, there were hardly any rich landowners of English birth left in England. It was a land ruled by Frenchmen, especially William's favourite Normans.

After winning the Battle of Hastings, William set about building a string of castles in strategic areas across the country. Two of his best known being the Tower of London and Windsor Castle. These ensured effectively that the many rebellions by the English people or his own followers did not succeed. By the end of William's reign over 80 castles had been built throughout his kingdom, as a permanent reminder of the new Norman feudal order.

William also opened the relations with the Continent and extended the civilization and commerce. Norman-French culture, language, manners and architecture were introduced. The Church was brought into closer connection with Rome, and the church court were separated from the civil courts.

William the Conqueror died in 1087. Normandy went to his eldest son Robert, and England to his second son William, who became William Ⅱ, but was known as William Rufus because of his red hair.

The line of Norman Kings ended in 1154, with Stephen's death. Henry Ⅱ, the first "Plantagenet" king, accedes to the throne on 19 December 1154. The Plantagenets were a huge powerful family not just in England but throughout Europe. King Henry Ⅱ's father owned vast lands in Anjou, an area as big as Normandy around the modern town of Tours. Henry's wife Eleanor ruled the even larger territory to the south called Aquitaine. Plantagenet Kings were thus the richest family in Europe and ruled England and half of France.

Their name came from planta genista, the Latin for yellow broom flower, which the Counts of Anjou wore as an emblem on their helmets.

Henry Ⅱ was not only king of England, but also ruled over most of Wales, Normandy, Anjou, Gascony and other parts of France (acquired through his marriage to Eleanor of Aquitaine). His reign represents a reversion in power back from the barony to the monarchical state in England; it was also to see a similar redistribution of legislative power from the Church, again to the monarchical state. This period also presaged a properly constituted legislation and a radical shift away from feudalism.

Under the Plantagenets England was transformed, although this was only partly intentional. The Plantagenet kings were often forced to negotiate compromises such as *Magna Carta*[4]. These constrained royal power in return for financial and military support. The king was no longer just the most powerful man in the nation, holding the prerogative of judgement, feudal tribute and warfare. He now had defined duties to the realm, underpinned by a sophisticated justice system. A distinct national identity was shaped by conflict with the French, Scots, Welsh and Irish, and the establishment of English as the primary language.

Under the Plantagenets huge advances were made regarding constitutional reform. The origins of Common Law originated under Henry Ⅱ as did trial by jury, and the first Parliament was held in 1265.

The English Middle Ages were characterised by civil war, international war, occasional insurrection, and widespread political intrigue amongst the aristocratic and monarchic elite.

☞ Notes

1. **the Hundred Years' War with France** 英法百年战争，从1337年到1453年英国和法国之间的一系列战争，贯穿于法国国王菲利普六世、约翰二世、查尔斯五世、查尔斯六世、查尔斯七世整个统治时期，以及英国国王爱德华三世、理查二世、亨利四世，亨利五世和亨利六世的统治时期。
2. **the War of the Roses** 玫瑰战争。中世纪的英国(1455—1487)，亨利六世、爱德华四世和理查三世统治时期的一系列内战。在长达32年间，同一个家族的两个分支为争夺英国王位所展开的艰苦斗争，他们均为爱德华三世的后裔，约克家族和兰开斯特家族。这场争夺王权的战争被称为玫瑰战争，是因为兰开斯特的标志是红玫瑰，而约克家族的象征是白玫瑰。
3. **the Doomsday（或 Domesday）Book** 《末日审判书》(史学家称之为《土地赋税调查书》)，是1086年由威尔士国王征服者威廉下令编撰的对英格兰和威尔士部分土地的“大调查”的记录稿。

4. **Magna Carta**(或 **Great Charter**) 《大宪章》。1215 年 6 月 15 日英王约翰被迫签署的宪法性的文件。其宗旨为保障封建贵族的政治独立与经济权益，又称《自由大宪章》或《1215 大宪章》。这份书写在羊皮纸卷上的文件在历史上第一次限制了封建君主的权力，日后成了英国君主立宪制的法律基石。《大宪章》是英国宪法的基础，创造了“法治”这一理念。时至今日，《大宪章》中的 3 个条款目前仍然有效，包括保证英国教会的自由，确认伦敦金融城及其他城镇的特权，以及所有人都必须有合法的审判才能被监禁。

☞ Questions for comprehension and discussion

1. How many years did the Middle Age Britain last? What big events happened during the period?
2. Why did William invade England? Who was Harold Godwinson?
3. What is the consequence of Norman Conquest?
4. What changes did the Norman Dynasty make to England? What is the Doomsday Book?
5. What happened in England under the Plantagenets?

1.6 Tudor Britain (1485-1603)

With Henry Ⅶ's accession to the throne in 1485, the Wars of the Roses came to an end, and Tudors would continue to rule England for 118 years. They brought peace to England after 150 years of virtually continuous warfare, encouraged new religious ideas, overseas exploration and colonisation.

Tudors were a Welsh-English family that ruled England from 1485 to 1603. The first Tudor king was Henry Ⅶ. He became king after the battle of Bosworth field, which ended the War of the Roses. He was the last king of England to win his throne on the field of battle. When Henry Tudor married Elizabeth of the Yorks, he created the Tudor rose, containing both the White Rose of York and the Red Rose of Lancaster. It symbolized the end of a struggle between York and Lancaster. He was successful in restoring the power and stability of the English monarchy. He founded a long-lasting dynasty and was peaceably succeeded by his son, Henry Ⅷ, after a reign of 23 years.

Tudor England had two of the strongest monarchs ever to sit on the English throne: Henry Ⅷ and his daughter Elizabeth Ⅰ. They are famous for many things, including Henry Ⅷ and his six wives, the exploration of America and the plays of William Shakespeare.

Henry Ⅷ was the first English monarch to be educated under the influence of the Renaissance, and his tutors included the poet Skelton; he became an accomplished scholar, linguist, musician and athlete.

Henry Ⅷ in his youth was much like William Shakespeare's description of King Henry Ⅴ — he was much more interested in arms and armor, swordplay, jousting, hunting, and women than in kingship. He wrote love poems and composed songs such as "*Pastime with Good Company*"[1]. Throughout his life, he also loved regal fashion — after all, what was royalty if one could not dress like a royal?

King Henry Ⅷ successfully united England and Wales under one system of government. The two countries were joined in 1536. The Laws in Wales Acts of 1535 and 1542 attempted to regularise the relationship between the two nations, by introducing the English legal system in Wales. English became the official language of administration.

Henry built a navy and made England stronger and more important in Europe.

Henry Ⅷ brought religious upheaval to England. When he became king, most people belonged to the Catholic Church, which was headed by the Pope, in Rome. Henry Ⅷ wanted a male heir, but his wife (Anne Boleyn) had not given birth to a son. Henry wanted to divorce her and take a new wife. The Roman Catholic Church refused to grant the divorce. In order to gain his divorce, Henry had to establish the Church of England and end Catholicism. He passed a law in 1534 making himself head of the Church of England. This led to the formation of the Protestant Church of England. The Protestant movement was known as the Reformation[2]. The year 1535 Henry ordered to close down of Roman Catholic Abbeys, monasteries and convents across England, Wales and Ireland. This act became known as the "Dissolution of the Monasteries"[3].

Henry Ⅷ had three children — Mary (by Catherine of Aragon), Elizabeth (by Anne Boleyn) and Edward (by Jane Seymour). Each became a monarch — Edward Ⅵ, Mary Ⅰ (or Mary Tudor) and Elizabeth Ⅰ in that order.

Elizabeth Ⅰ — the last Tudor monarch — was born at Greenwich Palace on 7 September 1533, the younger daughter of Henry Ⅷ and his second wife, Anne Boleyn. She came to the throne in 1558, when she was 25. Elizabeth liked hunting and enjoyed court masques (entertainment of poetry, songs and dancing). She was very well-educated and was fluent in six languages. She did not marry and was known as the Virgin Queen.

Elizabeth Ⅰ's rule is remembered as the Golden Age of English history. Under her rule, England advanced in such areas as foreign trade, exploration, literature, and the arts.

Elizabeth Ⅰ was one of western civilization's first true cult figures. Her tastes in fashion set the standard for the aristocracy and the rest of society; her love of music, drama, and poetry fostered an atmosphere in which many of England's greatest writers such as William Shakespeare found encouragement and financial aid.

Under Elizabeth's leadership, England experienced the true cultural reawakening or renaissance of thought. And at Queen Elizabeth's direction, Oxford and Cambridge universities were reorganised and chartered as centers for learning and scholarly endeavor.

During the Elizabeth Age, great adventurers discovered many new lands. Sir Francis Drake made the first voyage around the world claiming new lands for England and introducing new materials and foods. The American State, Virginia, is named after her.

The Tudor exploration brought to Britain many things such as more trade, discovery of tobacco, discovery of potatoes and maize, better knowledge of the world, colonising other countries, more accurate maps, better ship building, vocabulary/language, and better navigation. The peak of England's power at sea was the triumph over the mighty Spanish Armada[4] in 1588, which secured the nation's position as a world power.

The Tudor dynasty ended when Elizabeth Ⅰ died childless on 24th March 1603 after 45 years on the throne. The Throne passed to their cousins, the Scottish Stuarts, unifying England and Scotland.

During 118 years of Tudor rule, England had a lot of changes. The development of trade and industry was promoted, America was discovered and the Renaissance spread into England. All these helped to prepare the conditions for the establishment of the capitalist mode of production in England and the country became richer than ever before. The Tudor Monarchy thus served as the transitional stage from feudalism to capitalism in English history.

☞ Notes

1. **Pastime with Good Company** 《与好伙伴一起消磨时光》，也被称为《国王的民谣》(*The King's Ballad*)，是16世纪初英国国王亨利八世加冕后不久谱写的一首民歌，被认为是最著名的一部作品，成了文艺复兴时期英国和欧洲其他国家的一首流行歌曲。人们认为此歌是为阿拉贡的凯瑟琳(亨利的第一任妻子)而写。
2. **Protestant Reformation** 新教改革。英国都铎王朝时期的宗教改革，是16世纪欧洲宗教改革的重要组成部分。这虽然只是一场封建君主为了加强王权，维护封建统治而被迫发动的改革运动，却在客观上促进了资本主义的发展。在这场改革运动中，新兴的资产阶级和新贵族们支持了封建君王，但却同封建教会进行了艰苦复杂的政治和宗教斗争。
3. **Dissolution of the Monasteries** 解散修道院法令。1534年，英国议会通过了《至

尊法案》，宣布英国国王及其继承人是英国教会的唯一最高首领，一切旧惯例、规定、外国的法律和权威与此法令相抵触者均无效。修道院的解散，使英王与罗马教皇之间的关系进一步恶化。

4. **Spanish Armada** 西班牙无敌舰队。为16世纪后期西班牙著名的海上舰队，是由西班牙国王腓力二世在1588年所派出，意图征服英格兰却失败的舰队。无敌舰队之役是英西战争中一个大型的战役，同时也是英国历史中最有名的战争。由于损失百艘以上的大战舰及超过14000名士兵，国势鼎盛的西班牙从此停滞不前，英格兰则成为海上强权，开启了伊丽莎白一世的盛世。

☞ Questions for comprehension and discussion

1. Who was the first Tudor king? What did he do on his reign?
2. What kind of person was Henry Ⅷ? Why did he break with the Roman Catholic Church?
3. What do you know about Elizabeth Ⅰ? Why is Her rule remembered as the Golden Age of English history?
4. What did the Tudors do for Britain?
5. Why is the Tudor Monarchy so important in English history? (It served as the transitional stage from feudalism to capitalism)

1.7 Stuart Britain (1603-1649)(1660-1714)

The Stuart (Stewart) dynasty ruled Scotland (1371-1714) and England (1603-1714), with an interregnum of eleven years.

After Elizabeth Ⅰ died in 1603, King James Ⅵ of Scotland (from 1567) became king of England (as James I). He was the first monarch to rule both countries and the first to call himself "King of Great Britain". However it was not until 1707 that an Act of Parliament[1] formally brought the two countries together. England and Scotland officially became one country — Great Britain. The Stuarts were thus the first kings of the United Kingdom.

James's years as the first of the Stuart kings of England were often troubled years. Conflicts between Catholics and Protestants continued. Conflicts also arose between Anglicans[2] and Puritans. When James insisted on the "Divine Right of Kings"[3], he ran into conflicts with Parliament as well. He dissolved Parliament many times, ruling much of the time without a lawmaking body. In 1605, he survived the famous Gunpowder Plot. When the plot failed, bonfires were lit in celebration. Today, the date of 5th November is still annually celebrated in England as Guy Fawkes Day, named after the conspirator who was caught in the cellar with gunpowder.

King James Ⅵ and Ⅰ died in 1625 and his son Charles Ⅰ took the throne, becoming King of Great Britain and Ireland till 1649.

Charles Ⅰ hoped to follow his father's footsteps and tried to rule without Parliament. After seeing his rights as king slashed by Parliament, Charles miscalculated by swarming into the Palace of Westminster with several hundred soldiers to arrest five Members of Parliament and a peer he accused of treason. They all escaped, but London was scandalized and the king was forced to flee the city.

Now members of Parliament felt that no one was safe. King Charles felt that there was no turning back. Then he raised an army to go to war against the Parliament of his own country, which led to the Civil War in Great Britain.

The War was a series of armed conflicts and political machinations between Parliamentarians (Roundheads) and Royalists (Cavaliers). It lasted nine years (1642-1651) in three stages, also known as the First, Second, and Third Civil Wars. The first (1642-1646) and second (1648-1649) civil wars pitted the supporters of King Charles Ⅰ against the supporters of the Parliament, while the third war (1649-1651) saw fighting between supporters of King Charles Ⅱ and supporters of the Parliament. The Civil War ended with the Parliamentary victory at the Battle of Worcester on 3 September 1651.

The Civil War led to the trial and execution of Charles Ⅰ in 1649, the exile of his son Charles Ⅱ, and the replacement of the English monarchy with first the Commonwealth of England (1649-1653) and then with Oliver Cromwell, the Lord Protector (1653-1659). He held his post until his death in 1658, when his son Richard Cromwell briefly took over. England became a Republic for eleven years from 1649-1660, the only time when there was no King or Queen in Britain.

When Richard Cromwell lost the confidence of Parliament and abdicated, Charles returned to London in time for his thirtieth birthday and to rule Great Britain (Scotland, England and Wales). Charles Ⅱ was crowned King of Scotland in 1651. Charles saw London recover from the Plague (1665) and Great Fire of London (1666) and the Dutch Wars[4]. Many new buildings were built at this time. St. Paul's Cathedral was built by Sir Christopher Wren and also many churches still to be seen today. Having suffered a stroke, Charles converted to Catholicism on his death-bed and passed away a few hours later. As Charles Ⅱ had no children, his younger brother James succeeded him, and became King of England and Scotland (as James Ⅱ) from 1685.

James tried to make England a Roman Catholic country by forcing people to follow his

Roman Catholic faith. He was very unpopular because of his persecution of the Protestants, and he was hated by the people. He was forced to give up the crown in the Glorious Revolution[5] of 1688. Mary, daughter of James Ⅱ and her Dutch husband, son of William Ⅱ of Orange, were invited by parliament to be King and Queen following James abdication . They became joint monarchs as King William Ⅲ (1688-1702) and Queen Mary Ⅱ (1688-1694).

Queen Anne, sister of Mary Ⅱ, was the last of the Stewart monarchs. She was Queen of Great Britain and Ireland from1702 to 1714. She died at Kensington Palace in London aged 49. As none of her 18 children survived her, under the terms of the *Act of Succession* of 1701 she was succeeded by George, Elector of Hanover, great grandson of James Ⅰ, who was proclaimed as George I. He was the first of the Hanoverian monarchs.

☞ Notes

1. **Act of Parliament** 《国会法案》此处是指《联合法案》(Act of Union)之一，即1706年由英格兰国会通过的《苏格兰联合法案》和1707年由苏格兰国会通过的《英格兰联合法案》。它标志着苏格兰与英格兰的结合。
2. **Anglican** 圣公会、英国国教(Church of England)、英国国教徒。安立甘宗是新教主要宗派之一，与信义宗、归正宗合称新教三大流派，中国常称其为圣公会。该宗在英格兰为国教，称英国国教会。英国其他地区的圣公会均非国教，组织上也不从属于英国国教会。
3. **Divine Right of Kings**(或 divine-right theory of kingship) “君权神授”理论，是封建君主专制制度的一种政治理论。认为国王的权力是神授予的，具有天然的合理性，国王代表神在人间行使权力，管理人民。
4. **the Dutch Wars**(或 the Anglo-Dutch Wars) 盎格鲁·荷兰战争，17、18世纪英国与荷兰为争夺控制海洋贸易路线而发生的系列战争。
5. **the Glorious Revolution**(或 the Revolution of 1688) 光荣革命，或称1688年革命。1688年，英国资产阶级和新贵族发动的推翻詹姆士二世的统治，防止天主教复辟的非暴力政变。这场革命没有流血，因此历史学家将其称为“光荣革命”。君主立宪制政体即起源于这次光荣革命。

☞ Questions for comprehension and discussion

1. Why there was an interregnum of eleven years in the Stuart Monarchs? When did England and Scotland officially become one country — Great Britain?
2. What happened during James I's reign of England?
3. How did Charles Ⅰ rule as the King of Great Britain and Ireland?

4. What do you know about the Civil War? What was the outcome?
5. What did Charles Ⅱ experienced?
6. Who was the last of the Stuart monarchs? Why?

1.8 Georgian Britain /Hanoverian (1714-1834)

By the *Act of Succession* of 1701, on the death of Queen Anne, a new family of monarchs now took over the throne — the Hanoverians, from north Germany.

There were a lot of better qualified people available to be king of England — unfortunately most of them were Catholic. Prince George Louis was declared king of Great Britain, France and Ireland on 1 August 1714 at the age of 54. He set the record as the oldest monarch on accession in British history.

When George Ⅰ arrived in England, he knew little about British politics nor could he speak very much English. George therefore became very dependent on the Whigs[1] who had arranged for him to become king.

George spent most of his time in his beloved Hanover, in Germany. He made little effort to learn the English and customs of the country. So his lack of English prevented him from holding council and it led to the cabinet system of government. The cabinet is a council which contains the leaders of the biggest party in Parliament, and its chief is called the Prime Minister. Sir Robert Walpole, leader of the Whig Party, became England's first Prime Minister (1721 to 1742).

On 11 January 1727 George Ⅰ died and was succeeded by his son George Ⅱ, who preferred Germany to England, but unlike his father, learned to speak English.

In 1735, George Ⅱ gave Sir Robert Walpole a gift of 10 Downing Street, now the permanent London residence of the British prime minister.

The coming of George Ⅲ to the throne in 1760 brought the first British born king. He was the first monarch since Queen Anne to put British interests well before those of Hanover. He was the longest-serving Hanoverian monarch.

During his reign, Britain lost its American colonies but emerged as a leading power in Europe. Australia was colonised. His reign was the age of some of the greatest names in English literature — Jane Austen, Byron, Shelley, Keats and Wordsworth. It was also the time of great statesmen like Pitt[2] and Fox[3] and great captains like Wellington and Nelson. Many other famous events happened during his reign.

In 1769 Captain James Cook's first voyage to explore the Pacific made him the first European to land on New Zealand.

In 1770 he "discovered" the south east coast of Australia, landing in Botany Bay.

In 1773 the "Boston Tea Party" was the first sign of the troubles that were to come in America. The American Colonies proclaimed their independence on July 4th 1776. The loss of the American colonies brought about changes in Britain with the appointment of Pitt the Younger as prime minister, whose legislative programme was to bring about the end of royal power. In 1775 James Watt developed the steam engine. The 1790s saw the French Revolution. The wars with France continued until Napoleon's defeat at Waterloo in 1815.

In 1801, under the *Act of Union*, Great Britain (England, Scotland and Wales) and Ireland were united into a single political entity-the United Kingdom of Great Britain and Ireland . The English capital of London was adopted as the capital of the Union. George was thus the first king of the new nation.

In 1813, Jane Austen's *Pride and Prejudice* was published.

George Ⅲ ruled for 50 years and fathered 15 children. He was mentally unfit to rule in the last decade of his reign. His eldest son — the late George Ⅳ — acted as Prince Regent from 1811 and succeeded him when he died in 1820. George Ⅳ was deeply unpopular for his extravagant lifestyle and scandalous private life, but he was an enthusiastic supporter of the arts and his residences, particularly Carlton House and Brighton Pavilion, set new standards of taste.

George Ⅳ died on 26 June 1830. His only child, Princess Charlotte had died in childbirth in 1817, so the crown passed to George's brother who became William IV.

The death of George Ⅳ was not regretted by the nation.

William IV was king of the United Kingdom of Great Britain and Ireland from 1830. He became known as the "Sailor King" after joining the navy from just 13 years old.

His reign saw the passing of the *Reform Act* of 1832[4]. During his reign England abolished slavery in the colonies in 1833. In 1834 Fire destroyed the Palace of Westminster. 1834 *Poor Law Act*[5] was passed, creating workhouses for the poor. In 1836, Births, marriages and deaths must be registered by law. In 1836, Dickens published *Oliver Twist*, drawing attention to Britain's poor.

William died on 20 June 1837, without surviving children, and was succeeded by his niece Victoria, who was the only child of Prince Edward (Duke of Kent), the fourth son of King George Ⅲ.

☞ Notes

1. **the Whigs** 辉格党，17 世纪末在英国出现的两个正在形成中的政党——辉格党和托利党(the Tories)之一。"辉格"一词起源于苏格兰的盖尔语，意为马贼。"托利”一词起源于爱尔兰语，意为不法之徒。1679年，当议会讨论詹姆士公爵(即后来的詹姆士二世)是否有权继承英国王位时，议员们展开了激烈争论。赞成的人被对方称为“托利”，反对的人则被对方称为“辉格”。渐渐地，双方各自都以此自称。大约19世纪30年代，托利党改称保守党，辉格党改称自由党。

2. **Pitt** 皮特，此处是指英国两位政治家老威廉·皮特(William Pitt the Elder)和小威廉·皮特(William Pitt the Younger)：老威廉·皮特，第一代查塔姆伯爵(William Pitt, 1st Earl of Chatham, 1708.11—1778.5)，英国辉格党政治家、首相，7年战争中英国的实际领导人。小威廉·皮特(1759—1806)，是查塔姆伯爵老威廉·皮特的次子，于1781年进入政坛，是英国的一位政治家和出色的演说家。小威廉·皮特毕业于剑桥大学，1784年，在英王乔治三世的全力支持下就任首相，是英国历史上最年轻的首相，就职时年仅24岁，同时也是英国历史上任期最长的首相之一(1783—1801, 1804—1806)，两个任期加起来将近19年，仅次于第一位英国首相罗伯特·沃波尔(Robert Walpole)。小威廉·皮特更被公认为英国首相中的“第一智者”。
3. **Fox** 查尔斯·詹姆士·福克斯(Charles James Fox, 1749.1—1806.9)，英国辉格党资深政治家，自18世纪后期至19世纪初年任下议院议员长达38年之久，是皮特担任首相期间的主要对手。
4. **The Reform Act of 1832** 《1832年改革法案》，或《人民代表法》(The Representation of the People Act 1832)，也称为《大改革法案》或《第一次改革法案》(Great Reform Act or First Reform Act)，是英国在1832年通过的关于扩大下议院选民基础的法案。该议案改变了下议院由保守派独占的状态，加入了中产阶级的势力，是英国议会史上的一次重大改革。
5. **1834 Poor Law Act** 《济贫法》，也叫《济贫法修正案》(The Poor Law Amendment Act 1834 (PLAA))，1834年英国议会通过的一项取代1601年发布的济贫法，史称《新济贫法》(New Poor Law)。这项新法律取消对无业贫民的一切金钱和实物的救济，只允许一种救济方式，即把他们收容到习艺所中。

☞ Questions for comprehension and discussion

1. Why was Prince George Louis declared king of Great Britain? What record did he set as monarch in British history?
2. Was George Ⅰ a responsible king of Britain? Why not?
3. What was George Ⅲ different from George Ⅰ and George Ⅱ? What important events happened during his reign? How many years altogether did he occupy the throne in Britain?
4. Why George Ⅳ was deeply unpopular?

5. What important events happened during the reign of William IV?

1.9 Victorian Britain (1837-1901)

Victoria was Queen of the United Kingdom of Great Britain and Ireland (1837-1901) and empress of India (1876-1901).

Victoria's first language was German. At three years old she learnt to speak English and French. Later she learnt to speak Hindustani because she was ruler of India as well. Victoria didn't go to school. She was taught at home. As well as learning languages, Victoria studied history, geography, and the *Bible*. She was taught how to play the piano and learned how to paint, a hobby that she enjoyed into her 60s. Queen Victoria loved singing and going to the opera.

Queen Victoria was only 18 when she came to the throne. She reigned for exactly sixty-three years, seven months, and two days (June 20, 1837-January 22, 1901), which is longer than that of any other British monarch and the longest of any female monarch in history, and is known as the Victorian era. It was a period of industrial, cultural, political, scientific, and military change within the United Kingdom, and was marked by a great expansion of the British Empire.

Whilst Victoria was Queen there was a tremendous change in the lives of British people: Britain became the most powerful country in the world, the most visible sign of economic growth was the steady increase in Britain's population. Since the Romans it had fluctuated between two and six million, but from 1750 it grew exponentially, nearly trebling in a century to reach 21 million by 1851. This increased to 37 million by 1901. The increasing number of people caused a huge demand for food, clothes and housing. Factories and machines were built to meet this demand and new towns grew up, changing the landscape and the ways people lived and worked. Railways, originally built to transport goods, meant people could travel easily around the country for the first time. Railways brought new foods to towns and cities.

When Queen Victoria opened the Great Exhibition[1] on 1 May 1851, her country was the world's leading industrial power, producing more than half its iron, coal and cotton cloth. The Crystal Palace itself was a triumph of pre-fabricated mass production in iron and glass. Its contents were intended to celebrate material progress and peaceful international competition. All the world displayed its wares, but most-by far — of the objects on show were British.

Victoria's reign saw a marked improvement in the standard of living of working people. More people were living longer, and enjoying more comfortable lives. The Victorian era saw considerable expenditure on monuments to civic pride. Libraries, wash-houses and swimming baths were all funded as part of a determination to provide working people with the means to improve themselves. Civic identity and civic engagement were more powerful forces in Victorian than in early 20th-century Britain.

In addition, no other country was as urbanised as Britain. In 1851 half the population inhabited a town or city, by 1901 three-quarters did so. The British Empire reached its largest size during the Victorian age. By the end of Victoria's reign, nearly one quarter of the world's land and one quarter of the world's people were part of the British Empire.

Throughout the reign of Queen Victoria, the United Kingdom was the world's leading power. Its naval supremacy was unchallenged and its dominant influence in diplomacy and international power were acknowledged on all sides. It was, however, the strength of Britain's economy that underpinned this pre-eminence.

Britain had progressed from being what Napoleon dismissed as a "nation of shopkeepers" and had become instead "the workshop of the world"— on the back of the world's first industrial revolution. Its control of international trade routes and its dominance of financial services also ensured that — for a while at least-the country could withstand the challenge of other newly industrial nations in the second half of the queen's reign.

Victoria's reputation in Britain was also due to her personality. She maintained a very harmonious relation with her husband and almost set a standard for posterity. Accompanied by her beloved husband Albert, and surrounded by her many children in the sumptuous but homely surroundings of Balmoral Castle, Victoria became an icon of late-19th-century middle-class femininity and domesticity. Indeed, Victoria came to be seen as the very model of marital stability and domestic virtue. Her marriage to Albert represented the ideal of marital harmony. She was described as "the mother of the nation", and she came to embody the idea of home as a cosy, domestic space.

Victoria's achievements were so popular in Britain and her personality was so widely esteemed that the title "Victorian" was later applied to any person or time with the characteristics of decency, morality and self-satisfaction. Her time was thus called "the polite society" in English history.

When Victoria died in 1901, the British Empire as world power had reached its highest point. She had 9 children, 40 grand-children and 37 great-grandchildren. The Royal Family today is related to many European monarchies because of the marriages of Queen Victoria's children. Eight of Victoria's children sat on the thrones of Europe, those of Great Britain, Prussia, Greece, Romania, Russia, Norway, Sweden and Spain. Both

Queen Elizabeth, the Queen today, and her consort, the Duke of Edinburgh, are great-great-grandchildren of Queen Victoria.

☞ Notes

1. **the Great Exhibition** 世界博览会或万国工业产品博览会(the Great Exhibition of the Works of Industry of all Nations),有时也叫水晶宫博览会(the Crystal Palace Exhibition),是指1851年5月1日至10月11日历史上首次在伦敦海德公园的铸铁和平板玻璃建筑内举办的万国工业博览会。

☞ Questions for comprehension and discussion

1. What do you know about Queen Victoria's talents and hobbies?
2. Why was remarkable in the Victorian era?
3. What changes took place in Britain during Victoria's reign?
4. In what way was the standard of living improved?
5. Why was Victoria described as "the mother of the nation"?

1.10 Modern Britain (1902+)

Queen Victoria died in 1901 and her eldest son Edward Ⅶ became king, inaugurating the Edwardian Era. Edward was created Prince of Wales almost immediately after his birth. At an age (60 years old) when many men are about to retire from work, Edward at last got the job of being king. He married Alexandra of Denmark and kept Europe at peace during his life. He was known as Edward the Peacemaker.

The Edwardian Era was characterised by great and ostentatious displays of wealth in contrast to the sombre Victorian Era. With the advent of the 20th century, things such as motion pictures, automobiles, and aeroplanes were coming into use. The new century was characterised by a feeling of great optimism. The social reforms of the last century continued into the 20th with the Labour Party being formed in 1900.

Edward died in 1910, to be succeeded by George V, who reigned 1910-1936. When George V came to the throne, he changed the family name from Saxe-Coburg-Gotha[1] to Windsor because of the anti-German feeling at the time. Scandal-free, hard working and popular, George V was the British monarch who, with Queen Mary, established the modern pattern of exemplary conduct for British royalty, based on middle-class values and virtues. He understood the overseas Empire better than any of his prime ministers and used his exceptional memory for figures and details, whether of uniforms, politics, or relations, to good effect in reaching out in conversation with his subjects. George V ruled Britain during First World War 1914-1918. During his reign women were allowed to vote for the first time. Sinn Fein Easter Rising[2] in 1916 led to independent Parliament in Ireland in 1918.

George V was succeeded by his eldest son King Edward Ⅷ in June 1936. Edward's genuine concern for the underprivileged and his official overseas tours on behalf of his father made him popular in Britain and abroad. However, he ruled for just 325 days and was abdicated to marry Mrs Wallis Simpson, a divorced American woman, as he was not able to marry a divorced woman and become King.

Edward Ⅷ's younger brother, the Duke of York, was crowned George Ⅵ. When the Second World War broke out in 3rd September 1939, King George Ⅵ was three years into his reign. He and his wife Queen Elizabeth (later the Queen Mother), became inspirational figures for Britain during World War Ⅱ. King George Ⅵ founded the George Medal and the George Cross to honour the "acts of the greatest heroism or of the most conspicuous courage in circumstances of extreme danger". The George Cross is one of the nation's highest award for extreme bravery. (The Victoria Cross being the ultimate or highest symbol of bravery in battle.)

The Royal family played major symbolic roles in the war. They refused to leave London during the Blitz, the German word "Blitzkrieg" (lightning war) and were indefatigable in visiting troops, munitions factories, dockyards, and hospitals all over the country. All social classes appreciated how the royals shared the hopes, fears and hardships of the people.

World War Ⅱ ended with the unconditional surrender of the Axis powers[3].

The post-war years of George Ⅵ's reign were ones of great social change and saw the start of the National Health Service. The whole country flocked to the Festival of Britain held in London in 1951.

Queen Elizabeth Ⅱ is the 40th monarch (King or Queen) since William the Conqueror obtained the crown of England in 1066. As a teenager, Elizabeth saw the world go through WW Ⅱ, Nazi bombers attacked Britain. The girl who would be Queen wanted to do her part. On her 21st birthday, Elizabeth gave a speech. She pledged her life to help the people of the British Empire. "I declare before you all that my whole life whether it be long or short shall be devoted to your service and service of our great imperial family to which we all belong," she vowed.

On November 20, 1947, Elizabeth married Philip Mountbatten, Duke of Edinburgh, an heir to the throne of Greece. Before the wedding, Philip had given up his right to the

Greek crown. Elizabeth's father made him Duke of Edinburgh, Earl of Merioneth, and Baron Greenwich, etc.

In February 1952, Elizabeth and Philip were touring Kenya when the King George Ⅵ died and Elizabeth succeeded to the throne. She was then 26 years old. Her coronation, on June 2, 1953, was the first to be televised.

Elizabeth Ⅱ (Elizabeth Alexandra Mary Windsor) is a constitutional monarch, which means that although she is officially the head of the state, the country is actually run by the government, led by the Prime Minister. The Queen's title in the United Kingdom is Elizabeth the Second, by the Grace of God, of the United Kingdom of Great Britain and Northern Ireland and of Her other Realms and Territories Queen. She is also Head of the Commonwealth[4], a multinational body created after the dissolution of the British Empire, and Supreme Governor of the Church of England.

Her Majesty is a very busy person. Since she became queen, she is always in the public eye and is well-loved by the British people. She has no plans to retire or abdicate. On 9 September 2015, she surpassed her great-great grandmother Queen Victoria as the longest-reigning British monarch.

☞ Notes

1. **Saxe-Coburg-Gotha** 萨克森-科堡-哥达王朝(德文：Sachsen-Coburg und Gotha)，是一个源自德国，曾经统治萨克森-科堡-哥达公国(1826—1918)、比利时(1831年至今)、葡萄牙(1853—1910)、保加利亚(1887—1946)和英国(1901—1917)的欧洲王室。
2. **Sinn Fein Easter Rising** 新芬党复活节起义。Sinn Féin 爱尔兰语，意为"ourselves"或"we ourselves"，中文译为"我们自己"。新芬党是爱尔兰共和国的一个政党，活跃在爱尔兰共和国和北爱尔兰，1905 年由前爱尔兰共和国总统亚瑟·格里菲思建立。格里·亚当斯自 1983 年起任爱尔兰新芬党主席。新芬党也是爱尔兰共和军的官方政治组织，其主张是建立一个全爱尔兰共和国。the Easter Rising 复活节起义，也叫复活节暴动(the Easter Rebellion)，是爱尔兰在 1916 年复活节周期间(4 月 24 日到 4 月 30 日)发生的一场暴动，是爱尔兰共和党为结束英国在爱尔兰的统治，从英国获得独立并建立一个独立的爱尔兰共和国的尝试。起义在 6 天之后遭到镇压，起义领袖被交送军事法庭并被处死刑。尽管军事上是失败的，但它是自从 1798 年起义以来爱尔兰最重大的起义，可以被认为是通往爱尔兰共和国的最终成立道路上的一块重要的里程碑。
3. **the Axis powers** (第二次世界大战中的)轴心国，指德国、意大利和日本(Germany, Italy and Japan)。

4. **the Commonwealth** 英联邦，原名为 the British Commonwealth，或 British Commonwealth of Nations，是一个以英国为主导的国家联合体，由 54 个主权国家(含属地)所组成，成员大多为前大英帝国的殖民地或附属国。该组织元首为英国女王伊丽莎白二世，同时身兼英联邦王国内的 16 国的国家元首。基于其历史渊源，人们常常以“British Commonwealth”(英联邦)称之，用以区分世界其他联邦。

☞ Questions for comprehension and discussion

1. How many monarchs reigned in Britain since the death of Queen Victoria? Who reigned the shortest and who reigned the longest?
2. What were characteristics of the Edwardian Era?
3. What was George V popular for in Britain?
4. What happened during the reign of George Ⅵ? What role did the Royal family play?
5. What do you know about Queen Elizabeth Ⅱ? What are Her major titles?

☞ Questions on Chapter 1 for reflection and presentation

Review the whole chapter and write a short essay on any of the following questions.

1. “British history has been a history of invasion by Barbarian”, e. g. invasion from the Roman Empire, settlement of the Anglo-Saxons ... Please illustrate this point with examples. How does each of the invasions influence the British Empire, especially in terms of language? Who laid the foundation of the English State?
2. British Empire was ruled by so many monarchs, what are the most notable features of the Royal tree? Please give your comments on the monarch(s) that have the deepest impression on you, e. g. their personalities, qualities, talents or abilities, and contributions to the country
3. There have been many wars, battles, risings or rebellions and destructive disasters in the British history, please describe some of the important ones about their causes and consequences or impacts.
4. Why was Victorian Britain called “the workshop of the world”?

Chapter 2

Facts and Figures of the United Kingdom

The United Kingdom of Great Britain and Northern Ireland is a country made up of four separate countries. This country is inhabited not only by the English, the Scot, the Welsh and the Irish, but also by immigrants from all parts of the world. Knowing the origins of the different country names and formation of the national flag may not only facilitate understanding the making of the UK, it can also help avoid incorrect terms in reference to the national identity and citizenship among its ever growing population of mixed races.

Being an island country surrounded by the sea, the UK boasts a beautiful landscape with its greatly varied physical geography, mainly highlands in the north and west and mostly lowlands in the east and southeast. Although the climate in the UK is generally temperate, such description is still considered to be true, "In no country other than in England, can one experience four seasons in the course of one single day."

2.1 The Countries and Names

When people say England, they sometimes mean Britain, Great Britain, sometimes the United Kingdom, and sometimes the British Isles.

The UK's full and official name is the "United Kingdom of Great Britain and Northern Ireland", although most people just refer to it as United Kingdom or the UK. The British Isles includes many islands not even part of the UK.

Up until the 17th century there had been four "countries" in the British Isles: England, Scotland, Wales, and Ireland, each one having its own separate sense of identity, its own history, and even its own language. There was no such word as British. People were simply either English, Scottish, Welsh or Irish.

By the end of the 18th century, all this changed. The word British was used for the first time, "Rule, Britannia!"[1] song was composed and the Union Flag created.

England used to be known as Engla land, meaning the land of the Angles, people from continental Germany, who began to invade Britain in the late 5th century, along with the Saxons and Jute.

England is the biggest country in the UK. It occupies most of the southern two thirds of Great Britain. Nearly 84 per cent of the total population of the United Kingdom lives in England. The capital, seat of government, and the largest city in the United Kingdom is London, which is also the capital of England. The English language, today spoken by hundreds and millions of people around the world, originated as the language from England, where it remains the principal tongue today.

Britain is the official name given to the kingdom of England and the Principality of Wales[2]. The name Britain goes back to Roman times when they called England and Wales "Britannia" (or "Britannia Major", to distinguish it from "Britannia Minor", ie Brittany in France). The Roman province of Britannia only covered the areas of modern England and Wales. The area of modern Scotland was never finally conquered. 1536 Act of Union joined England and Wales. In 1543, during the Tudor times, England and Wales were united as one country. Scotland and Ireland remained separate kingdoms, with their own parliaments and laws until the much later.

Great Britain is the official name given to the two kingdoms of England and Scotland, and the principality of Wales. The term Great Britain was first used in 1603 when King James Ⅵ of Scotland became also James Ⅰ of England. The separate kingdoms of England and Scotland were ruled over by the same monarch, but both kingdoms kept their own parliaments. James Ⅰ was very keen to be King of Great Britain. From 1606 Scots were officially called English citizens. In 1707 the *Act of Union* meant that Scotland lost her Parliament and her independence and became part of a new country to be called "Kingdom of Great Britain", a single kingdom with a single Parliament (but Scotland has always retained its own legal system).

In 1801 a second *Act of Union* was passed and joined Ireland to "Great Britain", creating yet another new country, the "United Kingdom of Great Britain and Ireland".

After years of civil war, Ireland became a republic in 1921. The *Anglo-Irish Treaty*[3] removed most of the southern counties in Ireland from the UK when they chose independence. Six northern Irish counties (Northern Ireland, also known as Ulster) remained part of the UK. In 1922, the name changed to the United Kingdom of Great Britain and Northern Ireland, which was adopted in 1927. It is now the official name of the UK.

In brief, England and Wales form Britain; England, Scotland and Wales together form Great Britain; Great Britain and Northern Ireland together form the "United Kingdom of Great Britain and Northern Ireland" (UK). The United Kingdom is made up of: England (the capital is London), Scotland (the capital is Edinburgh), Wales (the capital is Cardiff), and Northern Ireland (the capital is Belfast). The capital of the UK is London.

The counties of Britain are territorial divisions of Britain for the purposes of administrative, political and geographical demarcation. England has 45 counties, the largest traditional one being Yorkshire. Wales has 22 counties and Scotland 30 counties.

England, as well as being divide into counties, is divided into nine governmental regions: South West, South East, London, East of England, West Midlands, East Midlands, Yorkshire and the Humber, North West, and North East. The Home Counties-the counties bordering London, are Berkshire, Buckinghamshire, Essex, Hertfordshire, Kent and Surrey.

☞ Notes

1. **Rule, Britannia!** 统治吧，不列颠尼亚！是英国著名的爱国歌曲。歌词取自詹姆斯·汤姆森(James Thomson)的同名诗作，由托马斯·阿恩(Thomas Arne)于1740年作曲。“不列颠尼亚”是不列颠的拉丁语旧称表达形式。
2. **the Principality of Wales** 威尔士公国(1216—1536)，在1267—1277年间最高峰时期包括现代威尔士的三分之二。历史上大部分时间与英国王室是“兼并和联合”的关系。公国是封建制下公爵或女公爵的封地。目前的威尔士亲王(Prince of Wales，也就是英国的查理斯王子)只是挂名的君主而已，并不具有实际的政治权利。
3. **Anglo-Irish Treaty** 《英爱条约》，是英国与爱尔兰于1921年12月6日签订的解除爱尔兰的条约。条约的主要内容是：把统一的爱尔兰分割为两部分，南部26郡，成立自由邦；北部6郡，则划归英国。自由邦名义上享有自治自决的全权，但其对外政策和一部分内政仍置于英国监督之下。自由邦必须效忠英王，其议会通过的法律，需经英国总督批准方能生效。

☞ Questions for comprehension and discussion

1. What is the official name of the UK? When was it officially adopted?
2. Who gave the name to England? Why does England dominate the UK?
3. What countries is Britain made up of? What was it called by Romans?
4. When was the term Great Britain first used and how was the United Kingdom of Great Britain formed?
5. How many counties and governmental regions is England divided into?

2.2 The Origin of the British Flag

The Union Flag, popularly known as the Union Jack[1], is the national flag of the United Kingdom. It is the British flag. It is a flag containing three other flags. It is called the Union Flag because it symbolises the administrative union of the countries of the United Kingdom. It is made up of the individual Flags of the Kingdom's three countries all united under one Sovereign — the countries of England, of Scotland and of Northern Ireland.

The flag also has an official or semi-official status in some other Commonwealth realms; for example, it is, by law, an official flag in Canada and known there as the Royal Union Flag. Further, it is used as an official flag in some of the smaller British overseas territories. The Union Jack also appears in the upper left-hand quarter of the flags of several nations and territories that are former British possessions or dominions.

One of the key components of the Union Flag is the flag of England, which is derived from St. George's Cross, a red cross on a white ground. The Cross of St. George[2] was introduced as the National Flag of England by Richard Ⅰ of England in 1194 A. D.

The origins of the earlier flag of Great Britain date back to 1606. After Queen Elizabeth Ⅰ of England died in 1603, King James Ⅵ of Scotland inherited the English throne and became King James Ⅰ of England. It was a Union of the Crowns, but not yet of the nations. Each country still kept its own parliament. On 20 October 1604 James proclaimed a new title for himself as "King of Great Britain". A problem arose, which flag should be hoisted on the king's ships. Scotland is represented by the flag of St. Andrew[3], a diagonal white cross form (called a saltire) on a blue field. English sailors resented the Scottish colours and the Scots scorned the cross of St. George.

On 12 April 1606, a new flag to represent this regal union between England and Scotland was specified in a royal decree, according to which the flag of England and the flag of Scotland would be joined together, forming the flag of England and Scotland for maritime purposes (for use at sea), thus making the first Union Jack (Jack being a shortening of Jacobus, the Latin version of James). Ashore however, the old flags of England and Scotland continued to be used by their respective countries. When the first flag representing Britain was introduced it became known simply as the "British flag" or the "flag of Britain".

When the red cross of England was put onto the flag of Scotland, a white border was added around the red cross for reasons of heraldry. (The rules of heraldry * demanded

The first Union Flag (1606)

that two colours must never touch each other.)

On 28th July, 1707, during the reign of Queen Anne, this flag was by royal proclamation made the National flag of Great Britain, for use ashore and afloat. The Royal Navy christened the British flag "The Union". On 1 January 1801, Ireland was united with Great Britain and it became necessary to have a new National Flag in which Ireland was represented.

Ireland is represented by the cross of St. Patrick[4], a diagonal red cross on a white background. So the cross St. Patrick was combined with the Union Flag of St. George and St. Andrew, to create the Union Flag that has been flown ever since.

The cross of St. Patrick was inserted so the position given to St. Andrew's Cross in one quarter was the same as that given to the Irish one in the diagonally opposite quarter; in heraldry this is known as "counterchanging". The "new" British flag is not symmetrical because of the counterchange.

As Scotland joined the Union nearly two hundred years before Ireland, St. Andrew's

Cross was placed uppermost in the top quarter nearest the flagstaff, this being the most honourable position according to heraldry, while the Irish Cross was given the second most honourable position, the top quarter of the fly. In order to avoid having the red of the Irish Cross directly upon the blue field of the Scottish one, an edging of the white field of the Irish Cross is used. The symbols of Scotland and Ireland are placed sided by side on the Union Flag. The St. Patrick's Cross remains in the flag even though today only Northern Ireland is part of the United Kingdom.

To summarize, the formation of the Union Flag (Union Jack) came about as the result of the progressive merging of the inhabitants of the British Isles under one throne. The Union Flag consists of the three heraldic crosses of St. George, St. Andrew and St. Patrick. The flags of the Patron Saints of England, Scotland and Ireland are represented on the Union Flag.

But, why doesn't the Welsh dragon  appear on the Union Flag?

The Welsh dragon does not appear on the flag because when the first Union Flag was created in 1606, Wales was already united with England from the 13th century. This meant that Wales was not a Kingdom but a Principality and it could not be included on the flag. (In 1536, under Henry Ⅷ, an Act of Union was passed making Wales, in effect a province of England.)

In November 2007, a Welsh MP, Ian Lucas, asked parliament why Wales is not represented in the Union Jack. What if Wales was represented, what would the flag look like? Below is Ian Lucas' version of the Union flag with Wales represented.

At the moment, the countries representing the UK, are still united under one flag. How long this will be so, no one knows. Even now, each of the countries which form the United Kingdom is fighting for its own independence. For the first time since 1707, the Scots now have their own Parliament in Edinburgh, and the Welsh their own national assembly in Cardiff.

Will the Union flag be replaced by four separate flags or will all the flags and the

Union Jack, be replaced by something else? Only time will tell.

☞ Notes

1. **the Union Jack** 联盟杰克。"Jack"一词可能起源于18世纪早期，但具体出处不明确。"Jack"也可能来源于继承了英格兰王位的苏格兰国王詹姆士四世的名字Jac，即Jacobus，Jacobus在拉丁文中是James的意思。另外，在1600年之前"Jack"是英国海军用语，指悬挂在军舰舰首的旗帜。当时英国皇家海军的规模、力量在国际上的影响力同样能解释为什么英国国旗的昵称是Union Jack。
2. **St. George** 圣·乔治，是英格兰的守护神(patron saint of England)，其勋章或徽章圣·乔治十字(St. George's Cross)即英格兰国旗。12世纪狮心王理查(Richard the Lion Heart)在中东十字军远征(Crusades)中使用了红十字旗，国王的士兵把它戴在上衣外面，以避免战斗中与敌方相混。据说真正的圣·乔治是4世纪的一名罗马士兵，他为基督教徒脱离迫害作出莫大贡献。4月23日是圣·乔治节，是英格兰的国庆节。
3. **Saint Andrew** 圣·安德鲁，是苏格兰的守护神，同时也是希腊、俄罗斯和罗马尼亚等国家的守护神(patron saint of Scotland, Greece, Russia, Romania, etc.)。作为圣彼得的兄弟和最初的使徒之一，安德鲁据说是在希腊的佩特雷(Patras)被杀害的，他向判处他死刑的罗马当局请求，不要让他采用和耶稣一样的姿势在十字架上钉死。他的请求得到批准，于是他最终是在X形的十字架上被处死的，所以X形十字后来也就成了他的象征(圣·安德鲁十字或X形十字)。苏格兰人在每年的11月30日庆祝圣·安德鲁节，这一天也是罗马尼亚的国庆节。2006年苏格兰议会还把这一天定为官方的法定假日。
4. **Saint Patrick** 圣·帕特里克，爱尔兰传说中的主要守护神(the primary patron saint of Ireland)，是5世纪罗马、英国的基督教传教士和主教(Romano-British Christian missionary and bishop)，在爱尔兰被称为"爱尔兰的使徒"("Apostle of Ireland")。他的逝世日3月17日成为圣·帕特里克节(Saint Patrick's Day)，是爱尔兰的一个宗教和文化节日。

☞ Questions for comprehension and discussion

1. What are the different names for the British national flag?
2. How the Union Flag (Union Jack) came to be the UK's national flag? What were the flags of England and Scotland like respectively?
3. What led to the creation of the first Union Flag? In what way was each of the countries honoured on the Union Flag?
4. How was the flag of Ireland combined with the Union Flag of St. George?

5. Why doesn't the Welsh dragon appear on the Union Flag?

2.3 The Population Structure and National Identity

The population of the United Kingdom is considered an example of a population which has undergone the "demographic transition" — that is, the transition from a (typically) pre-industrial population with high birth and mortality rates and only slow population growth, through a stage of falling mortality and faster rates of population growth, to a stage of low birth and mortality rates with, again, lower rates of population growth. This population growth through "natural change" has been accompanied in the past two decades by growth through net international migration into the UK.

The mid-2014 population estimates show that the UK population was 64.6 m. The population of England was 54.3 m, which accounts for 84% of the UK population. Followed by Scotland at 5.3 m (8% of the UK population), Wales at 3.1 m (or 5% of the UK population) and Northern Ireland at 1.8 million (3% of the UK population).

The population of the UK increased by 4.2 million between 2001 and 2011. The UK Office for National Statistics (ONS) projected in 2011 that by 2035, the UK's population is expected to increase to just over 73 million people. This is an average annual growth rate of 0.6% per annum.

Rising immigration is the main reason for Britain's increasing population. Since 1945, immigration to the United Kingdom under *British Nationality Law*[1] has been substantial, in particular from the Republic of Ireland and from the former colonies and territories of the British Empire such as India, Bangladesh, Pakistan, the Caribbean, South Africa, Kenya and China Hong Kong. Other immigrants have come as asylum seekers, seeking protection as refugees under the *United Nations* 1951 *Refugee Convention*[2], or from member states of the European Union, exercising one of the *European Union's Four Freedoms*[3].

About 70% of the population increase between the 2001 and 2011 censuses was due to foreign-born immigration. 7.5 million people (11.9 per cent of the population at the time) were born abroad, although the census gives no indication of their immigration status or intended length of stay.

From April 2013 to April 2014, a total of 560,000 immigrants arrived in the UK, including 81,000 British citizens and 214,000 from other parts of the EU. The top countries represented in terms of arrivals were: China, India, Poland, United States, and Australia. The largest groups of people granted British citizenship were from India, Pakistan, Somalia, and the Philippines.

In June 2010, Britain's new Conservative-Liberal Democrat Coalition government brought in a temporary cap on immigration of those entering the UK from outside the EU, with the limit set as 24,100, in order to stop an expected rush of applications before a permanent cap is imposed in April 2011.

According to the UK Border Agency (UKBA), a department within the Home Office, all individuals wanting to settle in the UK should demonstrate their commitment by learning English and by having an understanding of British history, culture and traditions. Any individual seeking to apply for naturalization or infinite leave to remain must pass the official Life in the UK Test[4].

The 2011 Census shows that the ethnic composition of the United Kingdom was as follows: 87.1% White, 7.0% Asian, 3.0% Black, 2.0% Mixed, and 0.9% Other.

National identity and citizenship are not always the same thing in the UK. People in the UK are called British although they have different nationalities. However, most white people born in Great Britain, although British citizens, do not regard themselves as British and prefer to state their national identity as English, Scottish or Welsh.

A YouGov[5] poll carried out by the *Daily Telegraph* in 2007 found that fewer than one third of today's teenagers instinctively think of themselves as British rather than English, Scottish or Welsh. But, pressed to say whether they also think of themselves as British, the great majority say yes. Only 10 per cent of the teenage sample, many of them Scots, reject a British identity altogether.

An ICM poll published by the *Daily Mail* in 2007 suggested that majorities of voters in both Scotland and England now want the countries to split.

However, on 18 September 2014, people in Scotland voted in a Referendum on Scottish Independence. The "No" side won, with 55.3% voting against independence.

The UK government believes that Scotland is better off in the UK and the UK is better off with Scotland in it.

Moreover, people moving to Britain have brought their own cultures and languages and try to keep them alive. For example, the United Kingdom's de facto official language is English which is spoken as a first language by 95% of the population. Meanwhile, six regional languages: Scots, Ulster-Scots, Welsh, Cornish, Irish and Scottish Gaelic are protected under the *European Charter for Regional* or *Minority Languages*. Over 250 languages are spoken in London, making the capital the most linguistically diverse city in the world.

On the whole, people from all cultures and ethnicities can be found in every corner of the UK and each person in his or her own way has contributed to make the country the place it is today.

☞ Notes

1. **British Nationality Law** 《英国国籍法》，是英国有关公民身份及其他类别英国国籍的法律。主要的英国国籍法是《1981 英国国籍法》，制定了现行英国国籍的多个类别体系，即英国公民、英国海外领土公民、英国海外公民、英国侨民(海外)、英籍人士和英国保护人士。只有拥有英国公民身份的人和某些英联邦公民有在英国居留的主动权。
2. **the United Nations 1951 Refugee Convention** 《联合国 1951 难民公约》，是关于难民地位(身份)的关键法律文件，以确定谁是难民，他们的权利和国家的法律义务是什么。
3. **the European Union Four Freedoms** 欧盟"四大自由"。"四大自由"指商品的自由流动、人员的自由流动、资本的自由流动和从业的自由。促进人的自由流动是自 20 世纪 50 年代以来欧洲一体化的主要目标。广义的定义是该项自由使得一个成员国的公民可以到另一个成员国旅行、居住和工作(暂时性或永久性的)。欧盟在这一领域立法的基本思想是来自其他成员国的公民应与国内公民享有平等的待遇，而不应该受到歧视。
4. **Life in the UK Test** 《英国入籍考试》是一种基于计算机的考试，是对寻求无限期留在英国或归化为英国公民的要求的一个组成部分。它是用来证明申请人有足够的英国生活方面的知识和足够的英语语言能力。该考试是 2002 年的《国籍、移民和庇护法案》提出的要求。它包括 24 个考题，涵盖的主题有诸如英国社会、政府、日常生活和就业等。根据英国内政部 2013 年 3 月开始实施的《新入籍考试指南》，新的考试大幅减少了生活类内容，增加了英国历史、文化等专题。
5. **YouGov** 舆观。是一家全球网上市场调查公司，由斯蒂芬·莎士比亚(Stephan Shakespeare，现任首席执行官)和纳迪姆·扎哈维(Nadhim Zahawi，前任首席执行官)于 2000 年 5 月在英国成立，总部位于英国，是英国民意调查委员会(British Polling Council)的成员之一，并在英国信息专员公署(Information Commissioner's Office)注册登记。舆观 YouGov 集团在全球拥有 21 个分公司，地域横跨英国、美国、欧洲、北欧以及中东地区。

☞ Questions for comprehension and discussion

1. What is the UK's population according to the latest census? Why do not all the British citizens regard themselves as British?
2. What is the main reason for UK's increasing population? Why do people migrate to UK?
3. What were the top countries of arrival in the UK from 2013 to 2014? What were the

largest group granted British citizenship?

4. In what ways has the government tried to limit the immigration?
5. What are the six regional languages used in UK in addition to English?
6. When did the Scottish independence referendum in 2014 took place? What was the result?

2.4 The Landscape and Climate

The UK is an island country in north-western Europe. It is bordered by four seas: to the south by the English Channel; to the east by the North Sea; to the west by the Irish Sea and the Atlantic Ocean.

The total area of the United Kingdom is approximately 245,000 square kilometres (94,600 sq mi), comprising the island of Great Britain, the northeastern one-sixth of the island of Ireland (Northern Ireland) and many smaller islands.

England is the largest country of the United Kingdom, at 130,439 square kilometres (over 50,000 sq mi), accounting for just over half the total area of the UK. Scotland, at 78,772 square kilometres (30,410 sq mi), is the second largest, accounting for about a third of the area of the UK. Wales and Northern Ireland are much smaller, covering 20,758 and 14,160 square kilometres (8,010 and 5,470 sq mi) respectively.

The UK has a coastline which measures about 12,429 km. The heavy indentation of the coastline helps to ensure that no location is more than 125 km from tidal waters.

The UK Landscape is very varied, ranging from the Grampian Mountains of Scotland to the lowland fens of England which are at or below sea level in places. Most of the UK is made up of gently rolling hills with isolated areas of high ground such as Dartmoor in the south-west of England or the Mourne Mountains in Northern Ireland.

England consists of mostly lowland terrain. The upland areas include the Lake District, the Pennines, Exmoor and Dartmoor. The lowland areas are typically traversed by ranges of low hills, frequently composed of chalk.

Scotland and Wales are the most mountainous parts of the UK. The ten tallest mountains in the UK are all found in Scotland, with Ben Nevis as the highest mountain, at 1,343 m (4,406 ft).

The physical geography of Scotland is distinguished by the Highland Boundary Fault which traverses the Scottish mainland from Helensburgh to Stonehaven. The faultline separates the two distinctively different regions of the Highlands to the north and west, and the lowlands to the south and east.

Wales is mostly mountainous, though south Wales is less mountainous than north and mid Wales.

Ireland's main geographical features include low central plains surrounded by a ring of coastal mountains. The highest peak is Carrauntoohil, which is 1,041 metres (3,415 ft) above sea level.

Northern Ireland is home to the UK's largest lake, Lough Neagh, which covers an area of 396 sq km (153 sq miles). Other major lakes include Windermere in England's Lake District and Loch Lomond in Scotland. Another of Scotland's lakes, Loch Ness is famous for sightings of "Nessie", a mythical monster! The deepest lake in the UK is Loch Morar in the Highlands of Scotland with a maximum depth of 310 metres (1,017 ft).

Being a relatively small Island, the UK's rivers are not very long. The Severn, its longest river, is just 220 miles (354 km) in length, beginning in Wales and entering the Atlantic Ocean near Bristol in England. It is also the greatest river in terms of water flow in England and Wales. The best known river is, of course, the Thames which flows through Oxford and London. It is the longest, at 215 miles (346 km), in England. Other major rivers in England include the Trent and Mersey rivers, which drain rainfall from large areas of central England.

Being an island country and surrounded by seas, the climate of the UK is generally temperate, although significant local variation occurs, particularly as a result of altitude and distance from the coast. In general the south of the country is warmer than the north, and the west wetter than the east. Due to the warming influence of the Gulf Stream, the UK is significantly warmer than some other locations at similar latitude, such as Newfoundland.

July and August are normally the warmest months but they are also the wettest. Around the coasts, February is normally the coldest month, but inland there is little to choose between January and February as the coldest month.

The Lake District is England's wettest region, receiving an average of 130 inches (330 centimeters) of precipitation each year. The western and northern hills receive about 40 inches (102 centimeters) of rain, while the east coast receives about 20 inches (51 centimetres).

During June, July and August (the months of longest daylight) the mean daily duration of sunshine varies from five hours in northern Scotland to eight hours in the Isle of Wight.

During the months of shortest daylight (November, December and January) sunshine is at a minimum, with an average of an hour a day in northern Scotland and two hours a day on the south coast of England.

Probably the best months to travel in the UK are May, June, September and October. These months generally have the most pleasant temperatures and less rain. The sunniest parts of Britain are along the south coast of England.

☞ Questions for comprehension and discussion

1. What are the four seas that border the UK?
2. What are comprised in the UK's total area of 245,000 square kilometers?
3. Which of the UK's four countries is the smallest in terms of area?
4. Where are the most mountainous parts of the UK?
5. What word can describe the general feature of the UK's climate?

☞ Questions on Chapter Two for reflection and presentation

Review the whole chapter and write a short essay on any of the following questions.

1. What do you think of the UK's Immigration and Nationality laws?
2. If you plan to travel in the UK, which parts of the country do you want to visit most and why?

Chapter 3

Political and Legal Systems of the United Kingdom

The United Kingdom political system is a multi-party system. All of the several major political parties hold seats in Parliament and work around the nation to advance their aims.

The United Kingdom is a unitary democracy governed within the framework of a constitutional monarchy, in which the Monarch is the head of state and the Prime Minister is the head of government. Executive power is exercised by the Sovereign, Queen Elizabeth Ⅱ, via Her Majesty's Government (HMG)[1] and the devolved national authorities — the Scottish Government, the Welsh Assembly Government and the Northern Ireland Executive. Legislative power is vested in the two chambers of the Parliament of the United Kingdom, the House of Commons and the House of Lords, as well as in the Scottish parliament and Welsh and Northern Ireland assemblies. The judiciary is independent of the executive and the legislature. The highest court is the Supreme Court of the United Kingdom. England and Wales, Northern Ireland and Scotland each has its own legal system with distinct history and origins.

3.1 Government System

The United Kingdom has a constitutional monarchic, parliamentary democratic, and a unitary system of government. Her Majesty's Government, commonly referred to as the British Government, is the central government of the United Kingdom of Great Britain and Northern Ireland.

The UK is constitutional monarchy with the monarch (Queen Elizabeth Ⅱ) as head of the state. The Queen only rules symbolically, in reality, power belongs to Parliament.

The principle behind parliamentary democracy is that the people elect Members of Parliament (MPs) to the House of Commons in London at a general election, government is directly accountable to Parliament, and that at any time the government can be dismissed by the Commons through a vote of "no confidence".

The UK's unitary system of government means that the power is held in the centre, although some powers have been devolved to Scotland, Wales and Northern Ireland. However, the government remains responsible for national policy on all matters that have not been devolved, including foreign affairs, defence, social security, macro-economic management and trade. England is the only country in the UK that doesn't have its own parliament or government. Issues that effect England are decided by the UK government, which consists of MPs from all over the UK.

A key principle of the British Constitution is that the Government is responsible to Parliament, and Parliament is responsible to the Queen, at least in theory. This is called responsible government.

Her Majesty's Government is made up of three parts: the Monarch, Parliament, and the Cabinet. The UK government is normally formed by the political party with the most MPs in the House of Commons. The leader of the party is asked by the Queen to become Prime Minister. Then the new Prime Minister chooses a team of people from Parliament who will run the country with him. The UK government has responsibility for developing and implementing policy and for drafting laws. It is also known as the Executive.

The UK Parliament is made up of all MPs and is the highest legislative authority with "absolute sovereignty" in the UK, in other words, it is where politicians (MPs) meet to decide laws and make decisions on running the United Kingdom (Some issues in Scotland, Wales and Northern Ireland are now dealt with by their respective parliaments and assemblies). The UK Parliament has responsibility for checking the work of government and examining, debating and approving new laws. It is also known as the Legislature.

Parliament is made up of three parts: the Monarch, the House of Lords, and the House of Commons. The current monarch, Queen Elizabeth Ⅱ, performs a range of important duties, such as summoning and dissolving Parliament and giving royal assent to legislation passed by the UK Parliament, the Scottish Parliament, the National Assembly for Wales or the Northern Ireland Assembly.

The Queen formally appoints important office holders, including the prime minister and other government ministers, judges, officers in the armed forces, governors, diplomats, bishops and some other senior clergy of the Church of England. She also grants peerages, knighthoods and other honours. In instances where people have been wrongly convicted of crimes, she is involved in pardoning them.

In international affairs, the Queen has the power to declare war and make peace, to conclude treaties and to take over or give up territory.

The Queen holds Privy Council meetings, gives audiences to her ministers and officials in the UK and overseas, receives accounts of Cabinet decisions, reads dispatches and signs state papers.

The House of Lords is the upper house of the UK Parliament. It is made up of people who have inherited family titles and those who have been given titles because of their outstanding work in one field or another. Membership of the House of Lords is made up of Lords Spiritual and Lords Temporal.

The main job of the House of Lords is to "double check" new laws to make sure they are fair and will work. It scrutinises and amends Bills that have been approved by the House of Commons. While it is unable to prevent Bills passing into law, except in certain limited circumstances, it can delay Bills and force the Commons to reconsider their decisions.

The House of Commons is the lower house of the UK Parliament. It is the most important place for discussing policies and making laws. A person who sits in the Commons is called a Member of Parliament (MP). Each MP represents one of 650 constituencies in the UK and is a member of a political party, such as New Labour or the Conservative party.

The functions of the House of Commons are to make laws, to examine government policy and administrations to supervise finance. The government cannot legally spend any money without the permission of the House of Commons.

The Prime Minister heads the Government and appoints Ministers, who head individual Government departments. Every week the Prime Minister appears before the House of Commons and must answer questions put to him by the members of Parliament. He also has weekly meetings with the Queen, where she has a right and a duty to express her views on Government matters.

The Cabinet is the committee at the centre of the British political system and the supreme decision-making body in government. Cabinet ministers are the highest-ranking ministers in the government, and most government departments have one Cabinet minister (or more). Most Cabinet ministers are titled 'Secretary of State'-although some have traditional titles, such as the Chancellor of the Exchequer and the Chief Whip.

The main functions of the Cabinet are: to make final decisions on the policy present to the parliament; to exercise the ultimate executive power on the Parliamentary policy; and to divide and adjust powers among the administrative departments.

The two other main political parties also have their own "shadow cabinets"[2], whose responsibility is to criticize the policies and actions of the government, as well as offering an alternative program.

☞ Notes

1. **Her Majesty's Government** 女王陛下政府，是现今英国政府的官方名称，当英国君主是男性(国王)时称为英王陛下政府(His Majesty's Government)。"女王陛下政府"也是以前英联邦王国成员国政府使用的名衔。
2. **shadow cabinet** 影子内阁，指实行多党制的国家中不执政的政党，与执政党相对。1907年，英国保守党领袖奥斯丁·张伯伦首先使用这一名词。"影子内阁"负责领导下院中本党成员的一切活动，遇到议会辩论时，各"影子大臣"就会踊跃发言，在阐述本党观点的同时，专挑当任内阁的毛病和缺点进行攻击和施加种种压力，其存在的目的是为了促使当任内阁倒台，并最终取而代之。因此，"影子内阁"也称为"预备内阁"或"在野内阁"似乎更为确切。

☞ Questions for comprehension and discussion

1. What is the official name of UK's Government? What is it made up of?
2. What type of government is the British government?
3. Does the central government control over all its countries in all their affairs?
4. What is Parliament made up of? What is the difference between Parliament and the Government?
5. What are the Prime Minister's powers and responsibilities?
6. Who form the Cabinet and the Shadow Cabinet? What are their functions?

3.2 Major Political Parities and General Elections

The United Kingdom has several major political parties, all of which hold seats in Parliament and work around the nation to advance their aims.

There are three major political parties in the House of Commons: Conservative, Labour and Liberal Democrats.

The Conservative Party, founded in 1834 and colloquially referred to as the Tory Party or the Tories, is a centre-right political party and also a dominant party in the United Kingdom. It espouses the philosophies of conservatism and British unionism. After merging with the Liberal Unionist Party in 1912, it changed its name to the Conservative and Unionist Party, although that name is rarely used. As of 2014 it is the largest single party in the House of Commons with 305 MPs, governing in coalition with the Liberal Democrats.

The Labour Party tends to be associated with socialism, and promotes extensive social services and a heavy governmental role in society. It has traditional ties with trade unions and other representatives of the working class.

The Labour and Conservative parties have traditionally split dominance of the government. In the House of Lords, party members sit on either side of a central aisle, with the Government on one side and the opposition on the other. Members of other parties may pick a side to sit on, or sit in a central area to indicate lack of affiliation with one of the two major parties. The Liberal Democrats, founded in 1998, are a left of center party which promotes political and social liberalism. This party is opposed to military intervention in foreign affairs, cutting of social services, and heavy state involvement in personal affairs. It also promotes progressive environmental policy and ties with the rest of the European Union.

As well as the three major political parties, the UK also has various minor ones, some of whom have seats in parliament. In addition to an Assembly, Wales is also represented by several political parties, including Plaid Cymru[1]. This party works to represent Wales better in British parliament, and also promotes Welsh independence. As a party, Plaid Cymru feels that Wales is not being governed well from London, and does a great deal of work within Wales to improve life for residents.

Scotland's primary political party is the Scottish National Party, which is lobbying for Scottish independence. It is a left of center party which believes that Scotland would be better served if it was recognized as an independent entity by the European Union. Scotland has its own parliament for decision making.

Northern Ireland has an Assembly and Parliamentary representation, with the major political party being Northern Ireland's Democratic Unionist Party. The party supports a union between Northern Ireland and the rest of Britain. It also promotes cooperation with Ireland, along with progressive social policies for Northern Ireland.

The mixture of parties ensures an even distribution of opinions in Parliament. The system has sometimes been criticized for lacking efficiency, as it can result in prolonged debate in Parliament. Usually the various parties make cooperative ties with each other to work towards common goals.

The UK Parliament has a maximum duration of five years. All the Members of Parliament forming the House of Commons of the UK's Parliament are elected by the people. The general elections are held following a dissolution of Parliament. Candidates aim to win particular geographic constituencies in the United Kingdom. Each constituency elects one MP by the first past the post[2] system of election.

The Electoral Commission's Register of Political Parties lists the details of parties registered to fight elections, and their registered name, in the United Kingdom. Under current electoral law, only registered party names can be used on ballot papers by those wishing to fight elections. Candidates who do not belong to a registered party can use "independent" or no label at all.

As of 10 June 2011 the Electoral Commission showed the number of registered political parties as 419. In Northern Ireland there are 42 registered parties.

The party with the most seats, i. e. the most MPs, usually forms the government, and the second largest party forms Her Majesty's Loyal Opposition[3]. Almost all successful candidates are members of a political party. If no party has an outright majority, parties can seek to form coalitions.

For example, after the 1992 general election the largest party, the conservatives, had 21 more seats than all the others. This is called a majority. With such a majority they could outvote all the other parties, so they formed the Government. Their Party Leader, John Major, became the Prime Minister.

After the 1997 general election the picture was rather different: the Labour Party had a majority of 179 and its leader, Tony Blair, became Prime Minister. In the 2010 general election no single party won enough majority of seats to form the government alone. So in order to form a government two or more parties had to join together. The Conservative Party formed a new government, in coalition with the Liberal Democrats. The Prime Minister was David Cameron, leader of the Conservative Party and Nick Clegg, leader of the Liberal Democrats was his deputy.

After the 2010 general election, the coalition government enacted the *Fixed-term Parliaments Act* 2011 which set fixed term parliaments of five years. As such, the next general election was scheduled to be held on 7 May 2015, with subsequent elections held every five years on the first Thursday of May. However the Act also contains provisions for Parliament to be dissolved and an early election held if no government can be formed within 14 days after a vote of no confidence in the government. Similarly, the Act allows for an election to be triggered by a vote of two-thirds of MPs in the House of Commons calling for one. The coalition ended following Parliamentary elections on May 7, 2015, in which the Conservatives secured a clear lead over their rivals with an outright majority of 330 seats in the House of Commons, while their coalition partners lost all but eight seats, and incumbent Prime Minister David Cameron was able to form a majority single-party government.

☞ Notes

1. **Plaid Cymru** 威尔士布雷库姆党，亦即威尔士党（the Party of Wales），鼓吹威尔

士在欧盟中独立。

2. **the first past the post**(缩写为 FPTP 或 FPP) (选举体制)得票最多者当选，票数领先即入选。

3. **Her Majesty's Loyal Opposition** 女王陛下忠诚的反对党(又称 the Official Opposition)，通常为下议院中议席居第二多的党派，自 2010 年以来的反对党为劳工党。"女王陛下忠诚的反对党"的存在，不仅为国家提供了后备政府，以便一旦选民要求改变政策时，反对党便可接过政府的责任；而且，更为重要的是，使政府受到了有效的监督。反对党的真正目的是要在下次大选中击败现执政党，以便上台执政。

☞ Questions for comprehension and discussion

1. What are three major political parties in the House of Commons? What parties have traditionally split dominance of the government.?
2. What does Plaid Cymru promote in Wales?
3. What type is the Scottish National Party and what does it believe?
4. What is the major political party in Northern Island?
5. What are the advantages and disadvantages to have the mixture of parties in the parliament?
6. Who elect the Members of Parliament?

3.3 Legal System

The United Kingdom does not have a single legal system since it was created by the political union of previously independent countries. It has three legal systems: English law, Northern Ireland law, and Scots law.

"English law" refers to the legal system administered by the courts in England and Wales, which rule on both civil and criminal matters. English law is renowned as being the mother of the common law[1] and is based on those principles. English law can be described as having its own legal doctrine, distinct from civil law legal systems since 1189. There has been no major codification of the law, and subject to statute, the law is developed by judges in court, applying statute, precedent and common sense to the facts before them, to give explanatory judgments of the relevant legal principles, which are reported and binding in future similar cases (stare decisis). In the early centuries, the justices and judges were responsible for adapting the Writ system[2] to meet everyday needs, applying a mixture of precedent and common sense to build up a body of internally consistent law. As

Parliament developed in strength, subject to the doctrine of separation of powers, legislation gradually overtook judicial law-making, so that today judges are only able to innovate in certain very narrowly-defined areas.

The courts of England and Wales are headed by the Senior Courts of England and Wales, consisting of the Court of Appeal, the High Court of Justice (for civil cases) and the Crown Court (for criminal cases). The Supreme Court is the highest court in the land for both criminal and civil appeal cases in England, Wales, and Northern Ireland and any decision it makes is binding on every other court in the same jurisdiction, and often has persuasive effect in its other jurisdictions. On appeal, a court may overrule the decisions of its inferior courts, such as county courts (civil) and magistrates' courts (criminal). The High Court may also quash on judicial review both administrative decisions of the Government and delegated legislation. The ultimate body of appeal for all criminal and civil cases in England and Wales (and Northern Ireland, and for all civil cases in Scots law) is the Supreme Court of the United Kingdom, which took over this function from the Appellate Committee of the House of Lords (usually just referred to as "The House of Lords") in October 2009.

Northern Ireland law is a common law system. It is administered by the courts of Northern Ireland, with ultimate appeal to the Supreme Court of the United Kingdom in both civil and criminal matters. The law of Northern Ireland is closely similar to English law, the rules of common law having been imported into the Kingdom of Ireland under English rule. However there are still important differences.

The sources of the law of Northern Ireland are Irish common law and statute law. Of the latter, statutes of the Parliaments of Ireland, of the United Kingdom and of Northern Ireland are in force, and latterly statutes of the devolved Assembly. The courts of Northern Ireland are headed by the Court of Judicature of Northern Ireland, consisting of the Northern Ireland Court of Appeal, the Northern Ireland High Court of Justice and the Northern Ireland Crown Court. Below that are county courts and magistrates' courts.

Scots law is a unique legal system with an ancient basis in Roman law. It is based on civil-law principles, with common law elements dating back to the High Middle Ages. Thus Scotland has a pluralistic, or "mixed", legal system. Since the Acts of Union in 1707, it has shared a legislature with the rest of the United Kingdom. Scotland and England & Wales each retained fundamentally different legal systems, but the Union brought English influence on Scots law and vice versa. In recent years Scots law has also been affected by both European law under the Treaty of Rome and the establishment of the Scottish Parliament which may pass legislation within its areas of legislative competence as detailed by the Scotland Act 1998.

The chief courts are the Court of Session, for civil cases, and the High Court of Justiciary, for criminal cases. The Supreme Court of the United Kingdom serves as the highest court of appeal for civil cases under Scots law, with leave to appeal from the Court of Session not required as a general rule. Sheriff courts deal with most civil and criminal cases including conducting criminal trials with a jury, known as sheriff solemn court, or with a sheriff and no jury, known as sheriff summary Court. The sheriff courts provide a local court service with 49 sheriff courts organised across six sheriffdoms. The Scots legal system is unique in having three possible verdicts for a criminal trial: "guilty", "not guilty" and "not proven". Both "not guilty" and "not proven" result in an acquittal with no possibility of retrial.

While England and Wales, Northern Ireland, and Scotland diverge in the more detailed rules of common law and equity[3], and while there are certain fields of legislative competence devolved in Northern Ireland, Scotland, Wales and London, there are substantive fields of law which apply across the United Kingdom.

The constitution of the United Kingdom is the sum of laws and principles that make up the body politic of the United Kingdom. It concerns both the relationship between the individual and the state, and the functioning of the legislature, the executive and judiciary. Unlike many other nations, the UK has no single constitutional document. This is sometimes expressed by stating that it has an uncodified or "unwritten" constitution. Much of the British constitution is embodied in written documents, within statutes, court judgments, works of authority and treaties. The constitution has other unwritten sources, including parliamentary constitutional conventions.

☞ Notes

1. **the common law**　普通法，起源于中世纪的英格兰，是一种以判例形式出现的适用于全国的法律。"普通法系"的国家主要是英国和美国，都是强调分权、制衡和个人自由的国家。该法系与欧陆法系（又称"大陆法"）并称为当今世界最主要的两大法系。判例法和成文法（Case law and statute law）分别是普通法系和大陆法系的主要法律渊源。
2. **the Writ system**　令状制度。西方国家的令状制度，亦称强制侦查令状制度、司法令状制度，是指侦查机关只有在获得法官签发的令状后，才有权实施扣押、搜查、监听及拘捕等强制侦查行为的制度。侦查人员即使在紧急情况下采取强制侦查措施，也必须事后得到司法官员的认可，否则应立即纠正，且所取得的证据作为非法证据予以排除。

3. **equity** 衡平法，也称平衡法、公平法、公正法。它是英美法律的一个分支，它包括根据公平与正义比普通法更重要的思想而建立的一些法则。因此，在裁决法律诉讼时，如果在法律原则和公平原则之间产生分歧，那么公平原则应占上风，法庭并会按此作出裁决。现时，所有法院可同时适用衡平法和普通法。而当衡平法与普通法出现矛盾，便以衡平法为归依。

   衡平法最早始于英国，当时它是由衡平法法院所实施的法律体系，与普通法相对。衡平法可用这样一句格言来总结，“公正不会让在没有救济的情况下蒙受一种冤屈”。

   衡平法是现代英美法系的重要组成部分，和普通法、制定法并称为三大法律渊源，它成为与普通法制度并列的第二大法律体系。

☞ Questions for comprehension and discussion

1. What are the three legal systems in the UK?
2. Why is English law renowned as being the mother of the common law?
3. Who head the courts of England and Wales?
4. Why is the law of Northern Ireland closely similar to English law?
5. Why is Scots law a unique legal system?
6. Are all fields of legislative competence devolved in Northern Ireland, Scotland, Wales and London?

☞ Questions on Chapter 3 for reflection and presentation

Review the whole chapter and write a short essay on any of the following questions.

1. Compare the politics of the People's Republic of China and the United Kingdom. Try to find out the differences and similarities (if any) in running the country and exercising the State power.
2. The opinions of different parties are voiced in the UK's Parliament. The system has sometimes been criticized for lacking efficiency. What is your view of point on this issue?
3. What are the respective characteristics of English law, Northern Ireland law, and Scots law?
4. What are the functions of such chief courts as the Court of Session, the High Court of Justiciary, the Supreme Court of the United Kingdom, and Sheriff courts?

Chapter 4

Religion and Beliefs

Religion has had a significant impact on lives of people in Britain. People are free to choose and follow their own religious beliefs. With over 170 distinct religions counted, the religious make-up of the UK is diverse, complex and multicultural. For over 1,400 years religion in the United Kingdom has been dominated by various forms of Christianity, which exerted great influence on the politics and social life in UK.

Today, Christianity is still the major religion, followed by Islam, Hinduism, Sikhism, Judaism and Buddhism in terms of number of adherents. According to the 2011 UK Census, increasing British people follow no particular religion. Trends are showing that fewer individuals are viewing religion positively, with 79 per cent of people agreeing that religion is a cause of much misery and conflict in the world today. Regular church attendance has steadily decreased since the middle of the twentieth century, with more individuals rejecting religion.

4.1 History of Religion in Britain

Pre-Roman forms of religion in Britain included various forms of ancestor worship and paganism. Little is known about the details of such religions. In Roman Britain, Christianity was introduced to what are now England, Wales, and Southern Scotland. Forms of Christianity have dominated religious life in Britain for over 1,400 years.

The first evidence of Christianity in England was from the late 2nd century AD. This came at first by indirect means, probably brought by traders and soldiers. At that time England and Wales were ruled by the Romans. The native people, Celts, were polytheists (they worshiped many gods). During the 4th century Christianity became widespread in England.

In 407 the last Roman soldiers left Britain. Over the following decades Roman civilization broke down. In the 5th and 6th centuries Saxons, Angles and Jutes from Germany and Denmark invaded southern and eastern England and gradually conquered most of England. They introduced their own Teutonic religion. In the course of the 7th century, Christianity was again brought to Great Britain by Roman Catholic and Iro-Scottish missionaries.

In the Middle Ages, religion was a vital part of everyday life. Most people lived their lives genuinely believing in the reality of a spiritual realm all around them and in heaven or hell when they died. Everyone attended mass on Sunday. Mass was in Latin, a language that ordinary people did not understand. The Catholic Church provided for the religious aspects of people's lives-baptism of babies, marriages, confession, the last rites for the dying and burying the dead, and dominated the thinking of people. Monasteries and nunneries looked after the old and sick, provided somewhere for travelers to stay, gave alms to the poor and sometimes looked after people's money for them. Monks could often read and write when many other people could not, so they copied books and documents and taught children. Monasteries often had libraries. Church festivals and saints' days were "holy days", when people didn't have to work. The Church played a big part in government: Bishops sat in the House of Lords. They could raise an army for the king in times of war.

As the Early Modern era started, the way people looked at life and the world around them began to change. Some began to question traditional beliefs. For example, many Catholic churches suggested that people could pay indulgences in order to buy their way into heaven. Some felt that this was just a way for the church to make money. This led to conflicts about religion and many people died because of their views. In 1517, a German monk called Martin Luther protested about the Catholic Church and "the Reformation" began in Western Europe, which attempted to reform the Catholic Church and develop Protestant Churches. Protestants believed in worshipping God more simply, without the need for beautifully decorated churches and lots of money. They felt that there should be no distractions and it should just be God and his people. Catholics, on the other hand, always believed in making a church look divine in order that people could feel closer to God there. They also had different ideas on liturgy, prayer and communion. At that time, Protestant ideas were spreading in England despite persecution by the state.

In the 16th century, Britain broke free from the Roman Catholic Church. There was a period of religious conflict. In 1534 King Henry VIII founded the Church of England (Anglican Church) and split it away from the Pope when the Vatican refused to grant him permission to divorce his first wife. He became the leader of the church. In 1539, Henry authorized a new English translation of the *Bible* and from 1545 English replaced Latin as the language of church services. During the reign of Mary I, daughter of Henry VIII,

Catholicism was restored and many Protestants were burned. In 1558, Elizabeth became Queen. She changed the church back to Anglican and it has been the official religion ever since.

In the early 17th century king and parliament clashed over the issue of religion. In 1642 came Civil War[1] between king and parliament. Following the Civil War, many independent churches sprang up in England. The parliament was determined to crash down on the many independent churches. When James Ⅱ became the king of England and Scotland in 1685, he tried to make England a Roman Catholic country by forcing people to follow his Roman Catholic faith. He was hated by the people because of his persecution of the Protestants. In 1688, he was forced to give up the crown. Afterwards the *Bill of Rights* (1689) said that no Catholic could become king or queen and no king could marry a Catholic.

In the early 18th century England was noted for its lack of religious enthusiasm. It was an age of reason and the churches lacked vigor. In the mid-18th century things began to change. And in the late 18th century religious enthusiasm began to revive in England.

During the early 19th century religious revival continued. The Church of England regained its energy and many new churches were built. Throughout the Victorian age, religion was a dominant force in the lives of many people. The Protestant church of England was very powerful. Most people were members of the Anglican or Presbyterian Church, although there were some Catholics and increasing numbers of Non-conformists for example, Quakers and Methodists. Social life for ordinary people revolved around choir and Sunday School outings. Many employers insisted that their employees go to church. Religion inspired many of the great 19th century social reformers and British Protestant missionaries travelled all over the world. At the same time, there were developments in science, such as Darwinism; politics, such as Marxism and theology. Religion had a great influence over people's life, however, there was a growing seam of doubt.

By the 20th century, religion had declined in importance for many people in Britain. Although there have been significant political events related to religion, the number of regular Christian worshipers began to decline, and many people didn't believe in God. By the end of the 20th century only a small minority of the population attended church regularly. The substantial immigration to Britain since the 1920s has contributed to the growth of foreign faiths, especially of Islam, Hinduism, Sikhism and Buddhism.

Today, Britain has been variously described as a post-Christian[2] society. British society became more liberal, secular and materialistic.

☞ Notes

1. **(English) Civil War** 英国内战，也称清教徒革命(Puritan Revolution)，是1642年至1651年在英国议会派与保皇派之间发生的一系列武装冲突及政治斗争。此事件对英国和整个欧洲都产生了巨大的影响，并由此将革命开始的1640年作为世界近代史的开端。
2. **post-Christian** 后基督教。从广义上讲，指基督教在一个地区或社会中的重要性下降后的一段时期。

☞ Questions for comprehension and discussion

1. When and how was Christianity introduced to Britain?
2. What kind of role did religion play in Middle Age Britain?
3. How did Britain break free from the Roman Catholic Church?

4.2 Church of England

There are two established churches in Britain, that is, churches legally recognized as official churches of the State: Church of England in England and Church of Scotland in Scotland.

The Church of England (Anglican Church) is the established or state church in England. It is divided into two provinces — Canterbury in the South of England and York in the North. Each province has a head or Primate — the Archbishops of Canterbury and York. On any one Sunday more than a million people attend Church of England services, making it the largest Christian denomination in the country.

The Church of England traces its roots back to the early church, but its specifically Anglican identity and its links to the State date back to the Reformation. In the 1530s, Henry Ⅷ started the process of creating the Church of England after his split with the Pope. Henry was anxious to ensure a male heir after his first wife, Catherine of Aragon, who had borne him only a daughter. Henry argued the marriage to Catherine was not valid, because she was his brother's widow. He asked the Pope to annul the marriage in order to remarry, however the Pope would not cooperate. In 1534 after several attempts to persuade the Pope to grant an annulment, Henry passed the *Act of Succession* and then *the Act of Supremacy*. These recognized that the King was "the only supreme head of the Church of England called Anglicana Ecclesia", and Church of England became the official religion.

The Church of England is the established church, meaning, amongst other things: the Monarch is the Supreme Governor of the church; the Church performs a number of official functions; and the Church and State are linked.

Today the Monarch retains the title Defender of the Faith. He or she has to approve the appointment of archbishops, bishops and deans (on the recommendation of the Prime Minister); formally open each new session every five years of the General Synod; promise to maintain the Church in his or her coronation oath.

The Church of England also has a law-making role in Britain. Twenty-six bishops (including the two Archbishops) sit in the House of Lords and are known as the Lords Spiritual. They are thought to bring a religious ethos to the secular process of law. However, in an increasingly multi-cultural society, questions are being asked as to whether that role needs to be specifically fulfilled by Church of England Bishops.

The Church of England fulfils a civic responsibility too. Its bishops and priests are responsible for performing state weddings and funerals, acts of remembrances, memorial services as well as grand occasions like the coronation. After events like the Gulf War or major disasters, the country "comes together" to mourn under the spiritual guidance of the Church of England. In recent years, such occasions have become more ecumenical and multi-faith as the Church of England acknowledges Britain's changing religious landscape.

From the 18th century onwards the Church of England has also been faced with a number of challenges that it continues to face today.

- There has been the challenge of responding to social changes in England such as population growth, urbanization and the development of an increasingly multi-cultural and multi-faith society.
- There has been the challenge of engaging in mission in a society that has become increasingly materialist in outlook and in which belief in God or interest in "spiritual" matters is not seen as being linked to involvement with the life of the Church.
- There has been the challenge of providing sufficient and sufficiently trained clergy and lay ministers to enable the Church of England to carry out its responsibility.
- There has been the challenge of trying to overcome the divisions of the past by developing closer relationships between the Church of England and other churches and trying to move with them towards the goal of full visible unity in faith.

☞ Questions for comprehension and discussion

1. What are the established churches in Britain?
2. Who are the two Archbishops?
3. What was the cause of the Reformation?
4. What are the main challenges faced by the Church of England?

4.3 Religion and British Culture

Christian influence on values, beliefs, and practices in Western culture are abundant and well ingrained into the flourishing society of today. Nowadays, Britain is in many ways a secular state, but perhaps the national culture is still more Christian than we often notice. Trying to take all the religion out of it would be not so much like taking the raisins out of a fruitcake as like taking the chocolate out of a chocolate cake.

Christianity is deeply ingrained in British culture, influencing all aspects of people, such as their daily life, weddings and funerals, literature, mass media, values, language, customs and habits. So here are some of the places in British society where Christian heritage can easily be uncovered.

Festivals and Calendar

The shape of our week is religious — the seven-day cycle with a day of rest. Days and months are named after gods, while our years are numbered after the birth of Christ. The very notion of holidays perpetuates the age-old observation of "holy days".

In Britain, most annual celebrations are religious in their origins. Some important traditional festivals are Christian. For example, Christmas Day celebrates the birth of Christ. Easter celebrates the Resurrection of Christ. Good Friday commemorates the crucifixion and death of Christ. Valentine's Day began as a celebration of early Christian saints St. Valentine. Guy Fawkes Night marks the burning in effigy of the Catholic threat to national security. Mother's Day marks the halfway point of Lent, and one theory of its origin is that it was marked by visiting the region's "mother church" or cathedral. New Year's Day has no very religious origin, but new year resolutions are a Puritan tradition of spiritual improvement.

The academic year revolves around Christmas and Easter holidays, while in the more traditional universities the terms are religious too. Oxford, for example has Michaelmas, Hilary and Trinity, marking the feast days of the Archangel Michael, Hilary of Poitiers and the metaphysical constitution of God. St. Andrews University has two semesters, Martinmas and Candlemas. Durham has Michaelmas, Epiphany and Easter.

Language and literature

Christianity and *Bible* has a great influence on the English language and literature. English incorporated many words and phrases from the *Bible*. For example, most swearwords, along with milder exclamations, if they are not related to bodily functions or organs, are religious. Many are explicit: OMG, for Christ's sake, what the hell, good heavens, damn. Others are under cover: "Heck" is hell, "Dickens" is the devil, "goodness" is God, "strewth" is God's truth. Other phrases are not Biblical but obviously religious — singing from the same hymnsheet, preaching to the converted, pop idol, godsend, making a sacrifice, hell to pay.

When talking about British literature, few deny the influence and position of Christianity. British writers over the centuries have been greatly influenced by the *Bible*, such as Chaucer, Shakespeare, Milton, Blake, Eliot, etc. The core issues concerned by Christianity are the nature of man, the environment of man and the destination of man's life voyage, all of which are also the great concerns of English literature. The three issues has been debated repeatedly in Christian classics and British literary works.

Sport

Football may be a religion in itself, with its worship, rituals, vestments and tribalism, but it still has room for Christian traditions. Witness how players cross themselves and point heavenwards, or put their hands together and pray to the referee to avoid being booked or sent off.

Meanwhile, the fans sing hymn tunes — occasionally with the original words such as *Abide With Me* at cup finals. More often they are adapted, such as "three-nil" to the tune of *Amazing Grace*, "We are the famous CFC" to the tune of *The Lord of the Dance*, or "You're not singing any more" to the tune of *Bread of Heaven*.

Food and drink

There are brands and products that take their names from religious sources, whether for historical reasons or just because it sounds good. So there are Angel Delight, devil's food cake and hot cross buns.

Upholding the traditional connections between holy orders and alcohol are Bishops Finger, Blue Nun and Abbot Ale. And the biggest fish sales of the year are still on Good Friday.

Folklore

Certain superstitions are supposed to have religious roots. In medieval lore, Satan loved to take the form of a black cat and hated salt, a symbol of purity, hence the unluckiness of seeing the one and the remedy of throwing the other over one's shoulder.

Fear of the number 13 may have stemmed from Judas being the 13th member of the Last Supper. And nowadays in Britain, we still bless people when they sneeze.

Music

While Masses, oratorios and sacred cantatas have an important place in classical music, the pop charts may not seem a welcoming place for theology. In fact, in one way or another, religion is a recurrent theme for many of the most respected and/or best-selling music acts. Witness everything from the gospel of Elvis and Mariah Carey to the hymns of Bob Marley and Van Morrison.

☞ Questions for comprehension and discussion

1. How are religious festivals like Christmas, Easter and Good Friday related with Christ?
2. Do you know any English words or phrases related to Christianity? Please list some of them.
3. Do you know any folklore in Britain that has religious root? Please share it with your classmates.

☞ Questions on Chapter 4 for reflection and presentation

Review the whole chapter and write a short essay on any of the following questions.

1. Please give a brief introduction of religion history in Britain.
2. How is Church of England related to the Crown and linked with the State?
3. Christianity has a deep root in British culture. Would you like to illustrate the point with examples?

Chapter 5

Economy and Social Welfare

Britain was the first country to industrialize in the world. In the late 18th century, Industrial Revolution started primarily in Britain and brought it the world's leading economy. For a few decades from early 19th century to the 1870s, Britain, known as "workshop of the world", had the industrial, commercial, financial and sea power to edge out rivals abroad. By the late 19th century, as other nations industrialized, coupled with economic decline after two World Wars, Britain began to lose the economic supremacy.

Today, Although the prosperity hundreds years ago has gone, the Britain remains a great power with considerable economic, cultural, military, scientific and political influence internationally. In 2013, it has the sixth largest economy in the world and third largest in Europe after Germany and France measured by nominal GDP[1] (2013). London, the capital city, is one of the world's largest financial centers and leading cities, and has the largest city GDP in Europe. Pound sterling, the currency of Britain, is the world's third-largest reserve currency after the US dollar and the Euro.

5.1 Domestic Economy and Foreign Trade

Britain, a highly developed capitalist country, maintains a leading trading entity, economic power and financial center with significant worldwide influence. In 2013, Britain has the sixth largest national economy by nominal GDP ($2.49 trillion). It's also one of the largest economies in European Union.

In Britain, there are significant regional variations in prosperity, with the South East of England and southern Scotland the richest areas per capita. London has the largest city GDP in Europe. The main components of British economy are services (77.8% by GDP in 2013), industry (21.5%) and agriculture (0.7%).

Agriculture The British were pioneers in modern agriculture and were among the first to bring science and machinery to farming. Agriculture in Britain is intensive, highly mechanized and efficient. At present, it contributes about £ 8 billion, less than 1% of its gross value added[2] (GVA). Less than 2% of the population, about 0.45 million, produces about 60% of food needs, and about 40% comes from imports. Britain has favorable conditions for agricultural development, such as temperate climate with plentiful rainfall, skilled farmers, high technology, fertile soil and subsidies, which primarily come from the European Union.

Agriculture uses around 1.86 million hm^2, about 73% of the country's land area, among which around 2/3 is for livestock, 1/3 for arable crops. Pastoral farming, an important part of agriculture, is the breeding of livestock for meat, wool, eggs and milk. The most common meat animals in Britain are cattle, sheep, chickens and pigs. Britain is the second exporter of livestock after France. The output of beef cattle and milk amounts more than a half of pastoral farming.

The arable land in Britain is concentrated in the southern and eastern part of England, and eastern Scotland. The chief crops include wheat, barely, oats, potatoes, sugar beet, oil seed, fodder crops and horticultural crops.

Industry Britain is an industrialized country. Although the heavy industry gradually and relatively declined throughout the 20th century, Britain remains strong in the world with its industry, especially the manufacturing sector, accounting over 10% of economic output and employing 2.5 million.

The automotive industry is a strong part of the economy, and has been one of the chief exporting industries. The origins of the British automotive industry date back to the final years of the 19th century. By the 1950s Britain was the second-largest manufacturer of cars in the world and the largest exporter. However in subsequent decades the industry experienced considerably lower growth. Since the late 1980s many British car marques have been acquired by foreign companies including Mini and Rolls-Royce (BMW), Jaguar and Land Rover (TATA), Bentley (Volkswagen Group)[3], and etc. Although all large-volume producers in Britain are now foreign-owned, the automotive industry remains a strong part of the economy, and has been one of the chief exporting industries. Apart from an abundant automotive manufactures, Britain has a prosperous car parts industry, healthy retail and maintenance sector.

The aerospace industry of Britain has a high level of R&D[4] and manufacturing. It is the second largest in the world after the U.S., with the global market share accounting for 13%. The British aerospace industry has made significant contributions to the world history of aircraft.

Chemicals and Pharmaceuticals are another important contributor to Britain's manufacturing base. Within the sector, the pharmaceuticals industry is particularly successful. Some world famous pharmaceutical firms, like GlaxoSmithKline and AstraZeneca, have bases and major research and development and manufacturing facilities in the country.

Other important sectors of the manifesting industry include electronics, textile, food and beverage, tobacco, paper, printing and publishing. Some major manufacturing companies in Britain are world famous, such as Unilever, Cadbury Schwppes, British American Tobacco, Imperial Tobacco, HarperCollins[5].

Britain has large coal, natural gas, and oil resources, but its oil and natural gas reserves are declining and Britain became a net importer of energy in 2005.

Service The service sector dominates British economy, contributes around 3/4 of GDP, and employs around 21 million, 75% of the labor force. Services, particularly banking, insurance, tourism and business service are key drivers of British economy growth.

The financial services industry is one of the key pillars of British economy, covering banking, insurance, stock broking, foreign exchange, investment funds and other services. It's among the world's best in terms of scale and internationalization. London is one of the principal financial centers of the world, and a major financial exchange market. Apart from London, several other major Britain cities have large financial sectors and related services, such as Leeds, Edinburgh, Manchester, Birmingham. Britain's banking industry is well developed, with the largest number of foreign banks in the world. The Bank of England, established in 1694, is the central bank of Britain, and it's regarded as the model on which most modern central banks have been based in the world. There are many world famous banks like HSBC Bank, Barclays Bank, Lloyds Banking Group, and Royal Bank of Scotland Group[6], etc. British insurance market is the largest in Europe and the third largest in the world, after the USA and Japan. According to figures released by the Association of British Insurers in September 2013, out of the total 26.4 million households within Britain, 5.3 million had whole-life insurance policies and a further 0.5 million had fixed-term life insurance cover. London is the world capital for foreign exchange trading. The average daily volume counted around 5 trillion of dollars US.

Britain, among the earliest to develop tourism, is a major tourist source area and destination. It is important to economy development. The abundant natural, historical and cultural tourist resources, as well as sophisticated travel services make the country a good condition for development of tourism. According to World Tourism Organization, Britain, with over 31.2 million tourists arriving in 2013, ranked as the 8th biggest tourist destination in the world, after France, United States, Spain, China, Italy, Turkey, and

Germany. The British earned \$40.6 billion inbound travel, while spent \$52.6 billion in out bound travel.

Education and academic research in Britain is at a leading position in the world. It's an important education center, with many world famous universities, like University of Cambridge, University of Oxford, Imperial College, etc. Every year many students from all over the world are attracted to Britain, not only bring huge foreign exchange for the country, also absorbing a lot of talent for the country of knowledge-based economy.

Foreign Trade Britain is the fourth largest trading country in the world, accounting for more than 5% of the world's total trade volume. Its limited domestic market and inadequate home supply of raw materials compel the country to rely heavily on foreign trade. Since import and export activities are a key contributor to the overall economic growth, the British have few restrictions on foreign trade and investment.

The country's chief exports are machinery, vehicles, aerospace products, electrical and electronic products, chemicals and fuels. Exports of services are mainly banking, insurance, stock brokerage, consultancy, shipping and computer programming. The exports of goods and services account for more than one-third of its GDP.

Britain is also one of the largest importers in the world. About 40% of the domestic food supplies have to be imported. And since 2005, the country has become a net importer of energy, especially oil and coal. Besides, Britain imports raw materials and manufactures them into finished goods and exports these finished goods for profits.

☞ Notes

1. **GDP** 国内生产总值，是 Gross Domestic Product 的简写。国内生产总值是指在一定时期内(一个季度或一年)，一个国家或地区的经济中所生产出的全部最终产品和劳务的价值，常被公认为衡量国家经济状况的最佳指标。
2. **gross value added** 常简写为 GVA，是一个估算国民生产总值(GDP)的重要方法。GDP 和 GVA 的关系可以用一条公式来表达：GVA-生产的税收-生产的补贴 = GDP
3. **Mini and Rolls-Royce** (**BMW**), **Jaguar and Land Rover** (**TATA**), **Bentley** (**Volkswagen Group**) 汽车品牌 Mini 和劳斯莱斯(宝马)、捷豹和路虎(印度塔塔)、宾利(大众)。
4. **R&D** 常译为“研究与开发”，是 research and development 的简写。R&D 指在科学技术领域，为增加知识总量(包括人类文化和社会知识的总量)，以及运用这些知识去创造新的应用进行的系统的创造性的活动，包括基础研究、应用研究、试验发展三类活动。还可译为“研究与发展”或“研究与试验性发展”。

5. **Unilever, Cadbury Schwppes, British American Tobacco, Imperial Tobacco, HarperCollins** 联合利华集团、吉百利食品集团、英美烟草集团、皇家烟草集团、哈珀柯林斯出版集团、巴宝莉时装集团、锐步服装集团以及茵宝服装集团。
6. **HSBC Bank, Barclays Bank, Lloyds Banking Group, and Royal Bank of Scotland Group** 汇丰银行、劳埃德银行、苏格兰皇家银行及巴克莱银行。

☞ Questions for comprehension and discussion

1. What are the main farming types in Britain?
2. Please briefly introduce the automotive industry in Britain.
3. What kind of role is London playing in British and world economy?
4. What are Britain's chief exports?

5.2 Social Welfare

Britain has a long history of social welfare. As the first welfare state in the world, Britain has established a "from-cradle-to-grave" social welfare program for all citizens.

The social welfare program is funded out of national insurance contributions and taxation. It includes a number of social services. The most important ones are the National Health Service (NHS), the social security program and personal social services.

5.2.1 the National Health Service (NHS)

The NHS was set up in 1948. It aims to provide for every resident, regardless of income, a full range of medical service. The NHS is a rare example of truly socialized medicine. It is mainly financed through general taxation — provided by the British government and funded by the taxpayer. The principle is: there should be a full range of publicly provided services designed to help the individual stay healthy. All taxpayers, employers and employees, contribute to its cost so that those members of the community who do not require health service can help to pay for those who do.

The NHS is now a largely free service. All appointments and treatments are free to the patient (though paid for through taxes), as are almost all prescription drugs. Some forms of treatment may be charged for, such as drugs prescribed by family doctors and general dental treatment.

The NHS has come under much criticism, especially during the early 2000s. The sheer size of the National Health Service in the UK, the vast number of services available and the millions of people that the NHS serves, lead to certain problems with the system.

The main problems for the NHS are waiting lists, patient demand and high running costs.

5. 2. 2 Social Security

Britain has a very comprehensive social security system. Once the residents reach the age of 16 they are awarded a National Insurance number, which is used as a reference number for their subsequent access to the social security system.

The British social security system is designed to secure a basic standard of living for people in financial need. It is the largest single area of government spending. Each year nearly a third of government expenditure is devoted to the social security program, which provides financial help for people who are elderly, sick, disabled, unemployed, widowed, bringing up children or on very low income. Major items of the social security program include:

State Retirement Pension

A State Retirement Pension is paid to people reached retirement age. The current retirement age in Britain is 65 for men and 60 for women. In the 2030s the eligible age for the state pension is due to rise to 68. To qualify, pensioners need to have paid enough National Insurance contributions throughout their working life. The amount they are paid depends on the contributions they have made.

Jobseeker's Allowance

Jobseeker's Allowance is paid to eligible people over 18 years old and under retirement age who are out of a job but capable of working and actively seeking employment. It is also available to people who work 16 hours or less every week. the claimant must not have become unemployed voluntarily or have lost their job through misconduct. They are expected to look for work actively and mush have good reasons for rejecting any job that is offered. The amount paid is based on previous National Insurance contributions and personal wealth.

Income Support

Income Support is available for people on a low income. Recipients must be over 16 years of age to get Income Support. They must not work more than 16 hours per week and, if they have a partner, that partner can not work more than 24 hours per week.

Income Support is dependent on how much money a person earns and any capital or savings they have. People with savings may get paid a reduced amount, and those with savings over a certain amount are not eligible.

Sickness and Invalidity Benefit

A large variety of benefits is available for people unable to work because of sickness or disablement. For example:

Statutory Sick Pay is a benefit paid by employers for a maximum of 28 weeks to employees who have been off work sick for 4 or more days in a row.

Disability Living Allowance is a tax-free benefit for people that who need help looking after themselves, and there are different rates which apply to the extent of the disability.

Invalid Carer's Allowance is a taxable benefit for people who are over 16 years old and spend at least 35 hours a week caring for someone who is disabled. The claimant does not have to be related to, or living with, the person for whom they care for.

Child Benefit

Child Benefit has remained universal, payable to all families with children under 16 regardless of income. They can also apply if a child is between 16 and 19, and in full time non-advanced education, or a child of 16 or 17 years old who has recently left education or training but is registered for certain work or training. It is paid at a higher rate for the eldest or only child, and then at a lower rate for all subsequent children.

Housing Benefit

People on a low income, whether employed or not, may be eligible for help in paying all or part of their rent. If the salary plus savings are below a certain level, help may be available. This is paid by the local authority in which the person lives. Housing Benefit can't be paid for heating, hot water, energy or food. How much one gets depends on the income and circumstances.

☞ Questions for comprehension and discussion

1. What does NHS in Britain aim to do? How is it financed?
2. What does The British social security system secure?
3. At what age do men and women generally retire?

☞ Questions on Chapter 5 for reflection and presentation

Review the whole chapter and write a short essay on any of the following questions.

1. When did Britain become "workshop of the world"? How did Britain lose the economic

supremacy gradually?

2. Britain's agriculture is highly mechanized. Give examples to show this.
3. What kind of role is Service Industry playing in Britain? Give example to show this.
4. What is meant by the term " 'from-cradle-to-grave' social welfare program" in Britain?

Chapter 6

Education System

Education is an important part of British life. There are hundreds of schools, colleges and universities, including some of the most famous in the world.

Education in the United Kingdom is a devolved matter with each of the countries of the UK having separate systems under separate governments: the UK Government is responsible for England; the Scottish Government, the Welsh Government and the Northern Ireland Executive are responsible for Scotland, Wales and Northern Ireland, respectively.

6.1 Education Stages

Education in the UK is generally divided into three major stages: Compulsory Education (CE), Further Education (FE) and Higher Education (HE).

Education is compulsory for all children between the ages of 5 (4 in Northern Ireland) and 16, the compulsory school age (CSA). In England, compulsory education or training has been extended to 18 for those born after 1 September 1997. This full-time education does not need to be at a school and a growing number of parents choose to home educate.

Prior to the CSA children can be educated at nursery if parents wish though there is only limited government funding for such places. Many children attend pre-schools, day nurseries, nursery schools or nursery classes attached to primary or infant schools. In practice, most schools take children earlier.

The Early Years Foundation Stage (EYFS, 0-5 years) became a statutory requirement for all Ofsted[1]-registered childcare settings in September 2008, which includes registered childminders, day nurseries, nursery schools, playgroups, and nursery, reception or foundation classes in primary schools.

The first year of full-time school for four to five year olds is called Reception. After a year (or less with staggered intakes) in Reception, children move into Year 1, then move up a year group each year, as this is a standard national system. Schools can arrange classes in any way they want, and many, especially smaller schools, will have mixed age classes, so that a child can move up a year group in September, but stay in the same class for another year.

In a few areas in England, instead of infant (4 to 7 year olds) and junior (7 to 11) or primary (4 to 11), followed by secondary school (11 to 16/18), there is a system of lower, middle and upper schools. Lower schools are usually for 4/5 to 9 year olds, middle schools for 9 to 13 year olds and upper schools for 13 to 18 year olds.

In addition to year groups, schooling is divided up into key stages. Children (5-11 year olds) attend primary school for seven years (Key Stage1&2). The final year of junior or primary school for most children is Year 6, and the first year of secondary school Year 7.

Most children transfer at the age of 11, usually to their nearest secondary school (Key Stage 3), though the law allows parents in England and Wales to express preferences for other schools too.

Study of GSCE[2] subjects begins at the start of Year 10, generally taken in a number of subjects by pupils aged 14-16 in secondary education in England, Wales and Northern Ireland. Some subjects start earlier, for example Maths, English and Science, because these courses are too long to be taught within 2 years. Final examinations are then taken at the end of Year 11 (age 15-16). In Scotland, the equivalent of the GCSE is the Standard Grade.

The Education and Skills Act 2008 raised the compulsory education age until which students must continue to receive some form of education or training to 18 by 2015.

UK post-secondary qualifications are defined at different levels, with levels 1-3 denoting further education and levels 4-8 denoting higher education. Within this structure, a foundation degree[3] is at level 5, a Bachelor's at level 6, at Master's at level 7, and a Doctoral degree at level 8.

Further Education is not compulsory and may be at any level above compulsory secondary education. It therefore includes education for people over 16, usually excluding universities and is usually a means to attain an intermediate or follow up qualification necessary to attend university, or begin a specific career path. UK students planning to go to college or university must complete further education. It is primarily taught in FE colleges, work-based learning, and adult and community learning institutions. In addition, FE courses may be offered in the school sector, both in sixth form[4] (16-19) colleges, or, more commonly, sixth forms within secondary schools. This includes post-16 courses similar to those taught at schools and sub-degree courses similar to those taught at higher education colleges (which also teach degree-level courses) and at some universities.

Higher Education has a long history in the UK. Oxford and Cambridge dated from the 12th and 13th centuries, while Scottish universities of St. Andrews, Glasgow, Edinburgh and Aberdeen from the 14th and 15th centuries. The rest were founded in the 19th and 20th centuries.

Apart from a single private university, Buckingham, all universities with the power to award degrees are heavily state financed.

Around 30% of the 18 to 19 year old British students enter full-time higher education. Students in England, Wales and Northern Ireland may usually enter university from the age of 18, while students in Scotland usually enter university in the year they turn 18 (with many still being 17 upon starting), hence courses take an extra year compared to England, Wales and Northern Ireland.

☞ Notes

1. **Ofsted**(The Office for Standards in Education) 教育标准局。属于非内阁部门的公职机构，由枢密院任命(成立于 1992 年)。其主要任务是对公立学校例行督导，后来逐步扩大到对私立学校、继续教育学院、地方教育行政当局、新教师和在职教师培训以及幼儿园和保育机构的督导。自 2007 年 4 月起，其职能范围又扩大到对儿童福利和成人教育机构进行督导，因而更名为“教育、儿童服务和技能标准局”(The Office for Standards in Education, Children's Services and Skills)，简称仍为“教育标准局”。
2. **GCSE**(General Certificate of Secondary Education) 普通中学证书。是指完成中学教育最后两年(中四、中五)后取得的文凭。
3. **foundation degree** 基础学位。为高等职业教育学位，是介于高等教育证书和荣誉学位之间的中间层次的高等教育资格，相当于英国国家职业资格(NVQ)的 5 级。全日制学生的修业年限一般为两年，非全日制为三或四年。
4. **Sixth form** 中学里的六年级(最高年级)，也是准备进入大学深造的学生通过 GCSE 后的大学预科班(一年至两年)；也称继续教育阶段，主要是学术方向和职业方向学习。完成预科的学生主要参加普通教育高级考试(general certificate of education, advanced level，简称 GCE-A level)，而职业技校的学生除了要参加 GCE-A level 考试外，还要参加普通国家职业资格考试(General National Vocational Qualification，简称 GNVQ)。

☞ Questions for comprehension and discussion

1. How many stages is education in UK divided into?
2. Is the UK government responsible for education in all of its countries?
3. What is the compulsory school age in England and Northern Ireland respectively?
4. At what stages does secondary school begin and end?
5. Can students go to universities immediately when they finish secondary education? What must they do?

6.2 Types of Schools

The main categories of school in the UK are state schools and independent schools. The term "state school" refers to government-funded schools which provide education free of charge to pupils. Most are organised by Local Authorities (LA) and are free to all British children between the ages of 4 or 5-16.

All government-run schools, state schools, follow the same *National Curriculum*, the main aim of which is to raise standards, making sure all children have a broad and balanced education up to the age of 16 and to ensure that schools in all parts of the country are following the same courses. The *National Curriculum* specifies what children must study and what they are expected to know at different ages. This ties in with the national tests that check whether children are meeting these targets.

The most common state schools are: community schools, controlled by the local council and not influenced by business or religious groups; foundation schools, more freedom to change the way they do things than community schools; academies, run by a governing body, independent from the local council — they can follow a different curriculum; comprehensive schools and grammar schools.

Comprehensive schools were introduced all over the country in the 1960s and are the most popular secondary schools in the UK today. Such schools admit children without reference to their academic abilities and provide a general education. Pupils can study everything from academic subjects like literature to more practical subjects like cooking. Nearly 88% of secondary school pupils in England go to comprehensive schools, as do all pupils in Wales. These take children of all abilities and provide a wide range of secondary education for all or most of the children in a district from 11 to 16 or 18. All children in Scotland go to non-selective schools. (Most state education in Britain is nominally non-selective, but middle-class parents try to live near the best schools.)

Grammar schools are selective state secondary schools. They lay emphasis on advanced academic subjects rather than the more general curriculum of the comprehensive schools and expect many of their pupils to go on to universities. They select children at the age of 11 based on academic ability. Entry to grammar schools is through an exam called "the 11-plus" taken in the final year of primary education. Those children with the highest marks go to grammar schools. Those who do not do well will go to the secondary modern schools[1].

The grammar school/non-grammar school division is still common in Northern Ireland, but throughout the rest of Great Britain grammar schools are becoming increasingly rare. In the UK 93% of the children in England and Wales go to "state schools".

Independent Schools are fee-paying schools and also known as private schools and public schools. They receive their funding through the private sector and through tuition rates, with some government assistance. They are not part of the nation education system, and thus are independent of many of the regulations and conditions that apply to state funded schools, but the quality of instruction and standards are maintained through visits from Her Majesty's Inspectors of Schools. They are not obliged to follow the *National Curriculum*, though most will follow a course that leads to common entrance[2] or to scholarship examinations and prepare their students ultimately for the national examinations such as GCSE and A-Levels[3].

Most of the larger independent schools are either full or partial boarding schools, although many are now predominantly day schools. Regulations do not permit international students to attend State Schools-they must attend Independent Schools.

Those educated wholly in the private sector will typically attend nursery between the ages of 0 or 2 and 4; pre-prep (preparatory) from 3 or 4 to 7 or 8 and prep school from age 7 or 8 to 11 or 13, which prepares pupils to go to a public school.

The term public school refers to a group of older, more expensive and exclusive fee-paying private schools that provides secondary education, particularly in England, which cater primarily for children aged between 13 and 18. In Scotland, where the educational system is completely different from the rest of UK, the term "public school" in Scottish English and Scots is only used to describe Scottish state funded schools (since they are publicly owned) -although, in the media preference is now being given to the term "state funded school" to avoid confusion with the English term.

The entrance exams used by most public schools are known as Common Entrance exams and are taken at the age of 11 (girls) or 13 (boys). English, maths, science and humanities form the core curriculum with many schools offering modern foreign languages (usually French, German, Spanish and/or Mandarin), classics-Latin, Greek and classical civilisation — plus IT, music, art, drama, PE. Typically one or two extra-curricular activities will be built into the day — usually during lunch or immediately after school but some boarding schools weave activities in to their daily timetable, ensuring all children get more that just academic fare. Some schools will have predominantly class-based teaching, some a mix of class and specialists (usually music, languages, PE), others will mirror senior schools with pupils moving to specialist areas for lessons with specialist teachers.

In 2011 there were more than 2,600 independent schools in the UK educating some 628,000 children, comprising over 6.5 per cent of UK children, and more than 18 per cent of pupils over the age of 16.

Compared with state schools, independent schools achieve higher academic standards. Parents choose to pay fees in order for their children to have a better chance of getting into good universities and getting better jobs when they leave school. The most famous public schools are Eton, Harrow and Winchester.

In 2013 the Higher Education Funding Council for England published a study noting, amongst other things, that a greater percentage of students who had attended an independent school prior to university achieved a first or upper second class degree compared with students from state schools.

☞ Notes

1. **secondary modern schools** 现代中学，1944 年至 20 世纪 70 年代遍布英格兰、威尔士和北爱尔兰的中学，采用三分制。主要招收大多数在“11 会考”中分数未能达到前 25%的学生。一般修业 5 年，其目标是完成多数学生的义务教育任务。现在很多专业科目已发展成为现代中学的课程，例如，工艺美术、缝纫裁剪、烹调、汽车工程机械、手工艺、农业科学、商业等。如今，现代中学已经合并或改为综合中学，主要只在北爱尔兰还有保留，通常称为中学。
2. **common entrance(examinations)** (CE)公学入学会考。是英国私立中学入学考试，是学生在 11 岁或者 13 岁时参加的小学升中学的一种考试，从 1904 年开始实施。学生只有在被某学校录取之后才能参加该会考，因此，考卷将由相关学校审阅。但是，大部分私立学校会采用该校自己设置的笔试和面试，这种考试与 GCSE(普通中等教育考试)类似，包括一些必选的核心科目，例如数学、英语、科学等。
3. **A-Levels** 中学高级课程，是指英国普通高级中学教育和大学的衔接课程，是世界公认的英国高校入学考试课程，其考试成绩也是中学升入大学的考核标准。

通常是两年，第一年叫做 lower six form，学习 AS-level（Advanced Supplementary Level）课程，选择至少 4 门的 A-Level 科目进行学习；第二年叫做 upper six form，学习 A2-level 课程，着重其中至少 3 门科目的学习。因此 AS-level + A2-level = A-levels。与之相替代的是国际课程(International Baccalaureate)，学期也是两年，第一年是 AS，第二年是 A Two。在这两年的学习过程中，学生必须从一系列广泛多样的学科中选择 6 门科目学习，其中 3 组高等级，另外 3 组标准等级。除了这 6 门科目之外，学生还必须完成 3 个核心课程，1 篇拓展论文，1 门有关于“认识论”的课程，以及 CAS(创造、实践、服务)。

☞ Questions for comprehension and discussion

1. What are the most common state schools in the UK?
2. What are the differences between comprehensive schools and grammar schools?
3. What are the major characteristics of Public Schools?
4. What do children study in public schools?
5. Why do parents choose to pay to let children go to independent schools?

6.3 Homeschooling

In the UK education is compulsory, but schooling is not, children are not required to attend school. They could be educated at home.

Article 2 of Protocol 1 of the European Convention on Human Rights[1] states that: “No person shall be denied the right to education. In the exercise of any functions which it assumes in relation to education and to teaching, the State shall respect the right of parents to ensure such education and teaching is in conformity with their own religious and philosophical convictions.”

Education and Section 7 of the *UK Education Act* 1996 states that: “The parent of every child of compulsory school age shall cause him to receive efficient full-time education suitable — (a) to his age, ability and aptitude, and (b) to any special educational needs he may have, either by regular attendance at school or otherwise.” So homeschooling, or home education, where parents choose to educate their children outside school, remains a legal option for families — as long as they provide a suitable full-time alternative.

Home education in the UK is often termed “elective home education” (EHE) to signify the independent nature of practice from state provisions such as education for children with ill-health provided by the local authority in the family home. EHE is a collective term used in the UK to describe education provided otherwise than through the schooling system.

Homeschooling may involve an informal style of education described as unschooling, informal learning, natural or autonomous learning.

Parents may decide to exercise their right to home educate their child from a very early age and so the child may not have been previously enrolled at school. They may also elect to home educate at any other stage up to the end of compulsory school age. Parents are not required to register or seek approval from the local authority to educate their children at home. Parents who choose to educate their children at home must be prepared to assume full financial responsibility, including bearing the cost of any public examinations. However, local authorities are encouraged to provide support where resources permit.

Parents are required to provide an efficient, full-time education suitable to the age, ability and aptitude of the child. There is currently no legal definition of "full-time". Children normally attend school for between 22 and 25 hours a week for 38 weeks of the year, but this measurement of "contact time" is not relevant to elective home education where there is often almost continuous one-to-one contact and education may take place outside normal "school hours". The type of educational activity can be varied and flexible. Home educating parents are not required to: follow the National Curriculum, provide a broad and balanced education, have a timetable, have premises equipped to any particular standard, set hours during which education will take place, have any specific qualifications, make detailed plans in advance, observe school hours, days or terms, give formal lessons, mark work done by their child, formally assess progress or set development objectives, reproduce school type peer group socialization, and match school-based, age-specific standards. However, local authorities should offer advice and support to parents on these matters if requested.

Children whose parents elect to educate them at home are not registered at mainstream schools. Some parents may choose to engage private tutors or other adults to assist them in providing a suitable education, but there is no requirement for them to do so. Learning may take place in a variety of locations, not just in the family home.

Although Home-educated children do not have to follow the national curriculum or take tests, there are certain aspects of education that can be reasonably expected to be put in place. Firstly, it is expected that parents or other caregivers spend a significant amount of time being directly involved in a child's education. Secondly, children should have access to educational materials, physical activity, and socialization. Finally, there should be some evidence that a child's individual needs and interests are being met and that they are properly intellectually stimulated.

Just as school is not compulsory, exams and qualifications are not compulsory either. Home educated children often go directly into higher education or vocational courses without first passing through GCSEs and A levels. However, many institutions require proof of secondary level or pre-university level qualifications before admitting a student or providing employment. To meet those requirements home educated children take GCSE or iGCSE[2] exams privately. This option is also available for A levels. While some GCSE subjects require "controlled assessment" at a school, others don't. There is no controlled assessment for iGCSE or A level qualifications.

Parents may choose home education for a variety of reasons. The local authority's primary interest should lie in the suitability of parents' education provision and not their reason for doing so. The following reasons for home educating are common, but by no means exhaustive: distance or access to a local school, religious or cultural beliefs, philosophical or ideological views, dissatisfaction with the system, bullying, as a short term intervention for a particular reason, a child's unwillingness or inability to go to school, special educational needs, and parents' desire for a closer relationship with their children.

The findings of the research showed that bullying and fears about the suitability of school for their children's individual needs were among the main reasons that parents opted out of the school system. (BBC News, 23 February 2007)

Often, these reasons are intensely personal and ultimately made with the best interest of the child in mind. Luckily, homeschooling in the UK is widely-accepted and help is readily available.

The numbers of families retaining direct responsibility for the education of their children has steadily increased since the late 1970s following the formation of support groups such as Education Otherwise and Schoolhouse. A growing number of parents are apparently turning their backs on the traditional system.

☞ Notes

1. **European Convention on Human Rights**(ECHR) 《欧洲人权公约》，全名为《欧洲保障人权和基本自由公约》(Convention for the Protection of Human Rights and Fundamental Freedoms)，是一份保障欧洲人权与基本自由的国际公约，于1950年开始起草，其后在欧洲委员会(Council of Europe，COE)的支持下为欧洲各国所签署，于1953年9月3日正式生效。目前所有欧洲委员会的成员国均为本公约的缔约国之一，且新加入的成员也要求批准该公约。

2. **iGCSE**(The International General Certificate of Secondary Education) 国际普通中等教育证书，是目前国外 14 岁至 16 岁全世界考试人数最多的体系之一，是 CIE (Cambrige International examination)剑桥全球测试的一部分。其证书在说英文的国家和地区均会得到承认，此考试成绩是申请英国名校剑桥、牛津大学等相近英系大学的重要参考之一。

☞ Questions for comprehension and discussion

1. What kind of legal obligation do British parents have to the education of their children?
2. What does the term "elective home education" mean?
3. What are parents required or not required to do to educate the children at home?
4. Are exams and qualifications compulsory for home educated children?
5. What might be the common reasons for parents to choose home education?

6.4 University Degrees and Requirements

The universities in the United Kingdom (with the exception of the Open University[1]) share an undergraduate admission system operated by UCAS — the Universities and Colleges Admissions Service. Applications must be made by 15 October for admissions to Oxford and Cambridge (and medicine, dentistry and veterinary science courses) and by 15 January for admissions to other UK universities.

Each course in the UK sets it own entry, so they vary considerably. The formal entry requirements to most degree courses are two A-levels at grade E or above. In practice, most offers of places require qualifications in excess of this. So within a university different courses will have different requirements and universities as a whole may have certain requirements that all students will have to meet. For example, the Universities of Oxford and Cambridge generally require all students to attend an interview, other universities will not require this.

Many universities now operate the Credit Accumulation and Transfer Scheme (CATS)[2] and all universities in Scotland use the Scottish Credit and Qualifications Framework (SCQF) enabling easier transfer between courses and institutions.

Some subjects, particularly where highly competitive or that lead to a professional qualification, require that students be interviewed prior to being offered a place on the chosen course.

In January 2013 it was announced that the Russell Group[3] would establish an academic board to advise the British exams watchdog Ofqual (The Office of Qualifications and Examinations Regulation)[4] on the content of A-Levels.

Also, international students coming to the UK can still attend University even though they may not have taken A-levels and have not been educated in the UK system, but they will need to contact the administrator of that program to find out what credentials from their home country they will need to provide.

The standard first degree in England, Northern Ireland and Wales is the Bachelor's degree conferred with honours. Usually this is a Bachelor of Arts (BA) or Bachelor of Science (BSc) degree. Most bachelor's degrees take three years to complete, with some notable exceptions, such as Medicine taking five years. Often students can initially enroll in a 4 year program then leave after three years and be awarded a bachelor's degree.

The standard first degree for students studying arts or humanities in Scotland is either a Bachelor of Arts or a Master of Arts (the latter traditionally awarded by the Ancient Universities of Scotland for a first degree in an arts/humanities subject). The standard undergraduate degree for natural and social science subjects is the Bachelor of Science.

Some universities award a Master's as a first degree following an integrated programme of study (an "integrated master's degree"). These degrees are usually designated by the subject, such as Master of Engineering for engineering, Master of Physics for physics, Master of Mathematics for mathematics, and so on; it usually takes four years to read for them. Graduation to these degrees is always with honours. Master of Engineering in particular has now become the standard first degree in engineering at the top UK universities, replacing the older Bachelor of Engineering.

Undergraduate degrees (bachelor's degrees and integrated master's degrees) may be awarded "with Honours" (BA Hons) or may be "Ordinary" or "Pass" degrees. The degree classifications are based on a weighted average mark of the assessed work a candidate has completed: First class honours (1st), Second class honours, upper division (2 : 1), Second class honours, lower division (2 : 2), Third class honours (3rd), and Ordinary degree (pass).

Master's degrees such as Master of Arts (MA) or Master of Science (MSc) are typically awarded to students who have undertaken at least a year of full-time postgraduate study, which may be taught or, in many cases, involve an element of research. Degrees such as Master of Philosophy (MPhil) or Master of Letters/Literature (MLitt) are likely to be awarded for postgraduate degrees involving original research. A student undertaking a Master's would normally be expected to already hold an honours degree in a relevant subject, hence the possibility of reaching Master's level in one year.

A graduate diploma (GradD, GDip, GrDip) is generally a postgraduate qualification, although some graduate diplomas involve the study of undergraduate level courses. The diploma is normally taken following a bachelor's degree and a successful award allows progression to a master's degree without having received honours with the bachelor's degree.

The Master of Business Administration (MBA) degree is highly valued by those seeking to advance in business as managers and decision makers.

Doctoral degrees or doctorates, such as the Doctor of Philosophy degree (PhD or DPhil), are awarded following a programme of original research that contributes new knowledge within the context of the student's discipline. Doctoral degrees usually take three years full-time. Therefore in the UK it may only take seven years to progress from undergraduate to doctoral level-in some cases six, since having a Master's is not always a precondition for embarking on a Doctoral degree. This contrasts with nine years in the United States, reflecting differences in the educational systems.

Some doctorates, such as the Doctor of Clinical Psychology (DClinPsy) qualification, confirm competence to practice in particular professions. There are also higher doctorates-Doctor of Science (DSc) and Doctor of Letters/Literature (DLitt) that are typically awarded to experienced academics who have demonstrated a high level of achievement in their academic career; for example they may have published widely on their subject or become professors in their field.

☞ Notes

1. **the Open University**(OU) 开放大学。是英国一所远程教学和研究型大学，拥有皇家特许状，成立于1969年，并于1971年正式招生。开放大学大学总部设在白金汉郡米尔顿·凯恩斯新城，在各地区设有分部，且在欧洲大部分其他国家设有办事处和考试中心。除了授予各种继续教育非学历文凭和证书以外，该大学也授予本科和研究生学位。

   开放大学的特点是不论性别、学历和社会地位都可申请入学。入学年龄从21~70岁不等，60%的学生为30~40岁左右。学生中在职教师所占比例最大，其次为文、法、医、技术人员和家庭主妇。

2. **Credit Accumulation and Transfer Scheme**(CATS) 学分积累与转换方案。为英国许多大学用来测定、记录和奖励所通过的模块化(阶段)课程，促进课程和院系之间的运行手段。通常名义上150或300小时的课程学习(面授学时和自学时数)为15~30个学分，满足国家资格证书框架中4至7级中的某个级别。荣誉学位(本科3年)总共需要360学分(通常是4、5、6级各120学分)。基础学位大致相当于 240 学分(4 级和 5 级)，本科的合格或普通学位相当于 300 学分。研究生 1 年(7 级)，需获得 180 个学分，一般来说一门课程都是 15 分或者 30 分，只要通过了所有的考试(包括考试、报告、essay、presentation 等)，就可以拿到学分。通常情况下，15 个学分的课程在一个学期(3 个月左右)修完，30 个学分的课程要分为两个学期修完，但也会有特殊的情况。所以，每个学期平均要修 4~5 门课左右。

3. **the Russell Group** 罗素大学集团。成立于 1994 年，由 24 所英国一流的研究型大学组成，包含了著名的金三角名校，被称为"英国的常春藤联盟"，代表着英国最顶尖的大学。罗素集团名称的由来，是因为最初的 20 所院校的校长，每年春季固定于伦敦罗素广场旁的罗素饭店举行研究经费大会而得名。

4. **Ofqual** (**The Office of Qualifications and Examinations Regulation**) 英国资格认证和考试管理办公室。为英国资格标准的独立监管机构，负责度量英国的学位资格标准、教育质量与世界最好国家之间的差距等。

☞ Questions for comprehension and discussion

1. Do all the universities in the UK have their own undergraduate admission systems?
2. What are the common formal entry requirements to most degree courses?
3. What are the common categories of the UK higher education degrees?
4. What are the classifications of bachelor's degree?
5. What qualifications are needed for Master's degrees and Doctoral degrees respectively?

☞ Questions on Chapter 6 for reflection and presentation

Review the whole chapter and write a short essay on any of the following questions.

1. State the main categories of schools in the UK and compare the similarities and differences between China's state school and the UK state school.
2. Do you think it is possible for parents in China to educate their children at home? Why or why not? What would be the advantages and disadvantages of homeschooling?
3. If possible, would you choose to study in the UK's universities? Give some reasons.

Chapter 7

Daily Life of the British People

Nowadays, many aspects of people's life in the United Kingdom are changing, including people's values and norms of marriage, the size of family, the cost of living, and the ways of travelling. However, people still enjoy their life and love some of the traditional way of life, such as shopping, sports and pub culture.

7.1 Family and Marriage

Marriage in England and Wales is legally recognised in the forms of both civil and religious unions, and is open to opposite-sex and same-sex couples.

In 2013, Parliament passed the *Marriage (Same Sex Couples) Act*, legalising same-sex marriage in England and Wales. Same-sex weddings began on 29 March 2014; however, the provisions of the Act came into force on 13 March 2014. Prior to this, Civil partnerships[1] had been made available to same-sex couples in the UK in 2005, granting rights and responsibilities virtually identical to civil marriage.

Marriage in Northern Ireland is legally defined as between a man and a woman. Civil partnerships became available to same-sex couples in December 2005 and grant rights and responsibilities identical to civil marriage. There are residency conditions that have to be met prior to marriage. If one of the parties wishing to marry is subject to immigration control, notice of marriage can only be given at a register office, which both parties must attend together.

In the UK the age of sexual consent * for women is 16, but the national age of consent legislation does not apply to its dependencies. In England and Wales people cannot marry if they are aged 16 or 17 and do not have parental consent. Since 1 December 2010, the age of consent in Scotland is 16 (parental consent is not required) regardless of sexual orientation or gender. Prior to 2008, the age of consent in Northern Ireland was always 17 for heterosexuals and lesbian sexual conduct. In 2008 the age of consent for all individuals was lowered to 16 so it was inline with the rest of the UK.

Wedding ceremonies can either be conducted by "authorised celebrants" (usually, but not always, a minister of religion) or by an "authorised registrar". However, to be legally binding, it must take place with an authorised person or superintendent registrar present (e. g. vicar or priest) and have at least two competent people, who will be required to sign the marriage register as witnesses. Civil marriages may not take place in religious venues, but since the Marriage Act 1994 may take place in other licensed venues. The marriage register is signed by the couple, the celebrant and two witnesses.

Most weddings take place on Saturday afternoons, this is very much the "peak period" in any week for getting married. Before the Wedding takes place, brides have "Hen" nights and bridegrooms have "Stag" parties (similar to bachelor/bachelorette parties). For couples getting married in a church, "banns" announcing the proposed wedding are read aloud in the church three Sundays before the wedding. The groom chooses a Best Man who will look after the couple rings during the wedding ceremony. It is unlucky for the groom to see the bride on the wedding day before the service. Traditionally the bride wears a white dress and the groom wears a suit (top hat and tails). The bride may be attended by bridesmaids and pageboys. The groom and the bride say their vows, give each other rings, and sign a wedding register.

After the wedding ceremony guests are invited to attend a meal and further celebrations. This is known as the Wedding Reception. Guests leave presents for the bride and groom on a table in the room where the reception takes place. It is traditional for the Best Man, Bride's Father and the Groom to give a speech at the wedding reception. It is traditional at weddings to have a special wedding cake at the reception, often with two or more tiers — each tier may be made of a different type of cake to satisfy the tastes of all the wedding guests. It's also customary for the top tier of a three or four tier cake to be kept aside for the christening of the couples first child. It is traditional for the bride and groom to go away on a holiday, called a Honeymoon, after the wedding has taken place.

The family in Britain is changing. The once typical British family headed by two parents has undergone substantial changes since the twentieth century. In particular there has been a rise in the number of single-person households, which increased from 18 to 29 per cent of all households between 1971 and 2002. By the year 2020, it is estimated that there will be more single people than married people.

In the past, people got married and stayed married. Divorce was very difficult, expensive and took a long time. Today, people's views on marriage are changing. Many couples, mostly in their twenties or thirties, live together (cohabit) without getting married. Only about 60% of these couples will eventually get married. In the past, people married before they had children, but now about 40% of children in Britain are born to unmarried (cohabiting) parents. In 2000, around a quarter of unmarried people between the ages of 16 and 59 were cohabiting in Great Britain. Cohabiting couples are also starting families without first being married. Before 1960 this was very unusual, but in 2001 around 23 per cent of births in the UK were to cohabiting couples.

People are generally getting married at a later age now and many women do not want to have children immediately. They prefer to concentrate on their jobs and put off having a baby until late thirties. The number of single-parent families is increasing. This is mainly due to more marriages ending in divorce, but some women are also choosing to have children as lone parents without being married. On average 2.4 people live as a family in one home Britain. This is smaller than most other European countries.

☞ Notes

1. **Civil partnerships** 民事伴侣。英国《民事伴侣关系法》于 2004 年 11 月 18 日获得通过，2005 年 12 月 5 日实施，2005 年 12 月 21 日根据该法案的规定注册形成的民事伴侣关系正式生效。民事伴侣与异性结婚的夫妇在免除遗产税、社会保障和养老保险等方面享有相同的财产权，并且能够为配偶的子女尽父母的义务，合理地维护自己的配偶及其子女，以及他们的租赁权、终身人寿保险的理赔、在医院和其他方面行使亲属权利等义务。解除伴侣关系也需要一个类似于离婚的正式程序。

☞ Questions for comprehension and discussion

1. What is the difference between civil partnerships and civil marriage in terms of rights and responsibilities?
2. What is the age of sexual consent in all the countries of the UK now?
3. Who are required to sign the marriage register as witnesses?
4. What other words are similar to 'Hen' nights and 'Stag' parties?
5. What substantial changes has the British family undergone since the twentieth century?

7.2 Housing

Most people in England live in urban areas. Towns and cities are spreading into their surrounding environment to cope with the increase populations. In England, an average of 7,000 hectares of farmland, countryside and green space were converted to urban use every year between 1985 and 1998. This is almost the equivalent size of 9,600 international football pitches!

Most houses in England are made of stone or brick from the local area where the houses are built. The colours of the stones and bricks vary across the country.

The main types of houses in England are: Detached (a house not joined to another house), Semi-detached (two houses joined together), Terrace (several houses joined together), and Flats (apartments). In the large cities, people often live in flats. Almost half of London's households are flats, maisonettes or apartments (Information taken from Census 2001). In most towns, there are streets of houses joined together in long rows. They are called terraced houses. The most popular type of home in England is semi-detached (more than 27% of all homes), closely followed by detached then terraced.

House naming started many years ago with rich people naming their homes. The rich named their Halls, Houses, Manors, Castles, and Lodges according to ancestry, location, and family titles: Norfolk House (Duke of), Belvoir Castle (overlooking the Belvoir Valley); Castle Droge (named after a 13th ancestor) etc. Gradually over the years other people began to give names to their homes too. House names today are inspired by a bewildering array of sources: everything from location and local history to literature and legends. The most Common Themes for House names in Britain are as follows: Animals and birds (e. g. Badgers Cottage, Cuckoo Cottage, Fox Hollow, Kestrels, Magpies, Mole End, Nightingale Cottage, Robin Hill, Rookery Nook, Squirrels Leap, Swallow Barn); Trees (e. g. Orchard House, Woodlands, Treetops, Oaklands, The Willows, Yew Tree Cottage, The Laurels, The Hollies); Plants and flowers (e. g. Rose Cottage, Primrose Cottage, Honeysuckle Cottage and Lilac Cottage); Locations and views (e. g. Hillside, Hillcrest, Sunnyside, Woodside, Meadow View and Fairview); Historical (e. g. The Coach House, The Old School House, The Old Rectory, The Old Vicarage, The Old Post Office, Mill House, The Granary and The Grange); Fairytales and Old Favourites (e. g. Thimble Cottage, Pippins, The Little House, The Nutshell, Whispers, Wishing Well Cottage and The Nest); and Holidays and beauty spots (e. g. Ambleside, Blencathra, Eskdale, Rydal, Tarn Hows, Windermere, Larmona, Tresco and Kynance).

All houses in towns and cities have a number. Very few have just a name and majority do not have names. Street numbering was introduced by Act of Parliament in 1765. Every house in a town and city has a number followed by the name of the road it is in e. g. 26 Avebury Avenue. The first house in the road is number one and the last house is the number of buildings in the street. The number readily identifies the location of a property in a road and so makes it easier for the emergency services to find houses quickly. Odd numbers are usually assigned to the left side of the street and even numbers to the right.

More people in the UK are buying their own homes than in the past. About two thirds of the people in England and the rest of Britain either own, or are in the process of buying, their own home. Most others live in houses or flats that they rent from a private landlord, the local council, or housing association. People buying their property almost always pay for it with a special loan called a mortgage, which they must repay, with interest, over a long period of time, usually 25 years.

The cost of housing in England has increased much faster than people's wages making it impossible for first-time buyers to get on the housing ladder unless they are in especially well-paid jobs, are able to call upon rich relatives or are prepared to buy jointly with friends. Land Registry figures for England and Wales show that house prices tripled in the 20 years between 1995 and 2015. Growth was almost continuous during the period, save for a two-year period of decline around 2008 as a result of the banking crisis.

The gap between income and house prices has changed so much in the last 20 years that even in the most affordable regions of England and Wales buyers are forced to spend six times their income. In London in 1995, the median income was £ 19,000 and the median house price was £ 83,000, meaning that people were spending 4.4 times their income on buying a property. By 2012-13, the median income in London had increased to £ 24,600 and the median London house price had increased to £ 300,000, thus people were forced to spend 12.2 times their income on a house. However, in 1995 the Bank Base Rate was 6%, but was cut to 0.5% in March 2009, where it has remained to September 2015. The resultant cheap mortgages have partially ameliorated the affordability issues, but only in a small way.

In the United Kingdom public housing is often referred to by the British public as "council housing" and "council estates", based on the historical role of district and borough councils in running public housing. Mass council house building began in about 1920 in order to replace older and dilapidated properties.

Since the 1970s, non-profit housing associations have been operating an increasing share of social housing properties in the United Kingdom. From 1996 they have also been known as Registered Social Landlords (RSLs), and public housing has been referred to as "social housing" to encompass both councils and RSLs. Despite being non-profit based, RSLs generally charge higher rents than councils. However, the Government introduced a "rent re-structuring" policy in 2002, which aimed to bring council and RSL rents into line in England by 2012. Local planning departments may require private-sector developers to offer "affordable housing" as a condition of planning permission (section 106 agreement).

This accounts for another £ 700m of Government funding each year for tenants in part of the United Kingdom. As of 2012, Housing Associations are now also referred to as "Private Registered Providers of Social Housing" (PRPs).

Since the year 2000, "choice-based lettings" (CBL) have been introduced to help ensure social housing was occupied speedily as tenants moved. This can still favour the local over the non-local prospective tenant. In a number of local authority areas, due to the shortage of council housing, three out of four properties may be designated for priority cases (those living in poor overcrowded conditions, with medical or welfare needs, or needing family support) or homeless applicants in order to meet the councils' legal obligations to rehouse people in need. The percentage of properties set aside for vulnerable groups will vary dependent on the demand for council housing in the area. All local authorities have a Housing Strategy to ensure that council houses are let fairly and fulfil the council's legal obligations; deal with people in need; and contribute to sustainability of housing estates, neighbourhood regeneration, and social inclusion.

Governments since the early 1990s have also encouraged "mixed tenure" in regeneration areas and on "new-build" housing estates, offering a range of ownership and rental options, with a view to engineering social harmony through including "social housing" and "affordable housing" options. A recent research report has argued that the evidence base for tenure mixing remains thin. Social housing occupants may be stigmatised and forced to use a poor door that is separate and less convenient than the door the unsubsidised occupants use and social housing may be less desirably situated. Most UK social housing tenants have the right to swap homes with another tenant even if their landlords are different. This is called a "mutual exchange".

☞ Questions for comprehension and discussion

1. In what type of house do people in the large cities live? What is the most popular type of home in England?
2. What are the most Common Themes for House names in Britain?
3. In what way are houses in towns and cities numbered?
4. In what way do British people buy their property?
5. What is public housing often referred to in the United Kingdom?
6. What are the priority cases for which properties may be designated to meet the councils' legal obligations to rehouse people in need?

7.3 Transport

Transport in the United Kingdom is facilitated with road, air, rail, and water networks. Roads and motorways are the primary domestic transport routes. There are some 225,000 miles (362,000 km) of roads in Britain. Many of the roads are built on the old roads laid down by the Romans centuries ago. Roads in the UK are classified as M (Motorway), A, or B roads, as well as various categories of more minor roads: for internal purposes, local authorities may also use C, and U (the letter standing for "Unclassified") Each road is given a number which is combined with the prefix, for example M40, A40 and B1110.

Roads in the UK range from wide modern motorways down to narrow country lanes usually bordered by hedges, stone walls, grassy banks or ditches. Cities and towns tend to have compact streets because they date back to well before cars were invented, and were certainly not planned for large lorries (trucks).

Some motorways have tolls (pay a fee to drive). The first toll motorway, the M6 Toll, opened in December 2003 to ease motorway congestion in the West Midlands. The 43-kilometre expressway cuts journey times around Birmingham by an estimated 45 minutes.

Travel by car, van or taxi is by far the most common means of transport, accounting for 85 per cent of passenger mileage in the UK. Most people travel by car. About 75% of households have at least one car.

In the UK, vehicles drive on the left and on multi-lane carriageways drivers are expected to keep to the left lane except when overtaking. In Great Britain, the Highway Code applies to drivers. In Northern Ireland the Highway Code for Northern Ireland applies.

The speed limit in each location is indicated on a nearby traffic sign or by the presence of street lighting. Round signs show speed limits in miles per hour (mph) or use of the national speed limit (NSL) symbol. The National Speed limits are as follows:

Motorways and dual carriage ways: 112km/h / 70mph

Unrestricted single carriageway roads: 96km/h / 60mph

Built up areas e. g. towns and villages: 48km/h / 30mph

Residential areas: 35km/h / 20mph

Motorcycling is popular in Britain, both as a means of transport and as a pastime with over one million motorcyclists. A moped with an engine capacity up to 50cc can be ridden at the age of 16 with a provisional licence. A full motorcycle licence can be obtained at the age of 17 after passing a test. The maximum legal speed a moped can be ridden is 30 mph (50kph).

Local bus services cover the whole country. Single decker and double decker buses are found in towns and cities. The red double-decker and the red single-decker buses in London are famous all over the world. The main places a bus goes to are shown on the front of the bus. Some double-deckers have automatic doors and you pay the driver when you go in. On single-deckers you sometimes buy your ticket from a machine in the bus. Most London buses have a conductor who will come round and collect fares. Open top buses are used in the United Kingdom for sightseeing and seasonal summer services.

Coaches provide long-distance links throughout the UK: in England and Wales the majority of coach services are provided by National Express. Megabus run no-frills coach services in competition with National Express and services in Scotland in co-operation with Scottish Citylink.

There is a mature system of taxicabs throughout the UK. In London, the taxis are black but in the rest of the country they are different colours. London's black cabs, also known as hackney carriages, can be hailed in the street or hired from a taxicab rank. With the "for hire" sign lit, the driver is obliged to stop for you. The fare is calculated on a taximeter that charges by both time and distance.

The rail network in the UK is one of the most extensive in Europe. The Stockton and Darlington railway (1825) was the first public passenger railway in the world. The major stations in London are: Euston, St. Pancras, Victoria and Charing Cross. Eurostar is the high-speed train service linking London, Ashford, Paris, Brussels, Lille, Avignon, Calais, Disneyland Resort Paris and the French Alps.

The London Underground (also known as the Tube or simply the Underground) is a public rapid transit system serving a large part of Greater London and parts of the home counties of Buckinghamshire, Hertfordshire and Essex. The Tube is made up of 12 lines, each bearing a traditional name and a standard colour on the Tube Map. If you want to travel fast around London, taking the tube will get you to your destination quicker than bus or taxi. Trains generally depart every 3 or 4 minutes, less frequently at weekends and late at night. London's Underground Tube system is divided up into several Zones in concentric circles from Zone 1 (central London) all the way out to Zone 6 (outer suburbs). Most tourist places are in Zones 1 and 2. The cost of using the Tube depends on which zone you start in and how many zones you need to cross. Fares vary from £ 4 for an adult single trip within Zone 1-2 to £ 3. 80 for an adult single trip between Zone 1 and Zone 6. An off-peak

Day Travelcard for Zones 1-2 is available after 9:00.

There are 470 airports in England. London has five airports: Heathrow, Gatwick, Stanstead, London City and Luton. The first three have underground connections to the centre of London and are the main London airports. Heathrow and Gatwick Airports are the two main centres for overseas flights. London (Heathrow) Airport is one of the largest airports in the world and has two tube stations.

Shipping still remains the main form of cargo transport in to and out of Britain, despite the opening of the Channel Tunnel to France in 1994. The busiest sea port is Dover. Many ferries cross the seas between England and Spain, Ireland, the Netherlands and France.

☞ Questions for comprehension and discussion

1. What are the primary domestic transport routes in the UK? How are roads in the UK classified?
2. What is by far the most common means of transport?
3. How do passengers pay for the buses?
4. Are all the taxis in the UK of the same color?
5. How is London's Underground Tube system is divided up?
6. How many airports does London have, which are for overseas?

7.4 Sports

Sports play an important part in the life in Britain and is a popular leisure activity. Many of the world's famous sports began in Britain, including cricket, football, lawn tennis, golf and rugby. England's national sport is cricket although to football is the most popular sport. Some of England's football teams are world famous, the most famous being Manchester United, Arsenal and Liverpool. In the English Football League there are 92 professional clubs. These are semi-professional, so most players have other full-time jobs. Hundreds of thousands of people also play football in parks and playgrounds just for fun. The highlight of the English football year is the Football Association Cup Final each May. The first set of laws of the game of football, or soccer as it is known in the US, date from the formation of The Football Association in England in 1863.

Rugby originated from Rugby school in Warwickshire. It is similar to football, but played with an oval ball. Players can carry the ball and tackle each other. The best rugby teams compete in the Super League final each September. For many years Rugby was only played by the rich upper classes, but now it is popular all over the country. There are two different types of rugby-Rugby League, played mainly in the north of England, and Rugby Union, played in the rest of England, Scotland, Wales and Ireland. England, Scotland, Wales and Ireland, together with France and Italy, play in an annual tournament called the Six Nations. American Football derived from the game of Rugby also Baseball derived from the old English game of Rounders.

The world's most famous tennis tournament is Wimbledon, which is the oldest of all the major tennis tournaments beginning in 1877. It begins on the nearest Monday to June 22, at a time when English often have the finest weather. Millions of people watch the Championships on TV live.

Netball[1] is the largest female team sport in England. The sport is played almost exclusively by women and girls, although male participation has increased in recent years.

Over 3 million people participate in basketball in the UK.

Scotland is traditionally regarded as the home of golf. There are over 400 golf courses in Scotland alone. The most important golf club in Scotland is in the seaside town of St. Andrews, near Dundee.

Horseracing, the sport of Kings is a very popular sport with meetings being held every day throughout the year. The Derby[2] originated here, as did The Grand National which is the hardest horse race in the world. Horse racing and greyhound racing are popular spectator sports. People can place bets on the races at legal off-track betting shops. Some of the best-known horse races are held at Ascot, Newmarket, Goodwood and Epsom. Ascot, a small town in the south of England, becomes the centre of horse-racing world for one week in June. It's called Royal Ascot because the Queen always goes to Ascot. She has a lot of racehorses and likes to watch racing.

Another equestrian sport is polo, brought to Britain from India in the 19th Century by army officers. It is the fastest ball sport in the world. Polo is played with four men on horses to a team. A ball is hit with a stick towards the goal, one at each end of a 300 yard long by 160 yard wide field.

Table tennis was invented in England in 1880. It began with Cambridge University students using cigar boxes and champagne corks. Although the game originated in England, British players don't have much luck in international championships. Badminton takes its name from the Duke of Beaufort's country home, Badminton House, where the sport was first played in the 19th century.

In the nineteenth century, students at Oxford and Cambridge, Britain's two oldest universities, were huge fans of rowing. In 1829, the two schools agreed to hold a race against each other for the first time on the Thames River. The Oxford boat won and a tradition was born. Today, the University Boat Race is held every spring in either late March or early April. Fishing (Angling) is one of the most popular sports in the UK, with an estimated 3.3 million people participating in the sport on a regular basis. Fishermen can be seen sitting beside rivers and lakes.

Boxing in its modern form is based on the rules established by the Marquess of Queensberry in 1865. In the UK boxing is both amateur and professional, and strict medical regulations are applied in both.

Swimming is also a popular pastime and enjoyed by people of all ages.

Various martial arts, mainly derived from the Far East, are practised in the UK, such as judo and karate.

Darts is a very popular pub game. The game of darts, as it is today, was invented in the north of England in a town called Grimsby. However, the origins of the game date back to at least the Middle Ages.

☞ Notes

1. **Netball** 篮网球，又称为投球或英式篮球，是一种发源自篮球的团队球类运动，一般被视为是以女性为主的运动项目。
2. **Derby** 德比。英国中部的都市、英国的大赛马会(1780年德贝伯爵所创立，每年六月的第一个星期三在London附近Epsom举行，参赛马龄平均为三岁，这天称为Derby Day)、赛马会。

☞ Questions for comprehension and discussion

1. What is Britain's national sport and what is the most popular sport?
2. What world's famous sports began in Britain?
3. What is Baseball derived from?
4. What is the sport of Kings?
5. What were used for Table tennis by Cambridge University students in 1880?

7.5 Shopping

Not only are the British, in the words of Napoleon, 'a nation of shopkeepers', they are also a country of compulsive shoppers. Shopping is considered as Retail Therapy. It is the number one leisure activity, especially for women and accounts for around 37% of all money spent in England. A newspaper survey found that 20 per cent of women are compulsive shoppers.

The main shopping street in many British towns is called the High Street, where you should head for if you want to go shopping. A few small shops are owned by local people. Most are owned by national "chains" of stores. This makes many town centres look the same. Some towns also have street markets where fresh food and cheap goods can be bought. Away from the town centre, small "corner" shops provide groceries to local customers.

There are difference types of shops. Department stores are large retail stores. They sell a variety of good and services: Marks & Spencer (for clothes and food), Debenhams and John Lewis and British Home Stores (for clothes and household items), Boots (for toiletries), WHSmith (newsagents, stationers, CDs and DVDs). Greengrocers sell fruit and vegetables. General Stores sell a variety of good for the home.

Shopping centres have a variety of shops under one roof. They will have an eating area with fast foods and sit down menus, parking area and often a cinema (movie house). Bluewater is the largest out of town shopping development in Europe, located in a disused chalk pit at Dartford in Kent. With more than 300 shops and parking for 13,000 cars, it attracts around 30 million visitors each year. A corner shop is a small shop near houses. It has a limited variety of food but often has long opening hours.

Supermarkets are large self-service shops selling mainly food. Large supermarkets also sell household goods. Main Supermarkets are: Asda stores ltd supermarket, Budgens Supermarket, CO-OP supermarket, Iceland, Safeway grocery supermarket, Somerfield grocery supermarket, Waitrose supermarket, Tesco supermarket (Britain's largest supermarket chain), and Waitrose supermarket. Charity shops sell goods (clothes, books and small household items) that have been donated. The items are usually very cheap and of good quality. Off-Licence shops sell alcholic beverages. Chain stores are a number of retail stores under the same ownership selling the same goods. Each shop in a retail chain will have the same name, e. g. WHSmiths, Marks and Spencers, Sainsburys.

There some Most Popular Shops for fashion clothes: Burton-The most popular mens wear shops, Topman-Has famous designer clothes, and Next-Mainly fashion clothes. Top Shop-Hugely popular for girls with Clothes worn by Catherine of Cambridge (Prince William's wife), River Island-High Street fashion brands, and Miss Selfridge-aimed specifically at teenagers.

There are thousands of shops and many markets in London. Oxford Street and Regents Street are London's busiest shopping areas. Many of their smaller shops sell tourist souvenirs, but there are may other shops too. They have lots of department stores and clothes shops and there are big music shops, bookshops too. Off the eastern side of Regent Street, close to Liberty department store, you will find Carnaby Street, one of the icons of the "swinging sixties"[1]. It is a pedestrianised shopping street in London. The Knightsbridge area of London is the home to the biggest department store not only in the city but in the whole of Britain. Harrods in London is the famous department store that every tourist wants to visit. You can find anything from the cheapest to the most expensive things. Its domed, terracotta building is lit up spectacularly at night. Covent Garden is overflowing with street markets, curbside entertainment, trendy cafes, English pubs, and small boutiques. It is a must visit for all tourists to London. Charing Cross Road is where book worms go. Mainstream bookshops, such as Foyles, Borders and Blackwells, line the street but perhaps the most unique feature about this road are its rare, second-hand and specialist shops. Foyles is famous for five floors containing thousands of titles. Tottenham Court Road is the best place for electronics shops and furniture stores.

There are some luxury shops. Liberty of London Department Store in Regent Street is famous for selling beautiful fabrics. The shop looks like a Tudor house and has an elaborate clock outside. Selfridges Store has an extensive designer section for both men, women and children, constantly updated by the arrival of international labels. Hamleys, in Regent Street, is London's largest toy shop. It has six floors filled with all kinds of toys, from dolls and teddy bears to models, electronic toys and robots.

London markets sell all kinds of things, from fruit and vegetables to antiques, crafts and clothes. Greenwich Market is the place to buy new and second hand clothes, gifts, crafts and jewellery. Leadenhall Market is a Victorian covered market. It sells traditional game, poultry, fish and meat. The best time to visit is early lunchtime. Berwick Street Market is a lively market in the heart of Soho. It is central London's only surviving fruit and vegetable market. The market has the freshest and cheapest produce for miles around. There are fish, bread, cheese, herbs and spices stalls, and also sells fabrics and cheap household goods. Petticoat Lane Market is a great place for bargain clothes and shoes. Spitalfields Market has everything from arts and crafts, clothes, furniture to organic foods. Portobello Market a place to buy antiques, clothes, shoes, bric-a-brac and organic fruit and vegetables all in one place. Camden Market has become one of London's top attractions. You can find hippie cloths, traditional craft stalls, 70's nostalgia and vegetarian food. Borough Market is London's favourite food market, offering imported and organic products such as cheese, wines, fish and meat.

Peak shopping days are Saturdays and Sundays. In England, most retail shops are generally open 6 or 7 days a week. Typical opening times are: Mondays-Saturdays from 9 am to 5:30 pm. Some shopping centres stay open until 8 pm or later; Sunday from 10 am to 4 pm (or 11 am to 5 pm). Sunday shopping has become popular in recent years and most large shops in towns are open for business. Shops are only allowed to trade for 6 hours on Sundays. Large supermarkets are open for 24 hours except for Sundays. Many supermarkets and superstores otherwise open from 8 am until 10 pm from Mondays to Saturdays and 10 am to 4 pm (or 11 am to 5 pm) on Sundays.

On public holidays some shops open and some shops do not. As a general rule banks will be closed, most supermarkets and large stores will be open (although with reduced Sunday opening hours), and in larger towns many shops will open. Over the Christmas and New Year period, all shops are closed on Christmas Day (December 25) and some shops are closed on New Year's Day (January 1). However, an increasing number of shops are now opening on Boxing Day (December 26), which is when many start their "New Year" sales. It is likely that most shopping centres will be closed on Easter Sunday and there will be reduced shopping hours on Easter Monday (often from either 10 or 11 o'clock in the morning). Some rural shops still follow the tradition of an early closing day (usually a Wednesday) when the shops close at 1.00pm.

☞ Notes

1. **swinging sixties** "摇摆的60年代"。20世纪60年代大不列颠繁荣的时尚文化场景，"摇摆的伦敦"为其时髦的首都。20世纪60年代的时装潮流发生了巨变，以"解放身体"为主导思想，最具时代意义的设计，便是解放了女人双腿的迷你裙。"中性"(unisex)风格的兴起又使男装女装不分彼此。不得不提的是这个时期出现了摇滚乐史上最伟大的几支乐队，给时装史注入了一股新的灵感源。最经典的案例便是那时候利物浦来的四个男孩组成了The Beatles乐队，席卷了整个世界，当时不管男女，都冲进街角的理发店，拿着披头士的照片喊着要剪那个经典的Bob头，就是这一批摇滚的鼻祖让20世纪60年代变得不平凡。

☞ Questions for comprehension and discussion

1. What other word can be used to substitute compulsive shoppers? Why is shopping considered as Retail Therapy?
2. What is the main shopping street in many British towns called?
3. What is Britain's largest supermarket chain what does it sell?
4. What are the Most Popular Shops for fashion clothes?
5. Where are London's busiest shopping areas?
6. What market is central London's only surviving fruit and vegetable market?

7.6 Pubs

Pubs (short for public houses) are an important part of British life. They are popular social meeting places. People talk, eat, drink, meet their friends and relax there.

There are over 60,000 pubs in the UK (53,000 in England and Wales, 5,200 in Scotland and 1,600 in Northern Ireland). One of the oldest pubs, Fighting Cocks in St. Albans, Herts, is located in a building that dates back to the eleventh century.

Pubs often have two bars, one usually quieter than the other, many have a garden where people can sit in the summer. Children can go in pub gardens with their parents. Groups of friends normally buy "rounds" of drinks, where the person whose turn it is will buy drinks for all the members of the group. It is sometimes difficult to get served when pubs are busy: people do not queue, but the bar staff will usually try and serve those who have been waiting the longest at the bar first. If you spill a stranger's drink by accident, it is good manners (and prudent) to offer to buy another drink.

Most pubs belong to a brewery (a company which makes beer) but sell many different kinds of beer, some on tap (from a big container under the bar) and some in bottles. The most popular kind of British beer is bitter, which is dark and served at room temperature (not hot, not cold). British beer is brewed from malt and hops.

Although most people think pubs are places where people drink alcohol, pubs in fact sell soft drinks (non alcoholic) drinks too. British people drink an average of 99.4 litres of beer every year. More than 80% of this beer is drunk in pubs and clubs.

British pubs are required to have a licence, which is difficult to obtain, and allows the pub to operate for up to 24 hours. Most pubs are open from 11 to 11. Nearly all pubs sell pub lunches. One of these is the Ploughman's Lunch which is a great wedge of Cheddar cheese, some bread, some pickle, and an onion. Other typical pub foods are scampi (kind of shellfish) and chips (fried potatoes), pie and chips, and chicken and chips.

Pubs have traditional names which date back over 600 years. Some typical names are The Chequers, The White Swan, The Crown, The King's Arms, The Red Lion and The White Horse. People often refer to the pub by its name when giving directions: Turn left at the Rose and Crown. There is usually a sign outside the pub showing the pub's name with a picture.

Various games, especially darts, are common features of pubs; many of the old country pubs continue to promote traditional games, such as "Bat and Trap" (played in

Kent) which have been played for hundreds of years.

The legal age to purchase alcohol is 18. People aged 16 and 17, with the licensee's permission, may consume only 1 glass of wine, beer or cider with a table meal in specific areas of the premises, providing they're with an adult and the adult orders it (England & Wales only, Scotland no adult required to be present). It is illegal to sell alcohol to someone who already appears drunk. You may not buy alcohol for a drunk person on licensed premises. All off-sales are advised to ask for photographic ID if the person looks under 21. Purchasing alcohol on behalf of a minor will result in an £ 80 on-the-spot fine.

Fourteen-year-olds may enter a pub unaccompanied by an adult if they order a meal. Children may enter a pub with their parents until 9 p. m., which lets families enjoy reasonably priced pub meals together, and allows pubs to continue in their traditional roles as community centers.

The legal age for drinking in one's home is 5 provided parental consent is given. Children under 5 must not be given alcohol unless under medical supervision in an emergency.

In most pubs in Britain, you must go to the bar to order drinks and food and pay for your purchase immediately, there is no table service. Some pubs have a waiting service, where orders are taken by waiters at the tables and not paid for immediately. There is usually a sign in the pub which tells you that diners will be served at the table. It is customary to tip your waiter/waitress at the end of the meal (approx 10%). Sometimes this is included in the bill.

☞ Questions for comprehension and discussion

1. How many pubs are there in the UK?
2. What should you do if you spill a stranger's drink by accident in the pub?
3. Do pubs only sell beer?
4. Can people aged 16 and 17 in England and Wales consume alcohols?
5. What are bartenders called and how to tip them? How much are you expected to tip your waiter/ waitress?

☞ Questions on Chapter 7 for reflection and presentation

Review the whole chapter and write a short essay on any of the following questions.

1. When you are in the UK, what kind of leisure activities would you like best? Please give some reasons.

2. Please make a shopping guide for people of different ages in London.
3. You are now studying in a university in the UK and your parents are going to see you there. Please make a detailed travel rout for them so that they know what transports are the fastest and most convenient.
4. What is your view on the same-sex marriage or partnership? What are the possible reasons for the UK people's changing view of marriage and family?

Chapter 8

Famous People

With a long, rich and vibrant history, the UK boasts a lot of famous and influential people in different fields. Who can forget Britishers' contributions to science? It was after all a British man Charles Darwin who propounded the theory of evolution. And what a whole lot the world owes to Sir Isaac Newton, the physicist and his contributions to the scientific revolution? Britishers are also the ones who gave the world the democratic form of government, a concept that evolved from the constitutional monarchy form of government in the Great Britain. Coming to the contemporary times, isn't the UK music scenario responsible for the pop revolution that took the world by storm?

In this part, we will introduce some British monarchs, politicians, scientists, musicians and film stars, who helped shape the world. Some highly talented British writers and poets will be included in Chapter XI, together with their famous works.

8.1 Monarchs

The beginning of the monarchy in Britain could be traced back to the 9th century. From then on, there have been 12 royal houses ruling Great Britain: Normans, Plantagenet family, House of Lancaster, House of York, House of Tudor, House of Stuart, Commonwealth, House of Stuart, House of Hanover, House of Saxe-Cobourg-Gotha and House of Winsor. Until 1603 the English and Scottish Crowns were separate, although links between the two were always close-members of the two Royal families intermarried on many occasions. Following the Accession of King James VI of Scotland (I of England) to the English Throne, a single monarch reigned in the country.

The last four hundred years have seen many changes in the nature of the Monarchy in the United Kingdom. From the end of the 17th century, monarchs lost executive power and they increasingly became subject to Parliament, resulting in today's constitutional Monarchy.

Today, the British monarch is the country's titular official Head of State, and leader of the government. The current monarch is Queen Elizabeth Ⅱ. She plays a political role in the United Kingdom and does have official duties. She acts by the Royal Prerogative, which refers to a set of formal privileges the monarch holds under the national constitution. Although her personal political power is very limited, the monarch provides stability and continuity to the country even in the midst of changing political parties and ever-present controversies. The Queen is a national icon who represents her country and its people at home and abroad. Indeed, the monarch is the United Kingdom's public face and a living symbol of the nation's power and sovereignty.

Henry Ⅷ

Henry Ⅷ (1509-1547) is one of Britain's most famous and controversial kings.

The best known fact about Henry Ⅷ is that his demand for a male heir led him to marry six different women. Two of those wives were executed on his order. Henry's divorce from his first wife, Catherine of Aragon, led the king to split with the Catholic Church and found his own church, the Church of England, which in turn set the stage for the English Reformation and for religious battles which lasted for centuries. It also led to his famous clash with the Utopian socialist Sir Thomas More, who was tried for treason and executed.

Henry was succeeded by his only son Edward Ⅵ. His daughter with his second wife, Elizabeth I, eventually took the throne and became the queen.

Elizabeth Ⅰ

Elizabeth Ⅰ (1533-1603) is considered by many to be the greatest monarch in English history. When she became queen in 1558, she was 25 years old. She inherited a bankrupt nation, torn by religious discord, a weakened pawn between the great powers of France and Spain. Dedicated to her position as ruler, Elizabeth fought off rivals (such as Mary, Queen of Scots, a rival heir to the throne) and expanded England's power overseas. Most notably, she led the country in defeating the Spanish Armada in 1588. Her reign is considered one of England's high points: it featured luminaries such as Sir Walter Raleigh, Sir Francis Drake, Francis Bacon and William Shakespeare, and was the birth of England's global expansion and colonization.

Elizabeth Ⅰ ruled alone for nearly half a century, lending her name to a glorious epoch in world history. She dazzled even her greatest enemies. Elizabeth never married (she was known as "the Virgin Queen"). Her sense of duty was admirable, though it came at great personal cost. She was committed above all else to preserving English peace and stability.

One of the reasons Elizabeth saw such success as a monarch was because she carefully crafted her image. Always dressed in splendid jewels and finery, and often using language that emphasized her love for her people, Elizabeth inspired an intense loyalty and affection that few monarchs of any gender enjoyed before or since. Even in her later years, when England suffered economic setbacks and the queen began to show her age, her reputation among the populace held firm.

Queen Victoria

Queen Victoria's nearly 64-year reign (1837-1901) was the longest in British history. The period was known as the glorious "Victorian Era" — Britain's great age of industrial progress, artistic successes and political empire-building. Britain had a worldwide empire on which the sun never set.

Victoria was only 18 when she became queen. In 1840 she married her cousin Prince Albert and they had nine children. Many of their children or grandchildren eventually married into other Royal families of Europe, such as Spain, Russia, Sweden and etc. Victoria was thus known as the "Grandmother of Europe". In the early part of her reign, she was influenced by her husband. Albert taught her much about how to be a ruler in a "constitutional monarchy" where the monarch had very few powers but could use much influence. Victoria was deeply attached to him and she sank into depression after he died, aged 42, in 1861. She had lost a devoted husband and her principal trusted adviser in affairs of state. Gradually, Victoria withdrew from public life and focused on her family. Late in the 1860s she re-emerged into public life, and as years passed she increasingly regained favor.

During Victoria's long reign, direct political power moved away from the sovereign. A series of Acts broadened the social and economic base of the electorate. Despite this decline in the Sovereign's power, Victoria showed that a monarch who had a high level of prestige and who was prepared to master the details of political life could exert an important influence.

Elizabeth Ⅱ

The current monarch of UK, Queen Elizabeth Ⅱ was born on April 21, 1926 and proclaimed queen on February 6, 1952 following the death of her father, George Ⅵ. She is the eldest daughter of George Ⅵ and Elizabeth Bowes-Lyon. In 1947, she married Philip Mountbatten, a distant cousin, and they have four children: Charles, Prince of Wales, Anne, Andrew and Edward. She is also one of the longest monarchs on the throne.

Elizabeth has managed to maintain a division between her public and private life. She is the first monarch to send her children to boarding schools in order to remove them from the ever-probing media. She has a strong sense of duty and diligence and dispatches her queenly business with great candor, efficiency and dignity. Her knowledge of current situations and trends is uncannily up to date, often to the embarrassment of her Prime Ministers. Harold Wilson, upon his retirement, remarked, "I shall certainly advise my successor to do his homework before his audience." Churchill, who had served four monarchs, was impressed and delighted by her knowledge and wit. She possesses a sense of humor rarely exhibited in public where a dignified presence is her goal.

☞ Questions for comprehension and discussion

1. How many royal houses have ruled Great Britain?
2. When did British monarchs lose their executive power?
3. Who split with the Catholic Church and initiated English Reformation? Why did he do it?
4. Would you like to list some of Elizabeth I's achievements?
5. Why was Queen Victoria known as "Grandmother of Europe"?

8.2 Politicians

There are many famous political politicians in Britain, such as Oliver Cromwell, Winston Churchill, Clement Atlee, Margaret Thatcher... All but Cromwell were Prime Ministers.

As is known to all, Britain is a constitutional monarchy. The king or queen is the head of the country, and the Prime Minister is the head of the executive branch of government. The British monarch has a special relationship with the Prime Minister, regardless of their political party. The Prime Minister, appointed by the monarch from the political party that wins the most seats in the General Election, chooses around 20 Members of Parliament to form government ministers in the Cabinet. The monarch gives a regular audience to the Prime Minister at which he or she has a right and a duty to express views on Government matters.

The post is generally acknowledged to have begun with Sir Robert Walpole in 1721 when he obtained the post of First Lord of the Treasury. So far there have been 12 Prime Ministers during the reign of Queen Elizabeth Ⅱ. The incumbent Prime Minister is Therasa May, who was appointed Prime Minister of UK after the resignation of David

Cameron on 24 June 2016.

Oliver Cromwell

Oliver Cromwell (1599-1658) was a British bourgeois revolutionist, politician, militarist and religious leaders. He is best remembered as a freedom fighter who put Charles Ⅰ on the guillotine and who built up a republic country called the Commonwealth of England. Many think that Cromwell is a better fighter than a ruler because his ruling was not satisfactory enough and the regime immediately began to collapse after his death.

When Oliver Cromwell was born in Huntingdon in 1599. His parents belonged to the lower ranks of the gentry and he grew up to be a farmer and minor landowner. There was nothing to show that he would become one of the most influential men in the history of Britain. In his 30s, he turned strongly to Puritanism and become known for his outspoken views on the monarchy and the Church. It was his success as a soldier in the Civil Wars (1642-1646) that lifted him to power. But after he was given the title of Lord Protector and got the chief power of the country in 1653, he became more and more a tyrant. After he died in 1658, Charles Ⅱ returned and restored the monarchy from his son.

People have different views on Cromwell's rule. To some, Cromwell was a defender of principles and liberties, the champion of fairness and religious tolerance, while for others, he was nothing more than a tyrant and the murderer of a king. Nevertheless, the period of his rule was one of the key turning points in England's history. In winning the Civil War, parliament made sure that never again would a king of England be able to rule on his own. The military successes of Oliver Cromwell not only overthrew feudal system in England but also shook the foundation of the feudal rule in Europe.

Winston Churchill

Winston Churchill (1874-1965), former British prime minister (1940-1945, 1951-1955), is generally regarded as one of the greatest wartime leaders in the world history. He is particularly remembered for his courage, decisiveness, political experience, and enormous vitality while leading his country through World War Ⅱ, one of the darkest times in British history.

Churchill became Prime Minister on May 10, 1940, when the war had already begun. During his first speech to the House of Commons, he stated "I have nothing to offer but blood, toil and tears". His policy on fighting the Germans was to fight with everything that the country had. Churchill spurred everyone around him to prepare for war. He also actively courted the United States to join in the hostilities against Nazi Germany. Also, despite Churchill's extreme dislike for the communist Soviet Union, his pragmatic side realized he needed their help. Churchill knew that the war would be difficult but he gave many famous speeches on the radio and kept the spirits of the British people high. Churchill stayed in London during the Blitz and spent time visiting areas that had been bombed. The British people loved the fact that even though he could have moved away from the area to stay safe, he chose to remain with the people who were suffering.

Although most well known for leading the United Kingdom through WW II as prime minister, Churchill was also an awesome orator, a prolific writer and an earnest artist. He won the Nobel Prize in Literature for his works and oratory, and was the first person to be made an honorary citizen of the United States.

Clement Atlee

Clement Atlee (1883-1967) was Prime Minister from 1945 to 1951. He won a landslide victory over Winston Churchill and was the first Labor Prime Minister to have a majority in the House of Commons.

During his term he allowed India to have independence, in a move largely seen as the end of the British Empire. Thus, he moved the UK into the modern era on the world stage, while also reducing British power and influence. This structural change to the Empire allowed for the beginning of the Commonwealth.

Undoubtedly his greatest achievement was the introduction of the National Health Service which gave healthcare universally to the whole population. Notably, he was also very successful in the difficult task of moving from a wartime economy to a peacetime one. As the Cold War began, Atlee secured the position of the UK as a loyal ally to the United States of America in an alliance that has lasted to this day.

In 2004, Atlee was voted as the greatest British Prime Minister of the 20th century by MORI; an opinion which is also largely held by the British public.

Margaret Thatcher

Margaret Thatcher (1925-2013) was the first female prime minister of the United Kingdom. She served three consecutive terms (1979-1990), the longest of any British prime minister in the 20th century. Known for her steely resolve and determination, Thatcher is also remembered for her conservative social and economic policies. She cut social welfare programs, reduced trade union power and privatized certain industries. Her fierce attitude earned her the nickname "Iron Lady".

Her political platform was that of limiting government and public spending, letting market forces control the economy. She was a monetarist, a follower of Milton Friedman's economic theories, and saw her role as eliminating socialism from Britain. She also supported reduced taxes and public spending, and the deregulation of industry. She planned to privatize Britain's many government-owned industries and to end government subsidies to others. She wanted legislation to seriously restrict union power and abolish tariffs except to non-European countries.

With the revival of the world economy, British economy was also improved. Many of Thatcher's policies gained her popularity. Due to her disagreement with several Cabinet ministers, Thatcher resigned in 1991. The next year, she was made a baroness for her contribution to the country and also became a member of the House of Lords.

After her death, American president Obama said: "As a grocer's daughter who rose to become Britain's first female prime minister, she stands as an example to our daughters that there is no glass ceiling that can't be shattered. As prime minister, she helped restore the confidence and pride that has always been the hallmark of Britain at its best."

☞ Questions for comprehension and discussion

1. Do you know any famous British politicians in history? Who are they?
2. What do you know about British Prime Minister? Who is the incumbent Prime Minister?
3. Who was Oliver Cromwell? How do people comment on him today?
4. What was the greatest contribution of Winston Churchill?
5. What economic theory did Margaret Thatcher follow? And what did she do?

8.3 Scientists

Britain is a country with a fairly strong scientific research strength, and its scientific research and development (R&D) has maintained a very high level. There are many world famous higher education institutions like Oxford, Cambridge, London School of Economics, Imperial College of Industry, and many outstanding scientists like Newton, Darwin, Faraday, Cavendish, Maxwell, Thomson in Britain. As of now, British scientists have won over 70 Nobel prizes, more than those of any other countries except the United States. Statistics show that with about 1 per cent of the world's population, Britain conducts about 5.5 per cent of the world's scientific research.

Science and technology in the United Kingdom has a long history, producing many important figures and developments in the field. Major theorists from the UK include the 17th-century physicist Isaac Newton whose laws of motion and illumination of gravity have been seen as a keystone of modern science, 19th-century biologist Charles Darwin whose theory of evolution by natural selection was fundamental to the development of modern biology, and 20-century physicist and cosmologist Stephen Hawking whose theory of exploding black holes redefined the structure of the universe. Major scientific discoveries made by people from the UK include hydrogen by Henry Cavendish in 1766, electromagnetic induction by Michael Faraday in 1829, penicillin by Alexander Fleming in 1928, and the structure of DNA by Francis Crick and others in 1953. Major engineering projects and applications pursued by people from the UK include the steam engine improved by James Watt in 1765, the steam locomotive developed by Richard Trevithick and Andrew Vivian in 1804, the jet engine by Frank Whittle in 1941 and the World Wide Web by Tim Berners-Lee in 1989.

The UK continues to play a major role in the development of science and technology and major technological sectors include the aerospace, motor and pharmaceutical industries.

Isaac Newton

Sir Isaac Newton (1642-1727) was an English physicist, mathematician, alchemist, and philosopher. Newton was born in Woolsthorpe, Lincolnshire, and studied at University of Cambridge. His scientific breakthroughs, led to significant increases in our understanding of gravity, optics and mathematics. He is widely considered the greatest scientist of all time, "the father of modern science".

Newton developed an intense interest in mathematics and the laws of nature which ultimately led to his most famous work *Philosophiae Naturalis Principia Mathematica* (1687). In this book, Newton explained the three laws of motion and planetary movements. It laid the framework for modern physics and is generally considered to be one of the most important scientific books ever written. Newton also made great advancements into the study of optics. In particular he developed the spectrum by splitting white light through a prism. In mathematics, he shares the credit with Gottfried Leibniz for the development of differential and integral calculus.

The most popular anecdote about Newton is the story of how the theory of gravitation came to him, after being hit on the head with a falling apple. There is no proof that this story is true. However, his assistant John Conduitt later wrote that Newton had said he was inspired to think about gravity after seeing an apple fall in his garden around 1666.

Newton was the dominant figure in British and European science. He was knighted in 1705 and upon his death in 1727 was the first scientist given the honor of burial in

Westminster Abbey.

Michael Faraday

Michael Faraday (1791-1867) was a British physicist and chemist, best known for his discoveries of electromagnetic induction and of the laws of electrolysis. His biggest breakthrough in electricity was his invention of the electric motor.

Born in 1791 to a poor family in London, Michael Faraday was extremely curious, questioning everything. He felt an urgent need to know more. At age 14, he left school and became an apprentice at a local book binder. During his seven-year apprenticeship he read many books, including Isaac Watts' *The Improvement of the Mind*, and he enthusiastically implemented the principles and suggestions contained therein. Besides, Faraday was particularly inspired by the book *Conversations on Chemistry* by Jane Marcet. At this time he also developed an interest in science, especially in electricity.

Faraday's greatest achievement was in the development of electro-magnetism and electricity. Though people already knew of electricity, it was Faraday who played a pivotal role in providing a continuous source of electricity, through his electro-magnetic rotation model of 1821. Ten years later, in 1831, he began his great series of experiments in which he discovered electromagnetic induction. These experiments form the basis of modern electromagnetic technology.

Charles Robert Darwin

Charles Darwin (1809-1882) was a famous English biologist who laid down a framework for the theory of evolution — showing how Man evolved from lower life forms. At the time, his research and publication led to bitter controversy, but his theory of evolution and natural selection became accepted within the scientific community.

Darwin was born in to a wealthy and influential family. In 1825, he was sent to study Divinity at Christ's College, Cambridge University. Darwin was not a great student. Preferring to spend time in outdoor pursuits, he spent a lot of time examining natural science and beetle collecting. From 1831 to 1836, he was offered a place on the British ship HMS Beagle to act as an official natural scientist on a world voyage. His observations during the journey led him to develop a theory of evolution: the notion that species evolve as the fittest members survive and pass their traits on to future generations. Darwin announced his initial ideas of natural selection in 1858, and in 1859 he formally published *The Origin of Species.* The book was both popular and controversial: although Darwin was a religious man himself and once considered a career in the church, his theory of evolution was attacked by those who felt it was contrary to the teachings of the *Bible*. Today Darwin's theories are embraced by nearly all scientists and his theories are the starting point for the modern study of evolutionary biology, even as the religious arguments continue. Darwin published many other books and pamphlets on the topic in later years, most notably *The Descent of Man* (1871).

Stephen William Hawking

Stephen William Hawking (1942-) is an English theoretical physicist, cosmologist and author. He is regarded as the most brilliant theoretical physicist since Einstein. Despite suffering from motor neurone disease, he has made many important scientific discoveries and helped to explain science to the general public.

It was in Cambridge that Stephen Hawking first started to develop symptoms of neuro muscular problems. This quickly affected his physical ability. His speech became slurred and he become unable to even feed himself. At one stage, the doctors gave him a life span of three years. However, the progress of the disease slowed down and he has managed to overcome his severe disability to continue his research and active public engagements. At Cambridge a fellow scientist developed a synthetic speech device which enabled him to speak by using a touch pad. Nevertheless, it can still be a time consuming process for him to communicate. Stephen Hawking has taken a pragmatic view to his disability. He once said: "It is a waste of time to be angry about my disability. One has to get on with life and I haven't done badly. People won't have time for you if you are always angry or complaining."

Stephen Hawking's principle fields of research have been involved in theoretical cosmology and quantum gravity. Amongst many other achievements, he developed a mathematical model for Einstein's General Theory of Relativity. He has also undertook a lot of work on the nature of the Universe, The Big Bang and Black Holes. Hawking is best known for his attempts to explain in clear terms the origins of the universe and some of the most complicated aspects of the cosmos and physics. He was the first scientist to offer a theory of cosmology explained by a union of the general theory of relativity and quantum mechanics.

Tim Berners-Lee

Tim Berners-Lee (1955-) is an English computer scientist, best known as the inventor of the World Wide Web. His work has transformed almost every aspect of our lives.

Born in 1955 in London, England, Tim's parents were both mathematicians. Tim loved electronics from an early age. He graduated as a Physics major from Oxford University in 1976. Having invented the Web in 1989 while working at CERN and subsequently working to ensure it was made freely available to all, Tim is now dedicated to enhancing and protecting the Web's future.

Tim is a Founding Director of the World Wide Web Foundation, which seeks to ensure the Web serves humanity by establishing it as a global public good and a basic right. He is also the Director of the World Wide Web Consortium, a global Web standards organization he founded in 1994 to lead the Web to its full potential.

Sir Tim has received multiple accolades in recent years. These include being knighted by H. M. Queen Elizabeth in 2004, and elected as a foreign associate of the United States National Academy of Sciences in 2009. He was honored as the "Inventor of the World Wide Web" during the 2012 Summer Olympics opening ceremony, in which he appeared in person, working with a vintage NeXT Computer at the London Olympic Stadium. He tweeted "This is for everyone", which instantly was spelled out in LCD lights attached to the chairs of the 80,000 people in the audience.

Time magazine named Berners-Lee one of the 100 Most Important People of the 20th Century, and wrote: "Unlike so many of the inventions that have moved the world, the World Wide Web is Berners-Lee's alone...He designed it. He loosed it on the world. And he more than anyone else has fought to keep it open, nonproprietary and free."

☞ Questions for comprehension and discussion

1. Who was "the father of modern science"? What were his main achievement?
2. How did Stephen Hawking view his disability?
3. Why didn't Tim Berners-Lee patent the Web?

8.4 Musicians

Through its history, the United Kingdom has been a source of musical innovation in the modern and contemporary eras. British music drew its cultural basis from the history of the United Kingdom, from church music, from Western culture and from the ancient and traditional folk music and instrumentation of England, Scotland, Northern Ireland and Wales. Due to its linguistic and cultural links with many countries and its capacity for invention, innovation and fusion, Britain has had a great impact on popular music and has led to the development of many of the major trends in popular music.

Since the 20th century, forms of popular music have particularly flourished in Britain. The dominance of American popular music in the early-20th century led to the explosion of the British Invasion since the early 1960s, led by The Beatles. The Beatles helped to secure British performers a major place in development of pop and rock music. Since then, large number of rock and pop performers from United Kingdom became popular in the United States, and notable movements in British music, including the New Wave of British Heavy Metal and Britpop began. Today, the United Kingdom has one of the world's largest music industries. Genres originating in or radically developed by British musicians include blues rock, heavy metal, progressive rock, ska, hard rock, punk rock, Bhangra, electric folk, folk punk, acid jazz, trip hop, shoegaze, drum and bass, grime, Britpop and dubstep.

Many contemporary British musicians have had an impact on modern music. In this part, we will introduce some of the leading figures in British music industry of the past 50 years, including rock band The Beatles, pop band Spice Girls and Westlife, classical crossover soprano Sarah Brightman.

The Beatles

The Beatles were an English rock band formed in Liverpool in 1960, with members John Lennon (rhythm guitar, vocals), Paul McCartney (bass guitar, vocals), George Harrison (lead guitar, vocals) and Ringo Starr (drums, vocals). They were the foremost and most influential act of the rock era, and introduced more innovations into popular music than any other rock band of the 20th century.

They gained popularity in the United Kingdom after their first hit, *Love Me Do*, in late 1962. With the single of *I Want to Hold Your Hand* over the next year, they gained international popularity and lead the *British Invasion* of the United States pop market. From 1965 onwards, the Beatles produced some of their finest material, including the innovative and widely influential albums *Rubber Soul* (1965), *Revolver* (1966), *Sgt. Pepper's Lonely Hearts Club Band* (1967), *The Beatles* (1968) and *Abbey Road* (1969).

More than any other top group, the Beatles' success was very much a case of the whole being greater than the sum of its parts. They were the first British rock group to achieve worldwide prominence, and made rock truly an international phenomenon. According to the RIAA, the Beatles are the best-selling music artists in the United States. In 2008, the group topped *Billboard* magazine's list of the all-time most successful "Hot 100" artists. They have received 10 Grammy Awards, an Academy Award for Best Original Song Score and 15 Ivor Novello Awards.

Spice girls

The Spice Girls are an English pop girl group formed in 1994. The group consists of Melanie Brown (Scary Spice), Melanie Chisholm (Sporty Spice), Emma Bunton (Baby Spice), Geri Halliwell (Ginger Spice), and Victoria Beckham (Posh Spice).

They were signed to Virgin Records and released their debut single "Wannabe" in 1996, which hit number one in 37 countries and established them as a global phenomenon. Their debut album *Spice* sold more than 30 million copies worldwide, becoming the best-selling album by a female group in history. Their follow up album *Spiceworld* sold over 20 million copies worldwide. The Spice Girls have sold over 80 million records worldwide, making them the best-selling female group of all time, one of the best-selling pop groups of all time, and the biggest British pop phenomenon since Beatlemania.

Every member of Spice Girls was given a specific identity by the British press from the outset, and each label was as much an extension of their own personality as it was a marketing tool, since each name derived from their debut single and video *Wannabe*. They are *Scary Spice*, *Sporty Spice*, *Baby Spice*, *Ginger Spice* and *Posh Spice*. Each persona was exploited in the group's press articles and videos, which helped send *Wannabe* to the top of the charts upon its summer release in 1996. Several years later, the concept of "Girl power" exploded onto the common consciousness. The Spice Girls' version was distinctive. Its message of empowerment appealed to young girls, adolescents and adult women, and it emphasized the importance of strong and loyal friendship among females.

Westlife

Westlife were a famous Irish boy band, formed in July 1998 and disbanded in June 2012. The group's final line-up consisted of Kian Egan (lead, vocal harmony), Shane Filan (main vocal), Markus Feehily (main vocal, high vocal) and Nicky Byrne (vocal harmony). Brian McFadden (main vocal, vocal harmony) was a member from 1998 until his departure in 2004.

Westlife followed in the tradition of European boy bands. The group performed ballads and club-worthy pop songs for a devoted European audience, becoming one of the continent's most successful bands in the process. Some of their songs are world famous, like *What Makes a Man*, *Dreams Come True*, *I lay My Love on You*, *Queen of My Heart*, etc.

Although they never managed to find American success, Westlife sold more than 40 million records worldwide, including seven platinum-selling records in the UK. In 2012, the Official Charts Company listed Westlife 34th amongst the biggest-selling singles artists in British music history.

Sarah Brightman

Sarah Brightman (1960-) is an English classical crossover soprano, actress, songwriter and dancer. She has sung in many languages, including English, Spanish, French, Latin, German, Turkish, Italian, Russian, Mandarin Chinese, Japanese and Catalan.

Brightman began her career as a member of the dance troupe, Pans People in 1976, before joining Hot Gossip the next year, where she released several disco hit singles as a solo performer. In 1981, she made her debut in musical *Cats* and went on to star in several Broadway musicals, including *The Phantom of the Opera*, where she originated the role of *Christine Daaé*.

After a number of successful years on the musical stage, Brightman decided to resume her solo career with co-producer, Frank Peterson. Their collaboration resulted in a string of successful albums, beginning with *Dive* (1993), *Fly* (1995) and *Timeless/Time To Say Goodbye*(1997). Her duet with the Italian tenor, Andrea Bocelli, *Time To Say Goodbye*, topped charts all over Europe and became the highest and fastest selling single of all time in Germany. It subsequently became an international success, selling 12 million copies, worldwide. In the following years, Brightman released a series of highly personal and thematic albums: *Eden* (1998), *La Luna* (2000), *Harem* (2003) and *Symphony* (2008). Brightman has appeared in several films, including Repo! *The Genetic Opera* (2008).

Brightman is the winner of more than 180 gold and platinum awards in 40 countries. She is the first artist to have been invited to perform at two Olympic games, first at the 1992 Barcelona Olympic Games and, 16 years later in Beijing, with Chinese singer Liu Huan, performing the song *You and Me*. In 2012, Brightman was appointed as the UNESCO Artist for Peace.

☞ Questions for comprehension and discussion

1. What is "British Invasion"?
2. What is the influence of Beatles?
3. What is the cultural and social significance of the Spice Girls.

8.5 Film Stars

With a significant film industry for over a century, Britain has cultivated many world-famous film artists. There are many successful directors in Britain, including Alfred Hitchcock, David Lean, Charlie Chaplin, Michael Powell, Carol Reed and Ridley Scott, ect. Alfred Hitchcock pioneered many elements of the suspense and psychological thriller genres. He had a successful career in British cinema with both silent films and early talkies and became renowned as England's best director. David Lean has been nominated 7 times for the Academy Award for Best Director, for which he won twice. His films are often admired by fellow directors as a showcase of the filmmaker's art. Charlie Chaplin was not only a director, but one of the most famous film stars in 20th century. His comic work during the silent film era entertained audience of one generation after another.

Many British actors have achieved international fame and great success, including Michael Caine, Julie Andrews, Richard Burton, Sean Connery, Laurence Olivier, Vivien Leigh, Audrey Hepburn, Anthony Hopkins and so on. Michael Caine is renowned for his distinctive working class cockney accent; he has appeared in over 115 films and is regarded as a British film icon. Julie Andrews received an Academy Award, a BAFTA, 5 Golden Globes, 3 Grammys and 2 Emmys. Her famous works include *Mary Poppins* (1964), *The Sound of Music* (1965), *The Princess Diaries* (2001), etc. The Princess Anne in *Roman Holiday* (1953) played by Audrey Hepburn impressed global audience, and made Hepburn the first actress to win an Academy Award, a Golden Globe and a BAFTA Award for a single performance.

There are also a great number of younger British performers currently active in international cinema like Hugh Grant, Colin Firth, Ralph Fiennes, Orlando Bloom, Catherine Zeta-Jones, Jude Law, Kate Winslet, and Keira Knightley and so on. In this part, we will introduce some of the leading figures of younger generation.

Hugh Grant

Hugh Grant (1960-) is an English actor and film producer. As one of Britain's best known faces, he has received a Golden Globe, a BAFTA, and an Honorary César.

In 1994, Grant became an overnight international star with the leading role as Charles in *Four Weddings and a Funeral* (1994), which won him a Golden Globe Award, as well as a BAFTA Film Award for Best Actor. During the 1990s Grant established himself as a very original and resourceful actor. He delivered comic performances in mainstream films like *Mickey Blue Eyes* (1999) and *Notting Hill* (1999), and played a string of characters projecting a positive mindset, showing how do you stay optimistic when you are actually worried about a cascade of troubles. By the turn of the 21st century, he had established himself as a leading man skilled with a satirical comic talent. Grant has expanded his oeuvre with critically acclaimed turns as a cad in *Bridget Jones's Diary* (2001), *About a Boy* (2002), and *American Dreamz* (2006). He later played against type with multiple cameo roles in the epic sci-fi drama film *Cloud Atlas* (2012).

Outside of his acting profession, Grant has been a good athlete, he played cricket and football in his younger years. He enjoys playing golf, frequently taking part in Pro-Am tournaments. He has been an avid art lover since his younger years, and has been collecting fine art, a passion he inherited from his father.

Orlando Bloom

Orlando Bloom (1977-) is a famous English actor. In 2004, he was on *People* (USA) Magazine's "50 Most Beautiful" list and "Hottest Bachelors" list. In 2009, Bloom was named a UNICEF Goodwill Ambassador. As of May 2007, Bloom has appeared in four of the top 15 highest grossing films of all time.

At 16, Orlando Bloom was classically trained at London's Guildhall School of Music and Drama. Shortly after his graduation in 1999 he was cast as the elf Legolas in the feature film trilogy *The Lord of the Rings*, directed by Peter Jackson and based on the hit fantasy novel by J. R. R. Tolkien. The film came out in 2001 and made Bloom both a star and a favorite heartthrob to teenage girls. After having his breakthrough in *The Lord of the Rings* trilogy, he rose to fame by further appearing in epic fantasy, historical epic, and fantasy adventure films. His best-known roles include Legolas in the *Lord of the Rings* and *Hobbit* trilogies, Will Turner in the *Pirates of the Caribbean series*, Paris in *Troy*, and Balian de Ibelin in *Kingdom of Heaven*.

Bloom subsequently established himself as a leading man in Hollywood films such as *Kingdom of Heaven*, *Elizabethtown* and appeared in ensemble films such as *New York, I Love You* (2008) and *Main Street* (2009). He made his professional stage debut in *West End's In Celebration* at the Duke of York's Theatre in 2007 and starred in a Broadway adaption of *Romeo and Juliet* in 2013.

He has one child with Australian model Miranda Kerr, whom he married in 2010. They separated in 2013.

Kate Winslet

Kate Winslet (1975-) is a famous English actress. She has received an Academy Award, an Emmy Award, three Golden Globe Awards and a Grammy Award. She is the youngest person to receive six Academy Award nominations, and is one of the few actresses to win three of the four major American entertainment awards.

Brought up in Berkshire, Winslet studied drama from childhood. She made her film debut in *Heavenly Creatures* (1994), for which she received praise. She garnered recognition for her supporting role, the willful and passionate Marianne, in Ang Lee's *Sense and Sensibility* (1995) before achieving global stardom with the romantic disaster film *Titanic* (1997), which was the highest-grossing film of all time at that point. She won the Academy Award for Best Actress for her role in *The Reader* (2008) in 2009, and the Emmy Award for Best Actress in a Miniseries for playing the title role in *Mildred Pierce* in 2011, which helped stake her claim as being one of the most accomplished and versatile actresses of her generation.

In addition to acting, Winslet has narrated documentaries and children's books. She was awarded the Grammy Award for *Best Spoken Word Album for Children* in 2000 for narrating *Listen To the Storyteller*. She has also provided her vocals to soundtracks of her films, including the single "What If" from *Christmas Carol: The Movie* (2001).

Keira Knightley

Keira Knightley (1985-) is a famous English actress and model. She began acting as a child on television and made her film debut in 1995. She achieved international fame in 2003 after appearing as Elizabeth Swann in *the Pirates of the Caribbean* film series. In 2008, *Forbes* identified Knightley as the second highest-paid actress in Hollywood, with reported earnings of US $ 32 million in 2007, making her the only non-American on the list of highest-paid actresses that year.

Since the *Pirates of the Caribbean* films, Knightley has become known for starring in period drama films such as *Pride & Prejudice* (2005), *Atonement* (2007), *Silk* (2007), *The Duchess* (2008), *A Dangerous Method* (2011), and *Anna Karenina* (2012). She has also appeared in a variety of genres of Hollywood films, including the romantic comedy *Love Actually* (2003), the historical action *King Arthur* (2004), the psychological thriller *The Jacket* (2005), biographical action *Domino* (2005), the historical drama *The Edge of Love* (2008), the film Noir *London Boulevard* (2010), the dystopian science fiction *Never Let Me Go* (2010), the romantic drama *Last Night* (2010), and the dark comedy *Seeking* a *Friend for the End of the World* (2012).

Knightley earned nominations for the 78th Academy Award for Best Actress and the 63 th Golden Globe Award for Best Actress for her performance in 2005 adaptation of Jane Austen's novel *Pride and Prejudice*. Two years later she was nominated again for the 65th Golden Globe Award for Best Actress in a Leading Role for her performance in *Atonement*. In 2014, Knightley appeared in four films. In *The Imitation Game*, she was nominated for a Golden Globe and the 87th Academy Award for Best Supporting Actress.

☞ Questions for comprehension and discussion

1. Do you know any world-famous British actors or actresses? Who are they?
2. Which film made Hugh Grant known to the world? What do you know about the film?
3. What roles do you know Orlando Bloom played in epic fantasy, historical epic, and fantasy adventure films?

☞ Questions on Chapter 8 for reflection and presentation

Review the whole chapter and write a short essay on any of the following questions

1. What are the similarities and differences between British monarchs and Chinese emperors?
2. What contribution has Tim Berners-Lee made? Which is valued most? What if he had patented the Web?
3. Which British singer or actor/ actress do you like best/ admire most? Why?

Chapter 9

Famous Landmarks and Top Attractions

Britain's long history and pervasive culture spread worldwide through the English colonialism and language, and make it one of the most visited countries in the world. This piece of land offers travelers endless possibilities when it comes to fun things to see and do. It is simply bursting with fascinating history, exciting cities and rich cultural traditions. Historic sites are found at every turn, from old castles dotting the picturesque countryside and colleges dating back to the Middle Ages to ancient Roman sites and centuries old royal palaces.

Britain has a large selection of historic sites and landmarks including ancient castles, royal palaces, impressive stately homes as well as various states statues, bridges and diverse architectures. If you want to see the lavish palaces, castles and stately homes, Britain is a not-to-be missed place. If you want to see the typical Western churches, cathedrals, abbeys, temples and other religious sites, there are some of the world's finest in Britain. If you want to see some ancient arts collections, Britain is home to many splendid art galleries and museums documenting the history of human culture. If you want to find something that can provide days worth of excitement and entertainment to suit everyone in the family, there are also theme parks or amusement parks. Besides, there are many nature reserves, including parks, gardens, safari parks, as well as good markets and shops and other attractions in UK cities.

In this part, we will introduce some of the famous landmarks and top attractions in Britain, including 1) Landmarks and Historic Sites, 2) Castles, Palaces and Stately Homes, 3) Churches, Cathedrals and Abbeys, 4) Museums and Galleries, 5) Amusements and Theme Parks.

9.1 Historic Sites and Landmarks

Britain as we know today has witnessed the rise and fall of many cultures, civilizations and empires. From pre-historic peoples to Celtic tribes, Roman conquerors and Anglo-Saxon and Norman invaders, the country forged of many influences. The rise of the English state and its eventual transformation into the United Kingdom has also ensured that many remarkable historic sites and landmarks remain to remind us of the diverse story of the country.

Today, the historic sites and landmarks of Britain range from the most famous and popular tourist destinations — such as Palace of Westminster, Tower Bridge, Buckingham Palace, Stonehenge and Windsor Castle — to lesser-known and often hidden sites well off the standard visitor trails.

Due to the limited space, in this part, we will mainly introduce some of the most representative historic sites and landmarks — Palace of Westminster and Big Ben, Tower Bridge and Stonehenge.

Palace of Westminster and Big Ben

The Palace of Westminster (more widely known as the Houses of Parliament) lies on the northern bank of the River Thames in the City of Westminster, in central London. It is the seat of Parliament and one of the political centers in the United Kingdom. At the northwest end of the Palace rises the most famous of the towers, Big Ben (known as Elizabeth Tower since 2012), which is an iconic landmark of London and the United Kingdom in general. Since 1987 the Palace has been a part of UNESCO World Heritage Sites.

The first royal palace was built on the site in the 11th century, and Westminster was the primary residence of the Kings of England. After a fire in 1512, it served as the home of the Parliament of England and also as the seat of the Royal Courts of Justice. In 1834, an even greater fire destroyed the heavily rebuilt Houses of Parliament, and the most significant medieval structure to survive was Westminster Hall. The present building was rebuilt after the fire in a splendid example of Victorian neo-Gothic architecture.

The Palace of Westminster contains over 1,100 rooms, 100 staircases and 4.8 kilometers of passageways, which are spread over four floors. The ground floor is occupied by offices, dining rooms and bars; the first floor, known as the principal floor, houses the main rooms of the Palace, including the debating chambers, the lobbies and the libraries. The top-two floors are used as committee rooms and offices. The business of Parliament takes place in two places, the House of Lords and the House of Commons. The House of Lords is located to the south and decorated with red leather upholstery, and the House of Commons is located to the north of the building and is decorated with green leather upholstery.

The 150 year old Big Ben Clock Tower is one of London's top attractions. The name Big Ben actually refers not to the clock tower itself, but to the 13.8 ton bell housed within the tower. Striking the hour accurately, the Great Clock achieved standards of accuracy considered impossible by 19th-century clockmakers, and it has remained consistently reliable since it entered service in 1859. It has become a symbol of the England and London and has appeared in many films. Big Ben towers 96 meters high in the sky overlooking Westminster. It is open for tours for UK residents who have made arrangements with their MP.

Tower Bridge

Tower Bridge is a combined bascule and suspension bridge in London. It is close to the Tower of London, which gives it its name. Tower Bridge is a busy crossing of the Thames, with over 40,000 people passing every day. It is also an iconic symbol of London, one of the most recognizable landmarks in the world.

In the second half of the 19th century, as the population of London grew, London desperately needed a new bridge. Finally in 1876 the City of London Corporation[1] made the decision to build a new bridge to the east of London Bridge. A huge challenge faced the corporation-how to build a bridge downstream from London Bridge without disrupting river traffic activities. Over 50 designs were submitted for consideration. It wasn't until October 1884 that Horace Jones, the City Architect, in collaboration with John Wolfe Barry, offered the chosen design for Tower Bridge as a solution.

Construction of Tower Bridge started in 1886 and took 8 years to build. The bridge is 244 m in length with two towers each 65 m high. The two bridge towers are tied together at the upper level by means of two horizontal walkways which are designed to withstand the tension of the suspended sections of the bridge. The 61 m central span between the towers is split into two equal bascules, which, each weighing over 1,000 tons, can be raised to an angle of 86 degrees to allow river traffic to pass.

Stonehenge

Stonehenge is one of the most world-famous prehistoric monument located in Wiltshire, England. It is a circle of ancient huge stones erected from 3000 BC to 2000 BC. No written records are left about Stonehenge and many aspects of it remain subject to debate. The site and its surroundings were added to the UNESCO's list of World Heritage Sites in 1986.

Archaeologists believe Stonehenge was constructed in several phases. The first phase of building started around 3000 BC, when the outer circular bank and ditch were erected. A thousand years later, an inner circle of granite stones, known as bluestones, was added. It's thought that these mammoth 4-tonne blocks were hauled from the Preseli Mountains in South Wales, some 250 miles away-an almost inexplicable feat for Stone Age builders equipped with only the simplest of tools. Although no one is entirely sure how the builders transported the stones so far, it's thought they probably used a system of ropes, sledges and rollers fashioned from tree trunks.

Around 1500 BC, Stonehenge's main stones were dragged to the site, erected in a circle and crowned by massive lintels to make the trilithons (two vertical stones topped by a horizontal one). Also around this time, the bluestones from 500 years earlier were rearranged as an inner bluestone horseshoe with an altar stone at the centre. Outside this the trilithon horseshoe of five massive sets of stones was erected. Three of these are intact; the other two have just a single upright. Then came the major circle of 30 massive vertical stones, of which 17 uprights and six lintels remain. Much further out, another circle was delineated by the 56 Aubrey Holes, named after archaeologist John Aubrey, who discovered them in the 1600s. Like many stone circles in Britain (including Avebury, 22 miles away) the inner horseshoes are aligned to coincide with sunrise at the midsummer solstice, which some claim supports the theory that the site was some kind of astronomical calendar.

Stonehenge is one of Britain's great archaeological mysteries: despite countless theories about the site's purpose, ranging from a sacrificial centre to a celestial timepiece, in truth, no one knows for sure what drove the prehistoric people to expend so much time and effort on its construction.

☞ Notes

1. **City of London Corporation** 伦敦市法团，也称伦敦法团，是英国伦敦的市中心区——伦敦市的自治组织和地方政府。

☞ Questions for comprehension and discussion

1. What is the meeting place of UK Parliament?
2. What did Palace of Westminster site serve as in the 11th century? How about after the fire in 1512?
3. Where is Big Ben? What do you know about it?
4. When did Tower Bridge start building? How long did it last?
5. Why has Stonehenge been a famous archaeological mystery?

9.2 Castles, Palaces and Stately Home

Due to its long history, Britain has a large selection of historic buildings — the old castles, royal palaces, stately homes, fortified manors and the great country houses. These impressive architectural and historical heritage attract people from all around the world. There are the World Heritage Sites of Edward I's castles at Beaumaris, Caernarvon, Conwy and Harlech; Blenheim Palace, the Tower of London and the Palace of Westminster; and over 120 royal palaces, historic houses and gardens. In this part, we will introduce the notable Buckingham Palace, Tower of London and Windsor Castle.

Buckingham Palace

Buckingham Palace is the London residence and principal workplace of the reigning monarch of the United Kingdom. Located in the City of Westminster between The Green Park, Hyde Park and St. James's Park, the palace is often at the centre of state occasions and royal hospitality.

Originally known as Buckingham House, the building which forms the core of today's palace was a large townhouse built for the Duke of Buckingham in 1703. It was subsequently acquired by King George Ⅲ in 1761 as a private residence for Queen Charlotte and was known as "The Queen's House". During the 19th century it was enlarged and finally became the official royal palace of the British monarch on the accession of Queen Victoria in 1837.

Buckingham Palace's 19 state rooms, ballrooms and gardens are open to visitors during August and September while the Queen makes her annual visit to Balmoral. The state rooms are the nucleus of the working Palace and are used regularly by The Queen and members of the Royal Family for official and State entertaining. They house some of the Royal family's priceless works of art and furnished with some of the finest mahogany furniture. The Ballroom, the largest multi-purpose room in the palace, is used by the Queen for State banquets and other formal occasions such as the annual Diplomatic Reception. It has been used variously as a concert hall for memorial concerts and performances of the arts.

Tower of London

The Tower of London is one of London's most famous ancient sites. It is a historic castle located on the north bank of the River Thames in central London. Built by William the Conqueror (1066-1087) in the early 1080s, the tower has served variously as a fortress, armoury, treasury, mint, palace, observatory, refuge and prison in the past thousand years. In 1988, the Tower of London was added to the UNESCO list of World Heritage Sites.

The Tower of London is an imposing fortress with many layers of history, which has become one of the symbols of royalty-was built around the White Tower. William the Conqueror built the tower strategically at a bend in the River Thames to protect London and assert his power. The tower had the dual role of providing protection for the City through its defensive structure and the provision of a garrison, and of also controlling the citizens by the same means. The Tower literally "towered" over its surroundings until the 19th century.

Covering some 18 acres, it is home to amazing exhibits such as Line of Kings, the world's oldest visitor attraction (1652) with its remarkable displays of royal armor. Other highlights include the wonderful Yeoman Warder Tours, Crown Jewels exhibition, the Royal Mint, and exhibits and displays regarding prisons and executions. The most striking building is the central White Tower, which is an excellent example of the royal Norman castle from the late 11th century. This Tower is so renowned that it was referred to by Shakespeare in many of his plays. It contains the impressive Royal Armouries collections and even an 11th century Romanesque chapel. When the tower served as a prison from 1100 to the mid twentieth century, many people lost their heads there. Some famous prisoners include Sir Thomas More, King Henry Ⅵ, Anne Boleyn and Catherine Howard (wives of King Henry Ⅷ) and Rudolph Hess.

Windsor Castle

Windsor Castle, located in Windsor about an hour west of London, is the largest and oldest inhabited castle in the world. It has served as one of the official residences of British Royals. Queen Elizabeth Ⅱ spends many weekends of the year at the castle, using it for both state and private entertaining.

It was originally built by William the Conqueror in the 11th century after the Norman invasion and has been used and extended by succeeding English monarchs over the years. The earliest surviving buildings at Windsor date from the reign of Henry Ⅱ (1154-1189, king of England). Much of the castle, including the magnificent State Apartments and the 15th-century St. Georges Chapel can be visited.

The State Apartments, along the north of the ward, have a collection of some of the finest paintings by Rembrandt, Canaletto and Gainsborough. They are open to the public from March to October. Visitors can also view George Ⅳ's private apartments which are some of the most lavishly decorated rooms in the castle.

St. George's Chapel is one of the finest examples of Gothic architecture in England, and features lavish decoration and works in marble, glass mosaic. It is the spiritual home of the Order of the Garter, the senior order of British Chivalry established in 1348 by Edward Ⅲ. Within the chapel are the tombs of ten sovereigns, including Henry Ⅷ and his third wife Jane Seymour, and Charles Ⅰ. More recently Queen Elizabeth the Queen Mother[1] was buried here.

Also of note is the wonderful Great Park, a magnificent 6 mi-long park that most visitors will already have seen from the air as they fly into Heathrow[2]. And, of course, no visit to a royal palace would be complete without witnessing the Changing of Guard in the Castle Precincts.

At last, one important point is Windsor Castle is a working palace and may be closed for State functions so visitors are advised to check opening times before they visit.

☞ Notes

1. **Queen Elizabeth the Queen Mother** 伊丽莎白太后，即伊丽莎白二世的母亲。
2. **Heathrow** 伦敦希思罗国际机场(London Heathrow International Airport)。英国航空和维珍航空的枢纽机场以及英伦航空的主要机场、伦敦最主要的联外机场，也是全英国乃至全世界最繁忙的机场之一。

☞ Questions for comprehension and discussion

1. What is the present function of Buckingham Palace?
2. Where can visitors see the Guard Changing of Buckingham Palace?
3. What has the Tower of London served as in the long history?
4. Can you list some famous exhibits in the Tower of London?
5. What has the royal family used Windsor Castle for?

9.3 Churches, Cathedrals and Abbeys

Religion has had a significant impact on British history and culture. There are many splendid collection of religious buildings, including churches, cathedrals and abbeys[1] in Britain, which are one of the prime reasons tourists visit the country.

Some cathedrals of Britain span the millennium-from the cathedrals dating from the 1100s to the modern cathedrals found in Liverpool and Coventry. They display a wide array of architectural styles from Early English Gothic, to the majesty of the Renaissance at St. Paul's and the sixties modernism of Liverpool's Roman Catholic Cathedral.

In the Middle Ages and up to the Reformation in the 1500s, the Church enjoyed enormous power and wealth, and cathedrals are eloquent symbols of its dominant place in British society. These cathedrals were elaborate and brightly colored before much of the interior decoration and original medieval art was destroyed during the Reformation and the Civil War. During the Civil War, some cathedrals were used as garrisons, prisons and even stables. Today, many churches, cathedrals and abbeys remain and attract visitors from the whole world.

Westminster Abbey

Westminster Abbey is a large, mainly Gothic, church located next to the Palace of Westminster in the heart of London. It is one of the most notable religious buildings in the United Kingdom and is the traditional place of coronation and burial site for English and, later, British monarchs. Today, the Abbey is a living church owned by the royal family, where worship still takes place.

Westminster Abbey is a mixture of architectural styles, but considered the finest example of Early English Gothic. The original church was built in the 11th century by King Edward the Confessor. Most of the present building dates from 1245 to 1272 when Henry Ⅲ decided to rebuild an old abbey in the Gothic style. The building was later significantly expanded: the Chapel of Henry Ⅶ was added between 1503 and 1512, while the two West Front Towers date from 1745. St. Edward the confessor's shrine is at the heart of the Abbey Church and is surrounded by the tombs and memorials of many great men and women from British History.

Every monarch since William the Conqueror has been crowned here, with the exception of Edward V and Edward Ⅷ. For many years Westminster Abbey was the main burial site for royalty although now the royal family burial site is Windsor Castle. Gradually, it became one of Britain's most significant honors to be buried or commemorated in the abbey. The practice of burying national figures in the abbey spread to include nobles, generals, poets, politicians, doctors and scientists such as Clement Attlee, Chaucer, Charles Darwin, Charles Dickens, Samuel Johnson, Rudyard Kipling, John Herschel, Isaac Newton Winston Churchill, William Wilberforce, etc.

The interior of the Abbey is a veritable museum of English history. Among many highlights are the medieval coronation throne; Poet's Corner with its memorials to giants of literature; and the tombs of some famous people. More than a 1000 years worth of treasures such as paintings, stained glass and textiles are on view to the public within the church.

St. Paul's Cathedral

St. Paul's Cathedral in London is the seat of the Bishop of London and a major London landmark. It is located on Ludgate Hill at the highest point of City of London. At 111 m high, it was the tallest building in London from 1710 to 1962. St. Paul's is the second largest dome church building in the world.

The present St. Paul's Cathedral, built between 1675 and 1710, was designed in the English Baroque style by the famous architect Sir Christopher Wren. It is the fourth religious building on the site, with the immediate predecessor destroyed in the Great Fire of London in 1666.

The cathedral is one of the most famous and most recognizable sights of London. It has been the location of the thanks giving services at the end of the First and Second World Wars and for Queen Victoria's Jubilee celebrations and Queen Elizabeth's 80th birthday and her Silver, Golden and Diamond Jubilees. It was also the place where the wedding of Prince Charles and Lady Diana Spencer took place. It has been the location for the funeral services for Lord Nelson, the Duke of Wellington. Numerous other tombs and memorials are scattered throughout the Cathedral including that of Sir Christopher Wren, Florence Nightingale, T. E. Lawrence, Lord Kitchener, Sir Alexandra Fleming and the clergy from the cathedral over the years. It also has a number of memorials dedicated to specific conflicts such as the Falkland and the Gulf War.

St. Paul's Cathedral is an Anglican cathedral, the first Cathedral to be built after the English Reformation in the sixteenth-century. Although it is still a working church, with regular services.

☞ Note

1. **churches, cathedrals and abbeys** church 一般指广义的“教堂”，即所有宗教活动的发生场所；也可以指“教会”或社区、村镇的小教堂。cathedral 指“主教教堂”，大多规模宏伟，拥有精美华丽的装饰。abbey 指“修道院”、“寺”，通常规模大，有几座附属教堂等。

☞ Questions for comprehension and discussion

1. What is the function of Westminster Abbey?
2. Which famous people do you know are buried in Westminster Abbey?

3. Who designed the St. Paul's Cathedral? What is the architectural style?

9.4 Museums and Galleries

There are many splendid art galleries and museums in Britain, which are a key element in the mass communication of culture, creativity and ideas. It is estimated that there are about 2,500 museums in the UK. Over 1,800 museums have been accredited. Most of the permanent collections are free to enter. London is the UK's main cultural artery. The sheer number of museums and art galleries in London alone makes it the protagonist of the UK's cultural scene.

Visits to museums and art galleries have greatly increased in recent years, it is likely to exceed 100 million a year. According to 2013 research, 52% of adults living in England made at least one museum visit in the previous year. The top five most visited museums in the UK in 2013 were: British Museum, The National Gallery, Natural History Museum, Tate Modern and Science Museum.

The British Museum

The British Museum is located in the Great Russell Square of central London. It is among the oldest, largest and most visited and comprehensive museums in the world.

The British Museum was founded in 1753, largely based on the collections of the collector Sir Hans Sloane. The museum first opened to the public on 15 January 1759. Its expansion over the following two and a half centuries was largely a result of an expanding British colonial footprint. Its permanent collection, numbering some 8 million works, exhaustively illustrates the history of human culture — from ancient and living cultures that spans two million years of history. There are artifacts representing every history period from the Vikings to the Romans to the Egyptians and Medieval Europe with examples of pottery, jewellery, statues, paintings, sculptures and many more. Among the must-sees are the Rosetta Stone[1], the key to deciphering Egyptian hiero-glyphics, discovered in 1799; the controversial Parthenon Sculptures[2], taken from the Parthenon in Athens by Lord Elgin in 19th century; the large collection of Egyptian mummies; the Anglo-Saxon Sutton Hoo burial relics[3] and the Winged Bulls from Khorsabad[4]. Nearly six million visitors each year walk through its galleries.

National Gallery

The National Gallery is an art museum in Trafalgar Square in the City of

Westminster, in Central London. It is among the most visited art museums in the world, after the Musée du Louvre, the British Museum, and the Metropolitan Museum of Art. There are masterpieces on display from Reubens, Van Gogh, Turner, Leonardo Da Vinci, Monet, Rembrandt and many more.

Founded in 1824 to display a collection of just 38 paintings, today the Gallery houses the national collection of Western European painting, over 2,300, dating from the mid-13th century to 1900. There are masterpieces from virtually every European school of art. The modern Sainsbury Wing extension contains the gallery's earliest works: Italian paintings by early masters like Giotto and Piero della Francesca. The basement of the Sainsbury Wing is also the setting for temporary exhibitions. In the West Wing are Italian Renaissance masterpieces by Correggio, Titian and Raphael; in the North Wing, seventeenth-century Dutch, Flemish, Italian and Spanish Old Masters. In the East Wing are some of the gallery's most popular paintings: works by the French Impressionists and post-Impressionists, including one of Monet's water lily paintings and one of Van Gogh's sunflowers series. Its collection belongs to the public of the United Kingdom and entry to the main collection is free of charge.

Natural History Museum

The Natural History Museum in London is the largest museum of natural history in Europe, which exhibits a vast range of specimens from various segments of natural history. It is home to one of the largest natural history collections in the world from microscopic slides to mammoth skeletons. The building itself is impressive with cathedral like structure, frescoes and sculptures and the central hall is home to an astounding Diplodocus skeleton.

The museum is home to life and earth science specimens comprising some 80 million items within five main collections: botany, entomology, mineralogy, paleontology and zoology. The museum is a world-renowned centre of research specialising in taxonomy, identification and conservation. Given the age of the institution, many of the collections have great historical as well as scientific value, such as specimens collected by Charles Darwin. The Natural History Museum Library contains extensive books, journals, manuscripts, and artwork collections linked to the work and research of the scientific departments; access to the library is by appointment only. The museum is recognized as the pre-eminent centre of natural history and research of related fields in the world.

The museum is divided into four colored zones. The green zone concentrates on facts about life, the planet, environment and evolution. The red zone explores our ever changing planet, how it was shaped and its place within the universe. In the blue zone you can marvel at the diversity of life on our planet from blue whales to the smallest invertebrates. Finally the orange zone takes you into the Wildlife garden (open between April and October) and to the Darwin centre.

Tate Modern

Tate Modern is a national museum of modern and contemporary art in London. It's located in the Bankside area of the London Borough of Southwark.

The Gallery is housed in the former Bankside Power Station, which shut in 1981; in 2000, it opened as an art museum, and has enjoyed spectacular popularity ever since, about five million visitors a year. The building's vast size becomes apparent when visitors enter via the awe-inspiring Turbine Hall, which is 152 meters long and runs the length of the entire building. Visitors can see amazing work for free by artists such as Cézanne, Bonnard, Matisse, Picasso, Rothko, Dalí, Pollock, Warhol and Bourgeois.

Tate holds the national collection of British art from 1900 to the present day and international modern and contemporary art, which represents all the major movements from Fauvism. It includes important masterpieces by both Picasso and Matisse and surrealist works by Dalí, Ernst, Magritte and Mirò. American Abstract Expressionism works include those by Pollock as well as the nine Seagram Murals by Rothko. There is an in depth collection of the Russian pioneer of abstract art Naum Gabo, and an important group of sculpture and paintings by Giacometti. Tate has significant collections of Pop art, including major works by Lichtenstein and Warhol, Minimal art and Conceptual art.

☞ Notes

1. **Rosetta Stone** 罗塞塔石碑。石碑制作于公元前196年，上面用古希腊文、古埃及文和埃及当时的通俗体文字刻有古埃及国王托勒密五世登基的诏书，这使近代考古学家有机会对照各语言版本的内容，解读失传了千余年的埃及象形文的意义和结构，成为目前研究古埃及历史的重要里程碑。
2. **Parthenon Sculptures** 埃尔金石雕是英国大使埃尔金勋爵从土耳其奥斯曼皇帝手中买得的一部分巴特农神庙石雕，这是巴特农神庙雕塑中最精华的部分。石雕被肢解后运回英国，后卖给大英博物馆，成为该馆最珍贵的馆藏。现在希腊政府希望大英博物馆返还该石雕。
3. **the Anglo-Saxon Sutton Hoo burial relics** 出土于萨顿胡的盎格鲁-撒克逊船葬文物，主要指萨顿胡船葬的头盔。该头盔源自公元7世纪早期(盎格鲁撒克逊时期)，发现于英格兰萨克福郡的萨顿胡古墓遗址第一基地。头盔表面点缀着动物装饰和人物场景的装饰嵌板，这些图案流行于当时的日耳曼社会，源头可以追溯到罗马帝国。该头盔在墓室倒塌时被严重毁坏，现通过三维拼图将残余碎片精确拼合，头盔才得以重组。

4. **the Winged Bulls from Khorsabad** 豪尔萨巴德遗址出土的带翼公牛雕像。豪尔萨巴德是亚述古国的另一座首府，离摩苏尔只有几公里。城中的宫殿建于公元前717—公元前706年之间，由亚述国王萨尔贡二世建立。宫殿中的浮雕和雕像保存相当完好。

☞ Questions for comprehension and discussion

1. Who bequeathed his collection to the British Museum?
2. Can you list some of the world-famous collections in the British Museum?
3. Can you list some of the world-famous masters' paintings in the National Gallery?
4. What is Tate Modern based in?
5. Can you list some of the famous collections in the Tate Modern?

9.5 Amusement and Theme Parks

There are many famous amusement parks and theme parks in Britain, providing excitement and entertainment to children as well as adults. In order to attract more visitors, these parks have formed their own features. Due to the limited space, it is not possible for us to exhaust all these parks in the UK. In this part, we will mainly choose some of the most representative ones, including London Eye, Alton Towers Theme Park, Blackpool Pleasure Beach and Legoland Windsor.

London Eye

The London Eye is a giant Ferris wheel on the South Bank of the River Thames in London. It has now become one of the iconic sights of London. Opened in March 2000 the wheel is also known as the Millennium Wheel, a metaphor for the turning of the century. It is the most popular paid tourist attraction in the United Kingdom with over 3.75 million visitors each year.

The London Eye is 135 m high and the wheel has a diameter of 120 m. The whole structure weighs 2100 tonnes. When erected in 1999 it was the world's tallest Ferris wheel. Its height was surpassed by the 158 m tall Star of Nanchang in 2006, the 165 m tall Singapore Flyer in 2008, and the 168 m High Roller (Las Vegas) in 2014.

Visible from all over the city, the London Eye is one of the world's biggest observation wheels. There are 32 capsules attached to the wheel which travels gently at a speed of 0.26 m per second. Each rotation takes 30 minutes in which time visitors can marvel at the views that span up to 40km in all directions (depending on the weather). All the capsules are sealed, air-conditioned and wheelchair accessible. Each one represents one of the Boroughs, and holds up to 25 people, who are free to walk around inside the capsule, though seating is provided. In the capsule, there is a touch-screen equipped to explain what visitors are looking at. On a clear day visitors can see as far as Windsor Castle, 25 miles away, from the top of the wheel.

Alton Towers Theme Park

Alton Towers Theme Park is the UK's biggest and most popular theme park and is home to some of the world's most iconic rides, from Nemesis to The Smiler. From the fun and thrills of the theme park, to the soothing spa and themed hotels, the resort provides a range of attractions for the whole family to enjoy.

Based in the grounds a 15th century Staffordshire country estate, the park was converted into a fully-fledged theme park on 4 April 1980, and has since developed into a land of ten themed areas: Towers Street, Mutiny Bay, Katanga Canyon, Gloomy Wood, Forbidden Valley, Dark Forest, Cloud Cuckoo Land, X-Sector, Adventure Land and CBeebies Land. The theme park is also home to the historic Towers and Gardens. The SkyRide cable car system travels between Towers Street, Forbidden Valley and Cloud Cuckoo Land and takes in views of the gardens.

There are no less than 9 high-speed coasters, including Nemesis, Oblivion, Rita, Thirteen, and The Smiler. The Smiler is the new ride for visitors to watch out. The 18 m ride is the world's first 14-loop rollercoaster, with added psychological effects including optical illusions and blinding lights. There is a multitude of more child-friendly rides including the newly opened Cbeebies Land. There's also two hotels, an aquarium, "4D" cinema, monorail, cable car and acres of beautiful gardens to explore.

Blackpool Pleasure Beach

Blackpool Pleasure Beach is an amusement park and pleasure beach resort situated along the Fylde coast in Blackpool, Lancashire, England. The park was founded in 1896 and has been owned and operated by the Thompson family. It is one of the most visited tourist attraction in the UK, and one of the top 20 most-visited amusement parks in the world. In 2014 it was voted as the best theme park in the UK and the ninth best park in Europe by the Travelers' Choice Awards.

There are 12 exciting rides across the fantastic worlds of some of the world's most popular cartoons, including SpongeBob SquarePants, Avatar Airbender, Dora's World Voyage, and Rugrats Lost River. There are also family theme park rides for all ages, like Wallace & Gromit's Thrill-O-Matic, Tea Cups, Thompson Carousel, Dodgems, Go Karts, and a super scary Ghost Train. The park is also famous for its world famous roller coasters, including The Big One, the Big Dipper, Infusion, Valhalla, Ice Blast, and the thrilling latest addition Red Arrows Skyforce.

There are much more to offer than thrills and spills. Visitors can enjoy Blackpool Pleasure Beach's shows and events, such as the legendary stage shows like Hot Ice, Craig Christian, Ken Webster, and the Circus of Horrors. There's something for all ages at the amusement park.

Legoland Windsor

Legoland Windsor is a child-oriented theme park and resort in Windsor, Berkshire in England, themed around the Lego toy system. The park opened in 1996 on the former Windsor Safari Park site as the second Legoland after Legoland Billund in Denmark. In common with the other Legolands across the world, the park's attractions consist of a mixture of Lego-themed rides, models, and building workshops. The facilities are mainly targeted at children between three and twelve.

In 2015, the park had 2. 2 million visitors, making it the second most visited theme park in the United Kingdom after Alton Towers, and the 10th most visited in Europe. It has over 55 interactive rides, attractions, live shows, building workshops and driving schools, not to mention a staggering 80 million LEGO bricks, all set in 150 acres of beautiful parkland. The biggest attraction for children is the Miniland, which is a miniature park in Lego form, depicting towns and cities from around the world, using nearly 40 million Lego bricks in models often at 1:20 scale. Besides, the area features a number of animated models of European and American scenes.

There's also the option to extend a visit to a sleepover at the fully LEGO themed, 150 room Legoland Hotel situated right in the heart of the Resort. Plus in its 20th anniversary year, guests to the Legoland Windsor Resort in 2016 can enjoy the all new 4D cinema presentation —"The LEGO Movie 4D A New Adventure" and a new Star Wars Miniland model display.

☞ Questions for comprehension and discussion

1. When did the London Eye open? Why did it get the name "Millennium Wheel"?

2. Which theme park is the biggest one in the UK?
3. What kind of activities are mostly provided by Alton Towers Theme Park?
4. What else would visitors enjoy apart from the roller coasters?
5. Who do Legoland Windsor target at? How many LEGO bricks can be found in there?

☞ Questions on Chapter 9 for reflection and presentation

Review the whole chapter and write a short essay on any of the following questions

1. Can you list some of the common characteristics of the tourist attractions in the UK?
2. Do you know any other tourist attractions in the UK? Would you like to introduce it to your classmates?

Chapter 10

Etiquette and Manners in the UK

Etiquette is a code of behavior that delineates expectations for social behavior according to contemporary conventional norms within a society, social class, or group. Manners is a term usually preceded by the word good or bad to indicate whether or not a behavior is socially acceptable. Rules of etiquette are usually unwritten, but aspects of etiquette have been codified from time to time. Adjusting to foreign etiquettes is a major complement of culture shock, providing a market for manuals. The British are said to be reserved in manners, dress and speech. They are famous for their politeness, self-discipline and especially for their sense of humour.

10.1 Courtesy Manners

Many languages use different pronouns to denote formality or familiarity when addressing people. This also applies in daily greetings. The use of an inappropriately familiar form may be seen as derogatory, insulting or even aggressive. Conversely, forms that are inappropriately formal may be seen as impolitely snobbish or distant. The British, particularly the English, are known for politeness and courtesy.

The usual formal greeting is a "How do you do?", which is a greeting not a question and the correct response is to repeat "How do you do?" It is commonly said when people are introduced for the first time and it is usually with a handshake. This greeting can also be substituted with "Nice to meet you-Nice to meet you too", "Delighted to meet you-Delighted to meet you too." "Pleased to meet you-Pleased to meet you too." "Glad to meet you-Glad to meet you too."

And greetings like "Good Morning / Good Afternoon / Good Evening" are usually followed by another common greeting "How are you?" and the most common and polite response is "I am fine, thank you, and you?" Do not be tempted to give a full account of the state of your health, as this is simply a courtesy greeting and not usually an actual question.

Informal greetings may be "Hi-Hi or hello, I am..." "Morning / Afternoon / Evening" (the word "Good" is dropped in informal situations). This is commonly said among friends. They may show concern to each other by asking "How's you? -Fine thanks. You?"

Sometimes "cheers" is said instead of thank you. You may hear "cheers" said instead of "good bye", what is really said is "thanks and bye".

In many parts of Britain, using someone's first name also denotes a certain level of friendship. In social interactions with strangers, the last name and/or more formal mode of address is used, usually until the people involved agree to move to an informal level. However, this may not apply among young people, among members of particular groups (e. g. students) or in informal settings.

You should not be offended when people address you with a seemingly over familiar or "affectionate" name such as "love", "pet", "duck", "chuck", guy, son, ma'am, madam, miss, sir, "mate" or "darling"-these terms vary across the UK. Here you are dealing with regional dialects and cultural conventions that have no deep or hidden meanings.

The "affectionate" name "duck" is thought to come from the Anglo-Saxon word "ducis" which was meant as a term of respect; similar to the Middle English "duc", "duk" which denotes a leader, commander, general; from which comes the title "Duke" and the Old French word "ducheé"-the territory ruled by a Duke.

"Breaking a taboo" is usually considered objectionable by society in general, not merely a subset of a culture. The following DOs and DON'TS are advisable.

Do shake hands: A firm handshake, but with a lighter touch between men and women, is the most common form of greeting and is customary when you are introduced to somebody new. It is advisable to avoid explicit gestures and physical contact such as backslapping or hugging and to maintain a sufficient distance not to invade the personal space of anyone around you, except where this cannot be avoided (such as when using public transport, during the rush hour).

Do take your hat off when necessary (men only). Removing one's hat is also a form of respectful greeting: the origin of this is that knights were expected to remove their helmets when meeting their king; not doing so would be a sign of mistrust and hostility. Nowadays, it is becoming more common to see men wearing hats indoors. However, this is still seen as being impolite, especially to the older generations. Among many segments of the UK population, it is considered rude to wear hats or other head coverings indoors, especially in churches, schools, private homes and respected public institutions. In churches, however, ladies are often exempt from this rule or even obliged to cover their heads in some Catholic churches.

Do say "Excuse me". If someone is blocking your way and you would like them to move, say 'excuse me' and they will move out of your way. If you accidentally bump into someone, say "sorry". They probably will too, even if it was your fault! This is a habit and can be seen as very amusing by an "outsider". It is very good manners to say "please" and "thank you". It is considered rude if you don't.

Do stand in line. In the UK people like to form orderly queues and wait patiently for their turn, e. g. boarding a bus. It is usual to queue when required, and expected that you will take your correct turn and not push in front. "Queue jumping" is frowned upon. It is also good manners to offer your seat to someone who is elderly, or has problems walking or standing, or a mother with young children.

Do open doors for other people. Men and women both hold open the door for each other. It depends on who goes through the door first.

Do pay as you go. Pay for drinks as you order them in pubs and other types of bars.

Do not greet people with a kiss. Only close friends and relatives would kiss the cheek of the opposite sex when they meet. Women might kiss each other once on the right cheek, but men would not.

Do not ask personal or intimate questions. It is considered impolite to ask a lady her age, a person about his or her weight and whether someone is married. Talking or asking about one's personal wealth, possessions or success in business is widely viewed as vulgar. People will rarely say how much money they make or have in the bank nor will they request such information from someone else. It is impolite to ask colleagues about their salary and in some places of work it is forbidden. Even elsewhere, for example, where government employees' salaries are publicly known, it is still considered extremely rude to ask individuals how much they earn.

Don't stare at anyone in public. Unnecessarily long eye contact is also considered an invasion of privacy and can be interpreted as anything from being rude to being a sign of aggression and should therefore be avoided.

Don't talk loudly in public. Don't pick your nose in public. If your nostrils need de-bugging, use a handkerchief.

Don't yaw or cough in public. When doing this, always cover your mouth with your hand. Don't burp in public. If you can not stop a burp from bursting out, then cover your mouth with your hand and say "excuse me" afterwards.

Don't pass wind in public. Go somewhere private and let it out. If you accidentally pass wind in company say "pardon me". And don't litter or spit in the streets, on the buses, trains or shops.

☞ Questions for comprehension and discussion

1. What are appropriate and formal ways of greeting when people are introduced for the first time?
2. What are common greetings among friends?
3. Should students use last names to address each other in daily life? How address people in a polite way on a formal occasion?
4. In what settings should men take their hats off?
5. What are the common polite words to use or what are the inappropriate behavours in public places?

10. 2 Visiting People in Their Houses

"Drop in anytime" and "come and see me soon" are idioms often used in social settings but seldom meant to be taken literally. It is wise to telephone before visiting someone at home. You should not visit or phone someone after 10pm, unless you have been asked to, because most people will think this is too late. If you receive a written invitation to an event that says "RSVP" (abbr. Reply, if you please), you should respond to let the person who sent the invitation know whether or not you plan to attend. Never accept an invitation unless you really plan to go. You may refuse by saying, "Thank you for inviting me, but I will not be able to come." If, after accepting, you are unable to attend, be sure to tell those expecting you as far in advance as possible that you will not be there. When you accept a dinner invitation, tell your host if you have any dietary restrictions. The host will want to plan a meal that you can enjoy. The evening meal is the main meal of the day in most parts of Britain.

Although it is not necessarily expected that you give a gift to your host, it is considered polite to do so, especially if you have been invited for a meal. Flowers, chocolate, or a small gift are all appropriate. A thank-you note or telephone call after the visit is also considered polite and is an appropriate means to express your appreciation for the invitation.

British people place considerable value on punctuality. It is often considered impolite to arrive even a few minutes late. If you are unable to keep an appointment, it is expected that you call the person you are meeting. Some general tips follow:

You should arrive at the exact time specified for dinner, lunch, or appointments with professors, doctors, and other professionals. If you are invited to someone's house for dinner at 7:00 pm, you are expected to be there on the dot. An invitation might state "7:30 for 8:00", in which case you should arrive no later than 7:50. However, if an invitation says "sharp", you must arrive in plenty of time. If you are going to be late, it is polite to let the host know.

It is not always so important to be exactly on time for teas, receptions, and cocktail parties. You can arrive any time during the hours specified, unless you are asked to be on time.

However, you should arrive a few minutes early for public meetings, plays, concerts, movies, sporting events, classes, church services, and weddings.

Everyday dress is appropriate for most visits to peoples' homes. You may want to dress more formally when attending a holiday dinner or cultural event, such as a concert or theatre performance. However, wearing coats, boots or other outer garments inside someone's home is often frowned upon as well. Sitting down to eat at table wearing a hat or coat etc. is even worse.

Food may be served in one of several ways: "family style," by passing the serving plates from one to another around the dining table; "buffet style," with guests serving themselves at the buffet; and "serving style," with the host filling each plate and passing it to each person.

In the UK, the host takes the first bite unless he or she instructs otherwise. The host begins after all food is served and everyone is seated. In religious households, a family meal may commence with saying Grace, or at dinner parties the guests might begin the meal by offering some favourable comments on the food and thanks to the host. In a group dining situation it is considered impolite to begin eating before all the group have been served their food and are ready to start.

You may eat chicken and pizza with your fingers if you are at a barbecue, finger buffet or very informal setting. Otherwise always use a knife and fork.

It is ok to pour your own drink when eating with other people, but it is more polite to offer pouring drinks to the people sitting on either side of you. Only white wine or rosé is held by the stem of the glass; red by the bowl. Wines should be served in the sequence "white before red, light before heavy, young before old".

Never lick or put your knife in your mouth. Never chew with your mouth open. No one wants to see food being chewed or hearing it being chomped on.

It is impolite to put too much food in your mouth. Never use fingers to push food onto your spoon or fork. It is impolite to slurp your food or eat noisily. Never blow your nose on a napkin (serviette). Napkins are for dabbing your lips and only for that. Napkins should be placed across the lap — tucking them into your clothing may be considered 'common'. Never pick food out of your teeth with your fingernails.

Should a mobile telephone (or any other modern device) ring or if a text message is received, the diner should ignore the call. In exceptional cases where the diner feels the call may be of an urgent nature, he should ask to be excused, leave the room and take the call (or read the text message) out of earshot of the other diners. If you have accidentally taken too much food and cannot possibly eat it all, say "I'm sorry, but it seems that my eyes are bigger than my stomach." Or "I'm sorry. It was so delicious but I'm full." The main thing is not offend your host.

☞ Questions for comprehension and discussion

1. What should you do if you receive a written invitation to a dinner?
2. What is the appropriate time to arrive for an appointment with professionals, a cocktail or a public meeting respectively?
3. In what styles may food be served and how to conduct each?
4. Who will pour drinks for you and to whom you may offer pouring drinks, in what sequence?
5. How to use napkins properly at tables?

10.3 Eating Utensil Etiquette

Table manners may also include the appropriate use of utensils. The British generally pay a lot of attention to good table manners. Even young children are expected to eat properly with knife and fork.

If you are eating at a formal dinner party, you will come across many knives and forks. At the top of your plate will be a dessert spoon and dessert fork. Start with the utensils on the outside and work your way inward with each subsequent course.

The fork is held with the left hand and the knife held with the right or the other way round if you are left handed. Once a bite-sized piece of food has been cut, it is conducted straight to the mouth by the left hand. For other food items, such as potatoes, vegetables or rice, the blade of the knife is used to assist or guide placement of the food on the back of the fork. The tines remain pointing down.

The knife and fork are both held with the handle running along the palm and extending out to be held by thumb and forefinger. This style is sometimes called "hidden handle" because the palm conceals the handle.

If you put your knife down, you can turn your fork over. It is correct to change hands when you do this, too, so if you are right handed you would switch and eat with the fork in your right hand. When no knife is being used, the fork can be held with the tines up. Under no circumstances should the fork be held like a shovel, with all fingers wrapped around the base.

When eating soup, the spoon is held in the right hand and the bowl tipped away from you, scooping the soup in outward movements. Soup should always be taken (without slurping of course) from the side of the spoon, and not from the "end" as in most of the rest of Europe.

To be very polite, peas should be crushed onto the fork — a fork with the prongs pointing down. The best way is to have load the fork with something to which they will stick, such as potato or a soft vegetable that squashes easily onto the fork. It is sometimes easier to put down your knife and switch your fork to the other hand, so you can shovel the peas against something else on the plate, thus ensuring they end up on your fork.

When eating in formal situations, rest the fork and knife on the plate between mouthful, or for a break for conversation.

Always chew and swallow all the food in your mouth before taking more or taking a drink. Always say "thank you" when served with something. It shows appreciation. When eating rolls, break off a piece of bread before buttering. Eating it whole looks tacky. On formal dining occasions, it is good manners to take some butter from the butter dish with a bread knife and put it onto a side plate, to later butter pieces of bread roll. This prevents the butter in the dish from gathering bread crumbs as it is passed around. Knives should be used to butter bread rolls but not to cut them, and they should instead be torn with the hands.

It is impolite to have your elbows on the table while your are eating. Don't reach over someone to pick up food or other items. You should always ask for items to be passed. In the same vein, you should pass those items directly to the person who asked. It is also rude to slurp food, eat noisily or make noise with cutlery. Never eat off a knife when having a meal.

The knife must never enter the mouth or be licked. Food should always be chewed with the mouth closed. Talking with food in one's mouth is seen as very rude. Licking one's fingers and eating slowly can also be considered impolite.

To eat dessert, break the dessert with the spoon, one bite at a time. Push the food with the fork (optional) into the spoon. Eat from the spoon.

When you have finished eating, this should be communicated to other diners and waiting staff by placing the knife and fork together on the plate, with the fork on the left, its tines facing upwards. Napkins should be placed unfolded on the table when the meal is finished.

☞ Questions for comprehension and discussion

1. By what is the piece of food conducted straight to the mouth?
2. What does "hidden handle" mean?
3. What is the proper way to eat peas with the fork?
4. How can you reach the food on the table?
5. What is the polite way to end eating?

10.4 Business Etiquette

Face-to-face communication

Introductions depend upon the circumstances of a particular situation. Generally, the best practice is to be introduced by a third party, although this may not always be possible. A handshake is the typical greeting for a new introduction and should not be expected at subsequent meetings.

In a meeting, use the courtesy titles Mr., Mrs. or Miss and a surname when addressing others. Not until you have been asked to do so should you call someone by their first name. To address a man in public without mentioning his name use "Sir". The equivalent form of address for a woman is "Madam", but the connotations associated with the word means it has fallen out of common usage and may not always be well-received depending on the context.

Meetings are conducted depending on the people attending. If all the attendees are of the same level, ideas and opinions flow freely. However, if a senior ranking person is present, most of the speaking will be done by that person.

Usually, there's some seemingly meaningless small talk before the actual meeting starts, but in general, meetings are formal with an agenda and a clearly defined purpose. This is seen as a good way to start the meeting in a harmonious manner.

Beginning a conversation with someone new may be a daunting proposition because of

British cultural norms and expectations. It is generally advisable to open a conversation with a neutral topic, such as the weather or something dictated by the immediate situation, such as asking for a recommendation on something to do, eat or drink. It is good practice to start a conversation with open questions rather than subjective assumptions or personal points of view as the reaction of your counterpart is not always predictable. As you will find, many British people are tolerant and open-minded. Some people may derive their opinions from the tabloid press that often depicts the world in black and white terms.

Self-promotion is not appreciated in the UK. It is far better to self-deprecate. It is, of course, acceptable to be positive about your company and products.

The British often use diplomatic language in lieu of directness. In business situations, they're non-confrontational because they don't want to offend the other party. This can often lead the British to seem evasive in meeting situations when they are really searching for a way of saying something negative in a positive way.

In addition to being diplomatic, the British also use language in a coded manner preferring to say unpalatable things using more acceptable, positive phrases. Thus, "I disagree" becomes "I think you have made several excellent points there but have you ever considered..." And a lack of interest in an idea is often greeted with "Hmm, that's an interesting point." Another difficulty in verbal communication may come from the British penchant for understatement. This sometimes shows itself in seeming self-deprecation and presents a challenge in understanding how things, people and situations are really perceived by the British. For example, what might be described as "a bit expensive" may well really mean "very expensive" and "a little problem" might actually constitute "a huge stumbling block" for a British counterpart.

Humour is virtually all-pervasive in business situations. Indeed, the more tense and difficult a situation is, the more likely the British are to use humour. This does not imply that the British are not taking the situation seriously — it is merely that humour is used as a tension release mechanism and helps to keep situations calm, reserved and non-emotional.

As a general observation, people tend to be more open and friendly outside of London and in the North in particular; in fact, there is still a north-south divide in terms of cultural openness in the UK. Some exceptions exist, for example Scottish Highlanders or Welsh farmers will hardly say a word until you get to know each other. Discussions tend to be emotionless and may become tense, with the parties politely excusing themselves and withdrawing.

Punctuality

In general, the British value time-keeping for business arrangements. If you set up a meeting for two o'clock, the chances are your counterparts will arrive on time or just before. It is considered very impolite to arrive late for a business meeting. If your delay is inevitable and you arrive late, it is usually sufficient to excuse yourself with an apology. If, however, you are running more than a few minutes late, you should call ahead to apologise and give an indication of how long you will be; in the case of a longer delay that would compromise the value of attending the meeting, you should consider offering to postpone the meeting to a new time and/or day. The busier people are, the greater the likelihood that they will have to leave for another engagement, so respecting their time is very important.

Attending social events is slightly different, and guests may be expected to arrive about fifteen minutes after the specified time, but this is contingent on the nature of the event and the number of attendees. The golden rule is that the more important the appointment, the more time you should allow for potential delays.

Gift Giving

Gift Giving is not a usual part of British business etiquette, although reciprocation is good practice when gifts are received. Some organisations are encouraged not to accept any form of gift and some are prevented from doing so on legal grounds. However, where a gift is offered, it is important to ensure that it is not expensive enough to be considered a bribe or so inexpensive as to be considered an insult.

There is a large range of suitable gifts to choose from: company greeting cards, pens, books, diaries, alcohol, flowers, souvenirs from the visitors' country or invitations to a cultural event etc. If a gift is received in public, it is advisable to open it immediately and express your gratitude to the giver.

Usually, the successful conclusion of negotiations presents an ideal opportunity for gift giving. Here the meaning is an acknowledgement of the occasion. Ideally, such gifts will be gold, silver or porcelain and it is important to consider the suitability of the gift and the taste of the recipient. It is not usual to exchange business gifts at Christmas; however, it is still good practice to send a greetings card to express thanks to your business counterparts.

If you receive an invitation to dinner or a party at the home of one of your business colleagues, it is normal to bring a bottle of wine and possibly a small gift such as flowers or chocolates. When giving flowers beware that red roses (which signify romantic intentions) and white lilies (which express grief and are used for funerals) are best avoided.

Business dress codes

When it comes to business dress codes, classical conservative attire is the norm for both men and women in British culture and dark colours such as black, dark blue and charcoal grey are predominant. It is common for women to wear either trousers or a skirt in an office environment, and head scarves are accepted as part of religious freedom. Women in management positions often mirror male attire in so far as dark suits and blouses are worn — with little in the way of more flamboyant accessories being seen. Many senior managers are fond of quality and express their status through their choice of clothing. Shopping in designer boutiques is popular among British society and bespoke suits, designer shirts, silk ties and hand-made shoes are signs of affluence and status.

When in doubt about the dress code for a particular business event, it is advisable to be overdressed rather than risk making a poor impression. It is often better to find out in advance, so you can make any necessary changes before your introduction to the company. This will put you at ease and make you more relaxed in your encounters with the company representatives.

Entertaining

It is reasonably common to be invited out for lunch by a business contact in the UK, but more unusual to be asked to go for dinner. Business lunches are often seen as an extension of the meeting and it is usually acceptable to discuss business matters over the food. If in doubt over this matter, follow the lead of your host. The person who invites will invariably pay and there is no real need to offer to contribute to the cost. If you have invited a guest and they offer to contribute, they are probably doing so out of politeness and do not necessarily expect to be taken up on their offer.

Lunches can vary in style from a very informal pub meal to a much more elaborate formal meal at an expensive restaurant. The choice of venue can depend on a number of factors such as location, importance placed on the business opportunity (or guest), market sectors etc. If you are unsure where to take somebody it is best to err on the side of caution and go to a good quality restaurant.

Alcohol will usually be offered at lunch and some British business people will accept whilst others prefer to stick to soft drinks — this is an entirely personal decision and you will not be under pressure to drink alcohol in this situation. It is much more common for larger amounts of alcohol to be drunk at dinner and on these occasions you may find that you are placed under a small amount of pressure to join in the "drinking culture".

☞ Questions for comprehension and discussion

1. What is an usual practice to start the meeting in a harmonious manner? What topic are good to open a conversation with someone new?
2. What are typical manners of British people in business communications?
3. How do the British value time-keeping for business arrangements? What is the golden rule for important business appointments?
4. What important matters should be considered when gifts are offered in business situations?
5. What are signs of affluence and status in terms of business dress code?
6. What places are good to entertain your business partners?

☞ Questions on Chapter 10 for reflection and presentation

Review the whole chapter and write a short essay on any of the following questions.

1. Do you think your country has the same courtesy manners as in the UK and how are they practised?
2. When communicating face to face, how can you leave a good impression on your counterparts and business partners and establish a good relationship with them?
3. What gifts would you offer to your business partners and what places would you choose to entertain them? Why?
4. What are the differences between the Chinese and the British in entertaining guests?

Chapter 11

Festivals and Holidays

In Britain, people celebrate many holiday, such as Christmas, Easter, Lent, New Year and so on. Many of them are so popular as to be known and celebrated in many countries today.

Due to different histories and cultures in England, Wales, Scotland and Northern Ireland, there are also some festivals and holidays peculiar to each nation. They are celebrated at different times for different reasons. For example, the English people celebrate the Guy Fawkes Night (Bonfire Night) on December 5 for the successful destruction of Catholic conspirators' intended explosion in 1605. Many people light bonfires and set off fireworks and in some towns and cities, the municipality organizes a bonfire and professional firework display in a park. The Scottish celebrate Hogmanay on December 31 and Burns Night on January 25. Hogmanay is the New Year's Eve in Scotland, which is more important than Christmas to Scots. On Burns Night, the Scottish people hold a Burns Supper for the remembrance of the great Scottish poet Robert Burns. The Northern Ireland's national holiday is St. Patrick's Day on March 17. People celebrate the birth of St. Patrick, the saint priest who brought Christianity to Ireland and converted Northern Irish people to Christians. In Wels, Saint David's Day on March 1 is the feast day of Saint David, the patron saint of Wales. There are many holidays and festivals celebrated in one country that are not shared with the rest of the UK. But as a result of culture diversity and change of time, many holidays are no longer confined by geographical confinement and shared by people throughout the country.

11.1 Religious Festivals

Britain is basically a Christian nation, although different religions are practiced owing to immigration and belief change. As a result, Christian holidays are celebrated. The most important religious holidays are Christmas, Easter and Lent.

Christmas

Christmas Day, December 25th, traditionally celebrates Jesus Christ's birth. It is the greatest of Christian festivals. Apart from its religious significance, two points help to set it apart from other festivals and holidays: the custom of giving and receiving gifts, and the habit of spending it with the family.

Prior to Christmas Day, people decorate their homes and gardens. These decorations may include Christmas trees, small colored fairy lights, leaves and berries from holly trees and mistletoe bushes, and various other decorations with rich colors that spark the Christmas mood.

Many people spend Christmas Day with family members, with whom they exchange gifts and cards. Many children wake up to find a sock or stocking filled with small gifts on their bed or somewhere else in the house. These have supposedly been brought by a mythical figure called "Father Christmas" or "Santa Claus", who lives for most of the year at the North Pole. Later in the day, people may attend special church services, even if they do not usually go to church. Nearly everyone prepares and eats a special meal. This often includes roast turkey, potatoes and parsnips, and other vegetables. After the main course, Christmas pudding is often eaten.

Nearly all organizations, except hospitals and shelters for the homeless, are closed on Christmas Day. Some public houses and smaller stores selling food may open for a few hours in the middle of the day. Public transport services do not run to their normal timetables and may even not run at all. Many churches hold special services on Christmas Eve and Christmas Day. Some also organize shelter, food and company for the homeless or those who need help.

There are many Christmas symbols. These include leaves and berries from the holly tree and mistletoe bush, pine trees, candles and small lights. Figures associated with the season are Father Christmas or Santa Claus, the baby Jesus, Mary, Joseph and the other characters from the Nativity story. Presents and Christmas food, such as turkey, Christmas pudding and mince pies also symbolize Christmas. A special mention should be reserved for the robin Redbreast. This small bird, with its red feathered breast, is at its most beautiful in the middle of the winter and is often seen as a decoration on Christmas cards, wrapping paper and cakes.

Easter

Easter in the United Kingdom is an important Christian holiday. Easter Day occurs on the first Sunday after the first full moon on or after the vernal equinox, and it usually falls on a Sunday between March 22 and April 25, according to the church calendar. For many people, Easter marks the celebration of the resurrection of Jesus Christ after his crucifixion. In churches, it is generally a festive occasion with an emphasis on the dawn of a new life. In Battersea Park in London, there is a large Easter parade every year.

Many people celebrate Easter Day by decorating, exchanging or searching for eggs. The eggs may be fresh or boiled eggs laid by chickens or other birds, chocolate eggs or eggs made of other materials. Many children believe that the Easter bunny or rabbit comes to their house or garden to hide eggs. They may search for these eggs or find that the Easter bunny has left them in an obvious place.

Some businesses and attractions hold Easter egg hunts. These can be competitions to see who can collect the most eggs. In some parts of the United Kingdom, people roll hard boiled down slopes. In other places, there is a game in which people roll hard boiled eggs against other people's eggs. The winner is the person whose egg remains whole. After the game, the eggs are eaten. In some parts of Scotland, fondant filled chocolate eggs about the size of a hen's egg are covered in batter and deep fried.

On Easter Day nearly all non-essential businesses and organizations are closed. In England and Wales, stores are also closed. In Scotland, they are allowed to open. Public transport systems may run on a different schedule from other Sundays. In some areas there may be no public transport.

Lent

Lent is the Christian season of preparation before Easter. In Western Christianity, Ash Wednesday marks the first day, or the start of the season of Lent, which begins 40 days prior to Easter (Sundays are not included in the count). Lent is a time when many Christians prepare for Easter by observing a period of fasting, repentance and moderation. The purpose is to set aside time for reflection on Jesus Christ — his suffering and his sacrifice, his life, death, burial and resurrection.

For Christians, the Lent is one way of remembering the 40 days when Jesus went into the desert to fast and pray before beginning his work for God. It is a test of self-discipline too. There are many foods that some Christians do not eat in Lent, such as meat and fish, eggs, and milky foods. Some Christians just give up something they really enjoy such as cakes or chocolate. Not all Christian churches observe Lent.

Halloween

Halloween is a holiday annually celebrated on October 31. People believed that, at this time of year, the spirits of dead people could come "alive" and walk among the living. They thought that it was important to dress up in costumes when venturing outside, to avoid being harmed by the spirits. This may be the origin of the Halloween costumes seen today. Common symbols of Halloween include pumpkins, bats and spiders.

Halloween celebrations in the United Kingdom include parties where the hosts and guests often dress up as skeletons, ghosts or other scary figures to reflect the day's theme. Other people gather together to watch horror films, either at home or at a cinema. Some children go trick-or-treating. This means that they dress up and go to other people's houses, knocking on the door for treat of sweets or a snack. Those who do not give out a treat may be tricked with a joke instead.

Halloween is not a bank holiday in the United Kingdom. Schools, businesses, stores and other organizations are open as usual. Public transport services run on their normal timetables.

☞ Questions for comprehension and discussion

1. What festival is the greatest in Britain? What is its significance and at what time is it celebrated?
2. How is Christmas usually celebrated in Britain?
3. How is Easter usually celebrated in Britain?
4. What is the purpose of Lent?
5. What would children do at Halloween?

11.2 National Holidays

National holidays refer to holidays celebrated throughout the Britain. Due to different histories and cultures of the four nations, it seems rather difficult to have national holidays that could be celebrated by the whole country.

New Year

New Year's Day is a public holiday in the United Kingdom on January 1 each year. It marks the start of the New Year in the Gregorian calendar.

The main celebration is on New Year's Eve (December 31), the last day of the year.

Many people see the old year out with a party, welcoming in the New Year with toasts of champagne, and exchanging good wishes for a "Happy New Year". It is traditional to stay up and see the old year out. Its exit is usually noisy. All over Britain there are parties, fireworks, singing and dancing, to ring out the old year and ring in the new. Just before midnight, many people turn on a television to show pictures of one of the four clocks on the Clock Tower on the Palace of Westminster in London counting down the last minutes of the old year. At midnight, as the New Year begins, the chimes of Big Ben, the bell inside the Clock Tower, are broadcast to mark the start of the New Year.

Many people make New Year's resolutions. These are promises to themselves that they will lead a better life in some way in the coming year. Common New Year's resolutions include stopping smoking, losing weight, eating more healthily, getting more exercise or spending less money. Some types of resolution that would lead to a healthier lifestyle are supported by government advertising campaigns.

In some areas, there are a number of customs associated with New Year's Day. In Scotland, New Year's Eve is celebrated with much drinking and revelry as Hogmanay, which traditionally lasts for a day or more into the New Year. Many people sing the song "Auld Lang Syne" at midnight as New Year's Day begins. New Year's Day is more important than Christmas to Scots. In Scotland and northern England, it is customary to go first footing. This is the first person to enter a house on January 1. There are many traditions and superstitions associated with first footing. A male first-footer brings good luck, but a female bad luck. In different areas there are different traditions about whether the first footer should have fair or dark hair, whether the person should bring coal, salt or other things and what food or drink that person should be served after arrival.

Nearly all schools, large businesses and organizations are closed. In some areas stores may be open, although this varies a lot. Public transport systems do not usually run on their normal timetables. In general, public life shuts down completely on New Year's Day.

Remembrance Day

Remembrance Day in the UK honors the heroic efforts, achievements and sacrifices that were made in past wars. Remembrance Day is an observance and not a public holiday in the UK. The main observance is on the second Sunday in November, but 2 minutes of silence is also made on November 11.

People stop work to observe a moment of silence at 11 a. m. on November 11, which is the time and date when hostilities formally ended after more than four years of battle during World War I. Poppies are worn as a symbol of respect and tribute on Remembrance

Sunday and/or November 11. The day is also marked by events such as memorial services, church services and parades. A national commemoration takes place at Whitehall, a road in the City of Westminster in central London.

Also referred to as Poppy Day or Armistice Day, Remembrance Day is observed in Commonwealth countries, including Australia and Canada. Other countries such as the U. S. have similar observances like Veterans Day.

Boxing Day

Boxing Day in the United Kingdom is the day after Christmas Day (December 26) or the Monday following if December 26 falls on a weekend. Traditionally, it was a day when employers distributed money, food, cloth or other valuable goods to their employees. In modern times, it is a bank holiday for sporting events and the start of the post-Christmas sales.

For many people Boxing Day is a time to recover from the excesses of Christmas day and an opportunity to spent time with family, friends and neighbors. Some people choose to go for a walk in the countryside, while other flock to the post-Christmas sales in large stores that often begin on Boxing Day. Some people even spend part of the night and early morning queuing to get into the stores when the best bargains are still available.

Boxing Day is also an important day for sports events. Traditionally, using dogs to hunt for foxes was a popular sport amongst the upper classes. Pictures of hunters on horseback dressed in red coats and surrounded by hunting dogs are often seen as symbolic of Boxing Day. Nowadays, fox hunting is outlawed. Horse racing and football (soccer) are now popular sports.

Queen's Official Birthday

The birthday of the British Monarch (currently Queen Elizabeth Ⅱ) in his/ her reign is a National Day in Britain. Queen Elizabeth Ⅱ was born on April 21, 1926, but her official birthday is on the second Saturday of June to coincide with a high probability of fine weather in the Northern Hemisphere for outdoor ceremonies.

☞ Questions for comprehension and discussion

1. How is New Year's Eve celebrated in England and Scotland?
2. What is the Scottish tradition concerning New Year's Day?
3. What do people usually do on Remembrance Day?
4. When are national celebrations held for Queen's Official Birthday?

11.3 Bank Holidays

In the UK, legal holidays are known as Bank Holidays, when most people have the day off work. Bank holidays do not count as normal working days even though, nowadays, most shops are open and some people work on them.

They've been called bank holidays since the late 19th century. The name originates because these were the days on which the banks were closed for trading. Bank employees didn't time off back then — they were too busy using the bank holiday to work on the accounts and tidy up the bookkeeping. The name, and the tradition of closing banks persisted into the 20th century, even though all that tidy bookkeeping was now done during normal business hours. But more recently, things have changed even more in a relatively short space of time. As in the USA, bank holidays have become excuses for shopping, sales and, in some cases, retail orgies. Besides, bank holidays tend to result in increased holiday activity, with many people going on a long weekend break.

Though many of the same holidays are observed in England, Wales, Scotland and Northern Ireland, there are slight variations, reflecting different national customs and priorities. England and Wales have the fewest bank holidays, with only 8, and Northern Ireland has the most generous allocation of holidays, with ten.

The public holidays in UK are as follows:

January 1st: New Year's Day
January 2nd: Bank Holiday (Scotland only)
March/ April: Good Friday
Easter Monday (not Scotland)
May (first Monday): May Bank Holiday
May (last Monday): Spring Bank Holiday
August (last Monday): Summer Bank Holiday (first Monday in Scotland)
December 25th: Christmas Day
December 26th: Boxing Day

- Northern Ireland celebrates two additional Bank Holidays: CMarch 17th: St. Patrick's Day

July 12th: Battle of the Boyne (Orangemen's Day)

- Public Holidays in Scotland

The Scots celebrate Hogmanay, a three or four-day New Year's blowout — so the official New Year's holiday includes an extra day, simply called 2nd January Holiday or

2nd New Year's Day.

The Summer Bank Holiday has been celebrated at the beginning of August in Scotland but the end of August elsewhere in the UK. Since most Scottish banks close at the end of the month as well, to correspond with the rest of the UK, in 2016 the holidays will be harmonized.

Since 2007, St. Andrews Day, the national day in Scotland, has been an optional or voluntary public holiday. Banks and schools may not necessarily be closed on Scottish public holidays since they mirror England and Wales for business reasons. Similarly, while Easter Monday is not observed as a public holiday in Scotland, in order to harmonize with the rest of the UK, the banks are closed.

Today, the banks are still closed on UK public holidays but not much else is. If you are planning a trip to UK that includes a national holiday, here's what you can expect:

- Banks are closed — obviously — so are Post Offices and other government offices and departments.
- Most office businesses, including travel and booking agencies are closed.
- Motorways are clogged.
- Queues at popular family attractions are longer than usual. In fact, if you are not fond of sharing your vacation time with hordes of kids, it's probably best to avoid bank holiday travel — when children are everywhere.
- Rooms may be harder to book or slightly more expensive during bank holidays.
- Most of the larger shops are open. This is a bit hit or miss. Some businesses hold big, bank holiday sales events while others shut their doors. The only exceptions are Easter Sunday and Christmas Day when the law requires the larger shops to close.
- Trains, buses and the London Underground operate reduced services so it is important to plan Bank Holiday travel on public transportation carefully.
- If a bank holiday date falls on a Saturday or Sunday then a "substitute" day will be given because most people do not work on Saturdays or Sundays anyway. (670 words)

☞ Questions for comprehension and discussion

1. What does "Bank Holiday" mean in Britain? How did it come in the past?
2. What might a tourist find in Britain during bank holidays?
3. How is the public transportation system working during bank holidays?

☞ Questions on Chapter 10 for reflection and presentation

Review the whole chapter and write a short essay on any of the following questions.

1. What are the similarities and differences between British and Chinese traditional festivals?
2. What are the differences between Chinese and British cultures reflected by different festivals?
3. Which British festivals are celebrated in China? What do Chinese people usually do?

Chapter 12

British Literature

British literature is hundreds of years old and remains popular in the whole world today. It is time-tested and well worn for many reasons: It represents writers from different time periods, and covers every major genre and style of writing as well. It teaches people about different time periods and faraway places. It also deals with universal themes and values that help people grow in everyday lives. British literature continues to be one of the most part of world literature.

In this chapter, we will introduce the brief history of British literature, and some famous English writers and their works.

12.1 Development of British Literature

English literature has a long history from the 5th century to the present, which can be mainly divided into eight periods: Old English Literature (450-1066), Medieval English Literature (1066-1500), The Renaissance Literature (1500-1660), The Seventeenth-Century English Literature (1603-1700), The Eighteenth-Century English Literature (1700-1798), The Romantic English Literature (1798-1832), The Victorian English Literature (1830s-1901) and The 20th-Century English Literature.

12.1.1 Old English Literature (450-1066)

English, as we know it, descends from the language spoken by the north Germanic tribes (Angles, Saxons and Jutes) who settled in England from the 5th century A. D. onwards. The language spoken by them is called the Old English, which is the foundation of English language and literature.

Old English Period is from their invasion to Norman Conquest in 1066. Much of the first half of this period, prior to the seventh-century, at least, was oral literature. People had no writing until they learned the Latin alphabet from Roman missionaries. The earliest written works in Old English were probably composed orally at first, and may have been passed on from speaker to speaker before being written. We know the names of some of the later writers (Cædmon[1], Ælfric[2] and King Alfred[3]) but most writing is anonymous.

Old English literature is mostly chronicle and poetry — lyric, descriptive but chiefly narrative or epic. The most important work in this period is *Beowulf*, which is the oldest poem in the English language and the longest epic poem in Old English. It tells the breathtaking story of a struggle between the hero, Beowulf, and a bloodthirsty monster called Grendel. *Beowulf* consists of more than 3000 lines. It had been passed from mouth to mouth for hundreds of years before it was written down in the 10th century or at the end of the 9th century.

☞ Notes

1. **Cædmon** 凯德蒙，第一位名字为人所知的英国诗人，成名于公元670年前后。
2. **Ælfric** 英国作家和本笃会僧侣，10世纪后半叶英国著名学者。
3. **King Alfred** 阿尔弗莱德王，9世纪后期出现的传奇英雄式的威塞克斯国王。

☞ Questions for comprehension and discussion

1. In literature, what is the Old English Period?
2. What are the characteristics of Old English?
3. What is oldest poem in the English language and the longest epic poem in Old English? What did it talk about?

12.1.2 Medieval English Literature (1066-1500)

From 1066 to around 1500, the language is known as Medieval English. This period sees a huge transition in the language, culture and lifestyle of England. Ideas and themes from French and Celtic literature appear in English writing at about this time. Much of the Medieval English writings were religious in nature; however, from about 1350 onward, secular literature began to rise. This period is home to the likes of Chaucer, Thomas Malory, Robert Henryson, William Langland and John Gower. Notable works include *Piers Plowman* and *Sir Gawain and the Green Knight*, etc.

The most popular and influential writer during this period was Geoffrey Chaucer (c. 1343-1400). He was considered the first great English poet. His works encompassed a variety of tones, styles, and genres. One of his most renowned works, *The Canterbury Tales*, is an epic story of pilgrims diverting themselves with the telling of tales on their way to Canterbury. Each pilgrim's tale takes on a narrative of its own. The poem is structured in a frame narrative, or "story within a story," a literary device that would go on to become one of the most popular storytelling techniques in the history of literature. *The Canterbury Tales represents Chaucer's final poetic achievements and is one of the monumental works in English literature.*

☞ Questions for comprehension and discussion

1. What kind of ideas and themes appeared in Medieval English writing?
2. Who was considered the first great English poet?
3. What did *The Canterbury Tales* talk about? What is its characteristic?

12.1.3 The Renaissance Literature (1500-1660)

English literature in the Renaissance Period is usually regarded as the highlight in the history of English literature. English drama and poetry developed at high speed and made a magnificent achievement in this period.

The Elizabethan Age was the golden age of English drama. Some of its excellent dramatists included John Lyly, Thomas Kyd, George Peele, Robert Greene, Christopher Marlowe, Ben Jonson, and, of course, William Shakespeare. Before the 16th century English drama meant the amateur performances of Bible stories by craft guilds on public holidays. Christopher Marlowe (1564-1593) broke through the old form of drama and became the first great dramatist of the Renaissance period. His plays explored the boundaries of the new world and the risks that mankind would run in the quest for power, for knowledge, for love. He was the greatest of the English dramatists before Shakespeare and paved the way for Shakespeare. William Shakespeare (1564-1616) is one of the most remarkable playwrights and poets the world has ever known. With his 37 plays, 154 sonnets and 2 long narrative poems, he has established his giant position in world literature.

Next to drama was poetry. In that period, writing poetry was a fashion. Many famous poets appeared, such as, Thomas Wyatt, Henry Howard, Philip Sidney, Edmund Spenser, Christopher Marlowe, William Shakespeare and Ben Jonson. Edmund Spenser (1552-1599) was recognized as the "poet's poet". He invented the Spenserian stanza, which became a popular verse form in the historical development of English poetry. His greatest work is *The Faerie Queene*. It set in the mythical world of King Arthur and his knights, praised the queen and promoted humanism.

In this period, there were also some famous prose writers. The great humanist, Thomas More (1477-1535), wrote his famous prose work *Utopia*, which has been regarded as the earliest work of Utopian socialism. The whole work is divided into two books. Book Ⅰ is a forcible exposure of the evil things in English society of that period; Book Ⅱ describes an ideal communist, Utopia. The conditions depicted in *Utopia* are markedly contrasted with those of English society, presenting a sharp criticism of current English society. Another famous figure was Francis Bacon, who wrote more than 50 excellent essays, which put him among the best essayists in English literature.

☞ Questions for comprehension and discussion

1. How did drama develop in the Elizabethan Age?
2. What do you know about William Shakespeare?
3. Who was recognized as the "poet's poet" in the Renaissance Period?
4. What did *Utopia* talk about?

12.1.4 The Seventeenth-Century English Literature (1603-1700)

The earlier 17th century, and especially the period of the English Revolution (1640-1660), was a time of intense ferment in all areas of life. The spirit of unity and feeling of patriotism ended with the reign of Elizabeth I. England was then convulsed with the conflict between the Royalists and the Puritans. That ferment was reflected in the literature of the era.

The main literary form of the Revolution Period was poetry. Among the poets, John Milton (1608-1674) was the greatest. He devoted almost 20 years of his best life to the fight for political, religious and personal liberty as a writer. His masterpiece, *Paradise Lost*, is the greatest English epic. The poem concerns the Biblical story of the Fall of Man: the temptation of Adam and Eve by the fallen angel Satan and their expulsion from the Garden of Eden. Milton's purpose, stated in Book I, is to "justify the ways of God to men". In 17th century, there was another group of poets — the Metaphysical Poets. The major members of this group are John Donne and Andrew Marvell. Their works were characterized by the inventive use of conceits, and by speculation about topics such as love or religion.

In the Restoration Period John Bunyan (1628-1688) occupied the most important place in the field of prose writing. His most important work, *The Pilgrim's Progress*, is regarded as one of the most significant works of religious English literature. It is an allegory, in which general concepts such as sin, despair, and faith are represented as people or as aspects of the natural world. The figures and places the hero, Christian, encounters on his journey stand for the various experiences every Christian must go through in the quest for salvation. Another important figure in this period is John Dryden (1631-

1700). As a poet, essayist and playwright who was made Poet Laureate in 1668, he is seen as dominating the literary life of Restoration England to such a point that the period came to be known in literary circles as the Age of Dryden.

☞ Questions for comprehension and discussion

1. What kind of conflict did the Seventeenth-Century English Literature reflect?
2. What was the main literary form of the Revolution Period? Who was the greatest poet in this period?
3. What did *Paradise Lost* concern?
4. What are the main concepts reflected in *The Pilgrim's Progress*?

12.1.5 The Eighteenth-Century English Literature (1700-1798)

The 18th century in England was The Age of Enlightenment or Age of Reason. Literature explored themes of social upheaval, reversals of personal status, political satire, geographical exploration and the comparison between the supposed natural state of man and the supposed civilized state of man. The two main literary characteristics of this age were realism and precision. They are found in their excellent form in the poetry of Alexander Pope, who perfected the heroic couplet, and in the prose of Joseph Addison who developed it into a clear, precise and elegant form of expression. The third characteristic of this age was the development of satire as a form of literature.

In the previous ages, it were the poetical works which were given prominence. Now, for the first time in the history of English literature, prose occupies the front position. It was an age of social, political, religious and literary controversies, and the prominent writers took an active part. A large number of pamphlets, journals and magazines were brought out in order to cater to the growing need of the masses who had begun to read and take interest in these controversial matters. Poetry was considered inadequate for such a task, and hence there was a rapid development of prose. In fact the prose writers of this age excel the poets in every respect. The graceful and elegant prose of Addison's essays, the terse style of Swift's satires, the artistic perfection of Fielding's novels, and the sonorous eloquence of Gibbon's history, have no equal in the poetical works of the age. In fact, poetry also had become prosaic. Its subject-matter had become criticism, satire, controversy and it was also written in the form of the essay which was the common literary form. Poetry became polished, witty and artificial, but it lacked fine feelings, enthusiasm, the poetic glow of Elizabethan Age and the moral earnestness of Puritanism. In fact, it became more interested in the portrayal of actual life, and distrusted inspiration and imagination.

Another important feature of this age was the origin and development of the novel. This new literary form, which gained great popularity in the succeeding ages, and which at present holds the prominent place, was fed and nourished by great masters like Daniel Defoe, Samuel Richardson, Henry Fielding, Tobias Smollet and others who laid its secure foundations. The realism of the age and the development of an excellent prose style greatly helped in the evolution of the novel during the eighteenth century.

The eighteenth century was deficient in drama. Goldsmith and Sheridan were the only writers who produced plays having literary merit.

☞ Questions for comprehension and discussion

1. What were the two main characteristics of Eighteenth-Century English Literature?
2. What was the main literary form in the Eighteenth century?
3. Why did a large number of pamphlets, journals and magazines start to be brought out in the Eighteenth century?
4. How did the literary form novel develop in the Eighteenth century?

12.1.6 The Romantic English Literature (1798-1832)

The Romantic Period began in 1798, when William Wordsworth (1770-1850) and Samuel Taylor Coleridge (1772-1834) published *Lyrical Ballads*, and came to an end in 1832, when the last romantic writer Walter Scott died. In part, the Romantic movement was a rebellion in response to the Enlightenment of the century prior, which focused on the more scientific and rational thought. Characteristics of Romantic literature emphasize passion, emotion, and nature.

Romantic poetry was often written in common everyday language for all to relate. Nature was a focus of many famous poets such as Wordsworth and Coleridge. Wordsworth was known as the "father of English Romanticism." Any of his works can support the focus of nature. He once illustrated a liberating aesthetic: for all good poetry is the spontaneous overflow of powerful feelings. Robert Burns (1759-1796) writes lyric verse in Scottish dialect. After Shakespeare, Burns is perhaps the most often quoted of writers in English: we sing his *Auld Lang Syne* every New Year's Eve. The later Romantic poets George Gordon Byron (1788-1824) and Percy Bysshe Shelley (1792-1822) are revolutionary in thinking. Byron uses romantic themes to explain contemporary events. He created the concept of "Byronic hero". Shelley is best known for his lyrics. The most well known is *Ode to the West Wind* (1819), which is a mixture of death and rebirth. John Keats (1795-

1821) is marked by an attempt to make language beautiful. The worship of beauty is often evident in his poem.

The romantic era was also rich in literary criticism and other nonfictional prose. These prose writers were much influenced by the French Revolution in politics and by the Romantic Movement in literature. The best representative of these writers is Charles Lamb (1775-1834). Lamb's most well known literary work is *Tales from Shakespeare*, which he wrote with his sister(1807). They were stories retold from the plays of Shakespeare.

There were also some famous novelists in this period. Jane Austen (1775-1817) is the first important English woman novelist in English literature. Although she wrote during the romantic era, her work defies classification. In her masterpiece *Pride and Prejudice*, she revealed her endless romantic feelings through the realistic technique. With insight, humor, and irony she drew vivid and realistic pictures of English country life. Walter Scott's (1771-1832) main contribution to literature is largely in historical novel. He is generally considered the father of European historical fiction. From Walter Scott on, many British writers focus on history and many historical novels came into being.

☞ Questions for comprehension and discussion

1. What themes did Romantic literature emphasize?
2. Who was regarded as the "father of English Romanticism"? What is the common characteristic of his works?
3. Do you know anything about "Byronic hero"?
4. What kind of writing technique did Jane Austen employ in *Pride and Prejudice*?

12.1.7 The Victorian English Literature (1830s-1901)

The Victorian Period is named for the reign of Queen Victoria, who ascended to the throne in 1837, and lasts until her death in 1901. The period has been generally regarded as one of the most glorious in the English history. It was a time of rapid economic development as well as serious social problems. In all of English (and world) literature, it is in strong contention with the Romantic Period for the most popular, influential, and prolific period.

In this period, a new literary trend, critical realism, appeared in novel writing. The novel became the most widely read and the most vital and challenging expression of progressive thought. The greatest English critical realist of the time was Charles Dickens (1812-1870). He masterly depicted the life of English society at his age, and had the ability to sustain interest through all kinds of literary devices. He is a great humorist and satirist and his novels are characterized by a mingling of humor and pathos. His major works include *Oliver Twist*, *Great Expectations*, *David Copperfield*, *A Tale of Two Cities*. Another representative of critical realism in the 19th century England was William Makepeace Thackray (1811-1863). His masterpiece *Vanity Fair* gave a comprehensive view of English society in the early 19th century. The title is derived from Bunyan's *Pilgrim's Progress*, which means "a fair, wherein are sold all sorts of vanity". Charlotte Brontë (1816-1855) and her sisters Emily (1818-1848) and Anne (1820-1849) are understandably linked together, but their work differs greatly. Charlotte's writing is marked by an intensity of a volcanic imagination and fiery passions. In her masterpiece *Jane Eyre*, the heroine, after much adversity, achieves happiness on her own terms. Emily's *Wuthering Heights* is a powerful novel of critical realism, and it gives a faithful record of human relationships between the oppressor and the oppressed in Victorian England. George Eliot (1819-1880) was the pseudonym of Mary Ann Evans. Her most popular novels are *Adam Bed*, *The Mill on the Floss*, and *Silas Marner*. Thomas Hardy (1840-1928) is one of the representatives of English critical realism at the turn of 19th century. On account of his fatalist view of life, Hardy's most novels are tragic. His famous works include *The Return of the Native*, *Tess of the D'Urbervilles*, *Jude the Obscure*, and others. His masterpiece *Tess of the D'Urbervilles* tells a peasant girl Tess's misfortunes and final tragedy.

Poetry in Victorian Period in many respects showed a further development of themes and attitudes explored by the poets in Romantic Period. It seldom touched on the serious social problems, but was mainly concerned with the poet's personal tastes or spiritual questionings. The most important poets of the age were Alfred Tennyson (1809-1892) and Elizabeth Browning (1812-1889). Tennyson was very popular and gained the title of "Poet of the People". His poetic output was vast and extremely varied. *In Memoriam* is often regarded as the most important of his longer poems. Browning's chief contribution to English poetry is his skillful use of the "Dramatic Monologue". His monumental work and masterpiece is *Ring and the Book*, which is based on a murder trial in 17th century Rome.

The most important dramatist is Oscar Wilde (1856-1900). He is the representative among the writers of aestheticism and decadence. His best known comedies are *Lady Windermere's Fan*, *A Woman of No Importance*, *An Ideal Husband*, and *The Importance of Being Earnest*. These plays are noted for witty dialogues and humorous epigrams.

☞ Questions for comprehension and discussion

1. What became the most widely read literary form in the Victorian Period?

2. What are the characteristics of Dickens' novels?
3. What does *Vanity Fair* literarily mean? What does it talk about?
4. Who was the representative writer of aestheticism and decadence?

12. 1. 8 The Twentieth-Century English Literature

In 20th century, Britain declined in national fortune and power. The two World Wars cost many lives and made destruction of much property. Momentous changes occurred in its social and political life. An important feature of English literature in this century was realism and modernism coexisted and dominated English literature alternately.

This century witnessed a great achievement in English poetry. T. S. Eliot (1888-1965) and William Butler Yeats (1865-1939) are two dominating figures in modern poetry. Eliot uses elements of conventional forms, within an unconventionally structured whole in his greatest works, among which *The Waste Land* (1922) is the most important. In Eliot's view the wasteland stands for Western Europe, or for Western civilization as a whole. The poem reveals disillusionment and mental breakdown with contemporary society. Yeats uses conventional lyric forms, but explores the connection between modern themes and classical and romantic ideas. His main poems are *Sailing to Byzantium*, *The Wind Among the Reeds*, *The Wild Swans at Coole*, and *The Tower*. Other important poets of the century include realistic poets Thomas Hardy, A. E. Housman (1859-1936), Rupert Brooke (1887-1915), Philip Larkin (1922-1985), and modernist poets Wystan Hugh Auden (1907-1973), Ted Hughes (1930-1998), etc.

In the early years of 20th century, many writers show continuity with the Victorian tradition of critical realism in novel writing. John Galsworthy (1867-1933), an outstanding successor to realism, enjoyed a high reputation. In his trilogy, *The Forsyte Saga*, he dealt with several generations of a distinguished wealthy bourgeois family, and directed his attack and satire toward the propertied class. Between the two World Wars, modernism began to show its appearance in novel writing. James Joyce (1882-1941) and Virginia Woolf (1882-1941) use the "Stream of Consciousness" technique, and challenge traditional narrative methods of viewpoint and structure. Joyce's masterpiece *Ulysses* deals with the events of one day (18 hours) in Dublin, and tells the inner thoughts of the three characters through natural flow with frankness never seen before in literature. In *To the Lighthouse* and *Mrs. Dalloway*, Woolf abandons the strict linear time and space in favor of the internal consciousness. D. H. Lawrence (1885-1930) is concerned to explore human relationships in the modern world where the natural harmony between man and man, man and woman has been destroyed by Industry and modernization. His most important work is semiautobiographical novel *Sons and Lovers*. After the Second World War realism became the main current. A group of young writers known as "the Angry Young Men" began to publish their writings and expressed their anger and discontent for social injustice and oppression. *Lucy Jim* by Kingsley Amis (1922-1995) is an example. The period was also marked by a number of good novelists, including Anthony Burgess (1917-1993), William Golding (1911-1994), Doris Lessing (1919-2013), Iris Murdoch (1919-1999), and Martin Amis (1949-), etc.

In 20th century, the major tradition in English drama was realism. Playwrights of this period exposed social problems in their dramatic works. George Bernard Shaw (1856-1950) was the greatest English dramatist in this century. His achievement in drama brought English drama a second golden period. Shaw used the stage to criticize the injustice of capitalism. His best-known drama is *Pygmalion*, which even better known today in its form as the musical *My Fair Lady*.

☞ Questions for comprehension and discussion

1. What is the main feature of English literature in 20th century?
2. What do you know about "Stream of Consciousness" technique?
3. What was the major tradition in English drama?

12.2 Famous Writers and Their Works

For centuries, English literature has occupied a disproportionately large place on the global stage, with iconic figures such as William Shakespeare and Charles Dickens endowing the English literary tradition with a luster that it still retains. Many famous figures in English literature history have been mentioned in the previous part. In this part, we will introduce some of the highly talented British writers and poets, including "Bard of Avon", William Shakespeare; poets, William Wordsworth and George Byron; and novelists Jane Austen, Charles Dickens and Thomas Hardy. One of their famous works will be followed in each part.

12.2.1 William Shakespeare and *Hamlet*

William Shakespeare (1564-1616) is the grand literary figure of the Western world. He was widely regarded as the greatest writer in the English language and the world's pre-eminent dramatist. He wrote approximately 37 plays, 154 sonnets, 2 long narrative poems, and a few other verses. His plays have been translated into every major living language and have dominated world theater more than 400 years. His words are so famous that his quotes, from "To be or not to be" to "Parting is such sweet sorrow," take up more than 70 pages in recent editions of *Bartlett's Familiar Quotations*.

Shakespeare was born in Stratford-upon-Avon, Warwickshire. His father William was a successful local businessman and his mother Mary was the daughter of a landowner. At the age of 18, he married Anne Hathaway, with whom he had three children: Susanna, and twins Hamnet and Judith. Their only son Hamnet died aged just 11. Sometime between 1585 and 1592, he began a successful career in London as an actor, writer, and part-owner of a playing company called the Lord Chamberlain's Men. He appears to have retired to Stratford around 1613, at age 49, where he died 3 years later.

Shakespeare produced most of his known work between 1589 and 1613. His early plays were mainly comedies (e. g. *Much Ado about Nothing*, *A Midsummer's Night Dream*) and histories (e. g. *Henry* Ⅴ). He then wrote mainly tragedies until about 1608, including *Hamlet*, *Othello*, *King Lear* and *Macbeth*, which often hinge on some fatal error or flaw in the lead character, and provide fascinating insights into the darker aspects of human nature. These later plays are considered Shakespeare's finest achievements. In his last phase, he wrote tragicomedies, also known as romances, and collaborated with other playwrights. Among those famous plays, He is also known for his poetry, especially his sonnets. It is generally thought that during the 1590s he wrote the majority of his sonnets.

Records of Shakespeare's private life are so sketchy that there are some speculation about his physical appearance, sexuality, religious beliefs, and whether the works were written by others. There were divided opinions as to whether Shakespeare wrote all the works known today or they were created by a group of people instead of one, there are even doubts about the existence of Shakespeare the person. Only a small minority of academics believe there is reason to question the traditional attribution, but interest in the subject continues into the 21st century.

Hamlet

The play opens on a cold night. Hamlet, Prince of Denmark, is visited by a mysterious ghost and told that his father was murdered by Claudius, the King's brother, who then took the throne and married Hamlet's mother, Gertrude. The ghost encourages Hamlet to avenge his father's death by killing Claudius.

Hamlet pretends to be mad and puts on a play for Claudius that reenacts his father's murder in order to confirm Claudius' guilt. He confronts Gertrude about his father's murder and hears someone behind the arras-believing it to be Claudius, Hamlet kills the man with his sword. But it turns to be Polonius, his beloved girl Ophelia's father. In the aftermath of her father's death, Ophelia goes mad with grief and drowns in the river.

Claudius realizes that Hamlet is out to get him. He arranges Hamlet to England, and plans to kill him. Hamlet escapes and arrives back in Denmark just as Ophelia is being buried. Ophelia's death prompts him to contemplate life, death and the frailty of the human condition.

Ophelia's brother, Laertes, comes to take avenge for his father and sister. Claudius encourages him to kill Hamlet with poisoned sword and wine. In the fight, the swords are swapped and Laertes is killed with the poisoned sword. Gertrude dies by accidentally drinking the poisoned wine. Hamlet stabs Claudius but he is fatally wounded too. Hamlet's revenge is finally complete. In his dying moments, he bequeaths the throne to Fortinbras, a Norwegian prince.

Themes of *Hamlet*

What separates Hamlet from other revenge plays is that the action we expect to see is continually postponed while Hamlet tries to obtain more certain knowledge about what he is doing. This play poses many questions that other plays would simply take for granted. Many people have seen it as a play about indecisiveness, and thus about Hamlet's failure to act appropriately. It might be more interesting to consider that the play shows us how many uncertainties our lives are built upon.

There are a number of themes in the play, including revenge, death, Hamlet's inability to act, incest and the state of Denmark, etc.

Revenge *Hamlet* is a revenge tragedy driven by someone unable to commit to the act of revenge. It is Hamlet's inability to avenge that drives the plot forwards. Once he decides to take action, he delays any action until the end of the play. To highlight Hamlet's inability to take action, Shakespeare includes some other characters like Fortinbras and Laertes, who are capable of taking resolute and headstrong revenge as required. What makes *Hamlet* unique is the remarkable way in which Shakespeare uses the delay to build Hamlet's emotional and psychological complexity. People may think perhaps lives could have been saved if Hamlet had acted earlier? Although Hamlet does ultimately kill Claudius in the final scene of the play, we cannot credit Hamlet with plotting the revenge-rather, it is Claudius' plan to kill Hamlet that backfires. Perhaps if Hamlet had acted earlier, lives could have been saved?

Death Throughout the play, Hamlet is obsessed with the idea of death, and considers death from a great many perspectives. Hamlet's grief and misery is such that he frequently longs for death to end his suffering, but he fears that if he commits suicide, he will be consigned to eternal suffering in hell because of the Christian religion's prohibition of suicide.

Incest Gertrude's incestuous relationship with her brother-in-law plagues Hamlet more than his father's death. Hamlet is not so angered by his uncle's incest — it is Gertrude, not Claudius that he blames. Gertrude has destroyed Hamlet's faith in women, which is perhaps why his feelings towards Ophelia become ambivalent.

The State of Denmark The political and social condition of Denmark is referred to throughout the play and the ghost is an embodiment of Denmark's growing social unrest. This is because the blood-line of the monarchy has been unnaturally disrupted by Claudius, an immoral and power-hungry king. Besides, at the end of the play, Hamlet bequeaths the throne to the rash and violent Fortinbras, which brings much uncertainty to Denmark's future.

At the time this play was written, Queen Elizabeth was 60 and there was concern about who would inherit the throne. The state of Denmark in Hamlet could be a reflection of Britain's own social unrest.

☞ Questions for comprehension and discussion

1. What famous quotes do you know from Shakespeare's words?
2. What did Shakespeare's tragedies mostly hinge on?
3. What does *Hamlet* mainly talk about? What's the theme of the play in your opinion?

12.2.2 William Wordsworth and *I Wandered Lonely as A Cloud* (*The Daffodils*)

William Wordsworth (1770-1850) was one of the great Romantic poets of 19th-century England. Wordsworth's publication of *Lyrical Ballads* with another poet, Samuel Taylor Coleridge, marked a major change of poetic style and the beginning of the English Romantic Movement.

Wordsworth studied at Cambridge University and then traveled in France during the Revolution, an experience which affected deeply his own political leanings. On his return to England he met Coleridge, and in 1798 they published the collection *Lyrical Ballads*. It included both Coleridge's *The Rime of the Ancient Mariner* and Wordsworth's *Tintern Abbey*, a rumination on man and nature inspired by the "steep and lofty cliffs" and "pastoral farms" around the stone ruins of the ancient church. Critics hooted at

Wordsworth's poems and his politics early in his career, but in later years he became accepted as a key voice in the Romantic movement. His other works include *Poems in Two Volumes* (1807) and *The Excursion* (1814). He was poet laureate of England from 1843 until his death in 1850. His autobiographical epic, *The Prelude* was published by his wife after his death. It is Wordsworth's most famous work, and is considered by many to be the crowning achievement of English romanticism.

Known as one of the "Lake Poets[1]", Wordsworth is most often described as a "nature" writer. On the one hand, Wordsworth always paid close attention to details of the physical environment around him (plants, animals, geography, weather). At the same time, he was a self-consciously literary artist. In his opinion, "poetry is the spontaneous overflow of powerful feelings". His poems celebrated the glories of nature and the human spirit while using the simple language of the "common man" — a radical idea for the time.

I Wandered Lonely as A Cloud (*The Daffodils*)

By William Wordsworth

I wandered lonely as a cloud
That floats on high o'er vales and hills,
When all at once I saw a crowd,
A host, of golden daffodils;
Beside the lake, beneath the trees,
Fluttering and dancing in the breeze.

Continuous as the stars that shine
And twinkle on the Milky Way,
They stretched in never-ending line
Along the margin of a bay:
Ten thousand saw I at a glance
Tossing their heads in sprightly dance.

The waves beside them danced, but they
Out-did the sparking waves in glee:
A Poet could not but be gay
In such a jocund company:
I gazed — and gazed — but little thought

What wealth the show to me had brought:

For oft, when on my couch I lie
In vacant or in pensive mood,
They flash upon that inward eye
Which is the bliss of solitude;
And then my heart with pleasure fills,
And dances with the daffodils.

Analysis of *I Wandered Lonely as A Cloud*

I Wandered Lonely as a Cloud (also commonly known as *The Daffodils*) is a lyric poem. The inspiration for the poem came from a walk Wordsworth took with his sister Dorothy around Glencoyne Bay, Ullswater, in the Lake District, when they came across a "long belt" of daffodils. He would draw on this to compose the poem in 1804. This poem is well-loved because of its simple yet beautiful rhythms and rhymes, and its rather sentimental topic. The poem consists of four six-line stanzas, each of which follow an ababcc rhyme scheme and are written in iambic tetrameter, giving the poem a subtle back-and-forth motion that recalls swaying daffodils.

Summary

In the first stanza the speaker describes a time when he meandered over the valleys and hills, "lonely as a cloud". Finally, he came across a crowd of daffodils stretching out over almost everything he could see, "fluttering and dancing in the breeze". By comparing himself to a cloud and personifying the daffodils several times, the speaker signifies his close identification with the nature that surrounds him. In the second stanza the speaker goes into more detail about the daffodils. They reminded him of the Milky Way, because there were so many flowers packed together that they seemed to be never-ending. The speaker guesses that there were ten thousand daffodils, which were "Tossing their heads in sprightly dance". In the third stanza the speaker compares the waves of the lake to the waves of daffodils and decides that even though the lake is "sparkling" the daffodils win because they have more "glee". He then comments that he, like any other poet, could not help but be happy "in such a jocund company". He looked at the scene for a long time, but while he was there he was unable to understand what he had gained from the experience. In the final stanza, the poet describes what he gained from the experience.

Afterwards, when he was lonely or feeling "pensive," he could remember the daffodils, seeing them with his "inward eye" and be content.

Themes

The themes of the poem include: first, in order to understand oneself and one's place in the universe, one must connect with nature (e. g. Lines 15, 23, and 24). Nature's beauty uplifts the human spirit. Second, people sometimes fail to appreciate nature's wonders as they go about their daily routines (e. g. Lines 17 and 18). Third, nature thrives unattended. The daffodils proliferate in splendor along the shore of the lake without the need for human attention.

Figures of Speech

Alliteration[2]: Alliteration is found repeatedly in the poem. For example, the repeated /h/ sounds in "high o'er vales and Hills (line 2)", and the repeated /b/ sound and /ð/ sound in "Beside the Lake, beneath the trees" (line 5).

Simile[3]: In line 1, the speaker was compared to a cloud, making him at one with nature. The comparison to the cloud suggests free floating and drowsiness. The speaker is relaxed. A "host of golden daffodils" attracts his attention.

Hyperbole: In line 9, "They stretched in never-ending line" was used to express the vastness of the vision.

Personification[4] and Comparison: In line 13, the waves danced too, but they do not produce the glee the daffodils have created.

☞ Notes

1. **Lake Poets** 湖畔诗人。是指 19 世纪英国浪漫主义运动中较早产生的一个流派。他们的诗作中的词句赞美大自然的湖光山色、抒发缠绵的爱情、歌颂纯真的友谊，多带有清新自然、青春亮丽、富有哲理的特点，其代表人物有威廉·华兹华斯、塞缪尔·泰勒·柯尔律治、罗伯特·骚塞等。
2. **alliteration** 头韵法。是英语语音修辞手段之一，指两个或两个以上单词的首字母相同，形成悦耳的读音，如 first and foremost(首先)，它是英语诗歌最常见的押韵之一。
3. **simile** 明喻。是将具有某种共同特征的两种不同事物作比喻的一种修辞手法。明喻的表达方法是：A 像 B。
4. **personification** 拟人。是把事物人格化的一种修辞手法，将本来不具备人物动作和感情的事物变成和人一样具有动作和感情的样子。

☞ Questions for comprehension and discussion

1. What is the most famous work written by William Wordsworth?
2. What is the rhyme scheme used in the poem *I Wandered Lonely as A Cloud*?
3. What figures of speech are used in the poem *I Wandered Lonely as A Cloud*?
4. How did William Wordsworth describe the Daffodils? What are the themes of the poem?

12. 2. 3 George Gordon Byron and *She Walks in Beauty*

George Gordon Byron (1788-1824), commonly known simply as Lord Byron, was a great English Romantic poet in the early 19th century and a leading figure in the Romantic movement[1]. Among Byron's best-known works are the lengthy narrative poems *Don Juan* and *Childe Harold's Pilgrimage* and the short lyric *She Walks in Beauty*. He is regarded as one of the greatest British poets and remains widely read and influential.

He was born with a club-foot and became extreme sensitivity about his lameness. Byron spent his early childhood years in poor surroundings in Aberdeen, where he was educated until he was ten. After he inherited the title and property of his great-uncle in 1798, he went on to Harrow and Cambridge. He travelled widely across Europe, especially in Italy where he lived for seven years. Later in life, Byron joined the Greek War of Independence fighting the Ottoman Empire, for which many Greeks revere him as a national hero.

Byron was often described as the most flamboyant and notorious of the major Romantics. His notability rested not only on his writings but also on his life, which featured aristocratic excesses, huge debts, numerous love affairs, and self-imposed exile. Although the poet was widely condemned on moral grounds by his contemporaries, Byron's influence on European poetry, music, novel, opera, and painting has been immense. He created the concept of the "Byronic hero". The figure of the Byronic hero pervades much of his work, and Byron himself is considered to epitomise many of the characteristics of this literary figure. The Byronic hero presents an idealized, but flawed character whose attributes include: great talent; great passion; a distaste for society and social institutions; a lack of respect for rank and privilege (although possessing both); being thwarted in love by social constraint or death; rebellion; exile; an unsavory secret past; arrogance; overconfidence or lack of foresight; and, ultimately, a self-destructive manner. These types of characters have since become ubiquitous in literature and politics.

She Walks in Beauty

by Lord Byron

She walks in beauty, like the night
Of cloudless climes and starry skies;
And all that's best of dark and bright
Meet in her aspect and her eyes:
Thus mellowed to that tender light
Which heaven to gaudy day denies.

One shade the more, one ray the less,
Had half impaired the nameless grace
Which waves in every raven tress,
Or softly lightens o'er her face;
Where thoughts serenely sweet express
How pure, how dear their dwelling place.

And on that cheek, and o'er that brow,
So soft, so calm, yet eloquent,
The smiles that win, the tints that glow,
But tell of days in goodness spent,
A mind at peace with all below,
A heart whose love is innocent!

Analysis of *She walks in Beauty*

She walks in Beauty is a romantic poem by Gordon Byron, written in 1814 and published in 1815. It is said that the poem was written upon Mrs. Wilmot, wife of Lord Byron's cousin. Byron met her at a party in a mourning dress of spangled black. He was amazed with her unbelievable beauty and was inspired infinitely to write the famous poem.

The woman is not described beautiful as for herself. The poem doesn't expose what the woman was wearing or the color of her dress or how tall she was or what the color of her eyes was. In fact, at the end of the poem the only specific fact the reader knows is that she has black hair. Nevertheless, there is no doubt that the lady has made a definite impression on the poet as well as the reader. To him, she is beautiful in the same way that "night" is beautiful, and, as he hastens to add, he means a particular kind of night, one of "cloudless climes and starry skies". There is no threat of a storm in this imagined landscape; there are no clouds to produce even a shower. Such a night is not really dark, for the sky is filled with stars. The light is soft and subdued; similarly, the dark lady has "tender" eyes, as unlike those of less subtle women as the light of a "starry" night is from that of "gaudy day". In this poem, readers find the woman's smile wins others, her mind is peaceful and her heart is pure. She is innocent and in the concluding stanzas it is very clear that these qualities are precisely why she "walks in beauty". Her physical appearance is lovely but readers will feel that what makes her maximally beautiful is the strength of her moral character.

The poem is short and undemanding. It doesn't comprise of great capacity of symbolic tools or device but there are few such as simile, metaphor[2], personification, alliteration and end rhyme[3].

Simile: Similes used in the poem are an extended comparison of comparing beauty of the woman with the night sky.

Metaphor: Lines 11 and 12 (Where thoughts serenely sweet express How pure, how dear there dwelling place.) are a metaphor. These particular lines in the short lyric highlight the clarity of thought Mrs. Wilmot possessed.

Personification: Line 6 (Which heaven to gaudy day denies) is a personification. Byron gave heaven individual emotions or qualities.

Alliteration: Alliteration is found repeatedly in the poem. For example, the repeated /cl/ sounds in "cloudless climes" are very musical, and the repeated /s/ sound, or sibilance, is rather soothing.

☞ Notes

1. **Romantic movement** 浪漫主义运动。18 世纪末及 19 世纪初西欧掀起的文学艺术运动，强调创作的绝对自由、反对古典主义的清规戒律；抨击社会的罪恶，对未来社会充满美好的理想；重视民间文学，酷爱描写中世纪和以往的历史；偏重于描写自然风光，厌恶资本主义文明和现实。
2. **metaphor** 暗喻、隐喻。比喻修辞的一种，主要是强调本体与喻体同时出现，但是却使用了特殊的比喻词的修辞手法。
3. **end rhyme** 尾韵法。和头韵法一样，是英语语音修辞手段之一，指词尾音素重复，如 great 和 bait，它是英语诗歌最常见的押韵之一。

☞ Questions for comprehension and discussion

1. How is George Gordon Byron's reputation? Why was he prized or criticized?

2. How did George Gordon Byron describe the woman in *She walks in Beauty*?
3. What figures of speech are used in the poem *I Wandered Lonely as A Cloud*?

12.2.4 Jane Austen and *Pride and Prejudice*

Jane Austen (1775-1817) was the first important English woman novelist, and one of the most widely read writers in English literature. Although she lived in the Romantic Period, she is one of the realistic novelists. Her realism, biting irony, social commentary as well as her acclaimed plots have gained her historical importance among scholars and critics.

Austen was born in Steventon, Hampshire, a small town in southwest England. She was educated primarily by her father and older brothers as well as through her own reading. The steadfast support of her family was critical to her development as a professional writer. From 1811 until 1816, with the release of *Sense and Sensibility* (1811), *Pride and Prejudice* (1813), *Mansfield Park* (1814) and *Emma* (1815), she achieved success as a published writer. Curiously, due to the lack of acceptance of women authors at the time, her major novels were published anonymously, and Jane Austen was not associated with them until after her death. In 1869, the publication of her nephew's *A Memoir of Jane Austen* introduced her to a wider public, and by the 1940s she had become widely accepted in academia as a great English writer.

Austen's novels were witty, warm and ironic portraits of the privileged classes of 18th- and 19th-century England. Her plots, though fundamentally comic, highlight the dependence of women on marriage to secure social standing and economic security. Her best-known work is *Pride and Prejudice.* The heroine Elizabeth — smart, witty and independent — and her dashing suitor Mr. Darcy — handsome and intelligent — are one of the most famous couples in English fiction.

Austen's stories have long been favorites in Hollywood. The many screen adaptations include *Pride and Prejudice* (both a 1995 BBC TV production with Colin Firth as Mr. Darcy, and a 2005 feature film with Keira Knightley as Elizabeth), *Emma* (1996, with Gwyneth Paltrow), and *Sense and Sensibility* (1995, with Emma Thompson and Kate Winslet). The 1995 Alicia Silverstone movie *Clueless* is a whimsical takeoff on *Emma.* Jane Austen herself was played by Anne Hathaway in the 2007 film *Becoming Jane.* Jane Austen's face will be on a £ 10 note, the Bank of England announced in July of 2013. The note is expected to go into circulation in 2017.

Pride and Prejudice

Pride and Prejudice is the story of Mr. and Mrs. Bennet and their five unmarried daughters. They live in the estate of Longbourn in Hertfordshire, a rural district about 30 miles from London. Without a male heir, Mr. Bennet's property is "entailed" to pass to Mr. Collins, the nearest male heir in the family. The main concern of Mrs. Bennet's life is to see that all her daughters — Jane, Elizabeth, Mary, Kitty, and Lydia — are married, preferably to men with large fortunes. She sees an opportunity for her eldest daughter Jane when Mr. Charles Bingley, a wealthy gentlemen from the city, occupies the nearby estate of Netherfield Park.

When Bingley meets Jane at a ball, he seems immediately smitten with her. Yet Bingley's snobby friend Darcy is rude to Elizabeth. Through the next few social gatherings, Jane and Bingley grow closer, and Darcy finds himself becoming attracted to Elizabeth's beauty and intelligence. Elizabeth, however, continues to consider him a snob. Wickham, an army officer Elizabeth finds charming, comes and claims Darcy wronged him in the past. Elizabeth's prejudice against Darcy hardens. Soon after, at a ball at Netherfield, Mrs. Bennet, much to Darcy's annoyance, comments that a wedding between Jane and Bingley is likely to soon take place.

Bingley departs suddenly, and Jane was informed that he is planning to wed Darcy's sister. Jane is crushed. Elizabeth is sure Darcy is deliberately separating Bingley and Jane. Elizabeth meets Darcy and grows angry when she learns that Darcy advised Bingley against marrying Jane. Oblivious, Darcy announces his love for her and proposes marriage. Elizabeth refuses his proposal, accusing him of ruining Jane's marriage and mistreating Wickham. In a letter Darcy explains that he intervened because he felt Jane did not truly love Bingley. Wickham, he writes, is a liar and a scoundrel. Elizabeth begins to feel she has misjudged Darcy and may have been rash in turning him down.

Next year, Elizabeth accompanies her aunt and uncle on a trip. During the trip, Elizabeth visits Pemberley, Darcy's estate. Darcy unexpectedly shows up and introduces her to his sister. Bingley also arrives and reveals that he is still in love with Jane. Elizabeth's trip is cut short by a letter from Jane announcing that Lydia has eloped with Wickham. Fearing a scandal that will ruin all the daughters' futures, the Bennets search for Lydia in London. Darcy tracked down the couple and paid off Wickham's massive debts in exchange for Wickham marrying Lydia. He saved the Bennet family's honor. Elizabeth finds out the truth about Darcy's assistance. She is impressed with his kindness.

Bingley and Darcy return to Netherfield and Bingley finally proposes to overjoyed

Jane. Darcy asks Elizabeth again to marry him. This time she accepts, telling him her prejudice against him had made her blind. Darcy acknowledges that his pride made him act rudely.

Themes of *Pride and Prejudice*

The central theme of *Pride and Prejudice* is consideration of pride and prejudice, and the impact these moral qualities have upon love, family, marriage, and by extension, society. In this story, each character represents a kind and degree of pride and/or prejudice. Austen examines the shades of pride and the degrees of prejudice. Characters are contrasted against each other to reveal the effects of the degrees of these moral qualities on love, family and marriage. In the end, the principal characters, after significant development, represent right-minded moral qualities that have beneficial effects on love, family and marriage.

Examples of pride

Darcy: From the beginning, Darcy is shown to be too proud of his own social standing. He looks down on people, especially the Bennets. This is made worse by his natural quietness, which makes him seem even more aloof.

Elizabeth: Elizabeth isn't naturally proud in the same sense as Darcy. But when she's slighted by him at the first ball, her pride is hurt. As a result, she compensates by becoming more proud of herself and defensive about her family.

Lady Catherine: Lady Catherine is incredibly proud, believing it to be the natural order of things that she be praised and obeyed.

Mr Collins: Collins' pride changes according to whom he's speaking. In the company of people he believes to be below him socially, he revels in taking the moral high ground and bragging about his standing. With those above him, his pride vanishes and he often humiliates himself.

Examples of prejudice

Darcy: Without knowing the Bennets — or almost anyone else, for that matter — Darcy seems to form opinions without taking the trouble to get to know them.

Elizabeth: Prejudice isn't Elizabeth's natural outlook. However, when Darcy offends her, she allows everything to feed the prejudice she develops against him. She's prepared to believe anything bad about him to fuel the impression she wants to create (for instance, Wickham's story).

Mrs Bennet: Mrs Bennet develops a more blatant prejudice against Darcy after his actions at the ball. She acts on this, insulting him within earshot. Her character's lack of depth is shown by her prejudice disappearing when Darcy proposes to Elizabeth.

Lady Catherine: She's prejudiced against anyone below her in social standing, unless they're prepared to play by her rules (that is, what she says goes). So she's prepared to tolerate Collins, but despises Elizabeth.

The Bingley sisters: Mrs Hurst and Miss Bingley are prejudiced against Jane and Elizabeth. This is mainly out of self-interest. They dislike Jane because they feel she isn't good enough for their brother; they dislike Elizabeth because Darcy likes her and Miss Bingley wants to marry him.

☞ Questions for comprehension and discussion

1. What are the characteristics of Jane Austen's novels? What do her novels mostly focus on?
2. What does *Pride and Prejudice* mainly talk about? What's the theme of the novel in your opinion?
3. What's Jane Austen's view on love and marriage?

12. 2. 5 Charles Dickens and *A Tale of Two Cities*

Charles Dickens (1812-1870) was an English writer and social critic, the greatest representative of English critical realism. He created some of the world's best-known fictional characters and is regarded as the greatest novelist of the Victorian era. His works enjoyed unprecedented popularity during his lifetime, and by the 20th century critics and scholars had recognized him as a literary genius. His novels and short stories enjoy lasting popularity.

Dickens was born in Portsea, Portsmouth. As a child, he experienced the fickle hands of fate. When he was ten years old, his father was put into prison for debt. Then he was taken from school and made to work long, 10 hour days, at a local boot blacking factory. The hard and dangerous work left a lasting impression on Dickens, and he later incorporated in his writings a sense of social injustice in Victorian Britain.

Despite his lack of formal education, he spent much time alone reading books especially the 18th century novels. He wrote 15 novels, 5 novellas, hundreds of short stories and non-fiction articles. In particular, his novels have the most colorful and eccentric characters which leave a lasting impression. He achieved this through his vivid memory of the various people he had met through his life, but also he added a touch of fantasy and exaggeration with his vivid floral style. His *A Christmas Carol* remains popular and continues to inspire adaptations in every artistic genre. *Oliver Twist* and *Great Expectations* evoke images of early Victorian London. His *A Tale of Two Cities*, set in London and Paris, is his best-known work of historical fiction. *David Copperfield*, which is said to be Dickens' favorite novel, impresses people with its good humor, tolerance, fun and the world now is still full of hope and sunshine.

Dickens was regarded as the literary colossus of his age. His creative genius has been praised by fellow writers — from Leo Tolstoy to George Orwell and G. K. Chesterton — for its realism, comedy, prose style, unique characterisations, and social criticism. On the other hand, Oscar Wilde, Henry James, and Virginia Woolf complained of loose writing and a lack of psychological depth.

A Tale of Two Cities

In 1775, Mr. Lorry, an official of Tellson's Bank in London, accompanies Lucie Manette to Paris. He has information that her father, Dr. Manette, who had disappeared 18 years ago, is alive. He had been wrongfully imprisoned in the Bastille and left there to die. After his release from prison, his former servant Dr. Manette's, a wine-seller in Paris, takes care of him. Dr. Manette has aged prematurely, having lost both his memory and his sense. Lucie take her father back to London. With love and compassion, Lucie plans to nurse her father back to health and sanity.

Years pass, Lucie marries Charles Darnay. He is a French aristocrat who has renounced his inheritance and now lives in London under an assumed name and works as a tutor. His uncle, the Marquis St. Evremonde, is a notorious man renowned for his cruelty and callousness.

In 1789, the French Revolution breaks out in all its fury with the storming of the Bastille. In London, Darnay has been happily married to Lucie for 11 years, and they have a daughter. On hearing that his former servant is endangered, Darnay secretly returns to Paris. He is caught and imprisoned. On hearing of her husband's capture, Lucie and Dr. Manette rush to Paris to save him. Dr. Manette, himself a victim of oppression, convinces the people of his son-in-law's innocence, and Darnay is discharged. Madame Defarge, however, seeks personal revenge against the Evremonde family, for the cruel Marquis killed her sister and brother. Largely because of her, Darnay is re-arrested and sentenced to death. There is no hope of saving him. Even the lives of Lucie and her daughter are in danger as the hard-core revolutionaries, like the Defarges, would like to eliminate anyone who has a connection with aristocracy.

Sydney Carton, who bears a striking resemblance to Darnay, sneaks into the prison and switches places with Darnay. The Darnay family flees back to England while Carton sacrifices his life for Darnay. The sacrifice is made to fulfill a promise to Lucie whom he loves. Carton feels noble about his action and knows that he will live in the hearts of the Darnays forever.

Themes of *A Tale of Two Cities*

Resurrection The major theme centers on resurrection, bringing people back to life from the seemingly inevitable clutches of death. Dr. Manette is rescued from long imprisonment and certain death and nursed back to health by the loving attention of his daughter Lucie. Darnay is twice saved from certain death by the compassion of Carton. These resurrected lives weave through the entire plot and hold the story together.

Cruelty of war The minor theme is the cruelty of war as seen in the French Revolution. While the French commoners' reasons for revolting were entirely understandable, and the French Revolution was widely praised for its stated ideals of "Liberty, Equality, and Fraternity", Dickens takes a more pessimistic view. By showing how the revolutionaries use oppression and violence to further their own selfish and bloodthirsty ends, in *A Tale of Two Cities* Dickens suggests that whoever is in power, nobles or commoners, will fall prey to the temptation to exercise their full power. In other words, Dickens shows that while tyranny will inevitably lead to revolution, revolution will lead just as inevitably to tyranny. The only way to break this cycle is through the application of justice and mercy.

☞ Questions for comprehension and discussion

1. What kinds of characters have been created by Charles Dickens?
2. What does *A Tale of Two Cities* mainly talk about? What's the theme of the novel in your opinion?
3. What's Dickens's view towards the French Revolution in your opinion?

12.2.6 Thomas Hardy and *Jude the Obscure*

Thomas Hardy, (1840-1928) was an English novelist and poet. A Victorian realist in the tradition of George Eliot, he was influenced both in his novels and in his poetry by Romanticism, especially William Wordsworth. He is best known for his novels *Far From the Madding Crowd* (1874), *Tess of the d' Urbervilles* (1891) and *Jude the Obscure* (1896).

Hardy spent most of his life in rural Dorset, which provided a background for his fiction. Trained as an architect, he spent five years in London at that profession before finding success as a novelist in the 1870s. He published several popular novels over the next 20 years, but *Tess of the d' Urbervilles* and *Jude the Obscure* received harsh criticism upon publication because they were called vulgar and pessimistic. The controversy drew much attention to the novels as well, and they were soon being read in Europe and North America, although Hardy never wrote another; he turned his pen to plays and poetry instead. Hardy's poetry, though prolific, was not as well received during his lifetime. It was rediscovered in the 1950s, when Hardy's poetry had a significant influence on the Movement poets of the 1950s and 1960s, including Philip Larkin.

Hardy always had a dream to be a poet and was well connected emotionally to his environment through observation and interaction, but the more practical occupation of architect and the experience of travelling and working on various restoration projects allowed him time to pen some of the most notable contributions to 20th Century literature. Inspiring many other authors including Virginia Woolf and D. H. Lawrence, many of Hardy's works have been widely read and adapted to the stage and screen.

Jude the Obscure

Jude Fawley dreams of studying at the university in Christminster, but his background as an orphan raised by his working-class aunt leads him instead into a career as a stonemason. As a youth, Jude teaches himself Classical Greek and Latin in his spare time with the hope of entering university. But before he can try to do this the naïve Jude is seduced by Arabella Donn, a rather coarse and superficial local girl who traps him into marriage by pretending to be pregnant. The marriage is a failure, and they separate by mutual agreement, and Arabella later emigrates to Australia, where she enters into a bigamous marriage.

After Arabella leaves him, Jude moves to Christminster and supports himself as a mason while studying alone. Jude meets and falls in love with his free-spirited cousin Sue. He arranges for her to work with Phillotson, the town schoolmaster, in order to keep her in Christminster, but is disappointed when he discovers that the two are engaged to be married. Once they marry, Sue regrets this and soon leaves Phillotson to live with Jude. Both Jude and Sue get divorced, but Sue does not want to remarry. Arabella reveals to Jude that they have a son in Australia, and Jude asks to take him in. Sue and Jude serve as parents to the little boy and have two children of their own.

Jude and Sue are socially ostracised for living together unmarried. Jude's employers dismiss him because of the illicit relationship, and the family is forced into a nomadic lifestyle, moving from town to town across Wessex seeking employment and housing before eventually returning to Christminster. Jude's son comes to believe that he and his half-siblings are the source of the family's woes. The morning after their arrival in Christminster, he murders Sue's two children and commits suicide by hanging.

Feeling she has been punished by God for her relationship with Jude, Sue left Jude once again for Phillotson. Jude is devastated and remarries Arabella after she plies him with alcohol to once again trick him into marriage. After one final, desperate visit to Sue in freezing weather, Jude becomes seriously ill and dies soon.

Themes and Analysis of *Jude the Obscure*

Jude the Obscure focuses on the life of a country stonemason, Jude, and his love for his cousin Sue. From the beginning Jude knows that marriage is an ill-fated venture in his family, and he believes that his love for Sue curses him doubly, because they are both members of a cursed clan. While love could be identified as a central theme in the novel, it is the institution of marriage that is the work's central focus. Jude and Sue are unhappily married to other people, and then drawn by an inevitable bond that pulls them together. Their relationship is beset by tragedy, not only because of the family curse but also by society's reluctance to accept their marriage as legitimate.

The horrifying murder-suicide of Jude's children is no doubt the climax of the book's action, and the other events of the novel rise in a crescendo to meet that one act. From there, Jude and Sue feel they have no recourse but to return to their previous, unhappy marriages and die within the confinement created by their youthful errors. They are drawn into an endless cycle of self-erected oppression and cannot break free. In a society unwilling to accept their rejection of convention, they are ostracized. Jude's son senses wrongdoing in his own conception and acts in a way that he thinks will help his parents and his siblings. The children are the victims of society's unwillingness to accept Jude and Sue as man and wife, and Sue's own feelings of shame from her divorce.

Jude's initial failure to attend the university becomes less important as the novel progresses, but his obsession with Christminster remains. Christminster is the site of Jude's first encounters with Sue, Jude's final moments and death, as well as the tragedy that dominates the book. It acts upon Jude, Sue, and their family as a representation of the unattainable and dangerous things to which Jude aspires.

☞ Questions for comprehension and discussion

1. Which novels are most famous written by Thomas Hardy?
2. What is the writing style of Thomas Hardy?
3. What is your view on Jude and Sue? Do you think their tragedy avoidable?

☞ Questions on Chapter 11 for reflection and presentation

Review the whole chapter and write a short essay on any of the following questions.

1. Can you list some of the famous dramatists, poets, and prose writers in the Renaissance Period? How did their works reflect the characteristics of the period?
2. Why did prose, instead of poetry, become the main literary form in the Eighteenth century? What was the main characteristic of this period?
3. What are the characteristics of Romantic English Literature? Please illustrate your point with examples.
4. Would you like to introduce your favorite English poem/ novel/ prose to your classmates? Please explain why you like it.
5. Would you like to analyze the similarities and differences between Chinese poems and English poems?

Chapter 13

Mass Media

The functions of mass media in the UK varies in the following aspects: it can provide information about political and social issues to the mass, give a platform for the people to know weather reports, provide a forum for people to write letters or call in to express their views or seek advice, and it can also carry advertising, entertainment, education, to engender a national culture.

13.1 The Press (Newspapers and Magazines)

Newspaper culture in the UK

The contemporary newspaper industry originate from the UK. From the end of 18th century to the beginning of 19th century, the UK has taken the lead in economy because of the Industrial Revolution. Therefore, an increasing number of people has the opportunity to read more newspapers. Most British people will read newspapers as the beginning of their days. Their choices of reading range from national newspapers to local newspapers, daily Sunday newspapers to weekly newspapers, and from morning newspapers to evening papers. The choice of British people for newspapers shows their class and level of education. Middle-class is the biggest group for reading newspapers, while the lower classes also account for a large percentage in the whole number of readers. People from either class of the society will buy newspapers based on their personal preferences. Therefore, Britain ranks the third as for newspaper popularity, only after Sweden and Japan.

At first, when the Parliament candidates want to express their opinions, they achieved this by making long speeches and distributing brochures. After that, the newspapers had been played an important role in helping the politicians express their ideas to the public in the UK. Therefore, not only politicians attach great importance to the power of the newspapers, the British merchants started to put their product information and advertisements on the newspapers and they must follow the Advertising Code. In addition, the British newspapers can print what they like without the regulation and the supervision of the government.

The main differences between national newspapers and local newspapers

The newspapers that are issued all around the country are called national newspapers. There are mainly three categories of national newspapers in the UK, which are: quality newspapers, popular newspapers and mid-market newspapers. They are different in terms of their style and content.

In the UK, there are 10 national daily newspapers that cover the important news throughout the country. Around half of them belong to quality newspapers or broadsheets (large-sheet newspapers). Quality newspapers are issued throughout the country and are distinguished from other newspapers by their seriousness. More sober and in-depth articles reflecting political and social importance and more comprehensive news are published on quality newspapers. In addition, quality newspapers publish reviews and feature articles regarding high culture, and are often read by middle-class of the society who are mostly well-educated. In the UK, there are daily newspapers and Sunday newspapers based on the frequency of circulation. Daily newspapers issue everyday while the Sunday newspapers only issue on Sunday. Sunday newspapers usually use part of the name of newspaper that is available on weekdays but differ in the following aspects: thickness and weight, special sections that are not found in the weekday editions, and the type and number of advertisements. Among the quality newspapers in the UK, there are six quality dailies and four quality Sundays. The quality dailies are as follows with their establishing time: *The Times* (1785), *The Guardian* (1821), *The Daily Telegraph* (1855), *Financial Times* (1888), *The Independent* (1986) and *i* (2010). And the quality Sundays are as follows with their establishing time: *The Observer* (1791), *The Sunday Times* (1822), *Independent on Sunday* (1990), and *The Sunday Telegraph* (1961).

While the quality newspapers cover serious news, the popular (tabloid) newspapers in the UK carry gutter news concerning scandals and gossips of famous people. They also publish catchy news in politics, sports and entertainment areas as well. This kind of newspapers is often smaller in size and has color photos and eye-catching headings. Usually, the articles on the newspapers are easy-reading short stories and show the readers more opinions instead of facts. There are four popular dailies with their establishing time: *Daily Mirror* (1903), *The Morning Star* (1930), *The Sun* (1964), and *Daily Star* (1978). And there are four popular Sundays with their establishing time: *Sunday People*

(1881), *Sunday Mirror* (1915), *Daily Star Sunday* (2002) and *The Sun on Sunday* (2012).

Mid-market newspapers aim for the middle market. There are four middle-market tabloid newspapers: *Daily Mail* (1896), *Daily Express* (1900), *Sunday Express* (1918), and *The Mail on Sunday* (1982).

Local newspapers are more regional-based and issued in local areas. They mainly cover local news and advertisements including morning, evening, Sundays and Dailies. In general, there are so many local newspapers in Britain including England, Northern Ireland, Scotland and Wales. There are some famous local newspapers such as: *Glasgow Herald*, *The Evening Standard*, and *The Evening News*.

Introduction of British newspapers and magazines

Newspapers:

The Times

The Times is a British daily national newspaper in the UK. It established in 1785 with the name *The Daily Universal Register* and then turned to *The Times* on 1 January 1788. *The Times* and its sister paper *The Sunday Times* are published by Times Newspapers, a subsidiary of News International, which is owned by Rupert Murdoch, head of News Corporation group.

Financial Times

Financial Times (FT) is an English-language international business newspaper printed as a broadsheet on light salmon paper. Founded in 1888, it has emphasized on business and financial news.

The Guardian

The Guardian is a British national daily newspaper founded in 1821 and is owned by the Guardian Media Group.

The Daily Telegraph

The Daily Telegraph is a daily morning broadsheet newspaper founded in 1855. It is published and circulated in throughout the Britain and the world.

Magazines:

The Economist

Since 1843, *The Economist* is a weekly international news and business publication, offering clear reporting, commentary and analysis on world current affairs, business, finance, science and technology, culture, society, media and the arts.

The Spectator

The Spectator is a weekly conservative magazine in the UK. It was founded in 1828, and is the oldest continuously published magazine in the English language.

The New Statesman

The New Statesman is a political and cultural magazine published in London and it was founded as a weekly review of politics and literature on 12 April 1913.

☞ Questions for discussion

1. What are the choices of Britons for reading newspapers?
2. How many categories of national newspapers and what are their differences?
3. What are the quality dailies and when are their establishing time?
4. What are the quality Sundays and when are their establishing time?

13.2 Television and Broadcasting

When it comes to the degree of popularity of the mass media in the UK, television ranks the first, with newspaper and radio following afterwards among the British people. The broadcasting media is a vital part of any Briton's everyday life. According to statistics, there are around 97% of the families throughout the country having a TV and a radio at home to receive the waves and signals from the broadcasting station for people to enjoy what they would like to listen and watch. Some 70 % people will listen to a radio on a daily basis. British people spend around 3. 5 hours per day to watch TV and many of them will read the TV-related part on the newspapers to know what will be shown on TV that day and the information of the programs. TV programs and shows are the most frequent topics in the conversations of British people.

At the beginning, broadcasting in the UK has been a public service with British Broadcasting Corporation (usually known as BBC) founded in 1926 being the only public service broadcaster. At that time, it was one of the biggest broadcast media in the world and the biggest in the UK. In 1955, private broadcasting is permitted to provide television and radio services for the people. There were Independent Television Network Limited, Channel Four Television Corporation, Channel Five Television Corporation, and British Sky Broadcasting Group as private broadcasters providing services to the people.

All the broadcasters must follow the regulations and basic principles for broadcasting. As for regulations, the Independent Television Commission (ITC) and the Broadcasting Standards Commission are two important regulating bodies in the UK. The Independent

Television Commission licensed and regulated commercial television services in the UK between 1 January 1991 and 28 December 2003. The ITC was formed by the Broadcasting Act 1990. (In 1990 the Broadcasting Act was passed in an attempt to guarantee standards of decency, accuracy in news coverage, and balanced presentations of controversial topics, while encouraging more competition in television and radio.) The Broadcasting Standards Commission is the statutory body for both standards and fairness in broadcasting. It is the only organization within the regulatory framework of UK broadcasting to cover all television and radio, both terrestrial and satellite. This includes text, cable and digital services. It has three main tasks, as established by the Broadcasting Act, 1996. These are: to produce codes of conduct relating to standards and fairness; to consider and adjudicate on complaints; and to monitor, research and report on standards and fairness in broadcasting. It was set up in 1997 to set standards, monitor violent and pornography and to respond to complaints about the broadcasts. As for the basic principles, Public broadcasting should serve the purpose of entertaining, informing and educating the nation. And there should not be political bias and the presentation of violence and pornography on television.

Brief Introduction of BBC and the Main Channels

Established in 1926 as a radio station, BBC is a main public service broadcaster in the UK. It moved into television in the year of 1936 and had long been considered one of the world's most respected media. It was the only radio and television broadcaster in the UK before the establishment of the ITV in 1955. In addition, BBC now also provides other services such as book publishing, newspapers, English teaching, a symphony orchestra, and Internet news services.

BBC has two TV channels: BBC1 and BBC 2, as well as some regional stations. It also has World Service in English and 43 other languages all around the world. The channel BBC 1 (since 1936) broadcasts general interest programs while the channel BBC 2 meets the minority and specialist interests of the audience. There is no commercials or advertisements on BBC 1 and BBC 2. The Independent Television (ITV, also as Channel 3 since 1955) broadcasts approximately 33% informative programs and 66% light entertainment programs. Channel 4 (since 1982) broadcasts 15% educational programs, and encourages innovation and experiment. Channel 5 (since 1997) is a general entertainment channel that shows both internally commissioned programs and foreign programs.

The funding of the channels and television licensing

BBC 1 and BBC 2 are funded through the license fees from viewers and the sale of the programs. Therefore, they do not rely on revenue through advertising and commercials. And BBC World is an advertiser-funded channel, with 24-hour news, information and analysis. ITV, Channels 4 and 5 are all profit-making channels. They get their revenue from advertising.

In the UK, any family who wants to enjoy the live television transmissions service must purchase a television license each year, which will cost around 50 pounds and 145 pounds for black and white TV set and color TV set respectively.

Popular programs and what British people watch on TV

Some of the most popular shows include *East Enders* and *Coronation Street*. *East Enders* is a soap opera that shows on the BBC 1. It is about the lives of several families who live in Albert Square in the working class East End of London. Much of the action takes place in and around the local pub, Queen Victoria. It is described as being faster-paced and more dramatic than its rival, *Coronation Street*.

Coronation Street, on ITV, is the world's longest running evening drama. It also focuses on working-class resident in a town in northern England. They all live on Coronation Street. Like a typical soap opera, the plot is juicy, and the characters move swiftly in and out of their tragedies and triumphs.

Other popular programs are reality TV shows such as *Pop Idol* (the original *American Idol*), *Big Brother*, *Survivor* and game shows like *The Weakest Link*.

Radio and the most popular radio stations

As for the radio services, there are 5 BBC radio networks and 3 independent national radio services and about 200 independent local radio services broadcasting throughout the UK. The independent radio services receive the license from the Radio Authority. The most popular British radio stations are as follows: Clare FM, Anna Livia, Live 95, Welsh Radio International, Imperial College Radio, Capital FM, and BBC Radio 2.

☞ Questions for discussion

1. What is the ranking of mass media in the heart of British people?
2. What are the main broadcasters in the UK and which category do they belong to?
3. What are the main functions of Independent Television Commission and Broadcasting

Standards Commission?

4. How many channels are there in BBC and what do they broadcast?
5. What are the main differences between the funding of BBC and the channels of private broadcasters?

☞ Questions on Chapter Twelve for reflection and presentation

Review Chapter 13 and write a short essay on any of the following questions.

1. What is the newspaper culture in the UK and can you list some of the national dailies after defining their main features?
2. How does the television and broadcasting industry develop in the UK?

Chinese Version

第1章　大英帝国的形成及其历代君主

英国的历史是一部征服和合并的历史。它几经改朝换代，先后被四十多位君主统治；它经历了国内战争、国际战争、不时的叛乱，以及贵族和君主精英之间广泛的政治阴谋，也遭遇过毁灭性的天灾人祸。然而，正是这些变化和事件，促成了这个国家在政治、军事、外交、经济、工业，以及语言和文化等各方面的演变和发展。

大英帝国的形成是300多年来贸易、移民与武力征服的结果。在其顶峰时期，它是历史上最大的帝国，曾经被描述为“日不落帝国”，因为它在地球上的广阔区域意味着太阳总是在它至少一个领土上闪烁着光辉。

1.1　不列颠的早期居民

约一万年前，大不列颠与欧洲相连，被冰雪覆盖。大约15000年前，天气变暖，冰山融化，海平面上升，大不列颠大约在8000年前成为岛屿。

人们所知道的最早的不列颠居民是伊比利亚人，他们在约公元前3000年的新石器时代来自于伊比利亚半岛，即现在的西班牙。约公元前2000年，宽口陶器人移居到现在的荷兰和莱茵兰地区。

约公元前700年铁器时代，凯尔特人来到不列颠岛。“铁器时代”一词源于一种叫做铁的新金属的发现。凯尔特人发现了如何用铁制造工具和武器。在铁器时代以前，不列颠用于制作工具的金属是青铜，即铜锡合金（故为青铜时代）。凯尔特人居住在欧洲大部分地区，特别是现在的奥地利、瑞士、法国南部和西班牙。凯尔特人来到不列颠有三高峰：戈伊德尔族的凯尔特人（盖尔人或盖尔语的人）在大约公元前600年第一批入侵不列颠。后来他们被公元前500—公元前400年到来的表亲布立吞族的凯尔特人（布立吞人或不列颠人）驱逐到了爱尔兰。布立吞人占领了今天的英格兰和威尔士。布立吞凯尔特人由小部落逐渐变成了较大的部落，有自己独特的身份，生活在整个不列颠他们自己特定的区域。当尤利乌斯·恺撒准备从罗马对不列颠发起侵略时，已经有更多的凯尔特人从高卢来到英格兰东南部定居了。这些主要是比利时的部落——比利其人，来自现在的比利时南部和法国北部。现在居住在不列颠的凯尔特人源于早年入侵的两个主要部落：戈伊德尔族的凯尔特人——苏格兰和马恩岛；布立吞族的凯尔特人——威尔士和康沃尔。

铁器时代居住在不列颠的凯尔特人都是武士兼农民，很擅长制造金属工具和武器。凯尔特人有许多不同的部落，每个部落由酋长（国王或女王）统治。部落首领带着他的士兵们驾着马车打仗。为防御敌人，他们在山顶建造了堡垒，并用土堤和木墙围着。

凯尔特人时期的不列颠没有城镇。大多数人是生活在农村的农民，他们用木头和泥筑成圆顶的房子。那时也没有什么道路，人们划着小船在河里行驶或在泥泞的小路上行走。有些不列颠的凯尔特人渡海去罗马帝国与其他凯尔特人进行贸易。

今天仍有很多凯尔特人生活在英国，他们主要居住在康沃尔郡、威尔士、苏格兰、马恩岛和爱尔兰等地。

不同部落的凯尔特人都讲着一种大致相同的语言。凯尔特一词来自希腊语 Keltoi，意思是野蛮人，正确发音大概是 Kelt。他们直到 18 世纪才被称为凯尔特人，罗马人把他们叫布立吞人，不叫凯尔特人。凯尔特人是“现代”的称呼，是对铁器时代所有的诸多部落的人们的统称。那些叫做盖尔人的凯尔特人居住在爱尔兰。

凯尔特语形成了较大的印度-欧洲语系的一个分支。在说凯尔特语的人于公元前 400 年左右进入历史时，他们已经分为几个不同的语言群体，而且还蔓延至西欧大陆、伊比利亚半岛、爱尔兰和不列颠等许多地区。

今天，凯尔特语这个词通常指的是爱尔兰、苏格兰、威尔士、康沃尔、马恩岛和布列塔尼半岛的语言和各自的文化，也被称为凯尔特诸民族。这些区域在一定程度上仍然是四种凯尔特语为母语的地方，它们分别是爱尔兰盖尔语、苏格兰盖尔语、威尔士语和布列塔尼语；再加上两个最近复兴的康沃尔语（布立吞语的一种）和马恩岛语（戈伊德尔语的一种）。也有人试图重建坎伯兰语（英格兰西北和苏格兰西南的布立吞语）。

1.2　罗马时代的英国

英国有记载的历史开始于罗马人的入侵。2000 年前罗马人来到英国，他们改变了这个国家。罗马帝国在英国留下了痕迹，即使在今天，罗马建筑的遗迹、堡垒、道路和洗浴遍布英国。

罗马人住在意大利国家中心城市罗马。公元前 55 年 8 月，罗马将军，尤利乌斯·恺撒皇帝入侵不列颠。他带着两个罗马军团，在几次战胜英格兰东南部的凯尔特部落（布立吞人）后撤回到法国。

次年夏天（公元前 54 年）恺撒再次来到英国，在肯特迪尔附近的沃尔默登陆。这次他带来了不少于五个军团（30000 步兵和 2000 骑兵）。罗马人越过泰晤士河，经过更多的战斗后，不列颠部落答应给罗马进贡，罗马人才平和地离开了英国将近一个世纪。

将近 100 年后的公元 43 年，克劳狄皇帝成功地组织了最后一次入侵英国的战争。奥鲁斯·普劳提乌斯将军率领 25000 人的 4 个军团，外加等量的辅助士兵。他们以 3 个师为单位穿过了英吉利海峡，分别在里奇伯勒、多佛和林普恩港口登陆。

最大的一场战役在靠近罗切斯特的梅德韦河岸打响，持续了两天才把凯尔特部落打退。

许多部落竭力反抗罗马人，侵略者花了大约 4 年的时间终于控制了英国南部。他们又花了 30 年征服所有的西部国家和威尔士高山峡谷地区。征服约克郡和英格兰北部的战斗在公元 70 年仍在进行。

第一个罗马城是加牧罗顿南姆，现在叫做科尔切斯特。罗马统治布列塔尼亚（不列颠）的地盘，直至遭受布迪卡起义的掠夺。当时伦敦被确立为管辖地，但直到加牧罗顿南姆事件后才变成一个要地。

罗马人称伦敦为“Londinium”。泰晤士河是英国和欧洲大陆之间货物运输的快捷通道，罗马人便把伦敦城建在河的主要过境点。

罗马人为什么来到英国不是很确定，一直认为有两个原因：

- 英国帮助高卢人（现在称为法国人）对抗罗马将军尤利乌斯·恺撒，罗马人因此很生气。
- 他们来到英国寻找财富——土地、奴隶，而且最重要的是铁、铅、锌、铜、银和金等矿藏。

英国（不包括苏格兰）成为罗马帝国的一部分长达近 400 年（公元 43 年至公元 410 年）！罗马人将英国划分为 4 个区域，分别以下列城镇为中心：伦敦、赛伦塞斯特、约克郡和林肯。他们撤离英国，是因为他们在意大利的家园遭到蛮族人的侵袭，急需每一个士兵上战场。

即使在今天，罗马帝国在英国人的生活中都发挥着重要作用。许多事物起源于罗马人：

- 语言是从罗马人的语言发展而来。罗马人说的和写的都是拉丁文，而许多英语单词来自拉丁语。
- 英国今天使用的日历有着 2000 多年的历史，起始于尤利乌斯·恺撒大帝。

它是基于地球绕着太阳的运动，所以被称为“阳历”。“阳历”一年有 365 天，每个闰年或每四年有 366 天。

- 月份的名称是取自罗马诸神和统治者的名字。事实上，七月就是以尤利乌斯·恺撒本人的名字命名的。
- 法律和法律制度最初来自罗马帝国。
- 人口普查。罗马帝国巨大，包括生活在大片地区的数百万人。为了管理所有人，罗马帝国开始采取普查，或“计数”所有在其境内的常住人口。今天，许多诸如英国的国家每 10 年都要进行一次人口普查。

罗马人还为英国留下了许多其他东西，如笔直的道路、庙宇、其他建筑物、暖气，澡堂、混凝土和渡槽。他们还很好地利用了英国的自然资源。罗马人还把基督教这门新宗教引入到了英国。

1.3　撒克逊时代的英国

最后一批罗马士兵于公元 410 年撤离英国，然后新的一批移民又乘船从北海来到英国，有来自德国北部的，也有丹麦和荷兰北部的，大多数是撒克逊人、盎格鲁人和朱特人，也有一些弗兰克斯人和弗里西岛民。

由于盎格鲁和撒克逊是三个入侵部落中最大的部落，便以盎格鲁-撒克逊人著称。他们是武士兼农民，高高的个子，金色的头发，手持大刀长矛和圆盾，好斗又凶猛。

历史学家也不确定为什么盎格鲁-撒克逊人来到英国。有的说，撒克逊士兵是应邀来到现在的英格兰，以帮助抵御来自苏格兰和爱尔兰的入侵者。另一个原因可能是因为他们的土地常常遭洪涝，很难种植庄稼，所以他们得寻找新的地方安身和耕种。

盎格鲁-萨克逊人统治英国长达 500 年（比罗马人还多 100 年）。然而，他们从不曾像罗马人那样“回家”过；今天住在英国的很多人的祖先都是盎格鲁-撒克逊人。甚至连“英格兰”这个名称都来自撒克逊语“Angle-Land”。

无论他们是通过和平协商，或是把英国人从他们的土地上赶走，盎格鲁-撒克逊人控制了英国的大部分地区，然而，他们从没能征服苏格兰、威尔士和康沃尔。生活在公元 700 年的历史学家比德写道：盎格鲁人居住在东英格兰、东中部和北部的诺森比亚。萨克逊人则迁到了苏塞克斯（以“南撒克逊人”命名）、埃塞克斯（东撒克逊人）、中塞克斯（中部撒克逊人）以及威塞克斯（西撒克逊人）。朱特人主要居住在肯特郡、汉普郡和怀特岛。七个主要王国（肯特、埃塞克斯、苏塞克斯、威塞克斯、东盎格利亚、麦西亚和诺森伯利亚）合称为七王国（或七国时代）。

盎格鲁-撒克逊有几位大国王，其中有麦西亚的奥法（他建造了 Offa 堤坝）和诺森比亚的埃德温（创立了爱丁堡或埃德温的山丘堡垒），但最著名的是艾尔弗雷德，英国历史上唯一被称为“大帝”的国王。他从 871 年到 899 年间是威塞克斯国王，后来成为了全英格兰的国王。

这些盎格鲁-撒克逊移民讲着同一种语言，每个部落都有一个首领，强者便成为“cyning”——盎格鲁-撒克逊语“国王”，每一个国王统治一个王国，领导一支小规模的军队。国王之间经常发生冲突和战争，以争当最强者。

罗马人所称的布立吞人（英国人）说的是拉丁语或当地的凯尔特语，新移民讲的是自己的语言，即现在被称为盎格鲁-撒克逊语或古英语。盎格鲁-撒克逊人自己称之为“Englisc”（古英语）。因而被新移民占领的国家就成了“英格兰”。

一部分英国人与新移民居住在一起，另一部分人则带着他们的拉丁凯尔特文化向西部和北部迁移。通过一些地名就能找到新“英国人”居住地的线索。例如，以-ham 结尾的地名显示这曾是撒克逊部落，Ham 在盎格鲁-撒克逊英语中的意思是“村”。

Burh（borough）表示盎格鲁-萨克逊城镇名，现在仍然出现在英国的一些地名里，例如 Peterborough（彼得伯勒）和 Scarborough（斯卡伯勒）。

最初的盎格鲁-撒克逊村庄是以酋长（村首领）的名字而命名的，以表明该村庄所属的部落。这些地名经常是在人名词尾加字母“ing”，地名的第一个部分最有可能就是当地酋长的名字。

住在黑斯廷斯村的就是 Haesta 的人——Haesta 是酋长。住在雷丁村的是 Redda 的人——Redda 是酋长。

后来，盎格鲁-撒克逊村庄都是以所在地的环境特征而命名，而不是以酋长的名字命名。牛津得名于一个赶牛过河的浅滩。

盎格鲁-撒克逊人为英国国家的形成打下了基础。首先，他们把国家划分为郡（后来的诺曼人称郡为县）。郡法庭和郡长官（或行政司法长官）负责执法，执法范围的广泛性如同中世纪初一样。其次，他们设计的窄条三圃田农耕制延用至 18 世纪。此外，他们还建立了采邑制。最后，他们还创立了议会（贤人会议），向国王提供建议，为今天仍存在的枢密院奠定了基础。

诺尔曼征服之后，盎格鲁-撒克逊人仍然保留着其身份，后来被称为诺尔曼统治下的英国人，最终发展成现代的英国人。

1.4 维京时代的英国

英国的维京时代始于大约 1200 年前的公元第九世纪，持续了 200 多年。

大约公元 800 年，与 400 年前盎格鲁-撒克逊人一样，凶猛的掠夺者穿过北海开始侵袭英国的海岸。他们是维京人（也被称为丹麦人，虽然他们不只是来自丹麦）。他们也像盎格鲁-撒克逊人那样在这里安了家，赶走了撒克逊人，抢占了部分国土。

维京人也被称为古斯堪的纳维亚人，意思是北方人。他们来自位于斯堪的纳维亚（北欧）的三个国家：丹麦，挪威和瑞典。他们是农民、渔民、海员和商人。许多海盗（维京人）是大航海家，乘着长船航行在欧洲其他地区和大西洋。维京工匠用木头、金属和骨头制作精美的物件；维京妇女织工熟练，制作精细的御寒纺织品。

大部分数维京人来英国只是寻找更好的土地耕种，因为他们家乡的土地不太适合种植庄稼或饲养动物：挪威是丘陵，瑞典被森林覆盖，丹麦很多地方都是沙质土壤。

一些历史学家认为，维京人离开他们的家园是由于过度拥挤，没有足够的土地供大家分享。在维京人的家中只有长子能继承家族的农场，其他兄弟不得不去别处谋生。

一些维京人想寻找宝藏致富，而英国是一个特别好的地方，可盗取的东西很多。

维京人首次入侵英国是在公元 793 年，最后一次是 1066 年，黑斯廷斯战役后征服者威廉成为了英国国王。

海盗们一直垂涎修道院里的财宝，所以首当其冲遭到袭击的就是位于英格兰东北部海岸小圣岛上的林迪斯法恩修道院。一些僧侣被淹死在海里，一些人被杀害，或者连同教堂里掠来的宝藏带走当了奴隶。

林迪斯法恩的掠夺标志着维京人在公元 793 年开始从斯堪的纳维亚向外扩张。

在随后的几年里，靠近海边的村庄、修道院和城市都处于海上入侵者的围困之中。很快，不列颠群岛（不列颠及其附近岛屿）都被海盗搅得没有安全之地，威尔士、苏格兰、爱尔兰、英格兰岛上的村庄和城镇都遭到了海盗的袭击。

公元 866 年维京人到了约克郡，并把约克郡（他们称之为约维克）变成了继伦敦之后的第二大城市。

维京人无论多少次被打败也不离开，最后，他们的努力都得到了回报。最终是诺曼底的维京人在 1066 年征服了英格兰，并从此改写了英国的历史。威塞克斯的萨克逊国王艾尔弗雷德在一场大战役中拼命奋战，也没能把他们赶走，最后不得不让给他们部分地盘，称之为丹麦区，覆盖着地图上连接伦敦和切斯特沿线靠东的地区，萨克逊人则住在沿线以南。

维京人定居在苏格兰沿海的岛屿——设得兰群岛、奥克尼郡和赫布里底群岛、苏格兰北部和西北部海岸周围、爱尔兰的部分地区——都柏林便是维京人的城市、马恩岛、威尔士的小部分地区、诺森比亚（包括现代的约克郡）、东英吉利亚、莱斯特、诺丁汉、德比，以及斯坦福和林肯等地。

定居英国的维京人在语言方面的长期影响有三点：超过一千个古斯堪的纳维亚词语最终成了标准英语的一部分；英格兰东部和东北部许多地方都有丹麦语地名；许多英国人名起源于斯堪的纳维亚语。

进入英语词汇的斯堪的纳维亚语包括“landing”、“score”、“beck”、“fellow”、“take”、“busting” 和 “steersman”。绝大多数外来词直到 12 世纪初才出现在文献里；包括许多现代词汇中发“sk-”音的词，如 skirt、sky 和 skin；其他在这个时期出现在文字资料里的词有：“again”、“awkward”、“birth”、“cake”、“dregs”、“fog”、“freckles”、“gasp”、“law”、“moss”、“neck”、“ransack”、“root”、“scowl”、“sister”、“seat”、“sly”、“smile”、“want”、“weak” 等，来自古斯堪的纳维亚语的“window” 意思是“wind-eye”。有些是英语中最常用的词汇，比如，“to go”、“to come”、“to sit”、“to listen”、“to eat”、“both”、“same”、“get” 和“give”。人称代词体系也受到了影响，以“they”“them” 和“their” 替代了其之前的形式。

英格兰有 1500 多个斯堪的纳维亚地名，主要在约克郡和林肯郡（丹麦区以前的边界内）：其中有 600 个以-by 结尾的词，斯堪的纳维亚语意为“村”，例如，Derby（德比）、Rugby（拉格比）、Whitby（惠特比）、Selby（塞尔比）和 Grimsby（格里姆斯比）；许多以-thorpe（或-thorp，-throp or-trop）结尾的意为“农场”，例如 Scunthorpe（斯肯索普）和 Grimethorpe（格里姆索普）；-toft 指的是房屋或土地所在的地点。这些地方都是早期维京人居留地的标记。

根据分析以-son 结尾的姓氏显示，斯堪的纳维亚人的影响仍然集中在北部和东部，与以前的维京人居住地相对应。中世纪早期的记载显示 60%的约克郡和林肯郡北部的人名受斯堪的纳维亚的影响。

1.5 诺曼时代的英国

英国中世纪是一个很长的时期，经历了始于 1066 年开始的诺曼（罗曼底）人征服、1348 年毁灭性的黑死病、英法百年战争与最终于 1485 年结束的玫瑰战争。

英格兰国王爱德华三世（称为“忏悔者”，因为他建造了威斯敏斯特教堂）在位 23 年后于 1066 年 1 月 5 日逝世。

诺曼公爵威廉是忏悔者爱德华的一个远房表亲，据说，爱德华国王曾答应把英格兰王位传给诺曼底公爵威廉，但是贤人会议却选择哈罗德戈德温为国王。

哈罗德是英国最有权势的戈德温伯爵的儿子和爱德华的妻弟。他是土生土长的英国人，也很受普通人的欢迎，但他与国王没有直接的血缘关系，不是皇家出生。哈罗德曾为爱德华赢得了许多战役。他说，让哈罗德继承王位也是爱德华的遗愿

（爱德华此说没有人证）。爱德华去世的次日，哈罗德成为了英国国王哈罗德二世。

于是，威廉率领他的军队入侵英国，在 1066 年 10 月重要的黑斯廷斯战役中打败并杀死了哈罗德。

威廉赢得黑斯廷斯战役后，也赢得了“征服者”的称号。他进军伦敦，并于 1066 年圣诞节在威斯敏斯特教堂加冕为王。

1066 年的诺曼征服是英国历史上最著名的事件，由征服者威廉建立的诺尔曼王朝统治英国长达半个世纪，直至被称为无政府状态的继承危机时期（1135—1154）。它改变了英国的历史进程，使英国与欧洲有了更紧密的联系，在接下来的 300 年中，英国的统治者和贵族都讲法语，而不是讲英语。

诺曼胜利改变了英国的统治方式，在撒克逊时期，伯爵常常与国王一样重要，但现在的国王享有绝对控制权，他统治着整个国家，他的规定就是法律。

征服者威廉用强有力的诺曼政府代替了软弱的萨克逊政权，并在英格兰建立了“封建制度”。根据此制度，国王拥有所有的土地。威廉把英国的大片土地分给他的贵族们，以换取他们服役和交租的承诺。这些地产分散于各处，使得那些土地拥有者不能轻而易举地联合起来反叛国王。他增加了传统的英国各郡的功能（自治行政区），将其列入中央的控制范围；他以限制每人一郡的做法来削弱贵族的权利。政府的所有行政功能（除了法院之外）都保持固定在特定的英国城镇，也会逐步加强，因而英国在欧洲拥有的行政机构最多。

1085 年，为了确定他的新领地范围和提高税收，威廉下令编写《末日审判书》，并于 1086 年出版。这本书是对英格兰大部分地区和威尔士部分地区进行“大调查”的记录稿，类似于现代的人口普查。

《末日审判书》记录了所有的土地和财产、每一个工厂和农舍，以及每头牛和猪，也记录了每一个土地拥有者和每一个宫廷的权利和义务。《末日审判书》让我们知道很多关于十一世纪的英国，例如，截至 1086 年，英国血统的富裕地主已经所剩无几。这是一个由法国人，特别是威廉的诺曼亲信们所统治的国家。

赢得黑斯廷斯战役后，威廉就着手在全国战略区域修建一个又一个的城堡，其中两个最著名的就是伦敦塔和温莎城堡。这些城堡有效地抵挡了英国人或者国王自己的追随者的许多叛乱。到威廉统治结束时，已有 80 多座城堡遍及他的王国，成为了新诺尔曼封建统治永久性的标志。

威廉还开放了与欧洲大陆的关系，传播文明、扩展商贸，还引进了诺曼法国文化、语言、礼节和建筑。教会与罗马的联系更为密切，并将教会法庭与民事法庭分离开来。

征服者威廉死于 1087 年，将他的诺曼底爵位传给了他的长子罗伯特，将英国的王位传给了二儿子威廉，成为威廉二世，又因他的红头发被称为威廉鲁弗斯。

随著斯蒂芬的逝世，诺曼王朝于 1154 年终结。首任“金雀花王朝”的国王亨利二世于 1154 年 12 月 19 日即位。金雀花王朝不仅在英国，而且在整个欧洲都是一个庞大而强大的家族。亨利二世的父亲在安茹拥有广袤的土地，所占面积与现代城市图尔周边的诺曼底相等。亨利的妻子埃利诺则在南部统治着更大的领土，称为阿基坦公国，因此金雀花的君王们是欧洲最富裕的家族，统治着英格兰和半个法国。其称谓源于拉丁文的 planta genista，意为黄色的金雀花，安茹伯爵们将其作为头盔上的徽章。

亨利二世不仅是英格兰的国王，而且还统治着威尔士的大部分地区、诺曼底、安茹、加斯科涅和法国其他地区（通过他与埃利诺的阿基坦的婚姻获得）。他的统治代表着权力从贵族回归到英格兰君主的逆转；也见证了类似的立法权力从教会再次回到君主制国家的重新分配。这一时期也预示着一个健全的立法以及封建制度的彻底转变。

英格兰在金雀花王朝的统治下进行了改革，尽管不完全是有意的。金雀花王朝的国王经常被迫协商对诸如《大宪章》的法令作出妥协。这些妥协约束了皇权，以换取金融和军事的支持。国王不再是这个国家掌握着审判的特权、封建贡品以及战争的最有权势的人。他现在的职责已经界定在特定的领域，复杂的司法体系为其基础。

金雀花王朝的巨大进步是关于宪法改革。普通法与陪审团审判均起源于亨利二世时期，第一届国会于 1265 年举行。

英国中世纪的特点是经历了国内战争、国际战争、时而的暴动，以及贵族和君主的精英中广泛的政治阴谋。

1.6 都铎王朝的英国

随着亨利七世于 1485 年即位，玫瑰战争结束，都铎王朝继续统治英格兰达 118 年。他们给 150 年几乎是连续作战的英格兰带来了和平，并鼓励新的宗教观念、海外探险和殖民地扩展。

都铎王朝是威尔士和英格兰家族，从 1485 年到 1603 年统治着英国。都铎王朝的开国之君是亨利七世，他在博斯沃思战役后成了国王，从而结束了玫瑰战争。他是英国最后一位在战场上赢得王位的国王。都铎王亨利与约克家族的伊丽莎白结婚后，创建了都铎玫瑰，组合了约克的白玫瑰和兰开斯特的红玫瑰，象征着约克和兰开斯特之间的斗争结束。他成功地恢复和稳定了英国君主制的地位，创建了长期持久的王朝，经过 23 年的统治之后，和平地将王位传给他的儿子亨利八世。

英国都铎王朝产生了两个最强的君主：亨利八世和他的女儿伊丽莎白一世。他们因很多事而出名，包括亨利八世和他的六个妻子的故事、探险美洲大陆以及威廉·莎士比亚的戏剧等。

亨利八世是第一个在文艺复兴的影响下接受教育的英国君主，他的导师包括诗人斯凯尔顿，使他成为了一个颇有成就的学者、语言学家、音乐家和运动员。

青年时期的亨利八世很像威廉·莎士比亚笔下描述的亨利五世国王——他更感兴趣的是武器和装甲、剑术、骑马、用长矛比武、狩猎和美女，而对王权没有兴趣。他写爱情诗、创作歌曲，如《与好伙伴一起消磨时光》。在他的一生中，他酷爱君主款式的时装——毕竟，如果不能穿得像个王室成员还叫什么皇族呢？

国王亨利八世成功地把英格兰和威尔士统一在同一个政治体系下，这两个国家在 1536 年合二为一。1535 年和 1542 年的威尔士法案试图规范两个国家之间的关系，将英格兰的法律制度引入威尔士，英语成为政府的官方语言。

亨利组建了海军，使英国在欧洲更加强大更加重要。

亨利八世给英格兰的宗教带来了剧变。他成为国王时，大多数人属于天主教会，由罗马教宗领导。亨利八世想要一个男性继承人，但他的妻子（安妮·博林）没有为他生育儿子。于是亨利想离婚，娶一个新王后，可是没有得到罗马天主教会的准许。为了离婚，亨利成立了英国国教，终结了天主教，并于 1534 年通过一项法律确立自己为英国国教的领袖。这一举动导致了英国新教的形成，新教运动被称为改革。1535 年亨利命令关闭遍及英格兰、威尔士和爱尔兰的所有罗马天主教寺院和修道院，被称为“解散修道院行动”。

亨利八世有三个孩子：玛丽（由阿拉贡的凯瑟琳所生）、伊丽莎白（安妮·博林所生）、爱德华（简·西摩尔所生）。每个孩子都依次当过君主：爱德华六世、玛丽一世（玛丽·都铎）和伊丽莎白一世。

伊丽莎白一世是都铎王朝的最后一个君主，1533 年 9 月 7 日出生在格林尼治宫，是亨利八世和他的第二任妻子安妮·博林所生。伊丽莎白 1558 年登基，时年 25 岁。她喜欢打猎，喜欢宫廷假面舞会（吟诗、唱歌、跳舞等娱乐）。她受过很好的教育，能流利地使用六种语言。她终身未婚，被称为“童贞女王。

伊丽莎白一世的统治被认为是英国历史上的黄金时代。在她的统治下，英国在对外贸易、探险、文学和艺术等领域都很先进。伊丽莎白一世是西方文明第一个真正的崇拜偶像之一。她对时尚的品位为贵族和社会其他阶层设立了标准；她对音乐、戏剧和诗歌的热爱营造了一种氛围，使许多像威廉·莎士比亚这样最伟大的英国作家获得了鼓励和资助。

在伊丽莎白的领导下，英国经历了真正的文化觉醒或文艺复兴。在伊丽莎白女王的指引下，牛津大学和剑桥大学进行了重组，被特许为学习和学术活动中心。

伊丽莎白时代，伟大的探险家发现了许多新的大陆。弗兰西斯·德雷克首次做了环球航行，声称为英国探寻新大陆、引进新材料和食品。美国的弗吉尼亚州就是以她的名字命名的。

都铎王朝的探险给英国带来许多东西，如更多的贸易、发现烟草、土豆和玉米、对世界有了更多的了解、在其他国家开拓殖民地、绘制了更精确的地图、建造了更好的船舶、丰富了词汇或语言、积累了更好的航海术等。1588 年战胜强大的西班牙无敌舰队使英国在海上的实力达到了巅峰，确保了世界强国的地位。

都铎王朝在伊丽莎白一世统治达 45 年之后，随着她 1603 年 3 月 24 日无嗣而终而结束，王位传给了他们的表亲苏格兰的斯图亚特家族，实现了英格兰和苏格兰的统一。

在都铎王朝 118 年的统治期间，英国发生了许多变化：促进了贸易和工业的发展，发现了美洲大陆，将文艺复兴传播到英国，所有这些都为英国建立资本主义生产模式提供了必备条件，国家变得比以往任何时候都更富裕。因此都铎王朝是英国历史从封建社会向资本主义的过渡阶段。

1.7 斯图亚特王朝的英国

斯图亚特王朝于 1371—1714 年间统治着苏格兰，1603—1714 年间统治英格兰，其间有一个 11 年的空位期。

伊丽莎白于 1603 年去世后，苏格兰国王詹姆士六世（自 1567 年）成为英国国王（詹姆士一世）。他是第一位同时统治两个国家的君主，自称“大不列颠国王”。但是直到 1707 年，一项议会法案才正式将这两个国家合并在一起，英格兰和苏格兰正式成为一个国家——大不列颠。因此，斯图亚特王朝成为了联合王国的第一任国王。

在詹姆士作为斯图亚特王朝第一位君主的年代里，英格兰经常是麻烦多多。天主教徒和新教徒之间的冲突未平，英国圣公会（新教、国教）和清教徒之间的冲突又起，詹姆士坚持“君权神授”理论，又与议会发生了冲突。他多次解散议会，很长时间没有立法机构。1605 年，他逃过了著名的“火药阴谋”一劫。阴谋失败后，人们点燃篝火庆祝。今天，英国仍然每年在 11 月 5 日这个日子庆祝盖伊福克斯日，以一个在地下室携带火药而被捕的同谋名字命名。

国王詹姆士六世和一世 1625 年去世，他的儿子查尔斯一世继承了王位，成为英国国王和爱尔兰国王，直到 1649 年。

查尔斯一世希望步其父的后尘，试图在他的统治下没有国会的干预。当意识到他作为国王的权利被国会逐步削减后，查尔斯便带领几百名士兵冲入威斯敏斯特宫，企图逮捕五名国会议员和一个被指控犯了叛国罪的叛徒，由于他的失算，这些人都跑掉了。这一丑闻震惊了伦敦，国王被迫逃离这个城市。

现在国会议员人人自危，查尔斯国王也觉得无法回头，便组织了军队去攻打他自己国家的国会，导致了英国内战。这场战争是国会议员（圆颅党）和保皇党（骑士）之间发生的一系列的武装冲突和政治斗争。战争持续了 9 年（1642—

1651)，分为三个阶段，被称为第一次、第二次和第三次内战。

第一次（1642—1646）和第二次（1648—1649）内战是国王查尔斯一世的支持者对国会支持者的战争，第三次内战（1649—1651）则是国王查尔斯二世和国会支持者之间的战争。内战于 1651 年 9 月 3 日在伍斯特战役以国会取胜而告结束。

这场内战导致了查尔斯一世在 1639 年被审判和处决，他的儿子查尔斯二世被流放，取代英国君主制的首先是英国联邦（1649—1653)，然后是护国公奥利弗·克伦威尔（1653—1659）。克伦威尔保持着这个职位直到 1658 年去世，由他的儿子理察·克伦威尔接管。英格兰从 1649 年至 1660 年的 11 年为共和国，是英国唯一没有国王或女王的时期。

当理察·克伦威尔对议会失去信任而退位时，查尔斯二世回到伦敦庆祝他三十岁生日，并开始统治英国（苏格兰、英格兰和威尔士)。他早在 1651 年就被加冕为苏格兰国王。查尔斯经历了伦敦从瘟疫（1665）和伦敦大火（1666)，以及荷兰战争等灾难中的恢复。很多新的建筑是在这个时期修建的，圣保罗大教堂是由克里斯多佛·雷恩爵士建造的，许多教堂今天仍然可见。中风后，查尔斯临死前几个小时皈依了天主教。由于查尔斯二世没有孩子，由他的弟弟詹姆士继位，自 1685 年成为英格兰和苏格兰国王（詹姆士二世)。

詹姆士试图通过强迫人们遵从他的天主教信仰使英国成为罗马天主教国家。因此，他对新教徒的迫害而被人们讨厌和憎恨。在 1688 年的光荣革命中，他被迫放弃皇冠。詹姆士二世退位后，他的女儿玛丽和她的荷兰籍丈夫，奥兰治王子威廉二世的儿子被议会邀请成为了国王和女王，成为英国的共同君主，威廉三世国王（1688—1702）和玛丽二世女王（1688—1694)。

玛丽二世的妹妹安妮女王是斯图亚特最后一个君王，从 1702 年至 1714 年为英格兰和爱尔兰女王。她 49 岁时在伦敦的肯辛顿宫去世。由于她的 18 个孩子都先她而逝，按照 1701 年的《王位继承法》条款，王位由詹姆士一世的曾外孙乔治继承，他是汉诺威选帝侯，亦称为乔治一世，成为汉诺威王朝的首位君主。

1.8　乔治时代 / 汉诺威时代的英国

依据 1701 年的《王位继承法》，安妮女王死后，一代新的君主——来自德国北部的汉诺威家族接过了王位。

本来有不少更好的人才可以成为英国国王，不幸的是他们大多数是天主教徒。1714 年 8 月 1 日，乔治·路易斯王子在他 54 岁的时候被宣布为英国、法国和爱尔兰国王。作为登基年龄最大的君主创下了英国历史纪录。

乔治一世抵达英国时，既不了解英国的政治，又不会说英语，因此对曾安排他成为国王的辉格党非常依赖。

乔治大部分时间都在他心爱的德国汉诺威度过。他不愿意费心去学习英语和了解英国国情，所以无法召开会议，导致了政府的内阁制。内阁是包含国会中最大的党派领导人的议会，其首领被称为首相。于是辉格党的领袖罗伯特·沃波尔爵士成为了英国第一任首相（1721—1742）。

乔治一世死于 1727 年 1 月 11 日，其子乔治二世继位。乔治二世也是喜爱德国胜于英国，与其父不同之处是他学习了说英语。

1735 年，乔治二世赐予罗伯特·沃波尔爵士一份礼物，唐宁街 10 号，现今英国首相在伦敦的常住官邸。

1760 年乔治三世继位，他是该朝代第一位在英国出生的国王，也是在安妮女王之后第一位置英国利益于汉诺威利益之上的君主，还是汉诺威王朝任期最长的君主。

在他的统治期间，英国失去了美洲殖民地，但却以领先力量在欧洲崛起；澳大利亚被英国开拓为殖民地；涌现出一批英国文学巨匠——简·奥斯丁、拜伦、雪莱、济慈和华兹华斯等；皮特和福克斯这样的伟大的政治家以及惠灵顿和纳尔逊船长也都产生于他的时代。许多其他有名的事件发生在乔治三世统治时期。

詹姆斯·库克 1769 年首次探索太平洋，成为登陆新西兰的欧洲第一人。

1770 年，他“发现”了澳大利亚东南部海岸，在植物湾（博特尼湾）登陆。

1773 年发生的波士顿茶叶事件成为了美国麻烦的第一个信号，1776 年 7 月 4 日美国殖民地宣布独立。失去了美国殖民地，随着小威廉·皮特出任首相，英国发生了很大的变化，他的立法纲领将终结王权。1775 年，詹姆斯·瓦特发明了蒸汽机。1790 年发生了法国大革命，与法国的战争持续到 1815 年，以拿破仑大败滑铁卢而告终。

1801 年，依据《联合法案》，大不列颠（英格兰、苏格兰和威尔士）和爱尔兰联合成为一个政治实体——大不列颠王国与爱尔兰联合王国，英格兰的首都伦敦成为联合王国的首都，因此乔治成为这个新国家的第一位国王。

1813 年简·奥斯丁的《傲慢与偏见》出版。

乔治三世统治了英国 50 年，亦是 15 个孩子的父亲。在他最后十年由于身患精神疾病而不宜统治，便由他的长子，后来的乔治四世从 1811 年开始担任了摄政王，并在他 1820 年逝世时继承了王位。乔治四世由于奢侈的生活方式和私生活丑闻很不得人心，但他却是艺术的热情支持者。他的府邸，尤其是卡尔顿宫和布莱顿穹顶宫，为艺术的品位创立了新的标准。

乔治四世于 1830 年 6 月 26 日去世。由于他唯一的孩子夏洛特公主在 1817 年分娩时去世，所以王位传给了乔治的弟弟，成为了威廉四世。

这个国家并不因乔治四世的去世而感到遗憾。

威廉四世从 1830 年起任大不列颠及北爱尔兰联合王国国王。因他从 13 岁就加入海军，故被称为“水手国王”。

在他统治期间，通过了 1832 年《改革法案》；1833 年英国废除了殖民地的奴隶制；1834 年大火烧毁了威斯敏斯特宫殿；1834 年通过了《济贫法》，为穷人设立了济贫所；自 1836 年起，出生、婚姻和死亡必须依法登记；1836 年，狄更斯的小说《雾都孤儿》面世，引起了对英国穷人的关注。

威廉于 1837 年 6 月 20 日无嗣而终，由他的侄女维多利亚继位。维多利亚是乔治三世第四个儿子爱德华王子（肯特公爵）的独生女。

1.9　维多利亚时代的英国

维多利亚是大不列颠和爱尔兰联合王国女王（1837—1901）和印度女皇（1876—1901）。

维多利亚的第一语言是德语，三岁时学说英语和法语，后来又学说印度斯坦语，因为她也是印度的统治者。维多利亚没有上过学，是在家里接受的教育。除了学习语言，她还学习历史、地理和圣经。她也学习弹钢琴和绘画，而且直到她 60 多岁这都是她的爱好。她喜欢唱歌和听歌剧。

维多利亚女王继位时才 18 岁，她的统治期确切地说是 63 年 7 个月零两天（1837. 6. 20—1901. 1. 22），比其他任何英国君主的年代都长，也是历史上统治期最长的女性，以维多利亚时代著称。这是英国历史上在工业、文化、政治、科学和军事等各方面都发生巨变的时期，大英帝国在此期间得到显著的扩张。

维多利亚时代，英国人民的生活发生了巨大的变化，英国成为了世界最强大的国家，经济增长最明显的标志就是人口的稳步增长，自从罗马时代，人口一直在 200 万到 600 万之间波动，但是从 1750 年开始呈指数级增长，到 1851 年达到了 2 100 万，一个世纪涨了近三倍，到 1901 年涨至了 3 700 万。人口的增长需要大量的食物、衣物和住房，为满足这些需要，建起了工厂和机器，新的城镇也在增长，改变了风景与人们生活和工作的方式。原来用于运输货物的铁路也第一次用来方便人们出行，铁路业把新的食物送到各个城镇。

1851 年 5 月 1 日，维多利亚女王举办世博会时，英国是世界领先的工业强国，铁、煤和棉布占世界的一半。水晶宫本身就是铸铁和玻璃预制批量生产的胜利，其展品的意图就是为了庆祝物质进步与和平的国际竞争。全世界都在展示自己的制品，但是到当时为止，展出的大部分物品都是英国制造的。

维多利亚时期，人们的生活水平得到了显著的改善，更多的人活得更长，也过得更舒适。维多利亚时期很多的开支都用于建设值得公民自豪的遗迹：部分资金用于修建图书馆、洗衣房、游泳池，其目的是改善劳动人民的生活。维多利亚时代公民的认同感和参与意识比 20 世纪初英国任何时期都强。

此外，没有一个国家像英国那样城市化，1851 年，英国的半数人口住在城镇，到 1901 年达到了四分之三。大英帝国的地盘在维多利亚时代扩展达到了最大化，到维多利亚统治结束时，几乎世界上四分之一的土地和四分之一的人都属于大英帝国。

整个维多利亚时期，联合王国都处于世纪领先地位，海上霸主的地位无可匹敌、外交和国际力量的主导影响力得到了各方的公认。然而，这一杰出地位的基础是英国的经济实力。

这个曾经被拿破仑认为是“店主的国度”现在发展成了“世界的工厂”，得益于第一次工业革命。她对国际贸易线路的掌控和对金融服务的主导也确保在女王统治的后期能够承受其他新兴工业国家的挑战，至少在一段时期之内是如此。

维多利亚在英国的声誉也缘于她良好的性格。她与丈夫一直保持着和谐关系，给后人树立了好的标准。在环境豪华而朴实的巴尔莫勒尔城堡里，有心爱的丈夫艾伯特的陪伴，有一群儿女围绕在身边，女王成为了 19 世纪末中产阶级女性和家庭的偶像。事实上，维多利亚被看做是婚姻稳定和家庭美德的典范。她与艾伯特的婚姻代表着和谐婚姻的理想。她被称为“国母”，体现出家是安逸舒适的空间。

维多利亚的成就在英国很受欢迎，她的性格广受尊敬，以至于“维多利亚的”头衔后来被用于具有体面、道德和自我满足特性的任何人或任何时间。她的时代被称为英国历史上的“上流社会”。

1901 年维多利亚去世时，大英帝国作为世界强国达到了顶峰。维多利亚有 9 个孩子，40 个孙子和 37 个曾孙。由于维多利亚子女们的婚姻，今天的皇室与许多欧洲君主都有关联，她的 8 个子女曾登上欧洲的王位：英国的、普鲁士的、希腊的、罗马利亚的、俄罗斯的、挪威的和西班牙的。今天的女王伊丽莎白及其丈夫爱丁堡公爵均是维多利亚女王的曾曾孙。

1.10　现代英国（1902+）

维多利亚女王于 1901 年去世，其子爱德华七世登基，开创了爱德华七世时代。爱德华几乎是一出生就被封为威尔士王子，到了很多人即将退休的年龄（60 岁），才终于得到了国王的职位。他娶了丹麦的亚历山德拉，一生致力维持欧洲和平，被称为爱德华和平使者。

爱德华时代的特点是招摇炫富，与阴郁的维多利亚时代形成了对比。电影、汽车、飞机等都在 20 世纪投入了使用，新世纪的特征是非常乐观。随着 1900 年工党的形成，19 世纪的社会变革一直持续到 20 世纪。

爱德华于 1910 年去世，乔治五世继位（1910—1936）。迫于当时的反德情绪，乔治五世即位后将王室的姓由萨克森-科堡哥达改为了温莎。乔治五世没有丑闻、努力工作、深得人心，与玛丽王后一起，基于中产阶级的价值观和美德，为英国皇室树立了现代模式的行为典范。他比他所有的首相都更了解海外帝国，凭借他对数字和细节的特殊记忆力，无论是在制服、政治还是各种关系等方面，他与他的臣民交谈都能达到良好的效果。乔治五世统治英国时正逢第一次世界大战（1914—1918）。他在位期间，妇女第一次被允许参加选举。1916 年新芬党的复活节起义导致了 1918 年爱尔兰独立议会的成立。

1936 年 6 月，乔治五世国王的长子爱德华八世继任了他的王位。爱德华对弱势群体的真正关心和他代表父亲对英国和海外的官方巡访使他很受欢迎。然而，为了能娶一个离了婚的美国女人沃利斯 · 辛普森夫人为妻，爱德华八世仅仅在位 325 天就退了位，因为国王不能娶一个离过婚的女人为王后。

爱德华八世的弟弟，约克公爵加冕成为乔治六世。国王乔治六世执政三年之后，1939 年 9 月 3 日爆发了第二次世界大战，在此期间他和他的妻子伊丽莎白王后（后来的王太后），成为了英国的精神偶像。国王乔治六世创立乔治勋章和乔治十字勋章，以奖赏“最伟大的英雄主义行为或在极端危险的情况下最突出的勇敢行为”（维多利亚十字勋章给予战场上的勇敢最高的象征）。

王室在战争中发挥了重要的象征性作用，在闪电战中他们也不愿离开伦敦，而是不知疲倦地访问军队、军需品工厂、船坞和全国各地的医院，社会各阶层都感激皇室成员与人民分享希望、分担恐惧和困苦。

第二次世界大战以轴心国无条件投降而告终。

乔治六世在战后统治时期是伟大的社会变革的时期，开始了国民健康服务。1951 年全国人民汇聚在伦敦举行了“英国节”。

伊丽莎白女王二世是自征服者威廉 1066 年获得英国王位后的第四十任君主（国王或女王）。青少年时的伊丽莎白经历了第二次世界大战和纳粹轰炸机对英国的袭击，那个后来成为女王的女孩想尽自己的一份力量。在她 21 岁生日时，伊丽莎白发表了一次演讲，她发誓要终身帮助大英帝国的子民。她发誓说：“我向你们宣告，我的一生无论是长是短，都将奉献并服务于你们和我们共同所属的伟大的帝国大家庭。”

1947 年 11 月 20 日，伊丽莎白嫁给了爱丁堡公爵菲利普 · 蒙巴顿，希腊王位的继承人。结婚前，菲利普放弃了他的希腊王冠，伊丽莎白的父亲授予他爱丁堡公爵、梅里奥尼思伯爵和格林威治男爵等爵位。

1952 年 2 月，伊丽莎白和菲利普亲王出访肯尼亚时，国王乔治六世去世，伊丽莎白继承王位，她当时 26 岁。她的曾加冕在 1953 年 6 月 2 日举行，首次进行了电视直播。

伊丽莎白二世（全名伊丽莎白 · 亚历山德拉 · 玛丽 · 温莎）是立宪君主，这意味着虽然她是正式的国家元首，实际上国家是由首相领导下的政府运作。女王在英国的头衔全称是伊丽莎白二世，承上帝洪恩，大不列颠及北爱尔兰联合王国与其属土及领地之女皇。她也是英联邦（大英帝国解体后创建的多国机构）元首和英国国教最高领袖。

伊丽莎白二世殿下非常繁忙，自她成为女王以来总是为公众所瞩目，深受英国人民的爱戴。她没有退休和退位的念头，2015 年 9 月，她超过了她的曾祖母维多利亚女王，成为了在位时间最长的英国君主。

*　　　*　　　*　　　*　　　*

第 2 章　英国概况

大不列颠及北爱尔兰联合王国是一个包含有几个国家的国家。居住在这个国家的不仅有英格兰人、苏格兰人、威尔士人和爱尔兰人，还有来自世界各地的移民。了解这个国家多个名称和国旗的形成渊源不仅有助于了解英国的形成历史，还能避免人们对这个人口日益增加的人种混杂的民族和公民身份的不正确称谓。

作为一个岛国，英国多姿多彩的自然地理使其拥有美丽的地貌，北部和西部主要是高地，东部和东南部主要是低地。虽然总体上英国的气候是温和的，但以下的描述仍被认为是真实的，“在任何国家都不能像在英格兰那样可以在一天中体验四季。”

2.1　不列颠诸国及其称谓

人们说到英格兰时，有时意指不列颠、大不列颠，有时指英国、有时指不列颠群岛。

英国的官方名称是“大不列颠及北爱尔兰联合王国”，虽然大多数人只是把它叫做 the United Kingdom 或 the UK。不列颠群岛则包括许多岛屿，甚至有些部分并不属于英国。

在 17 世纪之前，不列颠群岛上有四个国家：英格兰、苏格兰、威尔士和爱尔兰，每一个国家都有自己独立的身份、自己的历史，甚至有自己的语言。根本没有“英国人”这个词，人们或者是英格兰人，或者是苏格兰人、威尔士人和爱尔兰人。

到了 18 世纪末，所有这一切都发生了改变。“英国人”一词首次出现，谱写了歌曲“统治吧，不列颠尼亚！英国国旗也得以形成。

英格兰曾被称为英格拉的国土，即盎格鲁人的国土，他们来自欧洲大陆的德国，在五世纪后期与撒克逊人和朱特人一起开始侵略不列颠。

英格兰是英国最大的国家，占大不列颠南部的三分之二；几乎英国总人口的 84%都居住在英格兰；伦敦是英国最大的城市，既是政府所在地首都，也是英格兰的首府；今天全球数亿人所讲的英语也是起源于英格兰的语言，今天仍然是其主要的母语。

不列颠是英格兰王国和威尔士公国的正式名称。不列颠这个名字可以追溯到罗马时代，人们称英格兰和威尔士为“布列塔尼”（或“大布列塔尼”，以区别于“小布列塔尼”，即法国的布列塔尼半岛）。罗马时期的不列颠省只覆盖现代的英格兰和威尔士地区，现代的苏格兰从未被罗马人最终征服。1536 年的《联合法案》将英格兰和威尔士合并，并于 1543 年都铎时代联合为一个国家。

大不列颠是英格兰王国和苏格兰王国以及威尔士公国的官方名称。这个词初次使用是在 1603 年苏格兰国王詹姆士六世成为英格兰国王詹姆士一世之时。两个独立的王国英格兰和苏格兰被同一位君主统治，但两国都保留着自己的议会。詹姆士一世很想成为大不列颠国王，而且苏格兰人从 1606 年起就被正式称为英国公民。《1707 联合法案》使苏格兰失去了自己的议会和独立，苏格兰成为了一个被称为“大不列颠王国”的新的国家的一部分，只有一个议会的统一王国（苏格兰一直保留其自己的法律系统）。

1801 年的第二次《联合法案》获得通过，爱尔兰加入了大不列颠，创建了另一个新的国家“大不列颠及爱尔兰联合王国”。

经过多年的内战之后，爱尔兰于 1921 年成为共和国，《英爱条约》使爱尔兰南部大部分选择独立的县脱离了英国，6 个北爱尔兰县（北爱尔兰，也称为阿尔斯特）仍然是英国的一部分。1922 年更名为“大不列颠及北爱尔兰联合王国”，于 1927 年被采用，为现在联合王国的正式名称。

简而言之，英格兰和威尔士组成了不列颠；英格兰、苏格兰和威尔士组成大不列颠；大不列颠和北爱尔兰组成了“大不列颠及北爱尔兰联合王国”（简称联合王国）。

不列颠的区域按行政、政治与地域划分为若干个郡。英格兰有 45 个郡，传统上最大的是约克郡。威尔士有 22 个郡，苏格兰有 30 个郡。

英格兰除了划分为郡以外，还划分为九个政区：西南、东南、伦敦、东英格兰、中英格兰西 、中英格兰东、约克郡和亨伯河、西北、和东北。伦敦周边各郡分别为伯克郡、白金汉郡、艾塞克斯郡、赫特福德郡、肯特和萨里郡。

2.2 英国国旗的起源

联盟国旗，俗称联盟杰克，是联合王国的国旗，是英国国旗，是一面包含有三面国旗的旗帜。称之为联盟国旗是因为它象征着联合王国的国家行政联盟。它是由王国的三个国家的国旗组合而成，这三个国家联合成为一个主权国，他们是：英格兰、苏格兰和北爱尔兰。

该米字旗在某些其他英联邦王国也有着官方或半官方的地位，例如，在加拿大是法定的官方旗帜，被称为皇家联盟旗。此外，在一些较小的英国海外领土它被用作官方的标志。前英国属地或领地的一些国家和地区也将米字旗放在其国旗的左上角。

联盟国旗的一个关键组成部分是源自于圣·乔治十字架的英格兰国旗，其图案为白底上的红色十字。公元1194年，英格兰的理察一世提出将圣·乔治十字作为英格兰的国旗。

早期英国国旗的起源可追溯到1606年。英格兰女王伊丽莎白一世1603年去世后，苏格兰国王詹姆士六世继承了王位，成为英格兰的国王詹姆士一世。这只是一个王权的联盟，还不是国家间的联盟，各国仍保留着自己的议会。1604年10月20日，詹姆士宣布自己的新头衔为“大不列颠国王”。随之而来的问题是，国王的船上应该悬挂哪面旗帜呢？苏格兰是由圣·安德鲁勋章旗代表，图案为蓝底上的白色交叉十字（或称圣·安德鲁十字或X形十字）。英格兰水手不喜欢苏格兰的颜色，而苏格兰人又瞧不上圣·乔治十字勋章。

1606年4月12日皇家法令规定了一面代表英格兰和苏格兰之间的皇家联盟的新旗帜，据此，英格兰的国旗和苏格兰的国旗在海上联合使用，从而形成了最初的联合杰克（Jack是James在拉丁文中Jacobus的缩写）。然而，在陆地上，英格兰和苏格兰继续使用各自国家的旧国旗。这面代表不列颠的“米字国旗”1606年首次推出时，仅仅被称为“不列颠国旗”。

由于纹章学的原因，英格兰的红十字被置入苏格兰国旗后，在红十字周围添加了白边框。（纹章的规则要求两种颜色不能相互接触。）

1707年7月28日，安妮女王统治时期，王室便宣告该旗帜为“大不列颠国旗”，陆地和海上都可以使用。皇家海军将英国国旗命名为“The Union”。1801年1月1日，爱尔兰和大不列颠联合，需要有一面带有爱尔兰标志的新国旗。

爱尔兰由圣·帕特里克十字架代表，于是被结合到圣·乔治和圣·安德鲁联盟的旗帜，创造了联邦国旗，使用至今。

圣·帕特里克十字架被插入在圣·安德鲁十字架的四分之一的位置，与爱尔兰旗的斜对角线所占的四分之一相等，纹章学中称之为“交错”。

由于苏格兰比爱尔兰早约 200 年加入联合王国，圣·安德鲁十字被置于靠旗杆最近的顶端四分之一的位置，按照纹章学这是最尊贵的位置，而爱尔兰的十字架在次尊贵的位置，旗飘上端的四分之一处。为了避免爱尔兰十字直接接触苏格兰的蓝色底面，就用爱尔兰十字的白色底域镶了一道白边，苏格兰和爱尔兰的标志就这样并排置于国旗的图案上。虽然今天只有北爱尔兰保留为联合王国的一部分，但是圣·帕特里克十字架仍留在国旗图案中。

总而言之，国旗（联盟杰克）的形成是不列颠诸岛居民在逐步合并在同一个王权统治的结果。联邦旗帜由英格兰、苏格兰和爱尔兰三个守护神的十字架纹章图案组成。（国旗：为米字旗。旗中白边红色正十字代表英格兰守护神圣·乔治，白色交叉十字代表苏格兰守护神圣·安德鲁，红色交叉十字代表爱尔兰守护神圣·帕特里克。此旗是由英格兰的白底红色正十字旗、苏格兰蓝底白色交叉十字旗和爱尔兰白底红色交叉十字旗重叠而成。）

威尔士龙没有出现在联邦国旗上是因为 1601 年第一次创建该国旗时，威尔士早在 13 世纪就已经与英格兰联盟，这就意味着威尔士不是一个独立的王国，而只是一个公国，所以不能包含在国旗中（实际上，1536 年在亨利八世统治下通过了一项联合法案，使威尔士成为了英格兰的一个省）。2007 年 11 月，一位叫伊恩·卢卡斯的威尔士议员曾经质问议会为什么威尔士不能在国旗中表现。假如威尔士的标志也在国旗中表现的话，这该是一面什么样的旗帜呢？下面便是伊恩·卢卡斯的版本。目前，代表联合王国的几个国家仍然团结在一面国旗之下，至于能维持多久，谁也说不准。即使是现在，每一个组成联合王国的国家都在为自己的独立而战斗，苏格兰人在爱丁堡有自己的议会，威尔士人在卡迪夫有自己的国民大会。

联邦国旗会不会被四面独立的旗帜所取代，或者所有的旗帜以及国旗都将会被别的旗帜所取代呢？只有时间能告诉我们。

2.3　英国的人口结构及其民族认同

英国的人口被认为是经历了“人口转变”的范例，即从工业前高出生率和高死亡率人口的缓慢增长，经过了死亡率下降人口较快增长的阶段后，又进入到一个低出生率和低死亡率的人口较慢增长阶段。这种通过“自然变化”的人口增长在过去的 20 年里一直伴随着国际移民到英国的净增长而增长。

2014 年中期的人口统计显示英国人口为 6460 万。英格兰的人口为 5430 万，占英国总人口的 84%。其后依次是苏格兰的 530 万（英国总人口的 8%），威尔士的 310 万（或占英国总人口的 5%），和北爱尔兰的 180 万（英国总人口的 3%）。

2001 年和 2011 年之间英国的人口增加了 420 万。英国国家统计局（ONS）预计，2011 年到 2035 年英国的人口将增加到 7300 多万，平均年增长率为 0.6%。

英国人口增长的主要原因是日益增加的移民。自1945年以来，大量移民依据《英国国籍法》涌入了英国，特别是来自爱尔兰共和国和大英帝国的殖民地和属地，如印度、孟加拉国、巴基斯坦、加勒比海地区、南非、肯尼亚和中国香港的移民。其他移民或者是依据1951年《联合国难民公约》来寻求庇护的难民，或者是来自欧盟成员国的公民，他们要行使《欧洲联盟四大自由》之一所赋予他们的权利。

2001年和2011年的人口普查显示，其间所增加的人口大约70%是在国外出生的移民。有750万人（当时总人口的11.9%）是在国外出生，虽然人口普查并没有显示他们的移民身份或打算逗留多长时间。

2013年4月到2014年4月共有56万名移民抵达英国，包括8.1万名英国公民和21.4名万来自欧盟其他地区的公民，涌入人数最多的国家是：中国、印度、波兰、美国和澳大利亚。获得英国公民身份的最大群体分别来自印度、巴基斯坦、索马里和菲律宾。

为了能在2011年4月实施永久的上限之前阻止预期申请入籍的高峰，2010年6月，英国的新保守党和自由民主党联合政府对那些从欧盟以外进入英国的移民设置了2.41万的临时上限。

隶属英国内务部的边境管理局规定，所有欲在英国居留的个人都应该通过学习英语和了解英国历史、文化及传统来展示他们的贡献能力。任何申请入籍或永久居留的人都必须通过正式的《新英国入籍考试》。

2011年人口普查显示，英国的人种构成是：白人87.1%，亚洲人7%，黑人3%，混血人2%，以及其他种族0.9%。

在英国，国籍认同与公民身份并不总是一回事。人们虽然具有不同的国籍可还是被称为英国人。然而，大多数在英国出生的白人尽管是英国公民，却不认为自己是英国人，而更愿意称自己的民族身份为英格兰人、苏格兰人和威尔士人。

2007年《每日电讯报》的YouGov民意调查发现，今天的青少年只有不到三分之一的人本能地认为自己是英国人而不是英格兰人、苏格兰人或威尔士人。但是，如果硬要他们说是否也认为自己是英国人，大多数人还是说是，只有10%被询问的青少年完全拒绝英国身份，他们中的许多都是苏格兰人。

2007年《每日邮报》开展的ICM调查结果显示，大部分苏格兰和英格兰的选民都希望国家分裂。

然而，2014年9月18日，苏格兰人投票支持“苏格兰独立公决”，说“不”的一方获胜，以55.3%票反对独立。

英国政府认为，苏格兰留在英国更好，英国拥有苏格兰也更好。

此外，来到英国的人们也带来了自己的文化和语言，而且也努力保留着自己的文化和语言。例如，英国的官方语言是英语，95%的人口把它作为第一语言。同时，六种地方语言也受到《欧洲区域或少数民族语言宪章》的保护，他们是：苏格兰语、阿尔斯特苏格兰语、威尔士语、康沃尔语、爱尔兰语和苏格兰的盖尔语。伦敦有 250 多种语言在使用，使首都成了世界上语言最具多元化的城市。

总之，在英国的每一个角落都可以看到来自所有文化和种族的人，每个人都以他/她自己的方式为把英国建设成今天这样做出了贡献。

2.4　英国的地貌和气候

英国是位于欧洲西北部一个岛国，紧靠四大海洋：北依英吉利海峡；东濒北海；西临爱尔兰海和大西洋。

英国的总面积约为 24.5 万平方公里（9.46 万平方英里），包括大不列颠岛，（北）爱尔兰岛东北部的六分之一和许多较小的岛屿。

联合王国中最大的国家是英格兰，面积为 130439 平方公里（50000 平方英里），占联合王国总面积的一半以上；第二大是苏格兰，占地 78772 平方公里（30410 平方英里），约为联合王国面积的三分之一；威尔士和北爱尔兰的要小得多，分别占地 20758 平方公里和 14160 平方公里（8010 平方公里和 5470 平方英里）。

联合王国的海岸线约 12429 公里。海岸线的巨大凹进使得英国所有地方离潮汐水域都不超过 125 公里。

联合王国的地形千姿百态，从苏格兰的格兰扁山脉到英格兰位于或低于海平面的低地沼泽。联合王国大部分国土是平缓起伏的丘陵与高地，如英格兰西南部的达特姆尔高原和北爱尔兰的莫恩（马伦）山脉。

英格兰的地形大多是低地。高地包括湖区、奔宁山脉，埃克斯穆尔高地和达特姆尔高原。低地通常是连绵的低矮山丘，常常是白土构成。

苏格兰和威尔士是联合王国山最多的地区，十个最高的山峰都在苏格兰境内，其中本尼维斯山为联合王国最高峰，海拔 1343 米（4406 英尺）。

苏格兰的高地边界断层从海伦斯堡横穿苏格兰大陆延伸到斯通黑文，使得其自然地理显得非常特别。断层线将两个明显不同的区域分离，北部和西部为高地，而南部和东部为低地。

威尔士大部分是山地，虽然南部没有北部和中部的山多。

爱尔兰的主要地理特征是其低中平原被海岸山脉所环抱，最高的山峰是卡朗图厄尔山，海拔 1041 米（3415 英尺）。

联合王国最大的湖泊讷湖（内伊湖）在北爱尔兰，面积为 396 平方公里（153 平方英里）。其他主要湖泊包括英格兰湖区的温德米尔湖和苏格兰的罗蒙湖。苏格兰的另一个湖泊是尼斯湖，因在湖中出现传说中的水怪“尼斯”而闻名。英国最深的湖是位于苏格兰高地的莫勒湖，最深处达310米（1017英尺）。

作为一个相对较小的岛国，英国的河流都不是很长，最长的河流塞文河也只有220英里（354公里）长，它起源于威尔士，流入英国布里斯托尔附近的大西洋，也是英格兰和威尔士水流量最大的河流。当然英国最有名的河流还是流经牛津和伦敦的泰晤士河。泰晤士河是英格兰境内最长的河，全长215英里（346公里）。英格兰的其他主要河流包括特伦特和默西河，排出英格兰中部大部分地区的雨水。

由于是四面环海的岛国，联合王国的气候总的来说还算温和，但是也会出现明显的局部变化，特别是因海拔和离海岸距离所引起的变化。一般来说，南方比北方暖和，西部比东北多雨/潮湿。由于（墨西哥）湾流暖化的影响，联合王国比其他在相似纬度的地区明显要暖和一些，比如纽芬兰。

7月和8月通常是最热的月份，但也是雨水最多的时候。在沿海地区，2月通常是最冷的月份，但在内陆很难区分1月和2月哪个是最冷的月份。

湖区是英格兰最潮湿的地区，每年的降水量平均是130英寸（330厘米）。西部和北部丘陵地带的降雨量约40英寸（102厘米），而东海岸则大约20英寸（51厘米）。

6月、7月和8月（白昼最长的月份），各地区平均每天日照的时间也不同，苏格兰北部为5个小时，怀特岛是8个小时。

白昼最短的月份（11月、12月和1月）日照最少，苏格兰北部平均每天1个小时，英格兰南部海岸一天2个小时。

在联合王国旅行最好的月份可能是6月、9月和10月，一般来说这几个月的温度最适宜而且还少雨。联合王国阳光最充足的地方是英格兰南部海岸。

* * * * *

第3章　英国的政治和法律体系

英国是多党制的政治制度。各大政党都在议会中占有席位，并在全国各地推进其目标。

英国是一个单一的民主政体。在君主立宪制的框架内，君主为国家元首，首相为政府首脑。行政管理权由君主女王伊丽莎白二世通过女王陛下的政府和地方国家机关（苏格兰政府、威尔士议会政府和北爱尔兰政府）行使；立法权属于联合王国议会的两院——下议院和上议院，以及苏格兰议会、威尔士议会和北爱尔兰议会；司法机关独立于行政机关和立法机关；最高法院为联合王国最高法院。英格兰和威尔士、北爱尔兰和苏格兰都有各自的法律体系及其独特的历史和起源。

3.1　政府体系

英国具有一个君主立宪、议会民主和单一制的政府体系。“女王陛下政府”通常用来指称英国政府，即大不列颠及北爱尔兰联合王国的中央政府。

英国的君主立宪是指君主（伊丽莎白女王二世）为国家元首，但权力有限。女王只是象征性的统治者，实际上权力属于议会。

议会民主的基本原则是：在伦敦的下议院议会成员（议员）在大选中由人民选举，政府直接对议会负责，下议院可以随时通过“不信任”投票解散政府。

英国的单一制政府即中央集权制的政府。虽然有些权力已下放给苏格兰、威尔士及北爱尔兰，然而，中央政府仍保留负责所有没有被下放的政策，其中包括外交、国防、社会保障、宏观经济管理与贸易等。英格兰是英国唯一没有自己的议会和政府的王国，所有关于英格兰的问题都由来自英国各地的议员所组成的中央政府决定。

英国宪法的一个重要原则是政府向议会负责，议会对女王负责，至少在理论上如此。这就是所谓的责任政府制。

女王陛下的政府由三部分组成：君主、议会和内阁。英国政府通常由在下议院占议员人数最多的政党的组成，该党领袖由女王任命为首相，然后新首相从议会中挑选一个团队与他一起管理国家。政府负责制定和实施政策及起草法律条文，亦称为行政机关。

英国议会是由所有议会成员组成，是英国具有“绝对主权”的最高立法机关。换言之，议会是政治家（议员）们为治理英国制定法律和做出决策的地方（苏格兰、威尔士和北爱尔兰的某些问题现在由各自的国会和议会处理）。英国议会的职责是检查和审查政府的工作、讨论和批准新的法律，亦称为立法机关。

议会由君主、上议院和下议院三部分组成。现任君主女王伊丽莎白二世承担着一系列的重要职责，如召集和解散议会，御准由英国议会、苏格兰议会、威尔士国民议会或北爱尔兰议会通过的立法。

女王正式任命重要官员，包括首相和其他政府部长、法官、武装部队的军官、州长/总督、外交官、主教以及其他一些资深英国教会的神职人员。她还授予爵位、勋章及其他荣誉。在有人被误判有罪的情况下，也由她出面赦免。

在国际事务中，女王有权宣战和媾和、缔结条约和接管或放弃领土。

女王召集枢密院会议、谒见英国海内外的部长和官员、接受内阁对所做决定的汇报、审阅并签署政府文件。

英国议会的上议院（the Upper House），其成员有的是继承家族头衔，有的是因在某个领域的出色成就而被赋予了头衔。上议院的成员分神职议员和非神职议员。

上议院的主要工作是“复核”新的法律，确保他们是公平可行的。凡是下议院通过的法案都需经上议院仔细检查和修改。虽然它无法阻止法案成为法律，但在某些有限的情况下，它可以延迟法案并迫使下议院重新考虑他们的决定。

英国议会的下议院（the Lower House），是讨论政策和制定法律的最重要的地方。下议院成员即是国会议员（MP）。每个议员代表英国650选区之一，并且是某个政党的成员，例如新工党或保守党。

下议院的职能是制定法律、检查政府政策和监督行政的财政管理。在法律上，没有下议院的许可政府不能擅自使用任何经费。

首相领导政府、任命各个政府部门的部长。每周首相都要去下议院回答议会成员提出的各种问题。他还与女王每周有一次会晤，她有权利和义务表达她对政府事务的看法。

内阁是英国政治制度的中心委员会和政府的最高决策机构。内阁大臣是政府的最高级别官员，大多数的政府部门均有一位（或更多）内阁大臣。大多数内阁大臣为“国务卿”，虽然有些是传统头衔，如财政大臣和秘书长。

内阁的主要职能是：向议会提交最后决策，对议会的政策行使最终行政权，并划分和调整各行政部门之间的权力。

另外的两个主要政党也有其自己的“影子内阁”，其职责是对政府的政策和行为进行批评，同时也提供可选择的方案。

3.2 主要政党及大选

英国有多个主要政党，都在议会拥有席位，并在全国各地推进自己的目标。

下议院的三个主要政党是：保守党、工党和自由民主党。

保守党成立于1834年，俗称托利党，是中右翼政党，也是英国的执政党。它信奉保守主义与英国统一主义哲学。1912年与自由统一党合并之后，更名为保守与统一党，不过该名称很少使用。截至2014年，该党是下议院中最大的政党，有305名议员，与自由民主党联合执政。

工党常与社会主义有关，促进广泛的社会服务并提升其在社会中的重要角色。它与工会和工人阶级的其他代表具有传统的关系。

传统上工党和保守党是轮流执政。在上院，两党成员分坐在中央通道的两边，一边是执政党，另一边是反对党，其他政党则可以选择其中一边坐下，也可以坐在中间的位置，表明与两个主要政党之一没有联系。自由民主党成立于1998年，是左翼党派，促进政治和社会自由主义。该党反对军事干预外国事务、反对消减社会服务、反对政府过多介入个人事务；它还促进进步的环境政策，并与其他欧盟国家保持着联系。除了这三个主要政党，英国还有各种各样的小政党，其中有些在议会中也拥有席位。

威尔士除了有议会以外，也由几个政党所代表，其中包括威尔士党，该党致力于在英国议会更好地代表威尔士，并促进威尔士独立。作为一个政党，威尔士党认为伦敦管理不好威尔士，并为改善威尔士居民的生活做了大量的工作。

苏格兰的主要政党是苏格兰民族党，正在为苏格兰独立进行游说。这是一个左翼党，认为苏格兰如果能作为一个独立的国家得到欧盟的认可会对苏格兰更有利。苏格兰有其自己的议会做决策。

北爱尔兰有议会代表，其主要政党是北爱尔兰的民主统一党。该党支持北爱尔兰与英国其他地区的联盟，也促进与爱尔兰的合作以及北爱尔兰进步的社会政策。

英国这种多党派的混合确保其各自的意见在议会合理分配，但这种体系有时被批评为缺乏效率，因为它会导致议会冗长的辩论。通常各党派都是互相合作的关系，为实现共同的目标而努力。

英国议会的任期最长为五年。所有下议院的议员均为人民选举产生。议会解散后会举行大选。候选人致力于在特定的地理选区赢得选票。每个选区得票最多者当选为议员。

政党选举委员会注册簿上列有参加英国竞选的各政党的详细资料和名称。依照现行的《选举法》，包括《政党注册法》、2006 年《选举管理法》、和 2000 年《政党、选举与全民公决法》，那些希望参加选举的政党在选票上只能使用所注册的政党名称。那些不属于注册方的候选人可使用“独立”标签，或什么标签都不用。

截至 2011 年 6 月 10 日，选举委员会显示注册政党数目为 419 个，北爱尔兰有 42 个注册的政党。

通常，政府是由占议员席位最多的党派组成，占第二多席位的政党形成女王陛下忠诚的反对党。几乎所有成功的候选人都是某一政党的成员。如果没有哪个政党有绝对多数，政党之间可以寻求结成联盟执政。

例如，1992 次大选之后，最大的政党保守党比其他政党多出 21 个席位，被称为多数，于是胜过其他各党派而形成了政府，其政党领袖约翰少校成为了首相。

1997 年大选后的画面又有所不同：工党以 179 个席位成为了多数党，而其领导人布莱尔则成了首相。在 2010 次大选中，没有一个政党获得足够多的席位而单独形成政府。因此，为了形成政府，双方或更多的政党必须联合。于是保守党与自由民主党结盟组成了新政府。保守党的领袖大卫·卡梅伦为首相，自由民主党的领袖尼克·克莱格则成为了他的副手。

2010 年大选之后，联合政府制定了《2011 议会固定期限法案》，将议会的固定期限定为五年。因此，下一次大选定于 2015 年 5 月 7 日，此后每五年举行一次，均在5月的第一个星期四举行。不过，该法案还规定，如果政府在被投不信任票后14日之内没能组成新的政府，则解散议会，提前选举。同样，如果下议院中有三分之二的国会议员投票要求选举的话，该法案则允许发起选举。联合政府在2015年5月7日的议会选举后结束，这次选举保守党在下议院中获得了330个议席的绝对多数，明显领先于其对手，而其联盟伙伴仅获得8个议席，因而现任总理卡梅伦戴维便能组建一届由占多数的政党单独组成的政府。

3.3 法律体系

由于英国是由以前几个独立国家的政治联盟所创建的国家，其法律体系不是单一的。英国的法律体系分为三种：英格兰法、北爱尔兰法和苏格兰法。

"英格兰法律"是指由英格兰和威尔士法院管理的法律体系，就民事和刑事案件进行裁决。英格兰法律被誉为《普通法》之母，并以其原理为基础。英格兰法律具有其自己的法律原理，与自1189年所产生的民事法律制度截然不同，没有主要的法典编纂，受制于法令，由法官在法庭上对所面对的案例凭借先例和常识运用法规，对有关的法律原则做出解释判断，并做出判决，该判例适用于将来类似的情况（遵循先例、照章办事）。在早期，法院和法官负责修正令状制度以满足日常需要，并应用先例和常识的结合，建立一整套内部一致法。随着议会势力的发展，根据权力分立原则，立法机关逐渐取代法庭立法，所以今天法官只能在某些非常狭窄的领域内创新。

英格兰和威尔士的法院受英格兰和威尔士的高级法院领导，其中包括上诉法院、高等法院（民事案件）和皇家法院（刑事案件）。最高法院是英格兰、威尔士、北爱尔兰处理刑事和民事申诉案件的最高一级法院，它所做的任何决定均可制约同一管辖范围内的其他法院，并对其他司法管辖区产生有说服力的影响。上诉法院可以驳回下级法院——如县法院（民事）和地方法院（刑事）的判决。高等法院也可以撤销政府行政决策和授权立法的司法审查。英国最高法院是受理英格兰和威尔士所有刑事和民事案件（北爱尔兰和苏格兰法律中的民事案件）的最高上诉机构，它于2009年10月从上议院的上诉委员会（通常称为"上议院"）接管了该项职能。

北爱尔兰是普通法体系，由北爱尔兰法院管理，民事和刑事案件最终均可上诉到英国最高法院。因为普通法的规则是在英格兰的统治下被引入爱尔兰王国的，所以北爱尔兰法律和英格兰法律极为相似。然而，两者仍有一些重要的区别。

北爱尔兰的法律渊源是爱尔兰的普通法和成文法。爱尔兰议会成文法，以及联合王国和北爱尔兰成文法，还有后来的威尔士议会法令均在实施。北爱尔兰的法院是以北爱尔兰司法法院为首，由北爱尔兰上诉法院、北爱尔兰最高法院和北爱尔兰皇家法院组成，其下级则是县法院和地方（治安）法院。

苏格兰法是一种基于古罗马法的独特的法律体系。它基于民法原则，具有中世纪普通法的要素。因此，苏格兰是多元或“混合”的法律体系。自 1707 年联合法案颁布，苏格兰与英国其他各国共享同一个立法机构。苏格兰、英格兰和威尔士各自保留从根本上不同的法律制度，但联合法使英格兰法律影响着苏格兰法律，反之亦然。近几年来，苏格兰法律也受依据罗马条约的欧洲法律和苏格兰议会的权威的影响，苏格兰议会可以在其立法权限范围内通过立法（详见苏格兰法 1998）。

首席法院包括负责民事案件的最高民事法院和负责刑事案件的高等刑事法院。英国的最高法院是依据苏格兰法律受理民事案件的最高上诉法院，不需要按常规获得最高民事法院的准许而上诉。郡法院处理大多数民事和刑事案件，包括与陪审团一起进行刑事审判，被称为执行官法庭，或者只有一个执行官，没有陪审团，被称为简易法庭。郡法院为地方法院提供由六个辖区组成的 49 个治安法院的服务。苏格兰的法律体系的独特之处在于其对刑事审判判决有三种可能：“有罪”、“无罪”和“证据不足”。而“无罪”和“证据不足”则不可能再审，而是宣判无罪释放。

虽然英格兰和威尔士、北爱尔兰、苏格兰在普通法中的细则与公正方面存在分歧，虽然北爱尔兰、苏格兰、威尔士和伦敦均有某些领域的立法权限下放，但仍有大量本质性的法律适用于整个英国。

英国的宪法是构成其政治的法律和原则的总和。它涉及个人与国家的关系，以及立法机关、行政机关和司法机关的运作。与许多其他国家不同的是，英国没有单一的宪法文件。有时被描述为“不成文的”宪法。英国宪法的大部分都是体现在书面文件中、在成文法中、在法院判决、在权威的著作和条约中。宪法有其他不成文的来源，包括宪法惯例等。

*　　*　　*　　*　　*

第 4 章　宗教信仰

宗教对英国人的生活有着重大的影响。人们可以自由选择并遵循自己的宗教信仰。英国有 170 多个不同的宗教，其宗教构成是多元化、复杂的，融合了多种不同文化。在过去的 1400 年间，基督教以不同的形式统治着英国，对英国的政治和社会生活产生了巨大的影响。

直到今天，基督教仍然是英国的主要宗教，按教徒人数计算，排在基督教之后的依次是伊斯兰教、印度教、锡克教、犹太教和佛教。2011 年英国人口普查结果显示越来越多的英国人不再信教，而且越来越多的人并不看好宗教，有 79%的人认为宗教是世界上许多痛苦和冲突的原因之一。从 20 世纪中期开始，定期去教堂的英国人数一直在下降，越来越多的人开始拒绝信教。

4.1 英国宗教史

在罗马统治英国之前，英国有多种形式的祭祀和宗教活动，人们对这些宗教的具体情况了解甚少。罗马统治时期，基督教被传入英格兰、威尔士和苏格兰南部，自此，基督教开始了在英国长达 1400 多年的宗教统治。

据记载，基督教最早出现在英格兰是在公元 2 世纪末，最初可能是由商人和士兵间接传入英格兰的。那时，英格兰和威尔士在罗马人的统治之下，而本土凯尔特人是多神论者（信奉多个神）。直到公元 4 世纪基督教才在英格兰变得普遍起来。

公元 407 年，最后一批罗马士兵离开英国，在接下来的几十年里，罗马文明逐渐崩溃。公元 5、6 世纪，来自德国和丹麦的撒克逊人、盎格鲁人和朱特人入侵英格兰南部和东部，并逐渐征服了英格兰大部分地区。他们传入了自己的日耳曼宗教。公元 7 世纪，基督教再次由罗马天主教徒和爱尔兰、苏格兰传教士传入英国。

到了中世纪宗教成为人们日常生活的重要组成部分。许多人一辈子都虔诚地相信身边存在一个精神世界，而且他们死后将会去天堂或地狱。那时候所有人周日都要做弥撒，而所用的拉丁语普通人根本听不懂。天主教为人们提供婴儿洗礼、婚配、忏悔、临终的圣事礼仪和葬礼等宗教活动并支配着人们的思想。那时修道院和修女院会照顾老弱病人、向旅客提供住宿、施舍穷人，有时还替人看管钱财。很多平民不识字，而僧侣们基本都会读书写字，所以，他们也担负着抄写书籍文献和教授孩子的任务，而且修道院通常配有图书馆。那时的教会节日和圣徒纪念日被称作“神圣的日子”，这时候人们不必工作。此外，教会在政府中也扮演着重要的角色，如，主教是上议院成员，战时可以为国王召集军队。

随着早期现代时期的开始，人们看待生活和周围世界的方式开始发生改变。有些人开始质疑那些传统的宗教信仰。比如，天主教会向人们发售“特赦券”，宣称持券可以获取死后进入天堂的机会。而有些人认为这只是教会赚钱的一种方式。这些导致了宗教冲突，许多人因为这些反天主教的言论被处死。1517 年，德国修士马丁·路德抗议天主教会，并在西欧掀起了一股改革天主教会、创立新教的宗教改革浪潮。新教徒主张简单实在的形式来信奉上帝，反对铺张华丽的教堂和聚敛钱财。他们认为教徒个人可以直接与上帝相通，不必由神父做中介。而天主教则认为必须维护教会的神圣才能让人更接近上帝。新教与天主教在教会礼仪、祷告和圣餐仪式上也有区别。那时，新教在英国虽然受到压制，但新教思想仍然在蔓延。

16 世纪，英国与罗马天主教决裂，并开始了一段时期的宗教冲突。1534 年，由于罗马教廷拒绝了亨利八世与第一任妻子离婚的请求，亨利八世与罗马教皇决裂并创建了英国国教（圣公会），成为英国国教的最高领袖。1539 年，亨利八世下令翻译英文版《圣经》。1545 年，英语开始取代拉丁语，在教堂仪式中使用起来。在亨利八世的女儿玛丽一世统治时期，她恢复了天主教的地位并烧死了大量新教徒。1558 年，伊丽莎白成为女王。她重新确立了英国国教的地位，自此，英国国教的官方地位一直延续至今。

17 世纪早期，国王与议会之间就宗教问题冲突不断。1642 年，保皇派与议会矛盾激化，英国内战爆发了，随后英国出现了许多独立教派，议会也对这些教派进行制裁。1685 年，詹姆士二世成为英格兰和苏格兰国王，他试图强迫人们遵从他的天主教信仰，使英国成为罗马天主教国家。詹姆士对新教徒的迫害使他非常不得人心。1688 年，詹姆士被迫退位，随后 1689 年颁布的《权利法案》规定天主教徒不得继承英国王位，且国王或女王不得与天主教徒结婚。

18 世纪早期，人们不再热衷于宗教，这一时期是理性主义时期，教会开始沉寂。这一状况到了 18 世纪中期才有所改变。18 世纪后期，英国的宗教热情又开始点燃。

19 世纪早期，宗教复兴仍在继续，英国国教恢复活力，一些新的教派也出现了。在整个维多利亚时代，宗教成为很多人生活的重要组成部分。那时英国新教非常强大，大多数民众是英国圣公会、长老会的成员，除此之外也有一些天主教徒和渐渐增多的非国教徒，如贵格会和卫理公会。普通人的生活常常是围绕唱诗班和主日学校集会进行的。许多雇主要求员工去教堂。宗教使许多 19 世纪杰出的社会改革家深受启发，英国的新教传教士也在全世界布道。这一时期的科技、政治、神学领域也有很大的发展，如出现了达尔文主义、马克思主义与神学的发展。宗教极大地影响着人们的生活，但同时人们对基督教的疑虑也越来越多。

到了 20 世纪，宗教的重要性已经在许多英国人心里下降了。尽管一些重大的政治活动与宗教有关，但正规的基督教信徒人数开始下降，很多人已经不再信仰上帝。到了 20 世纪末，只有一小部分英国人按时去教堂。此外，自 20 世纪 20 年代开始的移民潮也促使伊斯兰教、印度教、锡克教和佛教等国外宗教在英国得以发展。

现在，从很多方面看来，英国已经成为一个“后基督教”社会，英国社会变得更加自由、世俗和物质化。

4.2 英国国教会

英国有两大国教，即国家法律上承认的官方教会，分别是英格兰圣公会和苏格兰长老会。

英格兰圣公会也称英国国教会或安立甘教会，是英格兰的国家教会，它分为南北两大教省，即南部的坎特伯雷教省和北部的约克教省，分别由坎特伯雷大主教和约克大主教管辖。每个周日，参加英国国教会礼拜的教众人数达到百万以上，使之成为英国最大的基督教教派。

英国国教会由早期的教会发展而来，但它隶属安立甘宗并与政府联系起来是从英国的宗教改革开始的。16 世纪 30 年代，亨利八世与罗马教皇决裂，创建了英国国教。那时，亨利的第一任王后凯瑟琳只生了一位公主，亨利迫切地希望有一个男性继承人，他以凯瑟琳是兄长的遗孀为由，提出是婚姻无效的。但是他向罗马教皇提出的离婚请求受到拒绝。1534 年，在几次争取无果后，亨利先后颁布了《继承法案》和《至尊法案》，宣布国王“为英国国教至高无上的领袖”，并且英国国教成为官方教会。

英国国教会作为国教，意味着君主是英国国教的最高领袖；国教要履行一些官方职能；教会与国家紧密相连。现在，英国君主仍然是国教的“信仰捍卫者”，国王或女王会（根据首相的建议）任命大主教、主教和高级神职人员；每五年正式召开一次圣公会主议会；在加冕仪式上发誓捍卫英国国教的信仰。

英国国教会也会参与英国的立法。26 位主教（包括两位大主教）作为上议院神职人员在上议院中占有席位，旨在将宗教信仰带到世俗的法律程序中。然而，在英国这样一个越来越呈现出多元文化的社会中，有人开始质疑将宗教信仰融入法律程序这一职责是否一定要由国教主教来履行呢？

英国国教会也要履行公民的职责。主教和神父负责主持皇室婚礼和葬礼、纪念仪式、悼念仪式以及君主加冕等重大仪式。在发生类似海湾战争或一些重大灾难事件后，国教会会感召全国人民一起哀悼。近年来，英国国教会已经意识到英国的宗教信仰情况发生了改变，其他的一些教派也参与到这样的活动中来。

从 18 世纪至今，英国国教会一直面临着许多的挑战：

- 由英国社会变化带来的挑战，如人口增长、城市化发展，以及英国已经越来越成为一个多元文化、多种信仰融合的社会。
- 教会履行职责面临着挑战。当今社会已经变得越来越物质化，人们对上帝的信仰和对宗教的关注不再需要通过教会来维系。
- 国教会无法提供足够多训练有素的神职人员，也没有足够的神父能履行教会的责任。
- 国教会仍需努力发展与其他教派之间的关系，克服长期以来的分歧，一起为实现“信仰里完全可目睹的联合”而努力。

4.3　宗教与英国文化

基督教对西方文化的价值观、信仰和实践有着巨大而深远的影响，在今天的发达社会中，基督教的影响也是根深蒂固的。如今，英国在许多方面都是一个世俗化的国家，但其民族文化中的基督教传统可能比我们平时注意到的那些还要多。要想将这些宗教传统移除可不像把葡萄干从水果蛋糕中挑出来那样简单，那可能会像从巧克力蛋糕中分离出巧克力一样的难。

基督教植根于英国文化中，影响着社会生活的方方面面，如人们的饮食起居、婚丧嫁娶、文学作品、大众传媒、价值取向、语言和风俗习惯等。所以我们很容易在有着基督教传统的英国社会中发现这样一些现象：

节日与日历

我们现在所用的星期制是带有宗教色彩的，即，一周七天，每周休一日。一周中的每一天和一年中的每个月都是以神的名字来命名。我们现行的公元纪年法是从耶稣出生的那一年开始算起。“假期”的概念也是由古老的“宗教节日”这一概念演变而来。

英国大多数周年庆典都起源于宗教。一些重要的传统节日就是基督教节日。例如，圣诞节是为了庆祝耶稣诞生。复活节是为了纪念耶稣复活。受难日是纪念耶稣的受难和死亡。情人节最初是用来纪念早期的基督教圣徒圣瓦伦丁。在盖伊·福克斯之夜，人们会点燃篝火，把危害国家安全的天主教极端分子盖伊·福克斯的人物模型付之一炬。英国的母亲节定在“四月斋”中期，关于它的起源有一个说法是，母亲节是为了纪念人们去当地“母教会”（mother church）或大教堂参加仪式。新年这一节日虽然并非起源于宗教，但“新年的决心”却反映了清教徒追求精神进步的传统。

英国学校的学期是按圣诞节和复活节进行划分的，在一些具有悠久历史和传统的大学里，学期的命名也具有宗教色彩。比如，牛津大学每一学年被划分为三个学期：“米迦勒学期（秋季学期）”、“希拉里学期（春季学期）”、“圣三一学期（夏季学期）”，它们分别用来纪念《圣经》中的天使长圣·米迦勒、普瓦捷的希拉里和神的形而上体系。圣安德鲁斯大学每学年被划分为圣马丁和圣烛两个学期。杜伦大学则包括米迦勒学期、主显节学期和复活节学期三个学期。

语言和文学

基督教和圣经对英语语言和文学有着巨大的影响。英语中的许多词和短语就来自圣经。比如，大多数表示咒骂或温和的感叹如果不与身体功能或器官有关，就与宗教有关。有很多明显的例子，如，我的天哪、看在上帝的份上、（用以加强语气或咒骂的）究竟、（表示惊讶或感叹的）天哪、（表示厌烦的）该死的。也有一些的不太明显的，如，“见鬼”是指地狱，“（表示烦恼或吃惊的）究竟、到底”是指魔鬼，“天哪”是指神，“（表示惊讶或厌烦的）哎哟”是指上帝的真理。还有一些短语虽然不是源自圣经，但显然也与宗教有关，如，唱同一个调子（在公开场合口径一致）、向皈依者布道（对已经有信念者做宣传）、流行偶像、意外的好运、作出牺牲、严厉惩罚。

在谈到英国文学时，很少有人会否认基督教的影响和地位。英国作家在几个世纪以来一直受到圣经的影响，如乔叟、莎士比亚、弥尔顿、布莱克、爱略特等。基督教的核心问题是人的本质、人的环境和人一生之旅的目的地，这些也都是英国文学关注的问题。在基督教经典和英国文学作品中，对这三个问题进行了反复的讨论。

运动

足球本身也许就是一种宗教，从球迷的狂热和崇拜、比赛特定的仪式、统一的服装和完善的组织结构就可以看出来。但是，足球也有一些基督教传统的影子。如，球员划十字并手指向天做出“上帝保佑”的手势，或是双手合十祈祷不要被裁判记名警告或罚下场。

同时，球迷们会高唱赞歌，比如有时会在决赛唱原版的“Abide With Me（与主同行）”，但更多的会唱一些改编的歌曲，如用 Amazing Grace（奇异恩典）的曲调唱“three-nil”、用 The Lord of the Dance（王者之舞）的曲调唱“We are the famous CFC（我们是举世闻名的切尔西）”，或用 Bread of Heaven 的曲调唱“You’re not singing any more”。

食物和饮料

有一些英国品牌和产品的名字是取自宗教，这样做可能有一些历史原因，或仅仅只是因为这样的名字比较好听。比如，Angel Delight（一种英国产的传统甜品粉）、devil’ food cake（魔鬼蛋糕）、hot cross buns（复活节的十字面包）。

有一些酒名能体现与圣职的传统联系，如 Bishops Finger（英国啤酒名）、Blue Nun（德国葡萄酒名）和 Abbot Ale（英式啤酒名）等。

民间传说

一些英国的迷信传说可能有其宗教根源。在中世纪的传说中，撒旦喜欢幻化成黑猫的形态，并且很讨厌盐，因为盐象征着圣洁。所以相传看见黑猫会给人们带来灾难，而往人的肩膀上撒盐就会驱灾辟邪。另外，人们对数字 13 的恐惧可能是由于在“最后的晚餐”中，背叛耶稣的犹大就是第 13 个人。至今在英国，如果有人打喷嚏时，人们往往也要送上祝福。

音乐

在古典音乐中，弥撒曲、清唱剧和神圣的康塔塔具有重要的地位，这些宗教音乐看起来与流行音乐榜似乎完全搭不上边。然而事实上，宗教主题总是一再以某种形式出现在许多最受尊敬和/或最畅销的音乐作品中，比如从有猫王埃尔维斯和玛利亚·凯莉的福音歌、鲍勃·马利和范·莫里森的赞歌里就可以看得出来。

*　　　　*　　　　*　　　　*　　　　*

第 5 章　经济和社会福利

英国是世界上第一个工业化国家，18 世纪后期，英国率先完成工业革命，成为世界经济的领头人。从 19 世纪初到 70 年代的几十年间，英国在世界工业、贸易、金融和海运等方面处于垄断地位，享有“世界工厂”的美誉。从 19 世纪末期开始，其他国家相继完成工业化过渡，第二次世界大战结束后，英国彻底失去了经济霸主的地位。

如今，英国虽然失去了百年前的辉煌，但它仍是一个在世界范围内拥有强大政治影响力，具有举足轻重地位的经济、文化、军事和科技强国。2013 年，英国的 GDP 排名居世界第六、欧洲第三，仅次于德国和法国。其首都伦敦是全球最大的金融中心和最为领先的城市之一，GDP 水平在欧洲城市中居第一位。英国的货币英镑是仅次于美元和欧元的世界第三大储备货币。

5.1　国内经济和对外贸易

英国是一个高度发达的资本主义国家，也是一个重要的贸易实体、经济强国和金融中心，具有很大的国际影响力。2013 年，英国的 GDP 总量为 2.65 万亿，是世界第六大经济体，也是欧盟最强的经济体之一。

英国的经济发展呈现出明显的地区差异，英格兰东南部和苏格兰北部是人均收入最高的地区，首都伦敦的 GDP 水平居欧洲之首。英国经济主要由服务业（2013 年 GDP：77.8%）、工业（21.5%）和农业（0.7%）构成。

农业　英国是现代农业的先驱，他们领先在农业中引进科学和机械，具有精耕细作、高度机械化、高效率等特点。目前，英国的农业年产值约为80亿英镑，农业占国内生产总值的比重不到1%。从事农业生产的人数约45万，不到总就业人数的2%，能供应全国近60%的粮食需求，其余的40%依靠进口。英国具备很多发展农业的良好条件，如气候温和，雨量充沛、农民技术水平高、农业技术发达、耕地土壤肥沃，还有来自欧盟的农业补贴等。

英国农用土地面积约为1860万公顷，占国土面积的73%，其中近2/3用于畜牧业，1/3用于种植业。畜牧业是英国农业的重要产业，农民饲养家禽来获取肉类、羊毛、鸡蛋和鲜奶等。在英国，农民主要饲养牛、羊、鸡和猪等牲畜，英国是欧洲第二大家禽出口国，仅次于法国。在畜牧业的产值结构中，肉牛、鲜奶和奶制品的产值占畜牧业产值的一半以上。

英国的种植业主要集中在英格兰的南部和中部，以及苏格兰的东部。主要的农作物有小麦、大麦和燕麦，其次还有马铃薯、甜菜、油料作物、饲料作物和园艺作物等。

工业 英国是一个工业化国家，尽管其重工业在20世纪已经逐渐衰落，但这种衰落是相对的，英国仍然是一个工业强国，它的制造业仍然比较出色，占全国总产值的10%以上，从业人员近250万人。

汽车行业是英国经济和工业出口的重要部分。英国的汽车工业开始于19世纪末期，到20世纪50年代，英国已经成为世界上第二大汽车制造国和出口国。然而接下来的几十年里英国汽车业发展缓慢。从20世纪80年代开始英国的汽车品牌陆续被外国公司收购，其中最有代表性的包括：Mini和劳斯莱斯（宝马）、捷豹和路虎（印度塔塔）、宾利（大众）等。尽管英国所有大销量的汽车品牌都已经被外国公司收购，但汽车行业仍然是英国经济和工业出口的重要部分。除了有众多的汽车制造企业外，英国还有大量的零部件生产商，完备的汽车零售及维修行业。

英国的航空航天业具有较高的研发和制造水平，占有全球13%的市场份额，全球排名第二，仅次于美国。英国的航天航空工业为世界航空业做出了杰出贡献。

化学及制药是英国制造业的另一个重要基础。其中，制药企业尤其成功，一些国际知名的制药公司，如葛兰素史克和阿斯利康，都将总部及主要的研发和制造工厂设在英国。

英国制造业的其他重要部分还包括电子工业、纺织业、食品、饮料、烟草、造纸、印刷和出版业等。英国一些著名的制造企业有联合利华集团、吉百利食品集团、英美烟草集团、皇家烟草集团、哈珀柯林斯出版集团、巴宝莉时装集团、锐步服装集团以及茵宝服装集团等。

英国拥有大量的煤、天然气、和石油储备，但其石油和天然气储量也在下降，2005英国成为能源净进口国。

服务业 服务业是英国经济的支柱产业，约占英国GDP的3/4，从业人数近

2100 万人，占劳动力总数的 75%。服务业主要包括银行业、保险业、旅游和商业服务等，这些都是促进英国经济增长的关键。

金融服务业是英国经济的支柱产业之一，不仅涵盖银行、保险、证券、外汇、基金、衍生产品等金融领域的方方面面，而且其发展规模和国际化程度均居世界前列。伦敦是世界最大的金融中心之一，也是全球重要的金融交易市场。除伦敦外，利兹、爱丁堡、曼彻斯特、伯明翰等城市也拥有大片金融服务区。英国的银行业很发达，银行数目之多，居全球首位。英格兰银行是英国的中央银行，它创立于 1694 年，被公认为是现代中央银行的鼻祖。另外汇丰银行、劳埃德银行、苏格兰皇家银行及巴克莱银行等也都是世界著名的银行。英国的保险业居欧洲第一、全球第三，仅次于美国和日本。2013 年 9 月，英国保险协会公布的数据显示，在英国 2640 万户家庭中，购买了终身寿险的有 530 万户，买了定期寿险的有 50 万户。另外，伦敦是世界最大的外汇交易中心，日平均交易额近 5 万亿美元。

英国是旅游业发展最早的国家之一，也是当今全球重要的旅游客源地和目的地，它对英国经济的发展具有重要意义。英国丰富的自然、文化和历史资源，以及便捷的交通服务使其具有得天独厚的旅游发展条件。据世界旅游组织统计，2013 年英国游客超过 3120 万人，居世界第八（落后于法国、美国、西班牙、中国、意大利、土耳其和德国），外国游客入境游花费 406 亿美元，而英国游客出境游花费达 526 亿。英国境内游的旺季是法定假日和夏季，其中八月是最火爆的。英国主要的景点集中在伦敦，其中最受游客欢迎的莫过于伦敦塔了。英国其他著名景点还包括大英博物馆、伦敦眼、威斯敏斯特大教堂、大本钟、剑桥城、牛津城、爱丁堡和巨石阵等。

英国的教育、学术研究处于世界领导地位，国际知名学府剑桥大学、牛津大学、帝国理工学院都位于英国，是美国以外全球最重要的教育枢纽。英国每年吸引不少来自世界各地的留学生慕名前来升学，不仅为国家带来丰厚的外汇，也为这个属知识型经济体系的国家吸纳不少人才。

对外贸易　英国是世界第四大贸易国，贸易额占世界贸易总额的 5%以上。由于国内市场需求有限、原材料供应不足，英国经济极其依赖对外贸易，进出口业务是其经济增长的一个关键因素。所以英国对对外贸易和外商投资的限制很少。

英国主要出口机械、汽车、航空设备、电器和电子产品、化工产品和燃料。劳务出口主要有银行业、保险业、证券经纪业、咨询、航运和计算机编程。商品和劳务出口约占国内生产总值的三分之一以上。

英国也是主要的进口国之一。大约 40%的粮食需要进口。自 2005 年以来，英国也成了一个能源净进口国，尤其是石油和煤。另外，英国还通过进口原材料，经过加工生产后，再出口成品赚取外汇。

5.2 社会福利制度

英国的社会福利体系建立已久，作为最早的福利国家，英国建立了一套面向全体公民、“从摇篮到坟墓”的福利制度。

英国社会福利制度的资金来源于国民保险费和税收，政府向国民提供一系列的社会服务，其中最重要的是国民保健制度（NHS）、社会保障制度和个人社会服务。

5.2.1 国民保健制度（NHS）

英国的国民保健制度建立于1948年，旨在向每个居民提供全方位的医疗服务，无论其收入多少。这个制度是一个少有的、真正的社会医疗制度。它的资金来源主要是国民税收，也就是说，由英国政府提供医疗保健服务，由纳税人提供资金。国民保障制度遵循的原则是：建立一套全方位的公共服务体系来帮助个人保持健康。所有的纳税人，包括雇主和雇员都要纳税，不需要卫生服务的成员可以为那些需要的人支付费用。

国民保健制度在很大程度上是一种免费服务。病人不需要就预约和治疗付费（虽然已通过税收支付），而且几乎所有的处方药都是免费提供。一些其他的医疗服务，如家庭医生开的药或一般牙科治疗则是要收费的。

英国的国民保健制度也受到许多的批评，尤其是在21世纪初。由于这一体系规模庞大、名目繁多，又要面向数以百万计的服务对象，现在已经出现了许多问题，主要包括漫长的候诊时间、病人的个性化需求和高昂的运营成本。

5.2.2 社会保障制度

英国的社会保障制度非常健全。居民满16岁就会获得国家保险号，这是以后使用社会保障系统的编号。

英国社会保障制度是用来在经济上保证公民的基本生活需要。这是政府最大的一笔单项支出，每年用于社会保障的经费占政府开支的近三分之一，用于向老年人、病人、残疾人、失业人员、寡妇、抚育幼儿者或低收入者提供经济支持。社会保障的主要内容包括：

国民退休金

国民退休金是支付给达到退休年龄的退休人员，英国现行的退休年龄是男性65岁，女性60岁，到20世纪30年代法定退休年龄将推延至68岁。要获取国民退休金，公民必须在就职期间缴付足够的国民保险金，缴纳保险金的多少将决定他们退休金的数额。

失业津贴

失业津贴是提供给年龄在 18 岁至退休年龄之间的、没有丧失劳动能力且正在积极寻找工作的失业人员。失业津贴同样适用于那些每周工作少于 16 小时的在职人员。故意失业者或因渎职失业者不得申请失业津贴。申请者必须要积极寻找新工作，并且不得无故拒绝新的就业机会。失业津贴支付的数额取决于之前缴纳的国民保险金及个人财富情况。

收入补助金

收入补助金是为低收入者设定，领取人必须年满 16 岁，且每周工作不超过 16 小时。如果有伴侣，则伴侣每周工作不多于 24 小时。

收入补助金取决于个人收入，以及个人拥有的资金或存款额。有存款者领取的补助金数额将有所减少，存款额达到一定数额者不得领取收入补助金。

疾病和伤残津贴

因疾病或残疾而无法工作的人员可以享受多种津贴。比如：

员工因病连续 4 天或更久无法工作者，将由雇主支付法定病假工资，最多持续 28 周。

残疾人士如需要人照料可以获得残疾人生活津贴，这是一项免税福利，津贴数额因残疾程度而异。

如年满 16 岁且每周需要至少 35 个小时照料一名残疾人，则有资格领取伤残照顾者津贴。这是一项应税福利，申领人与受照顾的残疾人不需要是亲属关系，也不需要一起居住。

儿童津贴

儿童津贴是一项很普遍的福利，有未满 16 岁子女的家庭，无论收入如何均可领取。儿童津贴同样适用于正在接受全日制非高等教育的 16 至 19 岁孩子，或年龄在 16 至 17 岁之间，刚结束教育或培训，且已登记某项工作或培训的孩子。一个家庭中长子（女）或独子（女）享受最高额津贴，其他孩子享受低额津贴。

住房津贴

低收入者，不论是否有工作，均有资格获得全部或部分租金的资助。只有工资加上积蓄低于一定水平，才能获取住房津贴。住房津贴由居民所在地政府提供，不得用于缴纳暖气、热水、能源或食物的费用，津贴的数额取决于受益人的工资水平和生活状况。

*　　　　*　　　　*　　　　*　　　　*

第 6 章　英国的教育体系

教育是英国人生活中的一个重要部分。英国有着数百所中小学和大专院校，其中有一些还是世界著名的。

英国的教育权限是下放的，每个国家都在自己政府的领导下有着各自的教育体系，英国政府负责英格兰的教育，苏格兰政府、威尔士政府和北爱尔兰政府则分别负责苏格兰、威尔士和北爱尔兰的教育。

6.1　教育阶段的划分

英国的教育通常分为三个主要阶段：义务教育、继续教育和高等教育。

义务教育是对 5 周岁（北爱尔兰是 4 岁）至 16 周岁的儿童，该年龄段称为义务教育学龄。英格兰把 1997 年之后出生的义务教育或培训延长至 18 周岁。这种全日制教育不一定非在学校进行，越来越多的家长选择在家里教育孩子。

如果家长愿意，也可以让义务教育学龄前的儿童上幼儿园，不过受政府资助的幼儿园数量有限。许多儿童上学前班、日托班、幼儿园或者是一些附属于小学的幼儿班。实际上很多学校都接受提前入学的孩子。

2008 年 9 月，对于所有在教育标准局注册的儿童场所（包括托儿中心，日托所、幼儿园、游戏班以及小学里的幼儿班或基础班），早期基础阶段（0~5 周岁）成为了法定的要求。

全日制学校的第一年称为幼儿班，一年后升入一年级，然后每年升一级，此为标准的国家体系。学校（尤其是较小的学校）也可以按自己的方法安排班级，许多学校都有混龄班，因此，孩子既可以在 9 月份升级，也可以在原来的年纪再读一年。

在英格兰的某些地区，学校不是按初小（4~7 周岁）、中小（7~11 周岁）或者是小学（4~11 周岁）之后是中学（11~16 或 18 周岁）来划分，而是按低年级、中年级和高年级的体系划分，低年级通常是 4 岁或 5 岁至 9 岁的学生，中年级是 9 岁至 13 岁的学生，高年级是 13 岁至 18 岁的学生。

除了按年龄群划分以外，学制也按关键阶段划分，儿童（5~11 周岁）上 7 年小学（1 和 2 关键阶段），大部分学生小学最后一年是六年级，中学的第一年是 7 年级。通常大部分学生在 11 岁时转入最近的中学（第 3 关键阶段），不过在英格兰和威尔士，法律允许家长根据偏好选择别的学校。

在 10 年级的时候学生开始学习《普通中学证书》科目，在英格兰、威尔士和北爱尔兰，一般是 14 岁到 16 岁的学生学习几门中学科目，有些科目也会早点开始，比如数学，英语和科学，这些课程太长，两年内很难完成。在 11 年级结束时（15~16 岁），学生进行结业考试。苏格兰与《普通中学证书》相等的是《标准等级》。

2008 年《教育与技能法案》提高了强制教育的年龄，到 2015 年所有的英国学生必须在学校接受教育和训练至 18 周岁。

高等教育，中学后教育或者是第三级教育是中等教育之后的非强制性的最后正规学习阶段。

英国中学后的资格证书按不同等级界定：1 至 3 级指的是继续教育，4 至 8 级为高等教育，其中的 5 级为基础学位，6 级为学士学位，7 级为硕士学位，8 级为博士学位。

继续教育是非强制性的，可以是高于义务中学教育的任何级别的教育。因此继续教育是为 16 周岁以上的人提供的教育，通常包括大学教育，并且通常意味着为了上大学或开始特定的职业生涯而获取必要的中间衔接的或高一级的资格证书。英国学生想上大学就必须完成继续教育。此种教育通常由继续教育学院、就业学习和成人学习以及社区学习等机构提供。此外，继续教育课程也可以由中学提供，较为普遍的是中学里的六年级（16~19 周岁）。其中包括为 16 岁后的学生所设的课程，类似于某些（也开设学位等级课程的）高等教育院校和某些大学所教的次学位课程。

英国的高等教育有着悠久的历史。牛津大学和剑桥大学可追溯到 12 世纪和 13 世纪，圣安德鲁斯大学、格拉斯哥大学、苏格兰大学、爱丁堡大学和阿伯丁大学从可追溯到 14 世纪和 15 世纪。其余的大学则建立于 19 世纪和 20 世纪。

除了唯一的一所私立大学白金汉大学以外，所有有学位授予权的高校都由国家资助。约 30%的 18 岁至 19 岁的英国学生进入全日制高等教育。英格兰、威尔士和北爱尔兰的学生通常是年满 18 周岁就可以上大学，而苏格兰的学生通常进入 18 周岁（许多人刚刚满 17 周岁）就可以上大学，因此与英格兰、威尔士和北爱尔兰相比，这些学生的课程要多一年。

6.2　学校的种类

英国的学校主要分为公立和独立（私立）两大类。公立是指受政府资助的学校，对学生提供免费教育。大部分是由地方政府创办，对所有四、五岁至十六岁的儿童免费。

所有政府办的公立学校都遵循同样的《国家课程大纲》，其主要宗旨是提升学生的标准，确保所有孩子享受广泛而均衡的教育，直至十六周岁，并且确保全国各地的学校都开同样的课程。《国家课程大纲》指定学生必须学习不同阶段所要求的内容，这一要求与国家测试紧密相连，以检测学生是否达到既定目标。

最普通的公立学校是：社区学校（由地方议会管理，不受商业和宗教影响）、基础学校（在变通方法上比社区学校享有更多的自由）、专科学校（由主管团体管理，独立于地方议会，可以有不同的课程）、综合学校以及文法学校。

综合学校于20世纪60年代引入全英国，是现今英国最受欢迎的中等学校，此类学校录取学生无需考虑学生的学术能力，提供的是通识教育，学生可以学习任何诸如文学之类的学术性科目和类似烹饪这类更具实用性的科目。将近88%的英格兰中学生和威尔士所有的中学生都上的是综合学校。综合学校接受具有各种不同能力的学生，并对所有或大部分11岁到16岁或18岁的学生提供广泛的中等教育。苏格兰所有的学生都上非选择性学校（英国大部分公立教育通常是非选择性的，但有些中产阶层的家长尽量住在最好的学校附近）。

文法学校是选择性的公立学校，其重点放在高级学术科目而非综合学校的更普通的课程，并且期望更多学生都能上大学。这类学校根据学术能力挑选年满11周岁的学生。进入文法学校需在小学最后一年参加一种叫做“11会考”的考试，分数最高的学生便能进入文法学校，而分数不怎么好的则上现代中学。

在北爱尔兰，文法学校与非文法学校的划分仍然很常见，但是在英国其他地方，文法学校现在却很少见。英格兰和威尔士93%的孩子都上公立学校。

独立学校是收费学校，亦称为私立学校和公共学校。他们的经费来源于私立机构和学费，也有一些政府援助。他们不属于国家教育体系，因此，独立于国家资助的公立学校的那些法规和办学条件，但是教育质量和标准却是通过女王陛下教育视察员的巡视得以维护。他们不必遵循《国家课程大纲》，但是大部分学校都会按照公学入学会考或奖学金考试的要求提供课程，并最终帮助学生通过诸如GCSE和A-Levels之类的全国考试。

虽然现在的私立学校主要是走读，但大部分还是要么完全寄宿，要么部分寄宿。法规不允许国际学生上英国的公立学校，他们只得上私立学校。

那些完全在私立学校接受教育的孩子通常在0岁或2周岁和4周岁上幼儿园；3~4岁到7~8岁上私立预科学校；7~8岁到11岁或13岁上私立小学，然后为上公共学校（私立中学）做准备。

“Public school”一词是指一批历史较久、收费较贵而又较独立的提供中等教育的私立学校，尤其是在英格兰，主要为13周岁到18周岁学生而设。然而，苏格兰的教育体系与英国其他地区完全不同，“public school”在苏格兰语和苏格兰人眼里仅仅是由苏格兰国家资助的学校（因为他们为公共所有），媒体更愿意称之为“国家资助学校”，以避免与英语的说法混淆。

大部分私立中学都采用一种叫做“公学入学考试”，女生 11 周岁男生 13 周岁参加该考试。核心课程是英语、数学、科学和人文学科，许多学校也提供现代外语（通常是法语、德语、西班牙语和汉语）、古典语文（拉丁语、希腊语和古典文明）、还有信息技术、音乐、艺术、戏剧、体育。通常白天还有一两种课外活动，常常是在午饭后或放学后，而寄宿学校则将课外活动穿插在白天的课表中，以确保学生获得更多的合理的学术课程进度。有些学校则是以课堂教学为主，有些是将课堂学习与专长（通常是音乐、语言、体育）相混合，还有些学校则借鉴高级中学的做法，让学生跟着专业老师学习专业课。

2011 年英国有 2600 多所私立中学，约 628000 名学生，为英国学生的 6.5%以上，16 周岁以上的学生超过 18%。

相比于公立学校，私立学校达到了更高的学术标准。家长选择缴费让孩子读书，是为了使孩子有更好的机会上好的大学，毕业后获得好一些的工作。最著名的私立中学当属伊顿中学、哈罗中学和温切斯特中学。

2013 年，英格兰高等教育基金会发表了一项研究，在获得一等学位或高级二等学位的学生中，那些上大学前就读于私立中学的学生的比例要大于就读于公立中学的学生。

6.3　在家上学

英国的教育是强制性的，但是上学并不是强制性的，不要求学生一定在学校学习，他们可以在家里学习。

《欧洲人权公约：第一议定书》第二条规定：“任何人都有受教育的权利。在行使与教育和教学相关的任何职能中，国家应尊重父母的权利，以确保教育和教学符合他们自己的宗教和哲学信念。”

1996 年《英国教育法案》第 7 节规定：“每一位义务教育适龄儿童的家长都应使其接受有效的全日制教育：1）要适合其年龄、能力和天分；2）要适合其可能有的任何特殊的教育需求，无论孩子是否定期上学校。”因此，让孩子在家里上学，或者是家庭教育仍然是父母的一项合法的选择，只要他们能提供一个合适的替代学校全日制教育的方式。

英国的家庭教育亦称为“选择性家庭教育”，表示其独立的性质，不是按国家规定执行的那种由地方政府为身体不好的儿童提供在家里接受的教育。选择性家庭教育是用于英国的统称，描述以非学校体系提供的另外一种形式的教育。

在家里接受教育是一种非正式的教育方式，可描述为非学校教育、非正式学习、自然的或自主学习。

家长有权决定他们的孩子从很小的年龄就开始进行家庭教育，所以孩子可能不曾在学校就读。他们还可以在任何一个义务教育阶段结束时选择家庭教育。家长选择在家教育孩子不需要登记或获得当地政府的批准。选择在家教育孩子的父母必须准备承担全部的财政责任，包括承担任何公开考试的费用，不过，也鼓励地方政府在资源许可的情况下给予支持。家长必须提供一个有效的、适合孩子的年龄、能力和才能的全日制教育。

目前对于“全日制”还没有法律上的定义。学校通常每学年 38 周，儿童每周上学 22 至 25 个小时，但这种“联系时间”与选择家庭教育无关，在家里常常是连续的一对一接触，而且教育可能发生在学校正常的“上课时间”以外的时间，教育活动形式多样、灵活机动。对于家庭教育的家长不做以下要求：遵循国家课程、提供广泛而均衡的教育、制定课表、拥有任何特定标准的处所、设置教育过程的时数、有任何具体的证书、提前制定详细计划、遵守学校的时间、天数或学期、讲授正式课程、批改孩子的作业、正式评估学习进展或制定目标、复制学校同龄儿童的社会化、匹配学校规定的特定年龄的标准。然而，如果有要求，地方当局应该在这些方面给家长提供建议和支持。

家长选择在家里接受教育的孩子不需要在主流学校注册。一些家长可能会选择聘请私人教师或其他成年人，以协助他们提供一个合适的教育，但没有要求他们必须这样做。学习可以发生在不同的地点，而不仅仅是在家里。

虽然不要求在家里接受教育的孩子遵循国家课程大纲和统一测试，但在某些方面，也期望能做到合理和到位：1）父母或其他照顾者能花费大量的时间直接参与孩子的教育；2）儿童应获得教育材料、有机会参与体育活动和社会化活动；3）应该有一些证据表明，孩子的个人需求和兴趣得到满足，他们的智力得到了恰当的刺激。

正如上学不是强制性的一样，考试也不是强制性的。在家里接受教育的孩子，不需要先通过 GCSEs and A levels 这些考试就直接进入高等教育或职业教育课程。但是，许多学校和机构在录取或雇佣他们之前也要求提供证明其中等教育水平或大学预科水平的资格证书。为满足这些要求，在家接受教育的学生可自主参加 GCSE or iGCSE（国际普通中等教育证书）考试，也可以选择考 A levels。有些 GCSE 科目要求某个学校的“管理评估”，有的则不要求。iGCSE or A level 证书是没有管理评估的。

家长选择在家里接受教育的理由多种多样，地方当局的主要兴趣应该在于家长教育的适用性，而不是他们这样做的理由。以下是家庭教育的共同原因，但绝不是详尽的：离当地学校路程远、宗教或文化信仰、哲学或意识形态观点、对体制的不满、怕孩子被欺负、(由于特殊原因的短期干预) 孩子不愿意或不能上学、特殊教育需求、以及家长希望与子女的关系更为密切等。

研究结果显示，家长选择退出学校体系的主要原因是怕孩子被欺凌和担心学校不能够满足孩子的个体需求。(BBC News, 23 February 2007)

通常，这些原因是极度的个性化，但是基本上都是考虑了孩子的最佳利益。幸运的是，家庭教育在英国被广泛接受，而且帮助也是随处可得。

随着诸如另类方式教育和家庭学校支持团体的形成，自 20 世纪 70 年代后期以来，保留直接对子女的教育负责的家庭稳步增加，越来越多的父母明显地放弃了传统的教育体系。

6.4　大学学位及其要求

英国的大学（开放大学除外）共享一个本科录取系统，由大学招生服务中心（UCAS）管理。牛津和剑桥（以及医学、牙科和兽医学课程）必须在每年 10 月 15 日前申请入学，其他英国大学则在次年元月 15 日前申请。

英国的每门课程都有其自己的入学要求，且差异很大。大多数学位课程的正式入学要求是两门高级课程成绩达到 E 级或以上，实际上，大多数录取要求都超过这个条件。所以，同一所大学内不同的课程有着不同的要求，而且大学作为一个整体可能要求所有学生都必须满足一定的要求。例如，牛津和剑桥的大学一般要求所有的学生参加一个面试，其他大学则不一定需要。

许多大学现在都采用学分积累与转换方案（CATS），苏格兰所有大学使用苏格兰学分和资格框架（SCQF），更便于课程和机构之间的转换。有些学科，特别是那些竞争激烈的学科或者是能够获得专业资格的学科，在录取学生选课之前还要求学生接受面试。

罗素集团在 2013 年 1 月宣布将建立一个学术委员会，就 A-levels 课程的内容给英国的考试监督机构（资格考试监管办公室）提供建议。

同时，国际学生即使可能没有考试 A-levels，没有在英国的教育体系受过教育，仍然可以上英国的大学，但需要联系某一课程的管理人员，弄清楚需要出具所属国家的何种证明。

英格兰、北爱尔兰和威尔士的标准是第一学位授予荣誉的学士学位，通常是文学学士（BA）或理学学士（BSc）学位。大多数学士学位需要三年才能完成，有一些值得注意的例外，例如医学专业是五年完成。通常，学生可以最初报考一个为期四年的课程，三年之后毕业并获得学士学位。

在苏格兰学习艺术或人文科学的学生的第一个标准学位是艺术学士，或者是艺术硕士（传统上，后者是由古老的苏格兰大学颁发的艺术或人文学科的第一个学位)。标准的自然科学和社会科学的本科学位是理学学士。

一些大学把硕士学位作为第一个学位，在完成综合学习计划（综合硕士学位）后授予。这些学位通常是按学科设置，如工程硕士、物理硕士、数学硕士等等，通常需要四年读完。这些学位总是伴有荣誉。特别是工程硕士，现在已经成为英国顶级大学工程专业的第一个学位，取代了工程专业的老学士学位。

大学本科学历（学士学位和综合硕士学位）可授予“荣誉”（荣誉学士学位）或可能是“普通”或“合格”的学位。基于对学生所完成学业的平均分数的评估，学位的类别可分为：一级、二级上、二级下、三级和普通学位（合格）。

文学硕士和理学硕士之类的硕士学位通常授予给那些至少从事了一年全日制研究生学习的学生，或者是课程学习，或者是涉及研究工作。研究型硕士或文学硕士学位可能只授予涉及创新研究的学生。通常是期望攻读硕士学位的学生已经获得相关学科的荣誉学士学位，这样才有可能在一年内拿到硕士学位。

研究生文凭（GradD，GDip，GDip）通常是研究生毕业证书，虽然有些研究生文凭也涉及本科水平的课程。攻读该文凭一般是获得学士学位之后，以及没有授予荣誉学士学位但获得了成功的奖励的学生。

工商管理硕士学位对于那些寻求企业管理和决策者职位的人具有很高的价值。

博士学位（PhD 或 DPhil）一般授予给那在某一学科背景中的原创性研究贡献了新知识的学生，通常需要三年的全日制学习。因此，在英国从本科读到博士水平一般可能只需七年时间，有时可能是六年，因为硕士学位不总是开始读博的先决条件。这个有别于美国的九年时间，反映出的是不同的教育体系。

有些博士学位，如临床心理学博士（dclinpsy）资格，需要通过特定的职业实践来确认其能力。也有更高的学位——理学博士（DSC）和文学博士（DLitt）通常授予给那些在所从事的学术领域表现出高水平成就的资深学者，例如他们可能在他们的学科领域广泛地发表了研究成果，或者成为了他们领域的教授。

*　　*　　*　　*　　*

第 7 章　英国人的日常生活

当今英国人的生活许多方面都在发生变化，包括人们的价值观和婚姻观、家庭规模、生活成本和出行方式等。然而，人们仍然享受和热爱着一些传统的生活方式，如购物、体育运动和酒吧文化等。

7.1 婚姻和家庭

在英格兰和威尔士，民事婚姻和宗教婚姻形式均被认可为合法，并且对异性和同性婚姻是开放的。

2013 年国会通过了《（同性伴侣）婚姻法案》，使同性婚姻在英格兰和威尔士合法化。同性婚礼开始于 2014 年 3 月 29 日；但是，该法案在 2014 年 3 月 13 日生效。在此之前，英国的同性夫妇在 2005 年就取得了民事伴侣关系，授予的权利与义务与民事婚姻几乎相同。

在北爱尔兰，婚姻被定义为一个男人和一个女人之间的法律关系。同性伴侣于 2005 年 12 月取得民事伙伴关系，并授予与民事婚姻相同的权利和义务。结婚前必须满足相应的居住条件。如果欲结婚的一方当事人受移民控制，则只能在登记处登记结婚，且双方必须一起到场。

在英国，女性的性行为允许年龄为 16 岁，但这一国家法定的允许年龄并不适用于其附属国。在英格兰和威尔士，16 岁或 17 岁的少年没有父母的同意不能结婚。自 2010 年 12 月 1 日起，无论是何种性取向或什么性别，苏格兰的性行为允许年龄为 16 岁（不需要父母同意）。2008 年之前，北爱尔兰允许异性恋者和女同性恋者发生性行为的年龄为 17 岁。2008 年对所有人的允许年龄都降至 16 岁，与英国其他地区一致。

婚礼既可以由“授权主礼者”（通常是牧师，但不一定）主持，也可以由“授权注册登记员”来主持。法定的结合则必须在一个授权人员或主管登记员（牧师或神父）和至少两名有决定权的在场的情况下举行，因为他们需要作为见证者签署婚姻登记册。民事婚姻不能在宗教场所举行，但自 1994 年起，《婚姻法案》允许其在获许的宗教场地进行。婚姻登记册由新人、主礼者和两名见证者共同签署。

多数婚礼都在周六下午举行。周六下午很像是每周结婚的“高峰期”。婚礼开始之前，新娘会办“女生之夜”，而新郎则有他们的“男性派对”（类似单身派对）。婚礼前的三个周日，教堂会为在此教堂举行婚礼的新人宣读他们的《结婚公告》。新郎选一个伴郎在结婚仪式中照看婚戒。新郎若在婚礼当天的仪式开始前看到新娘被认为是不吉利的。传统上，新娘身着白色礼裙，新郎身着西装（高帽和燕尾服式）。新娘在伴娘和花童的陪伴下入场。新郎和新娘互诉誓言，交换戒指，然后登记结婚。

婚礼过后，宾客们受邀参加进一步的庆祝活动，即我们常说的“婚宴”。宾客将送给新人的礼物放在举办婚宴房间的桌上，传统上伴郎、新娘的父亲与新郎会在婚宴中致辞。婚宴上历来会准备一个两层或多层的特制结婚蛋糕，并且为了满足所有来宾的口味，每一层都是不同的种类。另一个习俗是把一个三层或四层蛋糕的顶层留下来，为这对夫妻的第一个孩子受洗所备用。通常新人在婚礼后就去旅行，即所谓的度“蜜月”。

英国的家庭形式正经历着变化。曾经由父母两人组成的典型英式家庭在20世纪发生了巨大的改变，尤其是单身家庭数量的增长，1971年到2002年间从18%增长到了29%，至2020年，单身人士估计会超过已婚人士。

过去，人们结婚就不会离婚。离婚是一件劳神、耗财又耗时的事。而如今，人们对婚姻的看法却正在改变。许多伴侣（多为二三十岁）在没有结婚的状态下共同生活（同居），且这些伴侣中仅有60%最终会结婚。从前人们婚后才生子，而今，英国约40%的儿童都生于未婚（同居）父母家庭。2000年，英国约有1/4未婚人士同居，其年龄在16~59岁之间。同居伴侣也包括那些未婚先孕的人。这些做法在1960年以前十分罕见，但到2001年，英国约23%的新生儿都生于同居伴侣家庭。

现在大龄结婚已经比较普遍，很多女性也不想马上要孩子。她们希望专心于工作，将怀孕推迟到三十多岁。单亲家庭的数量也与日俱增，其主要原因虽是越来越多的婚姻都以离婚告终。而有一些女性则会选择不结婚，以单亲父母的身份来养育孩子。现在英国的家庭平均人口为2.4人，这个数字小于其他多数欧洲国家。

7.2 住房

英格兰多数人都居住在城市。小镇和城市正在向周边扩展来应对不断增加的人口。1985年到1998年间，英格兰每年平均7000公顷的农田、农村和绿地转为城市用地，几乎相当于9600个国际足球场的规模！

英格兰的多数房屋都是用所在地的石头和砖修建的，全国各地的石头和砖的颜色各异。英格兰的主要住房类型有：独立式（独门独栋）、半独立式（两所房子相连）、排房（多所房子相连）和公寓（套房）。在大城市，人们通常都住公寓。几乎一半伦敦家庭住在公寓、复式公寓或套房（来自2001年人口普查的信息）。多数小镇街上的房子挨家挨户连成一排，被称为“排房”。英格兰最流行的住房类型是半独立式（超过27%是这种型），其次是独立式，最后是排房。

住房的命名起始于许多年前富人为自己的房屋命名。富人们按照他们祖先的姓氏、所处的地名和家族的头衔来给他们厅堂、房屋、庄园、城堡和度假小屋命名，如“诺福克庄园”（公爵的住宅）、“贝尔沃城堡”（能俯瞰贝尔沃山谷）、“迦勒底城堡”（以第13代祖先命名）等。多年来，其他人也开始给他们的房子取名字。如今住房的名字有一系列稀奇古怪的灵感来源，从处所到当地的历史，从文学作品到传说故事，应有尽有，其中英国住房名称最常见的主题有以下一些：动物和鸟类

（如“獾别墅”、“布谷鸟别墅”、“福克斯山谷”、“红隼”、“喜鹊”、“鼹鼠别墅”、“夜莺小屋”、“知更鸟山庄”、“鸟群栖所”、“松鼠跃居”、“燕子仓”）；树类（如“果林别墅”、“林地”、“树梢”、“橡树地”、“柳树”、“紫杉树小屋”、“月桂”、“冬青树”）；植物和花卉类（如“玫瑰小屋”、“樱草花小屋”、“金银花小屋”、“丁香小屋”）；地点和风景类（如“山坡”、“山顶”、“向阳面”、“森林边”、“草原纵览、“集市风光”）；历史类（如“教练屋”、“老校舍”、“老教区长住宅”、“老牧师住宅”、“老邮局”、“磨坊”、“谷仓”、“田庄”）；童话与旧爱类（如“顶针小屋”、“皮蓬”、“小房子”、“坚果壳”、“私语”、“许愿井小屋”、“鸟巢”）；还有节日与景区类（如“安布塞德”、“布伦卡思拉”、“艾斯克代尔”、“赖德尔”、“豪斯湖”、“温德米尔湖”、“特雷斯科”、“康沃尔”）等。

小镇和城市所有住房都有编号。有名称的是极少数，多数都没有名称。1765年，《国会法案》提出给街道编号，小镇和城市的所有住房都会依据其所在的街道被编号（例如，埃夫伯里大道26号）。每条路上的第一间是1号，最后一间则是这条街上所有住房的数量。号码使得街道上房产的位置变得容易识别，也更容易让房屋在紧急服务中快速地被找到。奇数号码通常会分配给街道左侧的住房，偶数则会分配给右侧。

与过去相比，更多的英国人会购买属于自己的房子。英格兰和英国其他地方约2/3的人或者已经拥有自己的房子，或者在购房过程之中。剩下的多数人都住在从私人房东、当地议会或是住房协会那里租来的楼房或公寓里。人们在购房时通常会用一种叫做“抵押贷款”的特殊贷款方式付款，他们需要花很长时间（通常是25年）连本带利偿还这笔贷款。

英格兰房价的增长速度远远超过了人们薪水增长的速度，这让首次购房者买房变得不现实，除非他们薪水特别高，或者是能得到富裕亲戚的资助或准备和朋友合伙购买。英格兰和威尔士的土地登记数据显示，1995年到2015年的20年间，房价涨了三倍。除了在2008年左右因银行危机导致两年房价下跌外，其间的增长几乎是连续不断的。

在过去20年间，收入与房价间的差距变化太大了，即使在英格兰与威尔士价格最合理的地区，购房者也得花费他们收入的六倍去买房。1995年，伦敦的平均年收入是19000英镑，平均房价为83000英镑，这就意味着人们要花收入的4.4倍去购房。到了2012—2013年间，伦敦的平均收入增长到24600英镑，房屋均价增长到30万英镑，这样一来，人们就得花收入的12.2倍去购房。1995年，银行基准利率为6%，而在2009年3月降至0.5%，且一直持续到2015年9月。廉价抵押贷款因此使得部分购买力问题得到改善，但也只是杯水车薪。

在英国，英国大众所指的公共住房通常是指“廉租房”和“市政地产”，公共住房的运行基于区和市镇议会的历史地位。大量廉租房于1920年左右开始修建，以取代破旧的老住宅。

自1970年以来，非营利性质的住房协会在英国社会住房房产中所占份额逐渐增加。从1996年开始，他们也被称为“注册社会房东（简称RSL）”，公共住房被称为“社会住房”，同时为议会和RSL所有。虽是非营利性质，RSL收取的租金通常高于议会。然而2002年政府提出了“租金重组”政策，旨在把英格兰议会和RSL的租金于2012年前协调一致。地方规划部门可以要求私人开发商提供“经济适用房”，使之作为规划许可条件之一（协议第106条），这就占了英国部分地区政府资助租户金额的另一个70亿英镑。从2012年起，住房协会也被称为“社会住房私人注册供应商（简称PRP）”。

自2000年起，政府提出“基于选择出租”（简称CBL）来确保租户搬走后的社会住房能迅速出租，这种做法更利于本地的而不是外地的潜在租户。由于许多管辖区的廉租房短缺，3/4的房屋可以安排给需要优先考虑的情况（如居住环境恶劣拥挤的，有医疗和福利需求的，有家庭支持需求的）或无家可归的申请者，以符合议会安置有需求居民的法律义务。为这些弱势群体留出的房屋比率根据当地廉租房的需求而有所不同。所有地方政府有其《住房政策》来确保廉租房能公平租出的同时，也能符合议会的法律义务，能帮助有需要的人，还能有利于地方地产的持续发展、社区重建和社会融入。

自1990年起，政府为了构建社会和谐，提供了多种所有权和租赁选项（包含“社会住房”和“经济适用房”双重选项）来鼓励重建地区和新建地方地产的“混合业权”。但近期研究报告表明业权混合实现的几率甚微。社会住房住户会因为被迫使用与非补贴性住户相比有所不同的、破旧又不方便的门户而蒙羞，因此社会住房便不愿与之同建。

即使房东不同，多数英国社会住房租户也有权与其他租户交换住处，这种方式被称为“相互交换”。

7.3 英国的交通

英国的交通由公路、航空、铁路、水路组成。其中公路和高速公路是国内主要交通线路。英国公路约有225000英里（362000公里），多数公路都是在几个世纪以前罗马人修建的老公路的基础上所修建的。英国的公路分为M公路（高速公路）、A公路和B公路及各种类别的小路。为了方便，当地政府也用字母C和U（代表“未分类”）。每条路在编号后加上分类前缀，如M40，A40，B1110。

英国的道路，从宽阔的现代高速公路到狭窄的乡间小路，通常由篱笆、石墙、草堤或水渠隔开。城市和小镇的道路比较拥挤，因为他们的历史可以追溯到汽车发明之前，显然当时没有规划大货车（或卡车）的道路。

有些高速公路需要收费（通行费）。第一条收费高速上的 M6 收费站于 2003 年 12 月开放，以缓解西米德兰兹郡高速拥堵的状况。这条长 43 公里的快道把伯明翰附近的旅程缩减了约 45 分钟。

汽车、大巴和出租车是至今最常见的出行方式，占英国乘客里程数的 85%。多数人开车出行，约 75%的家庭拥有至少一辆车。

在英国，车辆靠左行驶。在多车道上，除超车外司机需要保持左侧车道行驶。在大不列颠，交通规则适用于所有司机，但北爱尔兰的交通规则仅在北爱尔兰适用。

每个地方的限速都显示在附近的交通标识或交通灯上。圆形标识显示每英里的限速（mph），也会用全国速度限制（简称 NSL）标识显示。全国速度限制如下：

高速公路和双向车道：112 公里/小时（70 英里/小时）

无限制单向道路：96 公里/小时（60 英里/小时）

建成区（如小镇和乡村）：48 公里/小时（30 英里/小时）

居民区：35 公里/小时（30 英里/小时）

摩托车在英国是一种盛行的交通方式和娱乐方式，约有超过 100 万人骑摩托车。年满 16 岁持有临时驾照可以骑排量为 50 毫升的机动脚踏车。年满 17 岁通过考试后可获得摩托车驾照。法律规定的机动脚踏车的最高时速为 30 英里/小时（50 公里/小时）。

全国地方巴士服务，小镇和城市都可以看到单层巴士和双层巴士。伦敦的红色双层巴士和单层巴士世界闻名。一辆巴士前往的主要地名显示在车的前部。有些双层巴士是自动门，你需要上车时付钱给司机。乘坐单层巴士则有时需要你在车里的一个机器上购票。多数伦敦的巴士都有售票员收费。敞篷巴士在英国用来观光和提供夏季的季节性服务。

整个英国都有大巴车提供长途服务。在英格兰和威尔士，英国国家快运公司（National Express）提供主要的长途大巴服务。在苏格兰，主打廉价大巴的一元大巴（Megabus）公司与国家快运公司相竞争，并与苏格兰地区长途汽车公司（Citylink）合作提供服务。

全国各地已有成熟的出租车系统。伦敦的出租车是黑色，其他地方的颜色各异。伦敦的黑色出租车也叫做“伦敦德士”，即可在街边招停也可从出租车行租用。如果“空车”的标志是亮的，司机就有义务为你停车。计价器根据时间和距离计算出费用。

英国铁路网是欧洲最发达的铁路交通之一。斯托克顿和达灵铁路（1825 年）是世界上第一条公共客运专线。伦敦主要站点为：尤斯顿站、圣潘克拉斯站、维多利亚站和查令十字街站。欧洲之星是连接伦敦、阿什福德、巴黎、布鲁塞尔、里尔、阿维尼翁、加莱、巴黎迪士尼乐园和法国阿尔卑斯山的最快列车服务。

伦敦地铁（又被称作“Tube”或直接叫做 Underground”）给大部分的大伦敦地区和部分白金汉郡、赫特福德郡和埃塞克斯郡等伦敦周边各郡提供了快速公共交通服务。伦敦地铁有 12 条线路，每一条都有一个传统名称且在地铁线路图上有一个标准颜色。如果你想快速玩遍伦敦，乘坐地铁肯定比巴士和出租车更快捷。列车每 3~4 分钟就有一趟，周末和晚间的车次要少一些。伦敦地铁系统呈同心圆分为几个区，从第 1 区（伦敦市中心）向外一直到第 6 区（远郊）。多数景点都在第 1 区和第 2 区。乘坐地铁的费用根据你上车的区域和跨经的区域而不同。第 1~2 区内单程成人票价为 4 英镑，第 1 区到第 6 区间单程成人票价为 3. 8 英镑不等。早上 9 点后即可购买第 1~2 区的非高峰期一日游交通卡。

英格兰有 470 个机场，其中伦敦有 5 个，分别是希思罗机场、盖特维克机场、斯坦斯特机场、伦敦城市机场和卢顿机场。前三个有地铁直达伦敦市中心，也是伦敦主要的机场。希思罗机场和盖特维克机场主营海外航线。伦敦希思罗机场是世界上最大的机场之一，内设两个地铁站。

尽管 1994 年开通了通往法国的英吉利海峡隧道，海运仍是英国进出口货物的主要方式。其中多弗港是最繁忙的港口。许多渡轮在英格兰与西班牙、爱尔兰、荷兰、法国等国之间的海域穿梭。

7.4 英国的体育运动

体育在英国人的生活中扮演了重要的角色，是一种受欢迎的休闲活动。世界上许多著名的运动开始于英国，包括板球、足球、草地网球、高尔夫球和橄榄球。尽管足球才是最受欢迎的运动，英格兰的国球却是板球。英格兰足球队世界闻名，其中最著名的有曼联、阿森纳和利物浦。英格兰足球联赛里有 92 个职业俱乐部，它们大多是半职业队，所以大多数球员有其他全职工作。大部分的人在公园和运动场踢足球只是为了娱乐。

英格兰足球最精彩的部分是在每年五月的足协杯决赛。足球（在美国叫做英式足球）比赛的第一套法规始于 1863 年英格兰足球协会形成的时候。

橄榄球起源于沃里克郡的橄榄球学校。它类似于足球，但是一个椭圆形的球。球员可以带球并互相抱住摔倒对手。最好的橄榄球队在每年 9 月参加超级联赛决赛进行角逐。多年以来橄榄球是富裕的上层阶级的专享，但现在已风行全国。英式橄榄球可分为两大阵营：联盟式橄榄球（主要是在英格兰北部）和联合会式橄榄球（在英格兰其他地方，如苏格兰、威尔士和爱尔兰）。英格兰、苏格兰、威尔士和爱尔兰，再加上法国和意大利，会举办一个年度巡回赛，被称为“六国赛”。美式足球源于橄榄球游戏，同样的棒球也源于一种被称做弧形球的古老的英国游戏。

世界上最著名的温布尔登网球锦标赛，是最古老的网球锦标赛之一，始于 1877 年。它是从 6 月 22 日前的星期一开始，这个时候英国往往有最好的天气。数百万人在电视上观看锦标赛的直播。

篮网球是英格兰最大的女性团队运动。这项运动几乎完全由妇女和女孩参与，尽管男性参与人数近年来有所增加。在英国有 300 多万人参与篮网球运动。

苏格兰在传统上被认为是高尔夫球的故乡。仅在苏格兰就有超过 400 个高尔夫球场。最著名的高尔夫俱乐部在苏格兰邓迪附近的圣安德鲁斯海滨小镇,。

赛马是一项非常受欢迎的皇室运动，一年中每天都会举行。德比起源于此，国家大马赛亦起源于此，这是世界上最难的赛马比赛。赛马和赛狗是非常受欢迎的运动。人们可以在合法的场外投注店下注。一些最著名的赛马会在阿斯科特、纽马基特、古德伍德公园和埃普瑟姆举行。每年六月中的一周，英国南部的小镇阿斯科特都会成为赛马世界的中心。因为英国女王总是去看赛马，它也被称为皇家阿斯科特赛马会，女王拥有很多赛马也喜欢看比赛。

另一个马术运动是马球，19 世纪由军官们从印度带到英国。这也是世界上速度最快的球类运动。马球由四人一组，骑在马背上持棍打球射入球场两端的球门，场地长 300 码，宽 160 码。

乒乓球于 1880 年起源于英格兰。剑桥大学的学生最开始用雪茄盒和香槟的软木塞打球。虽然这项运动起源于英格兰，英国球员却在国际赛事中无缘冠军。羽毛球得名于鲍弗特公爵的乡村住所“巴德明顿庄园”，19 世纪在这里人们第一次玩这项游戏。

19 世纪，来自英国最古老学府牛津大学和剑桥大学的学生都十分热衷于赛艇。1829 年，两所学校同意在泰晤士河上首次一决雌雄。牛津大学最终获得胜利，这项传统随之诞生。如今，每年春天 3 月底或 4 月初都会举行牛津剑桥赛艇对抗赛。钓鱼是英国最受欢迎的运动之一，约 330 万人定期去钓鱼。钓鱼爱好者在河边和湖边随处可见。

现代拳击的规则于 1865 年由昆士伯利侯爵创建。英国拳击运动有业余式和职业式两种，每种都有严格的医疗法规。

游泳也是一种流行且老少皆宜的娱乐方式。

各种主要来自远东地区的武术项目也在英国盛行，如柔道和空手道。

飞镖则是大伙喜爱的酒吧游戏。虽然如今的飞镖游戏诞生于英格兰北部一个叫格里姆斯比的小镇，它的起源却可以至少追溯到中世纪。

7.5　购物

用拿破仑的话说，英国不仅是“小店主之国”，也是强迫性购物者之国。人们认为购物是一种“购物疗法”，尤其对于女性，购物是排名第一的消遣活动。在英格兰，女性37%的钱都花在了购物上。一份报刊调查发现，20%的女性是强迫性购物者。

英国许多城镇的主要购物街道叫做“高街”，如果你要购物的话就一定要去那里。有些是当地人经营的小店，但多数都是全国性的连锁店，这也使得很多地方的市中心大同小异。有些城镇的街市可以买到新鲜食物和廉价商品。市中心以外的区域，可以在“街角小商店”找到当地人日用品。

商店种类不计其数。百货商店是大型的零售商店，提供各种类型的商品和服务：有玛莎百货（主营服饰和食品）、德本汉姆百货、约翰·路易斯百货、英国家庭百货（主营衣服和家居用品）、博姿（主营化妆品）、史密斯连锁书店（报刊经销商、文具、CD和DVD）。果蔬店卖水果和蔬菜。百货商店出售各类家居日用品。

购物中心里的商店琳琅满目，有可以点快餐也可以坐下来吃饭的美食区，有停车场，通常还有电影院。坐落在肯特郡达特福德一个废弃白垩矿场的蓝水购物中心是欧洲城外购物中心发展中最大的一个。购物中心有三百多家店，能泊13000辆车，每年吸引了约三千万顾客。街角商店是住宅附近的小商店，它提供的商品种类有限，但营业时间长。

超市是出售食物的大型自助商店，大型超市也卖家居用品。主要的超市有阿斯达超市有限公司、巴吉斯超市、合作社超市、冷冻食品超市、西弗韦日用超市、索莫菲尔德日用超市、维特罗斯超市、乐购（英国最大超市连锁）。慈善商店出售一些捐赠物品，如服装、书籍、小型家居用品。其销售的产品便宜，质量也不错。持卖酒执照的商店可销售酒精饮料。同一个股东旗下的连锁店销售同种商品，且每家连锁店的名称也相同，如史密斯连锁书店、玛莎百货、圣百利超市等。

最受欢迎的时尚服饰店有Burton（最受欢迎的男装店）、Topman（有著名设计师的品牌服装）、Next（主营时尚服饰）、Topshop（因威廉王子夫人凯特王妃爱穿而大受少女喜爱）、River Island（高街时尚品牌）、Miss Selfridge（目标客群为青少年）。

伦敦有成千上万的商店和市场，牛津街和摄政街是伦敦最热闹的商业区。街上有很多小店贩售旅游纪念品，当然也有其他商店。有数不清的百货商场、服装店，也有大型唱片店和书店。在摄政街左侧靠近自由百货商店处，是卡尔纳比街，这里是曾经“摇摆六十年代”的标志之一，现在是伦敦一条购物步行街。伦敦的骑士桥区有全市乃至全国最大的百货商场。伦敦哈罗斯百货是每个游客都想去的著名商场，可以买到从最便宜到最昂贵的所有商品。到了晚上，它半球状的陶色建筑灯光熠熠，引人注目。考文特花园里到处都是摊贩、街头艺术、文艺咖啡馆、英式酒吧和小精品店。是游客到伦敦必访之地。书虫们都回去查令十字街，这里有许多主流书店，如福伊尔斯书店、鲍德斯书店、布莱克维尔书店成行成市，但这条街最特别的还要算那些罕见的二手特种商品商店了。福伊尔斯书店因其五层楼包含了成千上万出版物而闻名。托特纳姆法院路是购买电子产品和家具的最好去处。

也有一些奢侈品店。位于摄政街的伦敦自由百货商场得名于服装质地精美。商店看起来像都铎时期的建筑，外壁上悬挂了一个精致的钟。塞尔福里奇百货店里各类男式、女式和儿童品牌很多而且经常进驻新的国际品牌。摄政街的汉姆利玩具店是伦敦最大的玩具店。它六层都是各式的玩具，从娃娃、泰迪熊到模型、电子玩具和机器人。

伦敦集贸市场出售各类物品，从水果蔬菜到古董、手工艺品和服饰。格林威治集贸市场是买新旧衣服、礼物、手工艺品和珠宝的去处。维多利亚风格的列登贺集贸市场出售传统游戏、家禽、鱼和肉，最好是在早午餐的时间过去。伯威克街市是苏荷区中心的热闹市场，是伦敦中心区仅存的果蔬市场，这里有远近闻名的最新鲜和价格最低廉的货物，如鱼、面包、奶酪、香料和佐料摊位，也有纺织品和廉价家居用品。衬裙巷市场是可以买到价格优惠服装和鞋的好地方。斯比塔菲尔德市场有工艺品、服装、家具和有机食品。波多贝罗市场可以在同一个地方买到古董、服装、鞋、小古玩和有机果蔬。卡姆登市场已成为伦敦的热门景点之一，在这里可以找到嬉皮服装、传统手工艺品、20 世纪 70 年代怀旧风和素食。博罗市场是伦敦最受欢迎的食品市场，有像奶酪、葡萄酒、鱼类、肉类等的进口商品和有机食物。

购物高峰期在周六和周日。在英格兰，多数零售店都是一星期营业 6 天或 7 天。一般营业时间为周一至周六早上 9 点到下午 5 点半。有些购物中心营业到晚上 8 点或更晚。周日营业时间为早上 10 点到下午 4 点（或早上 11 点到下午 5 点）。最近几年周日购物流行起来，从而城镇多数大型商店都开门营业，但周日超过六小时的营业是禁止的。大型超市除周日外每天 24 小时营业。许多超市和大型商店则周一到周六从早上 8 点营业到晚上 10 点，周日从早上 10 点营业到下午 4 点（或从早上 11 点到下午 5 点）。

公共假期间一些商店营业而有一些不营业。一般来说银行会关门，多数超市和大型商店会继续营业（虽然周日营业时间变少），在大一点的城镇很多商店都是开门的。在圣诞节和新年期间，所有商店在圣诞节（12 月 25 日）关门，有些商店在元旦（1 月 1 日）关门。但如今在节礼日（12 月 26 日）营业的商店变多，从这天起许多商店开始做促销活动。通常许多购物中心在复活节都会关门，有的在复活节当天也会缩短营业时间，通常早上 10 点或 11 点才开门。乡村地区的一些商店还有一周某一天（通常在周三）提早到下午 1 点关门的习惯。

7.6 酒吧

酒吧是英国生活的重要组成部分，也是流行的社交场所。人们可以在酒吧聊天、吃饭、喝酒、会友和放松。

英国有6万多家酒吧，其中英格兰和威尔士有53000家，苏格兰有5200家，北爱尔兰有1600家。位于赫特福德郡圣奥尔本斯的斗鸡酒吧所在的建筑可以追溯到11世纪，是最古老的酒吧之一。

酒吧通常有两个吧台，其中一个要相对安静一些，大多都有花园供人们夏季休憩。小孩可以和父母在酒吧花园娱乐。一群好友通常轮流买单，也就是说轮到谁，谁就要为所有人买单。酒吧忙的时候就很难得到服务，不需要排队，但酒吧工作人员通常会尽量招待那些久等的客人。如果你不小心把酒洒在到陌生人身上，礼貌的做法是请他再喝一杯。

多数酒吧都属于某个酿酒厂（也是制酒公司），但可以卖各式的啤酒，有些是用酒桶接的（从吧台底下一个大酒桶中接），有些是瓶装的。最受欢迎的英式啤酒是一种深色的、在适宜室温（不冷不热）下供应且带苦味的啤酒。英国啤酒用麦芽和啤酒花酿制。虽然多数人认为酒吧是喝酒的地方，其实酒吧也卖不含酒精的软饮料。英国人平均每天喝99.4升啤酒，80%都是在酒吧和俱乐部喝的。

在英国经营酒吧，若有经营执照（很难获得）就可以长达24小时经营。多数酒吧营业时间为早上11点到晚上11点。

几乎所有酒吧都卖酒吧午餐。其中一种叫做农夫午餐，包含一个大块的楔形切达奶酪，几片面包、一些腌黄瓜和一个洋葱。典型的酒吧食物还有挪威海螯虾（贝类）和薯条（炸土豆）、派和薯条、鸡肉和薯条。

酒吧的传统名称可以追溯到六百多年前。常见的名字有“首相别墅”、“白天鹅”、“皇冠”、“国王的武器”、“红狮子”和“白马”。人们在指路时通常用酒吧名做参照，如“在‘玫瑰与皇冠酒吧’左转“。酒吧外通常有带着酒吧照片和酒吧名的标识。

飞镖是众多的酒吧游戏中常见的一种。许多老的乡村酒吧会持续推广传统的游戏，比如在肯特郡流行的“蝙蝠和陷阱”游戏已有数百年的历史。

买酒的法定年龄为18岁。在有一个成年人陪伴并由成年人点单的情况下，年满16岁和17岁者在酒吧允许后可以伴随餐点买1杯葡萄酒、啤酒或苹果酒，只有英格兰和威尔士是如此，在苏格兰不需要成年人在场。

向醉酒者卖酒是违法行为。即使有执照许可，也不能给醉酒者买酒。如果客人看上去小于21岁，所有经销商都要查带照片的证件。为未成年人买酒会当场予以80英镑的罚款。

年满14岁后若只是在酒吧点餐，则不需要成年人陪同就能进入酒吧。小孩在晚上9点以后可以随父母进入酒吧，这样既可以让家人一起享受实惠的酒吧食物，也能让酒吧的社区中心的传统地位得以延续。

英国的多数酒吧都得去吧台点酒水和食物，然后立即付款，没有餐桌服务。调酒师被称为“酒吧男招待”或“酒吧女招待”，不需要给他们小费。如果想要给他们小费，习惯的做法是对他说，“来一杯吗?”就可以了。

有些酒吧有餐桌服务，等待时服务员在桌边帮你点餐并不需要立即付款。酒吧里通常会有提醒你这里有餐桌服务的标识。在结束用餐后给服务员约 10%的小费是一种习惯的做法，但有时候小费已经包含在账单里了。

*　　　　*　　　　*　　　　*　　　　*

第 8 章　英国著名人物

英国有着悠久的历史和丰富的文化，在不同的领域涌现出许多著名的人物。没有人会忽视英国人对科学做出的贡献，是查尔斯·达尔文提出了进化论、是艾萨克·牛顿和他的科学贡献造福了全世界！是英国人在君主立宪制的基础上带来了民主的政府模式。到了近代，是英国的音乐结构掀起了全球流行音乐的变革。

在这一部分中，我们将介绍一些英国君主、政治家、科学家、音乐人和电影明星，他们为社会的发展贡献了自己的力量。英国还有许多才华横溢的作家和诗人，我们将在第 11 章中与他们的作品一起介绍。

8.1　英国君主

英国的君主制最早可以追溯到公元 9 世纪。至今为止，一共有 12 个皇室家族统治过英国，包括诺曼王朝、金雀花王朝、兰开斯特王朝、约克王朝、都铎王朝、斯图亚特王朝、共和国时期、斯图亚特王朝、汉诺威王朝、萨克斯·科堡·哥达王朝和温莎王朝。在 1603 以前，英格兰和苏格兰是分开统治的，英格兰皇室和苏格兰皇室之间联系紧密，许多皇室成员彼此通婚。自从苏格兰詹姆士六世继承英格兰王位，成为英格兰詹姆士一世后，开始了一个君主统治英国的局面。

过去的 400 年里，英国君主政体的性质发生了许多变化。从 17 世纪末开始，君主失去了行政权，并开始越来越受制于议会，直到形成今天的君主立宪制形式。

现在，英国君主只是名义上的国家元首和政府领袖。现任英国君主是女王伊丽莎白二世，她在国家事务中担任政治角色，并有正式职责。女王在宪法规定的君主特权范围内行使王权，尽管其个人政治权力非常有限，但她的存在对保障国家的延续和政治的稳定起到了重要作用，尤其是在政党交替和矛盾频出的年代尤为重要。另外，女王也是国家的象征，在国内与国际事务中代表国家和人民。所以，君主是英国的代表，也是国家权力和主权的象征。

亨利八世

亨利八世（1509—1547）是英国最著名、最有争议的国王之一。

有关亨利八世最著名的一件事就是他为了获得男性继承人，先后娶了六个妻子，其中两个被他下令斩首。亨利与第一任妻子凯瑟琳离婚后，与天主教决裂并成立了英国国教，开始了英国的宗教改革，掀起了英国长达几百年的宗教斗争。著名的空想社会主义学家托马斯·莫尔因不满亨利的宗教统治，被判叛国罪并处以死刑。

亨利八世去世后由独子爱德华六世继位。王位最终由亨利与第二任妻子的女儿伊丽莎白一世夺得。

伊丽莎白一世

伊丽莎白一世（1533—1603）被普遍认为是英国历史上最杰出的君主。1558年，年仅25岁的伊丽莎白继位时，英国由于尖锐的宗教矛盾已经变得满目疮痍，而当时强大的法国和西班牙一直对其虎视眈眈。伊丽莎白一生勤理政务，击溃了政敌的威胁（如王位的另一位继承人，苏格兰女王玛丽），大力发展英国海军。最值得注意的是，1588年伊丽莎白带领英国击溃了西班牙的海上舰队。她在位的这段时间被称为英国历史上的黄金时期：不仅出现了沃尔特·罗利爵士、弗兰西斯·德瑞克爵士、弗朗西斯·培根和威廉·莎士比亚这些著名人物，而且开始了英国的全球扩张和殖民统治。

伊丽莎白统治了英国近半个世纪，她的名字与世界历史上这段辉煌时期紧密相连。甚至连她的劲敌也对她惊叹不已。伊丽莎白终生未嫁，是著名的“童贞女王”，尽管牺牲了个人幸福，她坚持自己的责任心，一生都致力于维护英国的和平与稳定。

伊丽莎白之所以能称为一名杰出的君主，还有一个原因是她会精心维护自己的形象。她总是身着精美的服饰，戴着华丽的珠宝，从她的语言里总是透露出对人民的关爱，她也理所当然地受到了人民的拥护和喜爱，这是在她之前，甚至之后的君主中从未出现过的。即使到了晚年，英国的经济状况大不如前，而伊丽莎白也已经老去，但人们依然爱戴她。

维多利亚女王

维多利亚女王（1837—1901）在位时间64年，是英国历史上统治时间最长的一位君主。“维多利亚时代”是英国历史上的全盛时期，这时英国的工业发展迅速，艺术繁荣兴盛，帝国地位得以确立。英国也成为著名的“日不落帝国”。

维多利亚继位时年仅 18 岁。1840 年她与表兄艾伯特王子结婚并育有九个孩子。他们的儿孙很多都与欧洲皇室联姻，如西班牙、俄国、瑞典等。维多利亚女王也被称为“欧洲的祖母”。继位早期，维多利亚深受其丈夫的影响。在“君主立宪政体”下君主的权力是极其有限的，但王权对国务仍然可以造成很大的影响，艾伯特教她如何在这种情况下做一名君主。维多利亚非常倚仗艾伯特，所以 1861 年当 42 岁的艾伯特去世时，维多利亚开始变得消沉，她不仅失去了一个可以依靠的丈夫，还失去了一个完全信赖的国务顾问。此后，维多利亚无心打理朝政并逐渐淡出政治生活，把重心转移到子女身上。直到 19 世纪 60 年代末，她才重新进入公众生活，并逐渐重获人民的爱戴。

在维多利亚漫长的统治时期，君主不再有直接的政治权利，一系列法案的出台扩大了选民的社会经济影响力。尽管王权被削弱，但维多利亚女王向人们展示了一个有威望的领袖、一个关心国家政务的领袖是如何发挥其重要影响力的。

伊丽莎白二世

现任英国女王伊丽莎白二世出生于 1926 年 4 月 21 日，在父亲乔治六世去世后，于 1952 年 2 月 6 日后受封为英国女王。她是乔治六世和伊丽莎白·鲍兹·莱昂的长女。1947 年，伊丽莎白与远亲菲利普亲王结婚，并育有四个孩子：查尔斯王子（威尔士亲王）、安妮公主、安德鲁王子和爱德华王子。她是英国历史上在位时间最长的君主之一。

伊丽莎白二世很注重将公众生活与私人生活分开。她是英国首位将孩子送到寄宿学校以躲避媒体的君主。她的责任感强，做事兢兢业业，履行女王职责时公正、高效又庄重。她对当前形势和趋势的把握精准全面，常常让首相感到尴尬。前首相哈罗德·威尔逊退休时曾说道，“我要忠告我的继任者，一定要在会见女王前做好功课。”英国另一位前首相，丘吉尔曾与四位君主共事，他对女王的学识和机智印象深刻，并感到愉快。私下里女王很幽默，但在公众场合总是表现得端庄得体、谨慎自重。

8.2　政治家

英国有许多著名的政治家，如，奥利弗·克伦威尔、温斯顿·丘吉尔、玛格丽特·撒切尔等……除了克伦威尔，其他几位都曾担任过英国首相。

众所周知，英国是一个君主立宪制国家。国王或女王是国家的首领，而政府行政部门的首脑则是首相。无论首相来自哪个政党，英国君主与其有着特殊的联系。君主从大选中赢得多数席位的政党中任命首相，首相再从该政党中选择 20 名左右议员组成内阁。君主定期与首相会面，行使其对政府事务发表意见的权利和义务。

首相一职始于1721年，是由罗伯特·沃波尔爵士担任第一财政大臣开始的。到目前为止，女王伊丽莎白二世已经与12位首相共事过。现任首相是特蕾莎·梅，她在戴维·卡梅伦2016年6月24日宣布辞职后被任命为英国首相。

奥利弗·克伦威尔

奥利弗·克伦威尔（1599—1658）是英国资产阶级革命家、政治家、军事家以及宗教领袖。他之所以被人们铭记是因为他是一位为自由而战的战士，他不仅把查理一世送上断头台，而且还建立了英格兰共和国。许多人认为作为一名战士，克伦威尔是优秀的，但作为一位统治者，他却并不合格。由于人民不满他的统治，克伦威尔死后不久共和国就被推翻了。

1599年，克伦威尔出生于亨廷顿的一个中等乡绅家庭，曾经当过农场主和小地主。那时谁都没想到他会成为一位在英国历史上具有影响力的大人物。30多岁时，克伦威尔成为一名忠实的清教徒，他对王权和天主教会的猛烈抨击让他开始小有名气。英国内战（1642—1646）期间，他在军队的卓越表现让他走上了权力之路。1653年，克伦威尔被封为护国公，开始掌握国家大权，可此后却渐渐变成一名独裁者。1658年克伦威尔去世后，查理二世复辟，从他儿子手中抢回王位，英国又恢复了君主制。

人们对克伦威尔的统治有不同的看法。有的人认为克伦威尔是一个捍卫原则和自由的勇士、维护公正和宗教宽容的胜利者；而有的人则认为他只不过是一个暴君和一个杀了国王的凶手。然而无论如何，克伦威尔的统治时期是英国历史上的关键转折点之一。内战的胜利让议会认识到再也没有一个国王能够独自统治英国了。克伦威尔在军事上取得的胜利不仅推翻了英国的封建制度，而且动摇了欧洲封建统治的基础。

温斯顿·丘吉尔

英国前首相温斯顿·丘吉尔（1874—1965）一直被公认为是世界历史上最伟大的战时领袖之一。第二次世界大战期间，丘吉尔带领英国走过了一段最灰暗的历史时期，领导英国取得了战争的胜利，他体现出来的绝佳的勇气、决断力、政治经验以及强大的生命力一直为世人所铭记。

1940年5月10日，丘吉尔担任英国首相，那时第二次世界大战已经开始。他在下议院所做的演讲中说道："我能奉献的唯有热血、辛劳和泪水。"他对战德国的原则就是倾全国之力全力对抗。他敦促身边的每一个人积极备战，不仅积极游说美国加入反对纳粹德国的斗争，还很务实地认识到需要寻求他一直厌恶的共产主义苏联的帮助。丘吉尔知道战事艰难，但他依然通过广播作了许多著名的演讲，使英国人民的抗战情绪高涨。在敌方发动伦敦大轰炸时，他留守伦敦并查看被炮轰的区域。当看到本可以躲避到安全区域的首相一直与自己共同遭受磨难时，英国人民倍感欣慰。

除了作为首相带领英国获得第二次世界大战胜利这一点值得称道外，丘吉尔还是一位杰出的演说家、多产的作家和专注的艺术家。他曾因为著作和演讲获得诺贝尔文学奖，也是第一位获得美国荣誉公民称号的名人。

克莱门特·艾德礼

克莱门特·艾德礼（1883—1967）从1945年到1951年担任英国首相。他在大选中以绝对优势战胜了丘吉尔获得首相一职，这也是工党首次在下议院获得多数席位。

艾德礼在任期间放弃了对印度的控制，大英帝国开始大规模解体。这一时期英国在步入现代化的同时，国力和影响力也在下降，大英帝国转化为英联邦。

毫无疑问，艾德礼最大的成就莫过于建立国民医疗服务制度，使英国变成一个福利国家。尤其值得一提的是，在艾德礼的领导下，英国成功地由战时经济过渡到和平时期。随着冷战的开始，英国成功地与美国结成忠诚的盟友，这种同盟关系一直持续到今天。

2004年，根据英国莫里调查公司的民意调查，艾德礼被评为20世纪最伟大的英国首相，这一结果受到了广大英国民众的支持。

玛格丽特·撒切尔

玛格丽特·撒切尔（1925—2013）是英国历史上第一位女首相。她连任三届（1979—1990），是英国20世纪任期最长的一位首相。撒切尔夫人最著名的是她钢铁般的决心和毅力，以及她所坚持的保守的社会经济政策。她削减社会福利、限制工会权力，并对一些产业进行私有化。由于态度强硬，撒切尔也获得了“铁娘子”的称号。

撒切尔的政治纲领是限制政府和公共开支，让市场控制经济。她信奉尔顿·佛里德曼的经济理论，实行货币主义的经济政策，并以消除英国社会主义为己任。她还减低税收、限制公共开支，并放松工业管制。她计划使英国许多国有产业私有化，并停止政府补贴。她希望通过立法来制约工会的权力，希望取消欧洲国家之间的关税。

随着世界经济的复苏，英国经济也得到了改善。撒切尔夫人的很多决策开始赢得人们的肯定。1991年，由于与几位内阁大臣出现意见分歧，她辞去了首相职位。1992年，撒切尔夫人因其对国家做出的突出贡献被封为女男爵并成为上议院议员。

撒切尔夫人去世后，美国总统奥巴马这样评价她：“从杂货店老板的女儿成长为英国首位女首相，撒切尔为我们的女儿们树立了榜样，告诉她们没有穿不透的玻璃屋顶。作为首相，她帮助英国重获其鼎盛时期特有的自信和尊严。”

8.3 科学家

英国是一个总体科研实力相当雄厚的国家，其科学研究与发展（R&D）一直保持着很高的水准。她拥有诸如牛津、剑桥、伦敦经济学院、帝国理工学院等世界著名的高等学府；她造就过像牛顿、达尔文、法拉第、卡文迪什、麦克斯韦、汤姆逊等诸多杰出的科学家。截至目前，英国共有 70 多位诺贝尔科学奖得主，仅次于美国。统计资料表明，英国以占世界 1%的人口从事着全球 5.5%的科研活动。

英国的科学技术发展历史悠久，涌现出许多重要的人物和发明。其中最重要的理论学家包括 17 世纪的物理学家艾萨克·牛顿，他的万有引力定律被奉为现代科学的基石；19 世纪的生物学家查尔斯·达尔文，他的自然选择进化论学说是现代生物学的基础；以及 20 世界的物理学家、宇宙论学家史蒂芬·威廉·霍金，他的黑洞爆炸论重新定义了宇宙的结构。英国的重要科学发现包括 1766 年亨利·卡文迪什发现的氢气、1829 年由米歇尔·法拉第发现的电磁感应现象、1928 年亚历山大·弗莱明发现了盘尼西林对细菌的作用，1953 年弗朗西斯·克里克等人发现的 DNA 结构。重要的工程项目及应用包括 1765 年詹姆斯·瓦特改良的蒸汽机、1804 年由理查·特里维西克和安德烈·维维安制造的第一部蒸汽机车、1941 年由弗兰克·惠特尔发明的喷气式引擎，以及 1989 年蒂姆·伯纳斯·李发明的万维网。

英国科学家将继续在科学研究及重要的科技领域扮演重要角色，包括航空航天业、汽车及医药工业。

艾萨克·牛顿

艾萨克·牛顿爵士（1642—1727）是一位英国物理学家、数学家和哲学家，他同时也对炼金术很感兴趣。牛顿出生在林肯郡乌尔索普，毕业于剑桥大学。他在科学上所取得的突破性成就，大大增进了人们对重力、光学和数学的理解。人们普遍认为他是迄今为止最伟大的科学家，奉他为“现代科学之父”。

牛顿对数学和自然规律有着强烈的兴趣，在他最著名的著作《自然哲学的数学原理》（1687）中介绍了基本力学三定律，还讨论了行星的运行。这本书奠定了现代物理学的框架，被普遍认为是历史上最重要的科学著作之一。牛顿在光学领域也取得了很大的成就，尤其是他用棱镜分裂白光，从而发现了光谱。在数学方面，他与莱布尼茨分别建立了微积分体系。

关于牛顿最有意思的一个趣闻是他被树上掉落的苹果砸到从而发现了万有引力定律。虽然无法证明这个故事的真实性，但他的助手约翰·康杜特在牛顿回忆录中写到，牛顿自己曾说过，他的确是在 1666 年左右因为看到苹果掉在花园里，所以受到启发开始考虑重力的问题。

牛顿在英国和欧洲科学界占有非常重要的地位。1705年，他被授予爵士爵位，并在1727去世后成为第一位葬在威斯敏斯特教堂的科学家。

迈克尔·法拉第

迈克尔·法拉第（1791—1867）是英国物理学家和化学家，他最杰出的贡献是提出了电磁感应学说和电解定律，在电力学领域最大的突破是发明了电动机。

法拉第1791年出生于伦敦的一个贫穷家庭，他从小就对一切充满好奇心和疑问，求知欲非常强。14岁时，法拉第辍学并开始在当地一家图书装订商家里做学徒。7年学徒生涯中，他阅读过大量的书籍，其中包括以撒·华兹的《悟性的提升》。法拉第按照书中讲述的学习原则与建议进行学习和实践。另外，他也从珍·玛西的著作《化学闲聊》中得到很多启发。通过大量的阅读，法拉第渐渐培养起对科学的兴趣，其中以电学为甚。

法拉第的最大的成就在于促进了电磁力和电力的发展。尽管当时人们已经发现了电，但是是法拉第在1821年通过“电磁转动”装置才提供了持续的电力。10年后的1831年，法拉第进行了一系列伟大的实验，并发现了电磁感应现象，这些实验成为现代电磁技术的基础。

查尔斯·达尔文

查尔斯·达尔文（1809—1882）是英国著名生物学家、进化论的奠基人，他向世人展示了人类是怎样从低级生物进化而来的。在他那个年代，他的研究和著作曾引发了激烈的争论，但最终他的进化论和物竞天择说被科学界广泛接受了。

达尔文出生于一个富有且颇具影响力的家庭。1825年，他被送到剑桥大学神学院学习神学。达尔文没有认真学习神学，反而对野外探索产生了兴趣。他花了大量的时间进行自然科学研究并迷上了收集甲虫。从1831年到1836年，他以博物学家的身份，参加了英国派遣的“小猎犬号”环球航行，做了五年的科学考察。在旅途中的一些发现让他形成了生物进化的概念：所有的生物都要按物竞天择、适者生存的原则进行发展和进化，只有优胜者的特性才会遗传给后代。达尔文在1858年公布了他关于物竞天择说的初步想法，并于1859年正式出版《物种起源》。这本书在当时很受欢迎，同时也有许多争议。尽管达尔文是一名教徒，甚至曾一度考虑在教堂供职，但他的进化论却与《圣经》相悖，所以他也遭到《圣经》信奉者的批判。现在，即使宗教争论仍在继续，达尔文的理论却几乎已经被所有的科学家接受，而且成为现代进化生物学研究的起点。之后几年，达尔文又出版了许多同主题的书籍和小册子，其中最著名的是1871年出版的《人类起源》。

史蒂芬·威廉·霍金

史蒂芬·威廉·霍金（1942— ）是英国理论物理学家、宇宙学家和作家，被誉为继爱因斯坦后最伟大的理论物理学家。尽管患有运动神经细胞病，霍金仍然取得了许多重要的科学成就，他还用通俗的语言向普通人解释科学原理。

霍金是在剑桥大学读书时开始出现运动神经疾病的症状，很快他的活动能力就受到了影响，他说话变得含糊不清，甚至无法自己吃饭。医生曾预计他只能再活三年，好在后来病情发展减缓，霍金也克服了种种障碍，继续进行科学研究和公众活动。剑桥的一位科学家为霍金设计了一种合成语音装置，使他能够用触摸板“说话”。即便如此，霍金与人交流仍然很耗时费力。对于自己的残疾，霍金一直是一种很务实的态度。他曾说过：“气恼我自己的残障是在浪费时间。人生必须不断往前走，而我到目前为止表现得还不错。如果你总是生气或抱怨，人们也不会有空搭理你。”

霍金的主要研究领域是理论宇宙学和量子引力学。他取得了很多成就，比如，他为爱因斯坦的广义相对论补充了数学形式。他还承担了许多研究宇宙性质的工作，如研究大爆炸和黑洞。霍金最著名的是他还用通俗的语言来解释宇宙的起源，以及关于宇宙和物理学中最深奥难懂的部分。他是第一位将广义相对论和量子力学相结合，来解释宇宙学理论的科学家。

蒂姆·伯纳斯·李

蒂姆·伯纳斯·李（1955— ）是英国计算机科学家，万维网的发明者。他发明的万维网已经改变了人们生活的方方面面。

1955年，蒂姆出生在英国伦敦，父母都是数学家。他很早就开始对电子学产生兴趣。1976年蒂姆毕业于牛津大学物理系。1989年蒂姆在CERN（欧洲量子物理研究所）工作时开发了世界上第一个Web服务器，随后又努力将Web无偿地向全世界开放，目前，蒂姆正在致力于加强和保护网络的未来。

蒂姆是万维网基金会的创始人，该基金会旨在保障网络为全人类服务，并将这一目标确定为一项全球公共利益和基本权利。蒂姆还担任了万维网联盟的主席，这是蒂姆1994年为保障万维网发展而创办的一个全球网络标准组织。

近年来，蒂姆获得了许多荣誉。2004年，英女王伊丽莎白二世向蒂姆颁发大英帝国爵级司令勋章；2009年，蒂姆获选为美国国家科学院外籍院士。2012年，蒂姆参加了伦敦奥运会开幕式，并获得了“万维网发明者”的美誉。他通过一台NeXT计算机在Twitter上发表消息说：“这是给所有人的”，体育馆内的LCD光管随即显示出文字来。

《时代》周刊将伯纳斯·李评为20世纪最杰出的100位科学家之一，并这样介绍他的个人成就："与所有的推动人类进程的发明不同，这是一件纯粹个人的劳动成果……他设计了万维网，然后把它开放给全世界。他比其他任何人都更努力地保持万维网的开放性、非营利性和自由性。"

8.4　音乐人

在历史上，英国一直都在不断地进行或接受着现当代音乐改革的洗礼。英国音乐具有独特的文化基础，深受英国历史、教堂音乐、西方文化，以及英格兰、苏格兰、北爱尔兰和威尔士各地悠久传统的民间音乐和乐器演奏的影响。由于与其他国家的语言、文化联系，以及自身强大的发明、改革及吸收能力，英国对流行音乐的发展起到了巨大的作用，引领了流行音乐的许多发展趋势。

20 世纪以来，许多流行音乐形式在英国蓬勃发展。20 世纪早期，美国对流行音乐有着主导性的影响，然而自从 20 世纪 60 年代开始，由披头士乐队引领的"英国入侵"爆发了。披头士乐队为代表的英国音乐人开始主导着流行乐和摇滚乐的发展。此后，大批的英国摇滚和流行乐者在美国大受欢迎，英国音乐发生了许多变化，如，英国重金属新浪潮和英伦摇滚流行起来。现在英国拥有世界上最大的音乐产业，英国音乐人开创并发展了许多新的音乐领域，如，布鲁斯摇滚、重金属乐、前卫摇滚、斯卡、硬摇滚、朋克摇滚、邦拉、电子民谣、民谣朋克、酸爵士、说唱，自赏、鼓打贝斯、尘垢、英伦摇滚和 Dubstep 电子乐。

许多当代英国音乐家对现代音乐有着极大的影响。在这一部分我们将介绍过去 50 年来在英国音乐产业中起领军作用的音乐人，包括摇滚乐队甲壳虫乐队、流行组合辣妹组合和西城男孩，以及古典跨界歌手萨拉·布莱曼。

披头士乐队

披头士乐队（又称甲壳虫、披头四、披头士）是一支来自英国利物浦的摇滚乐队，由约翰·列侬（节奏吉他、主场、作词作曲）、保罗·麦卡特尼（贝斯、主唱、作词作曲）、乔治·哈里森（主音吉他、主唱）和林戈·斯塔尔（鼓手）四名成员组成。他们是 20 世纪最重要、最具影响力的一支摇滚乐队，为流行音乐领域开创了许多音乐风格，这是 20 世纪任何一支摇滚乐队无法企及的。

1962 年下半年，他们的首支单曲《我愿意》在英国大获好评。1963 年，随着单曲《我想要握你的手》的发行，披头士风潮席卷全球，引领"英国入侵"的风潮，抢占美国流行音乐市场。从 1965 年开始，披头士乐队陆续发行了一些优秀专辑，包括极具创造力和影响力的《Rubber Soul》（1965），《Revolver》（1966），《Sgt. Pepper' Lonely Hearts Club Band》（1967），《The Beatles》和《Abbey Road》（1969）。

跟其他顶级乐队不同，披头士乐队很好地诠释了团体力量大于个体总和这一点。他们是首个获得世界影响力的英国摇滚乐队，真正使摇滚乐在全球范围内流行起来。根据美国唱片工业协会统计，披头士乐队是美国最受欢迎的乐队。2008 年，他们登上美国《公告牌》杂志“最热门 100 位艺术家”榜首。甲壳虫乐队一共荣获了 10 项格莱美大奖、1 项奥斯卡最佳原创歌曲奖和 15 项全英原创音乐奖。

辣妹组合

辣妹组合是一支成立于 1994 年的英国女子流行组合，成员包括梅兰妮·布朗（疯狂辣妹）、梅兰妮·切斯霍姆（运动辣妹）、艾玛·伯顿（宝贝辣妹）、洁芮·哈利薇尔（姜汁辣妹）以及维多利亚·贝克汉姆（时髦辣妹）。

1996 年，辣妹组合与维京唱片签约，同年发行首张单曲“Wannabe”，创下了 37 个国家排行榜首位的成绩，这使她们从英国迈向全世界。她们的首张专辑《Spice》全球销售超过 3000 万张，成为历史上最畅销的女团专辑。之后的《SpiceWorld》全球销量也超过 2000 万张。辣妹组合的全球累计专辑销量已超过 8000 万张，成为音乐史上最畅销的女子组合、全球销量最高的流行组合之一，也是继披头士之后最大的流行组合。

英国媒体在一开始就给辣妹组合的每个成员分配了独特的身份，每个标志既代表了她们的真实性格，又成为市场化的工具。这些身份标志都取自她们的首支单曲《Wannabe》，包括“疯狂辣妹”、“运动辣妹”、“宝贝辣妹”、“姜汁辣妹”和“时髦辣妹”。每个名字都被用在了乐队的报道和 MTV 中，这种创意使《Wannabe》在 1996 年夏天发行的时候一下子登上了榜首。几年之后，“女性主义”的概念已经潜移默化，“辣妹”也变得独一无二，它所传递的女权意识吸引着中青年女性，而女子之间坚实忠诚的友谊也得到认可和强调。

西城男孩

西城男孩是一支著名的爱尔兰男子歌唱组合，1998 年成立，2012 年解散，固定成员是奇恩·伊根（队长，和声部），尚恩·菲南（主唱），马克·菲海利（主唱，高声部）和尼基·柏恩（和音部）。布莱恩·麦菲登（第二主唱，和声部）1998 年加入，2004 年离队。

西城男孩延续了欧洲男子乐团的传统，演唱的民谣和俱乐部流行乐曲受到欧洲歌迷的热捧，一时成为欧洲最成功的乐队之一。他们的一些世界名曲包括《What Makes a Man》,《Dreams Come True》,《I lay My Love on You》,《Queen of My Heart》等。

尽管他们没有赢得美国市场，但在全球范围内售出了 4000 万张专辑，其中包括七张超白金专辑。2012 年，据英国官方排行榜公司统计，西城男孩的累计唱片销量居英国音乐史第 34 位，是英国销量最高的音乐人之一。

莎拉 · 布莱曼

莎拉 · 布莱曼（1960—　）是一位英国古典跨界女高音歌唱家、演员、作曲家及舞蹈家。她曾用多国语言进行演唱，包括英语、西班牙语、法语、拉丁语、德语、土耳其语、意大利语、俄语、汉语、日语及加泰罗尼亚语。

1976 年，布莱曼加入 Pans People 节目，成为一名舞蹈演员，第二年她加入 Hot Gossip 组合并发行了几首迪斯科独唱单曲。1981 年，她在音乐剧《猫》中首次亮相，此后主演了几部百老汇音乐剧，如在《歌剧魅影》中扮演女主角克莉丝汀 · 戴耶。

在音乐剧舞台上取得多年成功后，布莱曼与制作人弗兰克 · 彼得森合作，重新开始了独唱生涯。他们的合作带来了一系列专辑的成功，如，《潜》（1993）、《苍蝇》（1995）、《告别时刻》（1997）。这首布莱曼与意大利男高音歌唱家安德列 · 波切利合唱的"告别时刻"荣登欧洲排行榜榜首，成为德国历史上销售最快、销量最高的单曲，全球销量超过 1200 万张。在接下来的几年中，布莱曼发行了《伊甸园》（1998）、《月光女神》（2000）、《后宫》（2003）和《交响乐》（2008）等极具个人化和主题化特色的专辑。此外，她还出演了几部电影，如《遗传学歌剧》（2008）等。

布莱曼先后在 40 多个国家获得过 180 枚金奖和白金奖。她也是第一位应邀参加过两场奥运会开幕式的明星，第一次是在 1992 年巴塞罗那奥运会上，第二次是在 16 年后的北京奥运会开幕式上，与中国歌手刘欢合唱歌曲《你和我》。2012 年初，布莱曼获得了联合国教科文组织授予的"和平艺术家"称号。

8.5　电影明星

在英国电影业蓬勃发展的 100 多年中，英国已经涌现出许多世界著名的电影艺术家。其中著名导演有阿尔弗雷德 · 希区柯克、大卫 · 里恩、查理 · 卓别林、迈克尔 · 鲍威尔、卡罗尔 · 里德、雷德利 · 斯科特等。阿尔弗雷德 · 希区柯克开创了许多悬疑心理恐怖电影的元素，他对英国无声电影和早期有声电影做出的杰出贡献使其成为英国电影界的泰斗。大卫 · 里恩七次获得最佳导演奖提名，两次获奖，他的作品常常是后辈学习的范本。查理 · 卓别林不仅是一名导演，更是上世纪著名的电影明星，他在无声电影时代的那些喜剧作品让一代又一代的观众忍俊不禁。

许多英国电影演员也在国际影坛上享有盛誉，包括迈克尔 · 凯恩、朱莉 · 安德鲁斯、理查德 · 伯顿、肖恩 · 康纳利、劳伦斯 · 奥利弗、费雯 · 丽、奥黛丽 · 赫本、安东尼 · 霍普金斯。迈克尔 · 凯恩以他独特的"伦敦工人阶级"口音著名，他参演的影片超过115部，被视为魅力永恒的英国影坛偶像。朱莉·安德鲁斯获得过一项奥斯卡最佳女主角奖、一项英国电影电视艺术学院奖、5项金球奖、3项格莱美奖，2次艾美奖。她的著名作品有《欢乐满人间》、《音乐之声》、《公主日记》等。奥黛丽·赫本在《罗马假日》（1953）中饰演的安妮公主一直深入人心，她也因此成为首位因为一部作品同时获得奥斯卡最佳女主角奖、金球奖和英国电影电视艺术学院奖的女演员。

英国还有许多正活跃于国际影坛的年轻一代，如休·格兰特、科林·费尔斯、拉尔夫·费因斯、奥兰多·布鲁姆、凯瑟琳·泽塔-琼斯、裘德·洛、凯特·温斯莱特、凯拉·奈特莉等。在这部分，我们将介绍一些杰出的英国年轻演员。

休·格兰特

休·格兰特（1960— ）是一位英国演员及电影制片人。作为英国著名的演员之一，他获得过一次金球奖、一次英国电影学院奖和一次荣誉恺撒奖。

1994年，格兰特因在《四个婚礼和一个葬礼》（1994）中饰演男主角查尔斯而一夜爆红，获得了金球奖，以及英国电影电视艺术学院奖最佳男主角。20世纪90年代期间，格兰特将自己定位为一个独创又善于机变的演员，他陆续在《蓝眼睛米奇》（1999）、《诺丁山》（1999）等主流电影中扮演了一些喜剧角色，这些角色很好地诠释了人在有许多烦心事时如何保持积极阳光的心态。21世纪初，格兰特俨然成为讽刺喜剧演员的代表。他一改往日戏路，在一些影片中饰演纨绔子弟和花花公子的角色，如《BJ单身日记》（2001）、《单亲插班生》（2002）和《美国梦》（2006）。他还在剧情科幻片《云图》（2012）中一人分饰过多个角色。

除了演艺事业外，格兰特还是个不错的运动员，他年轻时曾玩过板球和足球。现在他喜欢玩高尔夫球，并经常参加职业选手和业余选手混合锦标赛。受父亲的影响，格兰特从少年时代起就对艺术有着狂热的热爱，有收藏艺术作品的习惯。

奥兰多·布鲁姆

奥兰多·布鲁姆（1977— ）是一位著名的英国演员。2004年，布鲁姆被美国《人物》杂志评选为“最美丽的50人”以及“最受欢迎的单身贵族”。2009年，联合国儿童基金会任命布鲁姆为亲善大使。截至2007年5月，在史上票房最高的15部电影中，布鲁姆参演了4部。

16岁时，奥兰多·布鲁姆在伦敦市政厅音乐戏剧学院学习演戏。1999年，毕业后不久的布鲁姆在彼得·杰克逊导演的《魔戒三部曲》中饰演“精灵王子”莱格拉斯。这部电影改编自托尔金的史诗奇幻小说，2001年上映后使布鲁姆一举成名，成为少女最喜欢的偶像。有了在《魔戒三部曲》中的精彩表现后，布鲁姆相继出演了一些史诗奇幻片、历史史诗片和奇幻冒险片，名气越来越大。他最著名的角色包括《魔戒三部曲》和《霍比特人三部曲》中的“精灵王子”莱格拉斯、《加勒比海盗》系列电影中的威尔·特纳、《特洛伊》中的帕里斯，以及《天国王朝》中的伊贝林的贝里昂。

布鲁姆通过《天国王朝》、《伊丽莎白镇》等影片确立了自己好莱坞一线影星的身份，随后出演了集段式电影《纽约，我爱你》和《小镇大街》。此外，2007 年布鲁姆还在伦敦西区出演了第一部舞台剧《辉煌人生》，2013 年他在百老汇新版舞台剧《罗密欧和朱丽叶》中饰演罗密欧。

2010 年，布鲁姆与澳大利亚模特米兰达·克尔结婚并育有一子，2013 年，两人离婚。

凯特·温斯莱特

凯特·温斯莱特（1975—　）是英国著名女演员，曾获得奥斯卡最佳女主角奖、艾美奖、三次金球奖和格莱美奖。她是目前为止获得六次奥斯卡提名的最年轻的演员，也是少数几位获得美国四大娱乐奖项中三项的女演员之一。

温斯莱特在伯克希尔长大，从小开始学习戏剧。1994 年出演首部电影《罪孽天使》开启了演艺生涯，并获得好评。1995 年，她在李安导演的《理智与情感》（1995）中扮演任性热情的配角玛丽安，获得了相当的人气，之后主演爱情灾难片《泰坦尼克号》（1997）名声大噪，这部影片也成为当时票房收入最高的电影。2009 年，她凭借《生死朗读》问鼎奥斯卡最佳女主角奖，2011 年凭借电视剧《欲海情魔》获得艾美奖迷你剧最佳女主角奖，进一步巩固了她在同辈人中成绩斐然、多才多艺的女演员地位。

除了演戏外，温斯莱特还为纪录片和儿童读物配音。她配音的《听故事的人》被评为 2000 年格莱美奖最佳儿童朗读专辑。此外，她还给一些配音的影片配乐，比如演唱动画片《圣诞颂歌》（2001）中的歌曲《如果》。

凯拉·奈特莉

凯拉·奈特莉（1985—　）是著名的英国女演员、模特。凯拉从孩童时开始演艺事业，她的第一部电影拍摄于 1995 年。2003 年，凯拉因饰演《加勒比海盗》系列中的女主角伊丽莎白·斯旺走红。2008 年《福布斯》杂志将凯拉列为好莱坞收入榜第二名，她以 2007 年 3200 万美元的收入，成为当年演员高收入榜上唯一一位非美籍女演员。

自从出演《加勒比海盗》大获成功后，凯拉又出演了一些时代剧，如《傲慢与偏见》（2005）、《赎罪》（2007）、《绢》（2007）、《公爵夫人》（2008）、《危险方法》（2011）和《安娜·卡列尼娜》（2012）。她还出演了一些好莱坞影片，如爱情片《真爱至上》（2003）、历史动作片《亚瑟王》（2004）、心理惊悚片《灵魂夹克》(2005)、动作惊悚片《多米诺》(2005)、历史片《爱的边缘》(2008)、犯罪剧情片《伦敦大道》(2010)、反乌托邦科幻片《别让我走》(2010),爱情片《一夜迷情》(2010)以及喜剧片《世界情缘》(2012)。

2005年,凯拉主演改编自简·奥斯汀小说的同名电影《傲慢与偏见》,并获得第78届奥斯卡金像奖最佳女主角及第63届金球奖提名。2007年出演剧情片《赎罪》,获得第65届金球奖最佳女主角提名。2014年出演了4部电影,凭《模仿游戏》获得金球奖以及第87届奥斯卡金像奖最佳女配角提名。

* * * * *

第9章 英国著名景点

随着英国的殖民扩张和英语的传播,其丰富悠久的历史文化也传播到世界各地,吸引着海外游客,使英国成为世界上游客最多的国家之一。这片土地几乎可以满足游客的一切需求,那充满魅力的英伦历史、富有朝气的城市生活以及丰富的文化传统总是让人流连忘返。从错落乡间的古城堡、中世纪建成的校园,到古罗马遗址和历史悠久的皇家宫殿,这里处处古迹,让人心驰神往。

英国有着数目繁多的古堡、宫殿、豪宅,雕像、桥梁等历史遗迹和地标建筑。如果你想游览富丽堂皇的皇宫、城堡或者豪宅,那么一定不要错过英国。如果你想参观教堂、修道院或者寺庙,这里也有许多世界上最为精致壮观的宗庙建筑让你尽兴。如果你想观赏古代艺术展览,这里也有许多优秀的画廊和博物馆,记录着人类文化的历史。如果你想找一个能让全家都玩得尽兴的地方,那不妨去一下主题乐园和游乐场。除此之外,英国还有许多的公园、花园和野生动物园等自然保护区,以及不错的购物市场和商店,一定可以让游客流连忘返。

在这一部分,我们将介绍一些英国著名的标志性建筑及名胜古迹,包括1)地标和古遗;2)城堡、宫殿和豪宅;3)教堂和修道院;4)博物馆和美术馆;5)游乐场和主题公园。

9.1 古迹和地标

我们今天所熟悉的英国有着悠久的历史,它经历了文化、文明以及帝国的兴起和衰落,从史前人类到凯尔特部落,再从诺曼征服到盎格鲁-撒克逊的入侵,这个国家有着举足轻重的地位。从英国崛起到发展成为现在的联合王国,这片土地上保留着许许多多卓越的历史遗迹以及地标建筑，它们也向游客展示着英国历史上那些丰富多彩的故事。

今天，这些历史古迹和地标建筑吸引着无数游客，其中既包括议会大厦、塔桥、白金汉宫、巨石阵、温莎城堡等世界闻名的景点，也包括一些默默无闻却又充满惊喜的地方。

由于篇幅有限，在这一节中，我们将主要介绍一些有代表性的古迹和地标，包括议会大厦和大本钟、塔桥，以及巨石阵。

威斯敏斯特宫和大本钟

威斯敏斯特宫（也称议会大厦）位于伦敦的中心威斯敏斯特市，它坐落在泰晤士河北岸，是英国议会的所在地，也是英国的政治中心之一。宫殿西北角的钟楼就是著名的大本钟（2012 年起更名为“伊丽莎白塔”），它是伦敦和英国的象征。1987 年，威斯敏斯特宫被联合国教科文组织列为世界文化遗产。

威斯敏斯特宫最初建于 11 世纪，一直作为英格兰王室的寝宫，1512 年的一场大火之后，宫殿开始成为英国国会的驻地，这里也曾作为皇家法庭使用。1834 年，一场更大的火灾几乎摧毁了重建后的大楼，保留下来的中世纪建筑中最重要的就是威斯敏斯特厅。现在我们所见的这座宫殿是大火后重建的，它是维多利亚新哥特式风格建筑的杰出代表。

宫殿分为四层，共有 1100 多个房间、100 道楼梯，以及总长 4. 8 公里的走道。首层有办公室、餐厅和酒吧；第二层为宫殿主要厅室，分布着议会厅、议会休息室和图书馆。顶部两层为委员房间和办公室。英国议会的工作地点有上议院厅和下议院厅两处。上议院厅位于威斯敏斯特宫南侧，厅内用红色皮革装饰。下议院厅位于威斯敏斯特宫北侧，用绿色皮革装饰。

这座有着 150 年历史的大本钟是伦敦最著名的景点之一。“大本钟”其实并不是钟塔本身，而是指塔内重达 13. 8 吨的这座大钟。这座钟整点报时，自 1859 年开始使用以来一直保持着高度的精确性，其精确程度很难让人相信它是由 19 世纪的工匠制作的。现在大本钟已经作为英国和伦敦的象征，出现在许多电影作品中。这座高达 96 米的大本钟塔楼俯瞰着威斯敏斯特市，英国国民如果要进入楼内参观，需要向议员提出申请。

塔桥

塔桥是伦敦的一座开合式悬索桥，因靠近伦敦塔而得名。塔桥横跨泰晤士河，每天有超过 4 万人在桥上通行。它不仅是伦敦的标志性建筑，也是世界上最著名的标志性建筑之一。

19 世纪下半叶，随着人口的增加，伦敦急需再建一座桥以缓解交通压力。

1876 年伦敦市法团决定在伦敦桥东侧再建一座桥，他们面临的问题是——如何才能在不影响交通的情况下建成这座桥呢？直到 1884 年 10 月，城市设计师霍勒斯·琼斯的一份设计方案才在 50 多份设计中脱颖而出，解决了这个难题。

塔桥 1886 年开始修建，历时 8 年完工。大桥全长 244 米，两座桥塔高 65 米，上方由两条水平通道相连，主要用来承受桥身悬浮段的张力。两座塔身之间相隔 61 米，分为等长的两段桥臂，当河中有船通过时，这两条重逾千吨的桥臂可提升到 86 度，让行船通过。

巨石阵

巨石阵是世界著名的史前文化遗址，位于英格兰威尔特郡。它由一些巍峨巨石环绕而成，建造于公元前 3000 年至公元 2000 年之间。目前没有发现关于巨石阵的文字记载，研究者们对巨石阵的研究仍存有争议。1986 年，巨石阵遗址及周边地区被列入联合国教科文组织世界文化遗产名录。

考古发现巨石阵的修建是分几个阶段完成的。第一阶段大约开始于公元前 3000 年，当时修建的是环形沟渠和土台。千年之后，人们在中间竖起了一圈蓝砂岩石柱，现在一般认为这些重达 4 吨的巨石是从约 250 英里外的南威尔士普利塞里山拖运过来的，这对于石器时代只有最简陋工具的劳工来说简直就是件无法完成的壮举。尽管没有人能确定古人是如何做到这一点的，但人们普遍认为他们有一整套绳索、雪橇和滚木等工具。

公元前 1500 年，巨石阵所需的巨石已经基本到位并被竖立排成一圈，石柱上横架着巨大的石楣梁，呈门廊状竖立（两个垂直的石柱上一块水平巨石）。这一时期，那些 500 年前运来的蓝砂岩石也被重新排列成马蹄形的内圈，中间有一块巨石作为祭坛。在巨石门廊外，竖着五组马蹄形的巨石，其中三组保存完整，另两组只剩下一根石柱。再外围就是 30 根石柱组成的主圈，其中只有 17 根直立石柱和 6 根平卧的石块还保持原样。在往外还有 56 个圆形大坑，这些大坑是 17 世纪由考古学家约翰·奥布里发现的，所以命名为“奥布里”坑。跟英国其他许多巨石遗址一样（如 22 英里外的埃夫伯里巨石遗址），石圈内的马蹄形石柱在夏至日时正好指向日出的位置，这与一些人对巨石阵为某种天文历法的猜测不谋而合。

巨石阵是英国一大考古之谜：人们对于古人建造它的目的有着诸多猜测，从祭祀台到天文计时仪，并无定论。事实上，没有人确切知道这些史前人类为什么会花费这么多的时间和精力在这样一项巨大的工程上。

9.2 城堡、宫殿和豪宅

在英国悠久的历史中，许多历史建筑得以保留下来，如，古城堡、皇宫、豪华宅院、驻防庄园和郊区宅院等。这些优秀的建筑和历史遗产吸引着世界各地的人们。这里有被列为世界文化遗产的，由爱德华一世修建的博马里斯城堡、卡那封城堡、康威城堡和哈莱克城堡；也有布莱尼姆宫、伦敦塔、威斯敏斯特宫；还有 120 多座皇家宫殿、古宅和园林等等。

白金汉宫

白金汉宫是英国君主在伦敦的主要寝宫及办公地点。宫殿位于威斯敏斯特城，坐落在格林公园、海德公园和圣·詹姆斯公园之间，是国家庆典和王室欢迎仪式举行场地之一。

1703 年，白金汉公爵建造了一大型建筑并将其命名为“白金汉屋”，这就是今天白金汉宫的主体建筑。1761 年乔治三世买下了这座府邸，将其作为妻子夏洛特女王的一处私人住宅，命名为“女王的家”。19 世纪宫殿开始扩建，1837 年维多利亚女王登基后，白金汉宫成为英王的正式寝宫。

每年的八、九月份，女王对巴莫纳进行年度例行访问期间，白金汉宫的 19 个国事厅、宴会厅和花园会对外开放。国事厅是白金汉宫的核心工作区，主要供女王及王室成员款待国事及官方活动的来客，这里有许多王室珍藏的艺术品，还有精致的红木家具。宴会厅是宫殿内最大的多功能厅，用于国宴及外交接待等正式场合使用，有时也会用来举办纪念音乐会和其他艺术表演等。

伦敦塔

伦敦塔是伦敦最著名的古迹之一，也是伦敦的标志性建筑。这座古老的城堡坐落于伦敦市中心，泰晤士河北岸。11 世纪 80 年代，威廉一世（1066—1087）修建了这座城堡，在此后近千年的岁月中，伦敦塔担任过各种角色，包括堡垒、军械库、国库、铸币厂、宫殿、天文台、避难所和监狱等。1988 年，伦敦塔被联合国教科文组织列入世界文化遗产名录。

伦敦塔围绕白塔而建，是一个具有悠久历史的堡垒，也是王室权力的象征。威廉一世将伦敦塔巧妙地修筑在泰晤士河的弯道上，既能保护伦敦，又能占领领土。伦敦塔以其牢固的防御结构和重要的驻军位置，肩负着保护伦敦城和控制臣民的双重任务。这座城堡一直统驭着周边领土，直到 19 世纪。

这座著名的城堡占地约 18 亩，这里陈列着大量珍贵的展品，比如世界上最早的（1652 年）展览“Line of Kings”就是在这里，展出过许多精致的王室盔甲。这里还有很多有意思的项目，游客不仅可以看到伦敦塔的守卫兼导游穿着传统服饰带队游览，还可以观赏御用珍宝展、皇家铸币厂，以及监狱和刑场展。伦敦塔内最著名的建筑莫过于位于城堡中心的白塔，它是 11 世纪晚期皇家诺曼底式城堡的典型代表，因为久负盛名，所以曾出现在莎士比亚的多部戏剧中。塔内有著名的皇家军械库展，还有一座11世纪诺曼底式教堂。12世纪到20世纪中期，在伦敦塔作为监狱期间，很多人在这里走上了断头台，这里也曾关押过一些著名的囚犯，如托马斯·莫尔爵士、亨利六世、亨利八世的妻子安妮·博林和凯瑟琳·霍华德，以及鲁道夫·赫斯等。

温莎城堡

温莎城堡位于伦敦以西一小时车程的温莎镇，是世界上最大、最古老的一座有人居住的城堡，也是英国王室的行宫之一。伊丽莎白二世常常在这里度周末、举行国宴并进行一些官方接待活动。

11世纪，威廉一世在诺曼征服后修建了温莎城堡，此后的英国君主使用并扩建了这座城堡。目前温莎保存下来的最早的建筑可以追溯到亨利二世时期(1154—1189年在位)。现在包括富丽堂皇的国家套房和15世纪的圣·乔治教堂在内的大部分城堡区域可以对游客开放。

国家套房里保留着许多精美的名画，其中不乏伦布兰特里、卡纳莱托和庚斯博罗的作品。这里每年3月到10月对游客开放，游客还可以参观乔治六世的住所，这里是城堡中最富丽堂皇的地方之一。

圣·乔治教堂是英国哥特式建筑中的精品，以其细致艳丽的彩绘玻璃著称。1348年开始，由爱德华三世制定的英国骑士勋爵最高级别“嘉德勋章”的授勋仪式就在圣·乔治教堂举行。这里还长眠着十位英国君主，包括亨利八世和他的第三任妻子、查理一世等。最后一位长眠于此的是伊丽莎白太后。

其他值得一看的还有精美的温莎公园，大部分游客在飞往希思罗机场的空中就可以将这座6英里长的漂亮花园尽收眼底。当然，对皇宫感兴趣的游客自然也不会错过城堡卫兵的换岗仪式了。

最后别忘了，温莎城堡是一座办公用的宫殿，在国事使用期间并不对外开放，所以游客来访前别忘了确认是否可以参观。

9.3 教堂和修道院

英国的历史和文化深受宗教的影响，这里有包括大小教堂和修道院在内的许多宗教建筑，英国的许多游客也是为此而来。

英国的一些大教堂有着逾千年的历史，这里不仅有12世纪的古老教堂，也有利物浦、考文垂的现代化大教堂。这些教堂从早期的英国哥特式风格，发展到具有文艺复兴庄严华丽特色的圣保罗大教堂，再到20世纪60年代具有现代风格的利物浦罗马天主教大教堂，展现了建筑风格的变化和发展。

从中世纪一直到16世纪英国的宗教改革，教会一直享有巨大的权力和财富，这些华丽的大教堂就是教会权利的象征。这些大教堂建造精美、色彩鲜亮，只是大部分室内装饰品和原有的中世纪风格在宗教改革和内战中被摧毁。内战期间，一些大教堂也被当做要塞、监狱，甚至马厩使用。现在依然有许多教堂和修道院吸引着来自世界各地的游客。

威斯敏斯特教堂

威斯敏斯特教堂（也称西敏寺）是位于伦敦市中心威斯敏斯特宫旁边的一座大型哥特式建筑风格的教堂，也是英国最负盛名的宗教建筑之一。这里一直是英国君主（以前是英格兰君主）加冕登基和安葬的地方。今天，威斯敏斯特教堂由英国王室管理，人们可以在这里做礼拜。

威斯敏斯特教堂融会了多种建筑风格，常被奉为早期英国哥特建造风格的典范。教堂最初是由“忏悔者”爱德华建于11世纪。现在保留的大部分楼体是在1245年到1272年间重建的，当时亨利三世决定重建一座威严的哥特式教堂。此后，教堂不断扩大：1503年到1512年间建成了亨利七世礼拜堂、1745年开始修建教堂西端的双塔。现在教堂的中心地带是圣·爱德华祠墓，主祠周围还有英国历史上一些著名人物的墓地和纪念碑。

威廉一世是第一位在威斯敏斯特教堂荣受加冕的国王，自此之后，王室的加冕礼就开始在这里举行，爱德华五世和爱德华八世除外。多年来，威斯敏斯特教堂也是皇室的主要墓地，现在皇室家族的墓地已经改在温莎城堡。在威斯敏斯特教堂安葬或竖立纪念碑已经逐渐成为一种极大的荣耀，目前安葬在教堂内的名人有英国贵族、将军、诗人、政治家、医生和科学家等，其中包括克莱门特·艾德礼、乔叟、查尔斯·达尔文、查尔斯·狄更斯、塞缪尔·约翰逊、鲁德亚德·吉卜林、约翰·赫歇尔、艾萨克·牛顿、温斯顿·丘吉尔、威廉·威伯福斯等。

威斯敏斯特教堂内部堪称一个名副其实的英国历史博物馆。在众多的景点中，游客不仅可以看到中世纪的加冕宝座，还可以看到诗人中纪念文学巨匠的纪念碑，以及一些名人的陵墓。这里还有一些千年珍宝，如绘画、彩色玻璃和纺织品等，可以让游客一饱眼福。

圣保罗大教堂

伦敦的圣保罗大教堂是伦敦的宗教圣地及主要地标建筑，它位于伦敦卢德门山顶，这是伦敦城的最高点。教堂高约111米，在1710年至1962年间曾是伦敦的最高建筑，也是世界第二大圆顶教堂。

1666年的伦敦大火烧毁了圣保罗大教堂的前身，著名建筑师克里斯托弗·雷恩爵士于1675至1710年间在这处旧址上建成了第四座教堂，这就是我们今天所见的这座英国巴洛克风格的大教堂。

圣保罗大教堂是伦敦最著名、最显眼的景点之一。这里不仅举办过第一次世界大战和第二次世界大战的感恩仪式，而且见证了维多利亚女王的周年庆、伊丽莎白女王的八十岁生日庆典，以及她的银婚、金婚及钻石禧年庆典，这里也是查尔斯王子和戴安娜王妃举行婚礼的地方。此外，这里也举办过纳尔逊、惠灵顿公爵等人的葬礼，许多名人的墓地和纪念碑也坐落于此，包括克里斯托弗·雷恩爵士、弗洛伦斯·南丁格尔、T. E. 劳伦斯、基钦纳勋爵、亚历山德拉·弗莱明爵士以及多年以来供职于此的神职人员。这里还有一些纪念福克兰岛战争和海湾战争战士的纪念碑。

圣保罗大教堂是16世纪英国宗教改革后建成的第一座大教堂，也是一座安立甘宗教堂。现在这所教堂仍在行使宗教职能，定期做礼拜。

9.4 博物馆和美术馆

英国有许多优秀的艺术馆和博物馆，它们是向大众传播文化、创意和想法的重要渠道。据估计，英国现有约2500家博物馆，其中超过1800家已经通过认证，大部分的永久收藏品已经向市民免费开放。伦敦是英国的文化中心，单看其博物馆和艺术馆的数量，就让人不得不感叹它的确是英国文化的核心。

近几年来参观英国博物馆和艺术馆的人大幅增加，每年去博物馆和艺术馆参观的游客总数已超过一亿人。根据2013年的一项调查，2012年参观过博物馆的英格兰居民达到52%。2013年最受欢迎的五大博物馆及艺术馆是：大英博物馆、国家美术馆、自然历史博物馆、泰特现代美术馆和科学博物馆。

大英博物馆

大英博物馆（又称英国国家博物馆、不列颠博物馆）坐落于伦敦市中心的罗素广场上。它是世界上历史最悠久、规模最宏伟、最受游客欢迎的综合性博物馆之一。

大英博物馆始建于1753年，大部分藏品来自于收藏家汉斯·史隆爵士的捐赠。1759年1月15日，博物馆正式向公众开放。在接下来的两个半世纪中，博物馆随着英国的殖民扩张而不断扩大、馆藏也愈加丰富。到了今天，馆内的永久藏品已近800万件，这些藏品记录着人类文化的发展——从古文化到现代文化，跨越了前后200万年的历史。这里有来自各个历史时期的文物，从维京人时代到罗马时期，从埃及文明到中世纪欧洲文明，藏品类型包括陶器、珍宝、雕像、绘画、雕塑等。其中最值得一看的有1799年发现的能解读古埃及象形文字的罗塞塔石碑、19世纪由埃尔金勋爵从雅典卫城帕特农神庙收来至今仍有争议的“埃尔金石雕”、古埃及木乃伊、出土于萨顿胡的盎格鲁-撒克逊船葬文物，以及豪尔萨巴德遗址出土的带翼公牛雕像。每年来到大英博物馆参观的游客有近 600 万人。

国家美术馆

国家美术馆（又称国家艺廊）是位于伦敦市中心威斯敏斯特城特拉法加广场的一座艺术博物馆。这是继法国卢浮宫、大英博物馆、美国大都会艺术博物馆之后，最受欢迎的一座艺术博物馆。这里展出了鲁本斯、梵高、特纳、达·芬奇、莫奈、伦布兰特和其他艺术家的作品。

国家美术馆成立于 1824 年，当时仅有 38 幅画作，后来逐渐拓展为今天的国家级美术馆规模，收集了从 13 世纪中期至 19 世纪，多达 2300 件西欧绘画作品。这里几乎收纳了欧洲每个艺术流派的作品。在现代塞恩斯伯里馆里展出了馆中最早期的作品，如早期意大利画家乔托和彼埃罗·德拉·弗朗西斯卡等人的画作。塞恩斯伯里馆的下层展厅中有一些短期展览。美术馆西翼展出的是意大利文艺复兴时期柯勒乔、提香和拉斐尔等人的作品；北翼中展出的是 17 世纪荷兰、弗兰德、意大利和西班牙大师级的作品。东翼中收藏的是馆中最受欢迎的作品：法国印象派和后印象派的画作，包括莫奈的一幅《睡莲》，和梵高向日葵系列中的一幅画作。

由于馆内的藏品属于英国公众，因此美术馆是以免费参观的方式向大众开放。

自然历史博物馆

伦敦自然历史博物馆是欧洲最大的自然历史博物馆，馆内陈列着大量来自不同自然历史时期的标本，是世界上最大的自然历史收藏馆之一，馆内藏品丰富，小至显微切片，大至庞大的猛犸象骨架，应有尽有。博物馆外观形似一座大教堂，里面有精美的壁画雕刻，中央大厅陈列一副巨型恐龙骨架，令人印象深刻。

馆内有动植物和岩石矿物等标本约 8000 万号，包括植物、昆虫、矿物、古生物和动物五种类型。自然历史博物馆是世界著名的生物分类、鉴定和保护研究中心。由于其历史悠久，许多馆内藏品具有重要的历史价值和科研价值，比如，里面有查尔斯·达尔文收集的标本。博物馆内的图书馆收藏着大量与科研相关的书籍、期刊、手稿和插图，游客只有预约才可以参观。英国的自然历史博物馆被公认为闻名世界的自然历史领域的研究先驱。

整个博物馆分为四个色区。绿色区陈列着关于生命、地球、环境和进化的相关展品。红色区主要研究地球的演化，包括地球的形成及其在宇宙中的位置。在蓝色区，游客会惊叹于地球上的生命是如此的丰富多样，这里不仅有蓝色的鲸鱼，还有微小的无脊椎动物。最后，橙色区会带你进入野生动物园（4 月至 10 月开放）和达尔文中心。

泰特现代美术馆

泰特现代美术馆是伦敦的一座国家级现当代艺术博物馆，位于伦敦南部的泰晤士河畔地区。

泰特美术馆是由原来的河岸发电站改建而成，发电站 1981 年关闭，于 2000 年该美术馆建成，广受游客的欢迎，每年来访的游客达到 500 万人。当人们走进长达 152 米、横穿整栋建筑的巨大涡轮车间时一定会感叹于它的宏大。在这里，游客可以免费观赏塞尚、博纳尔、马蒂斯、毕加索、罗斯科、达利、波洛克、沃霍尔和布尔乔亚等人的画作。

泰特专门收藏了 20 世纪初到现在的英国现代艺术作品，以及一些国际现当代艺术作品，包括自野兽派后所有主要的艺术流派。这里不仅有毕加索和马蒂斯的杰作，也有达利、厄恩斯特、马格丽特和米罗等人的超现实主义作品。美国抽象表现主义的作品包括波洛克的作品，以及罗斯科的 9 幅西格兰姆壁画。这里还详细收集了俄罗斯抽象艺术先驱纳姆·嘉宝的许多雕塑作品，以及贾科梅蒂的一组重要雕塑品及画作。泰特还收藏了里奇特斯坦和沃霍尔的波普艺术作品，以及极简艺术和观念艺术的一些作品。

9.5 游乐场及主题公园

英国有许多著名的游乐场及主题公园，可以让大人和小孩玩得尽兴。为了吸引游客，这些游乐场和公园各有各的特色，但由于篇幅所限，我们的介绍不可能将所有有特色的公园和游乐场包含在内。这一节主要将选择一些具有代表性的游乐场所，包括伦敦眼、奥尔顿塔主题公园、黑池游乐海滩和温莎乐高主题乐园。

伦敦眼

伦敦眼是一座矗立于伦敦泰晤士河南岸的巨型摩天轮，现在已经成为伦敦的标志性景点之一。伦敦眼于 2000 年 3 月对公众开放，也被称为“千禧之轮”，隐喻人类进入新千年。伦敦眼是英国最受欢迎的付费景点，每年有超过 375 万名游客登上巨轮游览。

伦敦眼高 135 米，转轮直径 120 米，整个结构重达 2100 吨。1999 年建成时，它是世界上最高的摩天轮，后来依次被 2006 年建成的南昌之星（高 158 米）、2008 年建成的新加坡飞行者摩天轮（高 165 米），和 2014 年建成的拉斯维加斯豪客摩天轮（高 168 米）超过。

作为世界上最大的景观摩天轮之一，人们可以从城市各个角度看到它。巨轮上有 32 个乘坐舱，回转速度约为每秒 0. 26 米，转一圈需要 30 分钟，（天气晴朗时）

舱中游客可以从各个角度看到40公里远的景色。所有的乘坐舱为密封舱，设有空调系统，可供轮椅上下，每个舱代表伦敦的一个行政区，可载客25人，舱内设有座位，游客可以在舱中自由行走，舱中还有触屏系统，向游客介绍他们所看到的美景。天气晴朗时，游客在巨轮顶端可以看到25英里外的温莎城堡。

奥尔顿塔主题公园

奥尔顿塔主题公园是英国最大、最受欢迎的一座主题公园，有着“复仇女神”、“微笑者”等世界上最具标志性的游乐设施。在这里，游客不仅可以寻求乐趣和刺激，还可以享受舒适的温泉及主题酒店服务，奥尔顿度假村可以给全家人提供舒适的享受。

公园修建在一座15世纪的斯塔福德郡庄园中，1980年4月4日建成为设施齐全的主题公园并向公众开放。现在公园内分为“塔街”、“兵变湾”、“加丹加峡谷”、“幽暗森林”、“禁谷”、“黑暗森林”、“幻境”、“X-sector”、“冒险园”和“Cbeebies land”儿童乐园十个主题区域。公园里还有历史悠久的塔楼和花园。空中缆车（SkyRide）穿梭于“塔街”、“禁谷”和“幻境”中，让乘客将园中景色尽收眼底。

目前公园里已经有至少9座高速过山车，包括“复仇女神”（Nemesis）、“湮没”（Oblivion）、“速度女王”（Rita）、“十三号”（Thirteen）以及“微笑者”（The Smiler）等。最值得游客期待的是“微笑者”过山车。这座高达18米的过山车是世界上首个绕14圈的过山车，加上视觉幻象和令人炫目的灯光等心理效应，游客会感到整个过程更为惊险刺激。公园里还有一系列受孩子们欢迎的游乐项目，如新建成的Cbeebies Land儿童乐园等。这里还有两座宾馆、水族馆、“4D”影院、单轨索道、缆车以及绵延数英亩的美丽花园，游客可以在这里休闲探秘。

黑池游乐海滩

黑池游乐海滩是位于英格兰兰开夏郡黑泽市菲尔德海岸上的一座游乐园及度假胜地，建成于1896年，由汤普森家族经营。它是英国最受欢迎的旅游景点之一，也是世界上最受欢迎的20大游乐园之一。2014年，被评为英国最佳主题公园，在“旅行者选择奖”欧洲最佳公园榜上位列第九。

公园内有“海绵宝宝”、“降世神通”、“朵拉的世界旅行”以及“淘气小兵兵”等多部世界流行卡通主题区，12座惊险刺激的游乐设施坐落其中。这里也有适合所有年龄层的家庭式游乐项目，如“超级无敌掌门狗刺激游戏”、“茶杯”、“汤普森旋转木马”、碰碰车、卡丁车以及超级恐怖的“幽灵列车”等。公园里还有很多世界著名的过山车，包括“大块头”（The Big One）、“北斗星”（the Big Dipper）、“注射器”（Infusion）、“瓦尔哈拉神殿”（Valhalla）、“冰风暴”（Ice

Blast）以及最新的刺激玩法“红箭飞行队”（Red Arrows Skyforce）。

游客在这里除了体验惊险刺激外，还可以观看黑池游乐海滩的现场演出及活动，比如极负盛名的舞台娱乐节目“热冰”（Hot Ice）、“克雷格·克里斯汀”（Craig Christian）、“肯韦·伯斯特”（Ken Webster）以及“恐怖马戏团”（Circus of Horrors）。这里的娱乐项目几乎可以让所有年龄层的游客尽兴而归。

温莎乐高乐园

温莎乐高乐园是一个面向儿童的乐高系列主题公园及度假村，位于英格兰伯克郡的温莎小镇。1996 年，温莎乐园由原来的温莎野生动物园改建而成，是继丹麦比隆乐高乐园后的全球第二座乐高主题乐园。跟世界上其他地区的乐高乐园一样，温莎的这座乐园中也包含了乐高主题的游乐设施、模型和建筑区，这些设施主要是为 3 至 12 岁的儿童设计的。

2015 年，温莎乐高乐园共迎来了 220 万游客，使之成为继奥尔顿塔主题乐园后英国的第二大主题公园、欧洲最受欢迎的十大公园之一。这里有超过 55 个互动游乐设施、景点、现场表演、建筑区和驾驶区，更别说在这 150 英亩的美丽公园中还有多达 8000 万块乐高积木。乐园中最受孩子们欢迎的莫过于“迷你城”了，这是一座由 4000 万块乐高积木，按照 1∶20 的比例搭成的微缩公园，它模仿了世界各地的一些城镇。并且，这里还有积木搭成的许多欧美影片中的动漫人物。

度假村的中心区域是一座具有 150 套房间的完全乐高主题的酒店，游客可以在这里休息娱乐。2016 年正值温莎乐高乐园建园 20 周年，乐园将以全新的 4D 影院呈现“乐高电影 4D 新冒险”节目，游客们还可看到《星球大战》电影著名场景的微缩版。

*　　*　　*　　*　　*

第 10 章　英国的礼仪和礼节

礼仪是指一个社会、社会阶层或社会群体之内符合时代及传统标准的社交行为准则。礼节常常有好坏之分，暗示一种行为是否为社会所接受。礼仪规范常常是不成文的，但其方方面面在不同时代会形成规约。适应外国礼仪是应对文化冲击的重要部分，历来有章可循。人们通常认为英国人在礼节、衣着和语言方面都较为保守，以礼貌、自律、特别是幽默感著称。

10.1　文明礼貌

为表正式或亲切，很多语言使用不同的人称代词称谓他人，这也适用日常问候。对亲昵人称的不当适用被视为对他人的贬低、侮辱甚至是攻击。相反，对正式人称的不当适用也被视为太势利，或对他人有距离感。英国人，尤其是英格兰人，以礼貌和客气而闻名。

常用的正式问候语是“您好吗？”这是一句问候语而非一个问题，正确的回答是重复一遍“您好吗？”人们通常在第一次见面时使用，同时握手。这句问候语也可替换为“见到你很高兴——见到你我也很高兴”等多种不同表达（Nice to meet you — Nice to meet you too；Delighted to meet you — Delighted to meet you too. Pleased to meet you — Pleased to meet you too. Glad to meet you — Glad to meet you too.）

诸如“早上好、下午好、晚上好”的问候语之后，通常会跟一句“你好吗？”而最常见的礼貌回答是“我很好，谢谢，你呢？”千万不要试图详细描述你的身体状况，因为这只是一句客套的问候语而非实际的问句。

非正式的问候语有“你好——你好，我是……”“早啊、下午好啊、晚上好啊”（非正式场合英语中的“好”可省略）。这些常常用于朋友之间，为表达关心，朋友间也会说“还好吗？——挺好的，谢谢。你呢？”

有时“cheers”会替代“Thank you”表达感谢之意，你也会听到用“cheers”替代“goodbye”，实际上是“谢谢，再见”。

在英国许多地方，直接称呼对方的名字也在一定程度上表达两人之间的友情程度。与陌生人交往时，通常会称呼对方的姓或使用其他更正式的称谓方式，直至彼此都愿意以较随意的方式称呼。然而，这些也许不适用于年轻人、特定群体的成员（比如学生）之间或其他非正式的场合。当人们使用表达亲密或爱意的称谓称呼你时，你不必感到不快，比如称你为“亲爱的”、“宝贝”、“乖乖”、“亲爱的”、“小伙子”、“孩子”、“夫人”、“女士”、“小姐”、“先生”、“老兄/老弟”或“心爱的”——在英国不同的地方这些称谓或有不同，但都是无潜在含义的友好表达，带有地方方言或传统色彩。

“duck”这一爱称来自盎格鲁-撒克逊语的“ducis”这一敬语，类似于中古英语中的“duc”“duk”，意为领袖、指挥官或将军，而“公爵”这一头衔和古法语中的“公爵领地（ducheé）”就是由这两个词演化而来。

“触犯禁忌”不仅仅被排斥在特定文化范围之外，更会被整个社会视为令人反感之举。以下是一些该做和不该做的注意事项。

一定要握手：认识新朋友时，一个有力的握手，或异性之间较轻柔的握手，是最常用的问候方式，也已成为惯例。避免过分亲热的举动，比如拍背或拥抱。和周围的人保持足够的距离，以免侵犯他人的私人空间，除非靠近他人在所难免（比如乘坐公共交通时或上下班高峰时）。

在必要时脱帽（仅男士适用）。脱帽也是表示尊重的问候方式：其渊源于古时骑士在面见国王时需要取下头盔；如不遵从则意味着不信任和敌意。如今，男士在室内戴帽子更加常见。然而，特别对老一辈人来说，这仍是不礼貌的。许多英国人认为在室内戴帽子或戴其他头罩是不礼貌的，特别是在教堂、学校、家庭和其他公共场所。但在教堂里，女士们常常无需遵从这一礼节，甚至在一些天主教堂里，她们还必须遮盖头部。

一定要说“对不起”。如果有人挡了路你想让他们挪动一下，请说声“excuse me”，他们会为你让路。如果你不小心撞到某人，请说声“sorry”。即便是你的错，他们也很可能会让开！也许在“局外人”看来甚为有趣，但这是英国人的习惯。说“please”和“Thank you”是很有礼貌的表现，但如果不说就是很无礼的行为。

一定要排队。在英国，人们喜欢井然有序地排队并耐心等待，比如乘公交车时。通常人们都会排队，等待轮到自己而不推搡前面的人。插队会被人嗤之以鼻。为长者、行动不便者或带孩子的母亲让座也是非常礼貌的行为。

请为他人开门。无论男女在出入时都会为彼此开门，取决于谁先出入。

走时记得付账。在酒吧或其他场所消费后，走时记得付账。

问候时不要亲吻对方。只有亲密的朋友和亲人之间才会在见面时亲吻异性的脸颊。女士之间可以在彼此的右脸颊上轻吻一下，但男士之间不会这么做。

不要问涉及隐私的问题。例如询问女性年龄、他人的体重或婚姻状况，这些都被视为是不礼貌的。谈论或询问他人的财产、所有物或生意上的业绩普遍被视为粗俗之举。人们很少谈论挣多少钱、在银行有多少存款，也不会向他人询问这些信息。问同事的薪水高低也是很不礼貌的，在有些工作场所此类问题是禁止询问的。在其他一些地方，比如在政府机构，公务员的薪水是公开的，即便如此，问别人挣多少钱仍然是非常无礼的行为。

不要在公共场所盯着任何人看。非必要的长时间目光接触也被认为是对他人隐私的侵犯，或者被理解为粗俗无礼或攻击性强，因此应该避免。

不要在公共场所大声说话或挖鼻孔。如果你需要清理鼻毛，请使用手帕。

不要在公共场所打哈欠或咳嗽。这样做时，请用手捂住嘴巴。

不要在公共场所打饱嗝。如果你实在控制不了，请用手捂住嘴并说声“Excuse me”。

不要在公共场所放屁。找一个隐蔽的地方，如果你无意中在人群中这样做了，要说“Pardon me”。不要在街上、公交车上、火车上或商店里随便扔垃圾或吐痰。

10.2　拜访朋友

“随时过来坐坐”和“常来看我”等习语常用于社交场合，但一般不能太当真。明智的做法是在登门拜访之前先打个电话，但晚上 10 点以后不应拜访他人或打电话，除非别人要你这么做，因为对大多数人来说这个时间都太晚了。如果你收到写有“请回复”（‘RSVP’）字样的书面邀请去参加某个活动，你应该回复邀请并告知邀请人你是否打算前往。除非你真的打算去，否则不要接受邀请。你可以这样拒绝邀请：“谢谢你邀请我参加，但我不能前往。”如果在接受邀请之后你不能去，尽早告知你无法到访。当你接受了聚餐邀请，如果你有任何忌口也要告诉主人，主人会精心准备，让你享受聚餐。晚餐是英国大多数地区的正餐。

尽管主人不期待你登门时送礼物，但这样做是非常礼貌的，特别是应邀聚餐的时候，鲜花、巧克力或其他小礼品都是合宜之选。一张感谢卡或拜访之后的一个电话都是礼貌之举，借此表达你的感谢。

英国人十分注重守时。即使只迟到几分钟，也常会被认为是不礼貌的。如果你因故不能赴约，最好给对方打电话告知。一些常见的注意事项如下：

赴午餐、晚餐或与教授、医生及其他专业人士见面时，你应准时赶到。如果你应邀晚上 7 点去某人家吃晚饭，你应该准时到那里。如果邀请函上的时间写着“7 点半到 8 点”，你应在 7 点 50 分之前到达。但是如果上面写着“×点整”，你就必须提前到达。如果觉得要迟到了，提前告知主人才是礼貌的。

对于茶会、招待会和鸡尾酒会，准时到场倒不是那么重要。你可以在活动开始后的任意时间到场，除非活动要求你必须按时到场。

但是对于参加会议、看戏、听音乐会、看电影、观看体育赛事、上课、去教堂，以及参加婚礼，你应该提前几分钟到场。

日常着装适合于一般的家庭拜访。在参加假日聚餐或诸如音乐会、戏剧等文化活动时，你可以穿得更正式些。但是在别人家里仍穿着大衣、靴子或其他外套会让人嗤之以鼻。如果戴着帽子、穿着靴子坐下来吃饭，那就更加糟糕了。

聚餐的方式有几种：“家庭式”，即在餐桌上互相传递盘子以分享食物；“自助式”，吃自助餐时宾客自助用餐；“服务式”，即主人把食物装盘并亲自递给每个人。

在英国，主人会率先吃第一口，除非他让客人这样做。当所有菜上齐，每个人都就位之后，用餐正式开始。在有宗教背景的家庭，饭前有谢恩祈祷；聚会时，客人会先夸赞饭菜表达对主人的感谢，再开始吃饭。在多人共餐的场合，在饭菜未上齐、用餐还未开始之前就开始吃是很不礼貌的。

在野餐、手抓自助餐或其他非正式聚餐时，你可以用手拿鸡肉或比萨，否则要用刀叉。

和他人共餐时，你可以自斟饮品，但主动给坐在你左右的人斟饮品会更礼貌。只有喝白酒或玫瑰红酒时才端着高脚酒杯的脚，喝红酒时要端着杯身。斟酒应依照一定顺序，即“先白酒后红酒，先低度酒再高度酒，先给年轻人斟酒再给年长者斟酒”。

不要舔舐餐刀或把刀含在嘴里。不要张着嘴咀嚼食物，没有人想听到咀嚼食物的声音。

一口吃进太多的食物是不礼貌的。不要用手把食物放到勺子或叉子上。啜食或发出“嗤喽”声也是不礼貌的。不要用餐巾擦鼻涕，只用它来擦嘴。餐巾应该平摊在膝上——把它揶进衣服也很“常见”。不要用指甲剔牙。

如果手机（或其他通信工具）收到来电或短信，不要接电话或查看消息。在特殊情况下，用餐者如果觉得这个电话非常紧急，他应征得主人的谅解，离开席间，在其他人听觉范围之外接电话（或查看消息）。如果你不小心取了太多的食物又不能吃完，请说声“对不起，看来我眼馋胃小”。或“对不起，太好吃了，可是我已经饱了。”重要的是不能冒犯主人。

10.3 餐具礼仪

餐桌礼仪也包括正确使用餐具。英国人大多很重视餐桌礼仪，即使是小孩子也要求正确使用刀叉。

如果你参加一个正式的晚宴，你面前将会有很多刀叉。摆在你盘子上方的是甜点匙和甜点叉。从最外层的餐具开始使用，根据上菜的顺序依次向内。

左手拿叉，右手拿刀，如果你是左撇子则反之。食物被切成一口的分量，即用左手的叉把食物送入口中。对于其他的食物，比如土豆、蔬菜或米饭，可以用右手的刀刃协助将食物放在叉子的背面，叉齿向下。

刀叉分别用两手握住其手柄，并用拇指和食指握住前端。这种方式有时被称为“隐柄式”，因为手掌遮住了手柄。

如果放下餐刀，你可以把叉子翻个面，换只手拿叉子，也就是说如果你是右撇子就换成左手拿叉。不用刀具时，叉子可以齿朝上使用。任何情况下都不要像握把铲子一样用五指包住叉柄。

喝汤时，右手拿汤匙，汤碗稍远离自己，舀汤时汤匙在碗中由内向外舀动。喝汤从汤匙边缘入口（不要发出太大声音），而不是像在欧洲其他地方一样从汤匙“末端”入口。

为了更加注重礼貌，吃豌豆时应把豌豆在叉子上压碎——叉齿向下。最好的方式是先在叉子上放点能粘住豌豆的食物，比如土豆或较软的蔬菜，这些都很容易用叉子压扁。有时把餐刀放下换只手拿叉，会更容易操作，这样你就可以用叉抵住盘中的其他食物盛起豌豆。

在正式场合用餐时，口含食物或与人交谈的间隙请放下刀叉。

吃菜或喝酒之前，要把嘴里的食物咀嚼吞咽干净。上菜时记得说“谢谢”，以表达感激。吃面包时，切出一小块来，再抹上黄油。整块一起吃看起来很俗气。在正式场合，用面包刀从黄油碟中取一些黄油放入面包碟中，再把黄油抹在面包上，这样做才是礼貌的。这就避免了在收拾面包屑时把黄油弄在盘子上。面包刀应只用来抹黄油，而不应用来切面包，面包应该用手掰碎。

用餐时把手肘放在桌子上是不礼貌的。不要伸长手去取食物或其他物品。你应该请他人递给你。同样地，在别人请你这样做时，你也应直接把食物或物品递给别人。咀嚼食物或用餐具发出很大的声音是很不礼貌的。用餐时也绝不要把餐刀放得太远。

一定不要让餐刀入口，也不要舔舐餐刀。永远闭着嘴咀嚼食物。含着食物的同时说话是非常粗鲁的。舔手指或吃得过慢也被视为不礼貌。

吃甜点时，用甜点勺切开甜点，一次只吃一口。用蛋糕叉（或直接）把食物放在甜点勺上，再用勺吃。

当你吃完后，应该把刀叉一同放在盘子上，叉子居左，叉齿向上，餐巾平铺在桌上，以向其他一同进餐的人和服务生示意你用餐完毕。

10.4　商务礼仪

面对面的交流

介绍自己的方式取决于场合的不同。总的来说，虽然不是每次都有机会，但最好是由第三方引荐。握手是相互介绍时最典型的问候方式，后续会面时也应如此。

会面时，使用先生、夫人或女士等敬称再加上对方的姓称呼对方。直到对方让你直呼其名，你才可以这样称呼。在公众场合若不提及对方姓氏，对男性要称“先生”（Sir）。同样，对女性要称“女士”（Madam），但这一称谓的内涵有时已不再常用，不一定适合所有语境。

会议交流的形式取决于与会者的身份。如果所有与会者地位相当，便可自由交流想法。然而，如果有身居高位者在场，则主要由他来发表意见。

通常，在会议正式开始之前，会有一些看似无意义的闲谈，但总的来说，会议是有正式议程和明确目的的。因此会议前的闲谈可视为一种使会议气氛融洽的良好方式。

由于英国的文化常规和背景的缘故，在英国和刚认识的人交谈也许是令人畏惧的。建议最好以较中立的话题开始交流，例如天气，或即时正提到的话题，如征询对方的建议，哪里有什么好玩的好吃的去处。以开放式的问题开始交谈是很好的方式，而非以发表个人主观看法开始，因为你无法估计对方的反应。你会发现，很多英国人宽容而思想开放。当然也有些人会受一些小报新闻的影响，把世界描述得非黑即白。

在英国，人们不太欣赏自我推销的人，表现得谦虚一些再好不过。当然，人们可以接受你正面评价自己的公司和产品。

英国人常常使用外交辞令来替代直言快语。在商务场合，人们不会正面冲突，因为他们不希望彼此冒犯。他们寻求正面的言辞去表达负面的含义时会显得有些闪烁其词。

此外，英国人还喜欢使用委婉的表达方式，以更能令人接受的、肯定的言辞表达否定或不认同。因此，“我不同意”就变成了“我觉得你的观点非常棒，但你是否考虑过……”。对一个观点不感兴趣，可能会表达成“嗯，很有趣”。与英国人交流的另一个难点是他们喜欢轻描淡写。有时，英国人会表面上自贬，这使人难以理解他们对人对事的真实看法。例如，描述一件东西“有一点贵”，可能意味着“非常贵”，描述一件事情“有点麻烦”，实际上这件事对英国人来说可能是“巨大的障碍”。

幽默在商务交往中无处不在。实际上，事情越是严重、棘手，英国人越是喜欢使用幽默。这并不意味着他们不严肃地对待此事——仅作为缓解紧张事态的方式，幽默有助于让人冷静、克制，不感情用事。

一般认为，伦敦以外的英国人特别是北方人更加开放和友善。事实上，在英国，文化的开放程度仍有着南北之分。当然也有例外，比如苏格兰高原地区的人们或威尔士农民很少主动与人攀谈，除非你们相识。讨论问题时他们会显得冷淡，甚至局促，有时会选择礼貌地离开或退避。

守时

英国人在商务活动中一般都很守时。如果你定好两点开会，你的同仁很可能会准时或提前到达会场。出席商务会谈迟到是非常不礼貌的。如果因不可避免的时间延误而迟到，你需要向其他人道歉，并请求谅解。但如果你迟到的时间稍长，你应该提前打电话道歉，并告知你需多长时间才能到达会场；如果因耽搁太久而可能错过会议的主要内容，你应该考虑推迟会议或择日再开会。人们越忙，就越有可能去赴其他的约会，所以尊重他人的时间是很重要的。

参加社交活动稍有不同，宾客可以在约定时间之后 15 分钟左右到场，不过这也得视活动性质和参加人数而定。黄金法则是约会越重要，你就越应该为潜在的延误留足时间。

赠送礼品

赠送礼品通常不是英国商务礼仪的一部分，虽然在收到礼品时回礼是好的做法。有些机构不鼓励接受任何形式的礼品，有些则依法律规定不允许接受任何礼品。然而，重要的是，是送礼也不要送太贵重的礼品，以免被认为是行贿，或者是太廉价的礼物让人觉得是受到侮辱。

可选的合适礼品有多种多样：公司贺卡、笔、书籍、日记本、酒、鲜花、来宾所在国家的纪念品或者文化活动邀请函等。如果当众接受礼品，建议立即打开并表达感谢。

通常，商务谈判圆满结束时是赠送礼物的最佳时机，此处表示的是致谢。最合适的礼物应当是金银制品或瓷器，重要的是要考虑礼物的适宜性和接受者的品位。在圣诞节期间交换商务礼品不太常见；然而，给商业伙伴邮寄贺卡以表感谢是良好的做法。如果你应邀去同事家参加晚宴或聚会，通常可以带一瓶酒作为礼物，可能的话鲜花或巧克力之类的小礼物也不错。送花时，最好避免送红玫瑰（意为爱情）和白百合（意为哀悼并通常用于葬礼）。

商务着装规范

谈到商务着装规范，在英国文化中，无论男女，都是首选经典而保守的着装风格，黑色、深蓝色或烟灰色一类的深色调最为盛行。在办公环境，女性穿裤子或穿裙子都很常见，为尊重宗教自由，戴头巾也可接受。管理层的女性在穿着上常常效仿男性——穿深色西装和衬衣——少见华丽装饰。很多高级管理人员注重服饰品质，以服饰的选择彰显自身的地位。在英国社会流行去设计师精品专卖店购物，定做西装、品牌衬衫、丝绸领带、手工鞋都是富裕和地位的标志。

当对某个商务活动的着装要求不太确定时，盛装打扮总好过穿着随便而给人留下坏印象。当然最好提前知晓着装要求，这样你可以在自我介绍之前做必要的更换。如此你便可更加自在而轻松地与其他公司代表见面。

宴请（款待、招待）

在英国，受到商务伙伴的邀请共进午餐很常见，但共进晚餐则较为少见。公务午餐常常是会晤的延伸，可以在吃饭的同时谈商务。如果对此不确定，那么就依东道主的意思行事。请客的人会买单，所以没必要主动要求一起买单。如果你请客，对方提议一起买单，多半是出于礼貌，并不一定真的需要如此。

午餐形式多样，可以在酒馆随便吃一顿饭，也可以在奢华的餐厅享用大餐。地点的选择取决于多种因素，如地理位置、商业机遇（或客人）的重要程度、市场领域等。如果你不确定带客人去哪里用餐好，出于谨慎最好选一家有档次的餐馆。

午餐通常会上酒，一些英国人愿意喝酒，而也有人坚持只喝软饮料——这完全取决于个人，在这种情况下你不必迫于压力而喝酒。喝酒更多是在晚餐的时候，量也更大，那时身处“酒文化”中，你会稍感压力。

*　　*　　*　　*　　*

第11章　节日和假日

在英国，人们庆祝许多节日，如圣诞节、复活节、大斋节、元旦等。今天，英国的许多节日受到大家的喜爱，已经在很多国家流传和庆祝了。

由于英格兰、威尔士、苏格兰和北爱尔兰有着不同的历史文化特色，他们各自有自己特有的节假日，会在不同的时间进行庆祝。例如，英格兰人在12月5日庆祝盖伊福克斯节（也称篝火之夜），以此来纪念1605年人们成功挫败天主教阴谋者试图炸议会、谋杀国王的企图。这一晚，许多人会点燃篝火并燃放烟花，有的市政会组织篝火晚会并在公园燃放大型烟火。苏格兰人会在12月31日庆祝新年之夜，这是苏格兰人的跨年夜，比圣诞节更重要。他们还会在1月25日举办彭斯晚餐来纪念苏格兰伟大诗人罗伯特·彭斯。北爱尔兰的国庆节是在3月17日圣·帕克里克节，人们在这一天纪念圣贤圣·帕克里克的生辰，感谢他将基督教带到北爱尔兰并把人们转变为基督教徒。在威尔士，每年3月1日的圣·大卫日是威尔士守护神圣·大卫的斋日。可见，许多节假日是某一国特有，而其他三国是不庆祝的。只是随着时间的推移和文化的传播，很多节日不再受到地域的限制，开始被整个英国的人们所庆祝。

11.1　宗教节日

由于移民和信仰变化，英国有很多不同的宗教，但英国大部分人是信奉基督教。因此英国人庆祝很多基督教节日，其中最主要的是圣诞节、复活节和大斋节。

圣诞节

每年的12月25日是圣诞节。圣诞节的传统是为庆祝基督的诞生，这是最重要的一个基督教节日。除了其宗教意义之外，还有两个特点使圣诞节看起来与其他节日不同：圣诞节时人们会互赠礼物并与家人共度佳节。

圣诞节前夕，人们会用各种装饰品装饰房间和花园，比如圣诞树、小彩灯、冬青树和槲寄生的叶子及浆果，以及其他各种可以营造圣诞氛围的彩色装饰品。

圣诞节这一天许多人会和家人待在一起，他们互换礼物和卡片。孩子们早晨醒来可以在床边或别的地方找到装满小礼物的袜子。相传这些都是由终年住在北极的神话人物“圣诞老人”（也称“圣克劳斯”）带来的。晚些时候，很多平时不怎么去教堂的人也会去参加教堂的特别仪式。这一天几乎每个人都会好好准备并吃上一顿大餐，这顿饭里通常有烤火鸡、土豆、萝卜和其他蔬菜。主菜吃完后，大家还会吃布丁。

圣诞节这一天除了医院和流浪者收容所外，几乎所有的组织机构都会关门歇业。有的酒吧和小商店会在中午营业几个小时。公共交通系统不会按平时的时间来营运，有的甚至会暂停服务。许多教堂在平安夜和圣诞节当天会组织一些特别活动。比如，有的会为那些无家可归的人或需要帮助的人提供住所和食物，并组织聚会等。

圣诞节有许多吉祥物，比如冬青树和槲寄生的叶子及浆果、松树、蜡烛和小灯等。圣诞节的吉祥人物有圣诞老人、神子耶稣、圣母玛丽、约瑟夫和《耶稣诞生记》中的一些其他人物。此外，圣诞礼物和火鸡、圣诞布丁、肉馅饼这些圣诞食物也是圣诞节的象征。其中特别值得一提的是红襟知更鸟，这种鸟胸前有一簇红橙色的羽毛，在冬季时尤其漂亮，所以常常被装饰在圣诞卡片、包装纸和蛋糕上。

复活节

复活节是每年春分第一次月圆后的第一个星期日，在英国，这是一个重要的基督教节日。根据教会日历，这通常是在 3 月 22 日到 4 月 25 日之间的某个星期日。对许多人来说，复活节是为了庆祝耶稣被钉死在十字架上之后得以复活。在教堂里，这是个很喜庆的日子，象征着新生活的曙光。在伦敦的巴特西公园，每年都有一个大的复活节游行来庆祝复活节。

许多人会在复活节当天画彩蛋、互赠彩蛋或玩寻找彩蛋的游戏。彩蛋可以是或生或熟的鸡蛋或鸟蛋，也可以是巧克力蛋或其他材料制成的蛋。许多孩子认为这一天会有复活节兔子跑到家中或花园藏彩蛋，所以他们会到处寻找彩蛋，有时候会在一些显眼的地方找到。

一些商家和景区会举行“寻找复活节彩蛋”的活动，人们比赛看谁能找到最多的彩蛋。在英国一些地方，人们会把煮熟的蛋从斜坡上滚下来。还有一些地方，人们用自己煮的鸡蛋撞别人的蛋，以此进行比赛，谁的蛋能最后保持完整谁就是赢家，等到比赛结束后，就可以把鸡蛋吃掉。在苏格兰的一些地方，人们把巧克力蛋做成鸡蛋大小，里面塞满软糖，外面裹满面糊再下锅油炸。

复活节这一天几乎所有非必需的企业和机构都会歇业。在英格兰和威尔士，商店也会关门。只有在苏格兰商店会照常营业。这一天公共交通的运营时间跟平时的周日不同，甚至一些地区可能根本没有公共交通在运行。

大斋节

大斋节（也称封斋期）是为复活节做准备的一段时间。在西方基督教中，大斋节由圣灰礼拜三开始，一直持续到复活节前日，一共四十天（不含周日）。大斋节期间，许多基督徒会斋戒、忏悔、节制来纪念基督耶稣的受难和牺牲、诞生和死亡、埋葬和复活。

大斋节不仅是基督教徒们用来纪念耶稣传教前在旷野守斋祈祷 40 天，也是检验自己是否自律的一段时间。大斋期间基督教徒会禁食鱼肉、蛋类和奶制品，有的教徒会禁食自己特别喜欢的一些食品，如蛋糕、巧克力等。不是所有的基督教徒都过这个节日。

万圣节

万圣节是在每年的 10 月 31 日。人们认为在每年的这个时候，死人的灵魂会回到故土找寻生灵，出门时只有把自己打扮成妖魔鬼怪才能吓走这些死魂，今天的万圣节服装可能就是这样来的。常见的万圣节标志有南瓜、蝙蝠和蜘蛛。

在英国，人们会举行万圣节晚会，主人和来宾们穿着应景的化妆服，打扮成骷髅、鬼怪或其他可怕的模样。有的人会结伴去电影院或待在家里看恐怖电影。有的孩子会玩“不给糖就捣蛋”的游戏，他们装扮成恐怖的样子，敲响邻居家的门并索要糖果，没有准备糖果的人家就会被孩子戏弄一番。

在英国，万圣节并不是一个公共假日。学校、企业、商店和其他机构会照常上班。公共交通也会照常运行。

11.2　全国性节日

全国性节日指的是整个英国都会庆祝的节日。由于组成英国的四个国家有着不同的历史和文化，所以几乎没有多少节日能够让英国各地一起庆祝。

元旦

元旦是在每年的 1 月 1 日，这是英国的公共假日，标志着公历新年的开始。

元旦的主要庆祝活动安排在跨年夜（12 月 31 日），这是旧的一年的最后一天。许多人会在一起聚会，一边喝着香槟，一边辞旧迎新，彼此祝福“新年快乐”。按照传统，这一天人们会熬夜守岁，跨年时常常非常热闹。英国各地到处都在举办派对，人们燃放烟火、唱歌跳舞，辞旧迎新。转钟之前，许多人会打开电视，关注电视上伦敦威斯敏斯特宫钟塔上的钟面，一起进行最后几分钟的跨年倒计时。午夜新年伊始，大本钟和钟塔里的钟一起敲响，宣告新的一年开始了。

元旦时很多人会作出“新年计划”，比如戒烟、减肥、健康饮食、积极锻炼、少花钱等。政府也会向民众积极宣传一些健康的生活方式。

各地也有很多新年的习俗。在苏格兰，跨年夜也称 hogmanay，人们喝酒狂欢，通常持续一天或更久。很多人在跨年时会唱着歌曲《友谊地久天长》来进行庆祝。对于苏格兰人来说，新年比圣诞节更加重要。在苏格兰和英格兰北部，人们有讲究“新年第一位访客”的习俗，这指的是在 1 月 1 日第一位走进屋里的客人。关于第一位访客有很多习俗和传说：如果第一位访客是男性则会给主人带来好运，如果是女性，主人就会倒霉；有的地区还会讲究第一位访客应该是金发还是黑发，应该带着煤还是盐，或是其他什么东西；而访客进屋后，主人应该用什么食品饮料来招待客人也是有讲究的。

元旦这一天几乎所有的学校、大型企业和机构都会放假。有些地区的商店可能会照常营业，不同的地区会有所区别。公共交通不一定能照常营运。整体而言，元旦这一天公共服务会完全停止。

阵亡将士纪念日

英国的阵亡将士纪念日是为了纪念在过去的战争中努力斗争、取得成就和做出牺牲的英烈。在英国这是一个纪念日，并不是一个假日。纪念活动主要在每年 11 月的第二个星期日举行，另外在 11 月 11 日也会有 2 分钟的默哀。

人们在 11 月 11 日上午 11 时会停下工作集体默哀，这一天的这一刻正是第一次世界大战四年多战火正式停止的一刻。人们佩戴着罂粟花，对阵亡将士表达尊重与悼念之情。这一天有许多纪念活动、教堂活动和游行。在伦敦中心西敏斯特城的怀特霍尔路上会举行全国性的纪念仪式。

阵亡将士纪念日在澳大利亚、加拿大等英联邦国家很重视，在有些地方也称其为罂粟花日或停战纪念日。其他国家也有类似的纪念日，比如美国的退伍军人日等。

节礼日

英国的节礼日是在圣诞节后的一天，也就是 12 月 26 日，如果 26 日是周末，则延至下一个星期一。节礼日的传统是雇主会在这一天向雇员发钱、食物、衣物或其他有价值的物品。现在，节礼日变成了一个举办体育比赛和圣诞后商家打折热卖的公共假日。

对许多人来说，节礼日是一个可以让人们在圣诞狂欢后休息恢复的日子，也是一个陪伴亲朋好友的日子。有的人选择在这一天去乡村散步，有的人则愿意去大商场赶圣诞节后的第一场促销。有些人甚至愿意通宵达旦地在卖场排队抢购减价商品。

节礼日也是一个重要的举行体育比赛的日子。以前贵族们流行在这一天驱狗猎狐，所以那些象征节礼日的图片上常常会出现穿着红外套、骑着马被猎狗拥簇的猎人形象。现在，猎狐已经被法律禁止，而赛马和踢足球（英式足球）变得流行起来。

女王的官方生日

在任英国君主（现任君主伊丽莎白二世）的生日为国庆日。伊丽莎白女王的生日是1926年4月21日，但她的官方生日却是每年6月的第二个周六，因为此时对于北半球的英国来说天气更怡人，更方便举行室外庆典活动。

11.3 银行假日（公假日）

在英国，法定假日也称银行假日（也叫公假日，银行关门歇业），这期间大部分人可以享受假期。现在虽然大多数商店会照常营业，有些人也会正常上班，但银行假日跟普通工作日还是有所区别的。

银行假日这种说法起源于19世纪末，由于当时银行在假日中会关门歇业而得此名。那时的银行假日并不是用来给职员休息，而是用来整理账目和账务的，尽管后来这些工作平时就完成了，但这个名字和银行暂停营业的传统却一直延续到了20世纪。到了现在，时间虽短，这些传统却发生了很大的变化，银行假日已经变成了购物和促销，有时甚至是商家疯狂促销的商机，这一点跟美国的情况差不多。此外，银行假日也催生了更多的假日活动，很多人会好好享受这些长周末。

在英格兰、威尔士、苏格兰和北爱尔兰，虽然很多公共假期是一致的，但也有一些区别，这也反映了不同民族风俗喜好的差异。英格兰和威尔士的银行假日数量最少，只有8个，北爱尔兰最多，有10个。

英国有这些公共假日：

- 1月1日：元旦
- 3月/4月：耶稣受难日
- 复活节星期一（苏格兰除外）
- 5月（第一个星期一）：5月银行假日
- 5月（最后一个星期一）：春季银行假日
- 8月（最后一个星期一）：夏季银行假日（苏格兰则是8月第一个星期一）
- 12月25日：圣诞节
- 12月26日：节礼日

北爱尔兰还有两个自己的银行假日：

- 3月17日：圣帕特里克节

- 7 月 12 日：庆祝博因河战役周年的公共假日

苏格兰的公共假日有一些区别：

- 苏格兰人非常重视元旦，一般会有三至四天的狂欢，他们新年的法定假日比英国其他地方多一天，就是 1 月 2 日或称为元旦第二天。
- 苏格兰的夏季银行假日在八月初，而英国其他地方则在八月末。由于大多数苏格兰银行在八月底也会与其他地方同步放假，所以 2016 年苏格兰的夏季银行假日时间会与英国其他地区时间统一。
- 苏格兰的国庆节叫做圣安德鲁日，从 2007 年开始，这一天就不再是强制公假日。出于商业目的，一些苏格兰的银行和学校会与英格兰和威尔士同步，不一定会在自己的公假日关门。同样地，即使复活节星期一不是苏格兰的公共假日，这里的银行为了与英国其他的银行同步，也选择在这一天停业。

现在，在英国的公共假日，银行仍然会关闭，但其他的商户却不一定如此。如果你选择在英国的公共假日去英国旅行，那么可能会遭遇以下情景：

- 银行肯定会关门，邮局和其他的政府机构和部门也会休息。
- 大多数办公场所，包括旅行社和订票机构都会关闭。
- 高速公路会很拥堵。
- 一些热门的适合全家人出游的景点会排起长队。如果你受不了在度假时看到大堆的孩子们，最好是避开银行假日，因为这时候肯定到处都是孩子。
- 银行假日期间宾馆的房间可能不太好订，价格也会比平时稍贵。
- 大部分大型商场会照常营业。不管能不能大挣一笔，一些商家会赶在大型假日或银行假日趁别家关门时进行大促销。唯一不会如此的是复活节和圣诞节当天，因为法律规定这两天大型商场要关门歇业。
- 银行假日期间，英国的火车和公汽，以及伦敦的地铁会减少班次，所以选择在这时出行一定要好好计划一下交通路线。
- 如果银行假日恰好排在周六和周日，那么会把假日移到另一天，毕竟大部分人周六和周日本来就不用上班的。

*　　　*　　　*　　　*　　　*

第 12 章　英国文学

英国文学有着数百年的发展历程，至今仍然在世界范围内受到人们的喜爱。英国文学之所以能经受历史的考验，有着蓬勃发展的生命力，不仅在于其每个时期总能涌现出一批杰出的作家，还在于它涵盖面广，几乎覆盖了每一个主要的文学流派和写作风格。英国文学带领读者在不同的历史时空中穿梭，领略风土人情，还引导人们思考那些普遍、永恒的主题，反映人们的价值观，帮助人们在日常生活中成长。英国文学一直是世界文学的重要组成部分之一。

在本章中，我们将向大家介绍英国文学的发展简史，第二部分向大家介绍一些著名的英国作家及其作品。

12.1 英国文学史简介

英国的文学史历时悠久，从公元5世纪一直延续到现在，共包括8个历史时期：古英语时期（450—1066）、中世纪英语时期（1066—1500）、文艺复兴时期（1500—1660）、17世纪文学（1603—1700）、18世纪文学（1700—1798）、浪漫主义时期（1798—1832）、维多利亚时期（1830s—1901）和20世纪文学时期。

12.1.1 古英语时期（450—1066）

正如我们所知，英语是从北方日耳曼部落盎格鲁人、撒克逊人和朱特人的语言发展而来，他们从公元5世纪开始定居在英格兰，他们的语言被称为古英语。古英语是英语和英国文学的基础。

古英语时期是从盎格鲁-撒克逊人在英格兰定居开始，持续到1066年诺曼人征服英格兰。至少在7世纪之前，也就是古英语的早期，文学形式都是口头相传的。那时英国人不会写字，这种状态一直持续到罗马传教士将拉丁字母传入英国。古英语最早的书面作品很可能也是先口口相传，然后才被书面记录下来的。我们现在只知道一些后期作家的名字（如凯德蒙、Ælfric和阿尔弗莱德王），大部分这一时期的作品都无法获知作者信息。

古英语时期的文学形式主要是史诗和诗歌，比如有抒情诗和描写诗，尤其是叙事诗。这一时期最重要的作品是《贝奥武夫》，这是最古老的一部英文诗，也是最长的古英语史诗。这部作品讲述了英雄人物贝奥武夫与嗜血怪物格伦德尔之间惊险的斗争故事。它共有3000多行，前几百年是由人们口头传播，直到10世纪或9世纪末才开始被文字记录下来。

12.1.2 中世纪英语时期（1066—1500）

从1066年到1500年左右的中世纪英语时期，英国的语言、文化和生活方式发生了巨大的转变，文学作品中也出现了法国及凯尔特文学的思想和主题。这一时期大部分文学作品是围绕宗教的，从大约1350年开始，也逐渐出现了一些世俗文学。这段时期出现的主要人物有乔叟、托马斯·马洛礼、罗伯特·亨利森、威廉·兰格伦、约翰·高尔等。杰出的作品有《耕者皮尔斯》、《高文爵士和绿衣骑士》等。

这段时期最受欢迎并最具影响力的一位作家是杰弗雷·乔叟（c. 1343—1400），他被誉为第一位伟大的英国诗人。他的作品中涵盖了多种基调、风格和流派。乔叟的著名作品《坎特伯雷故事集》是一部诗体短篇小说集，讲述了朝圣者们在去坎特伯雷的路上用讲故事的方式来打发时间，每一个朝圣者讲述的故事都是单独叙述，整首诗里“故事套故事”，是一个简单串在一起的故事集。这种文学手法成为文学史上一种流行的叙事手法。《坎特伯雷故事集》代表了乔叟的最终成就，是英国文学中最有纪念意义的作品之一。

12.1.3　文艺复兴时期（1500—1660）

文艺复兴时期的英国文学通常被认为是英国文学史上的一大亮点。这段时期，戏剧和诗歌得到的巨大发展，取得了辉煌的成就。

伊丽莎白时代是英国戏剧的黄金时代。这一时期优秀的剧作家有约翰·黎里、托马斯·基德、乔治·皮尔、罗伯特·格林、克里斯托弗·马洛、本·琼森，当然还有威廉·莎士比亚。在16世纪之前，英国戏剧只是由工艺演出行会在公共假日时表演圣经故事的一种业余表演。克里斯托弗·马洛（1564—1593）冲破旧的戏剧形式的束缚，成为文艺复兴时期的第一位伟大的剧作家。他在戏剧中探讨了新世界的界限，以及人类在追求权力、知识与爱情的过程中所面临的风险。马洛是莎士比亚之前英国最伟大的剧作家，他为莎士比亚的创作铺平了道路。威廉·莎士比亚（1564—1616）是世界上最著名的剧作家和诗人之一，他以37个剧本、154首十四行诗和2首长篇叙事诗确立了他在世界文学中的伟人地位。

这一时期除戏剧外，诗歌创作也得到繁荣发展。写诗成为一种潮流，一批著名的诗人涌现出来，如托马斯·怀特、亨利·霍华德、菲利普·锡德尼、埃德蒙·斯宾塞、克里斯托弗·马洛、威廉·莎士比亚和本·琼森等。埃德蒙·斯宾塞（1552—1599）在他的那个时代被称为“诗人中的诗人”，他创作的斯宾塞诗节成为英国诗歌发展史上的流行诗歌形式。《仙后》是斯宾塞最伟大的一部作品，它以亚瑟王和他的骑士世界为背景，歌颂女王，并宣扬了人文主义思想。

这段时期也出现了一些著名的散文作家。伟大的人文主义家托马斯·莫尔（1477—1535）撰写了著名的散文作品《乌托邦》，这是最早的一部空想社会主义作品。《乌托邦》分为2本书。第一本书有力地揭露了那个时期英国社会的黑暗；第二本书描述了理想的共产主义社会——乌托邦。《乌托邦》中描绘的情形与当时的英国社会形成强烈的对比，是对当时英国社会的尖锐批评。另一个著名的人物是弗兰西斯·培根，他写了50多篇优秀的散文，是英国最优秀的散文家之一。

12.1.4 17 世纪（1603—1700）

17 世纪早期，尤其是英国革命期间（1640—1660），英国的各个领域都处于激烈的矛盾中。伊丽莎白一世统治结束后，人们的统一精神和爱国情感也随之而去，英国也因为保皇党和清教徒的冲突而骚乱。这种骚乱也反映到这一时期的文学作品中。

英国革命时期的主要文学形式是诗歌。约翰·弥尔顿（1608—1674）是这一时期众多诗人中最著名的一位。作为一名作家，他几乎把自己生命中最美好的 20 年都投入到政治、宗教以及个人自由的奋斗中去。他的代表作《失乐园》是英国文学中最伟大的一部史诗，讲述了圣经故事中亚当和夏娃受到堕天使撒旦的诱惑并被逐出伊甸园的故事。弥尔顿在第一本书中表明了他要"向世人昭示天道的公正"的主旨。17 世纪英国诗歌的另外一支是玄学派诗歌，代表诗人有约翰·邓恩和安德鲁·马韦尔。玄学派的特点是采用奇特的意象创造性地阐述爱和宗教等主题。

王政复辟时期最受欢迎的作家是约翰·班扬（1628—1688）。他最重要的作品《天路历程》被奉为最杰出的英语宗教文学作品之一。在这部作品中一些普通概念，如罪、绝望、信念等被塑造成人物或自然界的某一物。主人翁基督徒在旅途中所遇到的人物或地点也代表了每一位基督徒在寻求救赎的过程中所必经的。这一时期另一位重要人物是约翰·德莱顿。他是一名诗人、散文家和剧作家，在 1668 年获得桂冠诗人的称号。在王政复辟时期，德莱顿驰骋英国文坛，于是这一时期也被称为"德莱顿时代"。

12.1.5 18 世纪（1700—1798）

18 世纪的英国处于启蒙主义时期或理性主义时期。这一时期的文学作品主要是围绕社会变革、个人地位、政治讽刺、地理探索，以及将人的所谓自然状态与文明状态相比较等主题。这一时期的文学作品具有真实和精确两大特点。这一点尤其体现在亚历山大·蒲柏的诗歌和约瑟夫·艾迪生的散文中。蒲柏使英雄双韵体这一诗体形式得以完善；艾迪生的文风清新秀雅、轻捷流畅。这一时期文学作品的第三个特点就是讽刺文学得以发展。

在 18 世纪以前，诗歌是英国文学作品的主流，而在这个时期，散文第一次在英国文学史上占据主要地位。这时的英国社会、政治、宗教和文学等领域出现了各种论战，一些著名作家积极参与其中，大量的小册子、期刊和杂志也涌现出来，迎合民众阅读和了解这些争论的需要。诗歌无法满足人们的这一需求，而散文得到了快速发展。这个时代的散文家在各方面都比诗人有更杰出的表现，如，艾迪生的散文优美典雅、斯威夫特的讽刺简洁有力、菲尔丁的小说具有完美的艺术性，吉本的史书文笔华美，这些都是诗歌无法企及的。事实上，这一时期的诗歌的创作也呈现出散文化的特点：内容以批评、讽刺和争论为主，形式也模仿散文。这一时期的诗歌精巧、机智、精雕细琢，缺乏细腻的情感和热情，失去了伊丽莎白时代的诗意和清教主义的道德热忱。诗歌主要用来描绘现实生活，缺乏灵感和想象力。

这个时代的另一个重要特点就是小说的兴起。小说作为一种新兴文学形式，后来越来越受到人们的欢迎，直至今天在文学作品中占有主导地位。而在那个时代，是丹尼尔·笛福、塞缪尔·理查逊、亨利·菲尔丁、托比亚斯·斯摩莱特等著名作家赋予小说以灵魂，为小说的发展奠定了坚实的基础，18 世纪的现实主义以及精美的散文形式也为小说的发展提供了助力。

18 世纪的戏剧没有得到发展，只有戈德史密斯和谢里丹的作品具有文学价值。

12.1.6　英国浪漫主义时期（1798—1832）

浪漫主义时期是从 1798 年到 1832 年。1798 年威廉·华兹华斯（1770—1850）和塞缪尔·泰勒·柯勒律治（1772—1834）合作出版了一本小诗集《抒情歌谣集》，这标志着英国浪漫主义文学的崛起。随着 1832 年最后一位浪漫主义作家沃尔特·司各特的逝世，浪漫主义时期也就结束了。就某种程度而言，浪漫主义运动是对 20 世纪启蒙运动注重科学理性的一次反拨，这个时期的文学特点是强调激情、情感和自然。

浪漫主义诗歌用日常平实的语言来描述生活。这一时期的许多著名诗人如华兹华斯、柯勒律治将自然作为诗歌的主题。华兹华斯被誉为“英国浪漫主义之父”，他的所有作品都是围绕大自然。他的创作理论是“好诗是强烈感情的自然流溢”。罗伯特·彭斯（1759—1796）用苏格兰方言来写抒情诗，他可能是继莎士比亚之后其作品最常被人引用的作者了。至今，人们在跨年夜还会唱起他写的《友谊地久天长》。浪漫主义后期的诗人乔治·戈登·拜伦（1788—1824）和波西·比希·雪莱（1792—1822）是革命诗人。拜伦总是用浪漫的主题来诠释对时事的理解，他在诗歌里塑造了一批“拜伦式”英雄。雪莱以抒情诗而闻名，他最有名的诗歌是《西风诵》，这首诗的主题是死亡和重生。约翰·济慈（1795—1821）的诗歌追求语言之美，在他的诗中总是体现出对美的尊崇。

浪漫主义时代的文学评论和其他非小说类散文也得到很好的发展。这些作家在政治上受到法国大革命的影响，文学上顺应浪漫主义潮流。其中最有代表性的人物是查尔斯·兰姆（1775—1834）。兰姆最为著名的作品是与姐姐合作创作的《莎士比亚故事集》，这是对莎士比亚创作的戏剧作品的复述。

这个时期也出现了一些著名的小说家。简·奥斯汀是英国文学史上第一位重要的女性小说家。虽然她的作品创作于浪漫主义时期，但文学界对她是批判现实主义作家还是浪漫主义作家一直存有争议。在她的代表作《傲慢与偏见》中，奥斯汀巧妙地将浪漫主义情怀与现实主义基调融为一体，用讽刺幽默的笔法，敏锐细腻地刻画了英国的乡镇生活。沃尔特·司各特主要的文学贡献是他的历史小说，这为他赢得了“西欧历史小说之父”的声誉。在他之后，许多英国作家也开始历史题材的创作，许多历史小说也相继出现。

12.1.7 维多利亚时期（1830s—1901）

维多利亚时代大致与维多利亚女王当政的时间一致，即从1837年女王登基到1901年去世。这一时期被公认是英国历史上最辉煌的一个阶段，既经历了经济的快速发展，也存在着严重的社会问题。维多利亚时代与浪漫主义时期一样，涌现出大量流传广泛、意义深远且丰富多彩的作品，这在英国文学史，乃至世界文学史上都是屈指可数的。

维多利亚时代，批判现实主义成为一种新的文学潮流出现在小说创作中。小说成为最受欢迎的读物，是小说家们用以表达进步思想的最重要而有力的方式。这个时期最伟大的英国批判现实主义者是查尔斯·狄更斯（1812—1870）。他娴熟地描绘当时英国的社会生活，并能运用各种文学技巧来吸引读者的兴趣。狄更斯既是一位杰出的幽默大师，又是一位尖锐的讽刺家，他的小说既幽默泼辣，又充满感伤情调。他的主要作品包括《雾都孤儿》、《远大前程》、《大卫·科波菲尔》、《双城记》等。19世纪英国的另一位批判现实主义代表是威廉·麦克皮斯·萨克雷（1811—1863）。他的代表作《名利场》全面描述了19世纪早期英国的社会状况。小说标题来自班扬的《天路历程》，意思是“一个出售各种名利的市场”。夏洛蒂·勃朗特（1816—1855）和艾米丽（1818—1848）、安妮（1820—1849）三姐妹常常被一起提及，但她们的作品风格却有很大差异。夏洛蒂的作品中一个明显的特点是具有丰富的想象力和炙热的情感。在她的代表作《简·爱》中，女主人公冲破重重逆境，最终靠自己的努力赢得了幸福。艾米丽的《呼啸山庄》是一部强烈的批判现实主义小说，它忠实地记录了维多利亚时代英国压迫者与被压迫者之间的关系。乔治·艾略特（1819—1880）是玛丽·安·伊万斯的笔名，她最著名的作品有《亚当·贝德》、《弗洛斯河上的磨坊》以及《职工马兰》。托马斯·哈代（1840—1928）是19世纪末的英国批判现实主义者之一。他的著名的作品有《还乡》、《德伯家的苔丝》、《无名的裘德》等。他的代表作《德伯家的苔丝》讲述了农村姑娘苔丝的不幸与悲剧命运。

维多利亚时代的诗歌从很多方面看都是在主题和风格上对浪漫主义诗歌的发展。这一时期的诗歌不再触及严重的社会问题，只是单纯地围绕诗人自己的喜好和精神探究。这个时期最著名的诗人是阿尔弗雷德·丁尼生（1809—1892）和罗伯特·布朗宁（1812—1889）。丁尼生非常受人欢迎，被誉为“人民诗人”。他的诗歌作品非常丰富多样，其中《悼念》通常被认为是他长篇诗歌创作中最重要的一部作品。布朗宁在诗歌上的主要成就是在诗歌中巧妙地运用“戏剧独白”。他的代表作品是《指环与书》，叙述了依据 17 世纪罗马发生的一场谋杀宣判。

19 世纪最负盛名的剧作家是奥斯卡·王尔德（1856—1900），唯美主义和颓废派的代表人物。他最著名的喜剧有《温德密尔夫人的扇子》、《无足轻重的女人》、《好丈夫》和《认真的重要性》，这些作品以其似是而非的怪论和机智诙谐的俏皮话而著称。

12.1.8　20 世纪

20 世纪英国的经济实力和综合国力衰退，两次世界大战让英国遭遇了巨大的人口损失和经济损失，社会和政治生活也发生了重大变化。在这期间英国文学有一个明显的特征，就是现实主义与现代主义并存，并交替处于主导地位。

这期间，英语诗歌取得了很大的成就。T. S. 爱略特（1888—1965）和威廉·叶芝（1865—1939）是现代诗歌的两个主要人物。爱略特善于将传统元素重构，在形式和内容上推陈出新。他最重要的一部作品是《荒原》（1922）。爱略特用荒原指代西欧，甚至整个西方文明，诗中反映了当时的社会和人们的幻灭感和悲观情绪。叶芝善于在传统的抒情诗中将现代主题与古典浪漫风格相结合。他的主要作品有《驶向拜占庭》、《芦苇中的风》、《库利的野天鹅》和《古堡》。20 世纪还有一些重要诗人，如现实主义诗人托马斯·哈代、A. E. 豪斯曼（1859—1936）、鲁伯特·布鲁克（1887—1915）、菲利普·拉金（1922—1985），以及现代主义诗人威斯坦·休·奥登（1907—1973）、泰德·休斯（1930—1998）等。

20 世纪早期，许多小说家沿袭了维多利亚时期批判现实主义传统，其中约翰·高尔斯华绥（1867—1933）享有很高的声誉。在他的代表作《福尔赛世家》三部曲中，作者通过讲述一个显贵的资产阶级家族的故事，对有产阶级进行了批判和讽刺。在两次世界大战期间，现代主义文学形式出现在小说创作中。詹姆斯·乔伊斯（1882—1941）和弗吉妮亚·伍尔芙（1882—1941）通过“意识流”的手法，打破传统的叙事方法和结构。乔伊斯在他的代表作《尤利西斯》中记录了都柏林一天里发生的事情，故事以意识流的方式，以前所未有的坦承态度展现了三个人物内心的思想活动。沃尔芙在她的作品《到灯塔去》和《达洛卫夫人》中突破传统的时空观，将意识流手法运用得出神入化。D. H. 劳伦斯（1885—1930）关注的主题是现代社会人与人之间的关系，在这个社会中男人与男人，男人与女人之间的自然和谐已经被工业化和现代化所破坏。他最重要的一部作品是半自传体小说《儿子与情人》。第二次世界大战后，现实主义文学开始回归。一批被称作“愤怒的青年”的新作家开始发表作品，抒发他们对社会不公和压迫的愤怒和不满，金斯利·艾米斯的小说《幸运儿吉姆》是“愤怒的青年”一派的代表作。这一时期还有许多杰出的小说家，如安东尼·伯吉斯（1917—1993）、威廉·戈尔丁（1911—1994）、多丽丝·莱辛（1919—2013）、爱丽丝·默多克（1919—1999）和马丁·

艾米斯（1949— ）等。

20 世纪英国戏剧的传统是现实主义，这一时期的剧作家纷纷在作品中揭露社会问题。乔治·伯纳·萧（1856—1950）是这一时期最优秀的剧作家，他将英国戏剧带入了第二个黄金时代。萧伯纳利用舞台来批判资本主义制度的不公。他最著名的一部戏剧是《卖花女》，我们现在所熟悉的音乐剧《窈窕淑女》就是改编自这部作品。

12.2 著名作家及作品

几个世纪以来，英国文学在世界文学舞台上一直占有举足轻重的地位，其标志性文学泰斗威廉·莎士比亚和查尔斯·狄更斯将英国文学的传统发挥到极致，这些文学的闪亮光芒一直延续至今。在上一节中我们提到了英国文学史上的许多名人大家，在这一节中，我们将介绍其中一些才华横溢的作家和诗人，其中包括"埃文河畔的诗人"威廉·莎士比亚、诗人威廉·华兹华斯和乔治·拜伦，以及小说家简·奥斯丁、查尔斯·狄更斯和托马斯·哈代。在人物介绍之后还将介绍他们的一部代表作品。

12.2.1 威廉·莎士比亚和《哈姆雷特》

威廉·莎士比亚（1564—1616）是西方的文学泰斗、最伟大的英语作家以及世界著名的剧作家。他的作品包括 37 个剧本、154 首十四行诗，2 首长诗以及一些杂诗。其戏剧被译成各种语言，400 多年来一直占据着世界舞台。莎翁语录广为人知，在最新一期《巴氏常用妙语辞典》中，他的经典语句占了 70 多页，包括著名的"生存还是死亡"以及"分别是甜蜜的哀伤"等。

莎士比亚出生于英国沃里克郡的斯特拉特福镇，父亲威廉是当地一名富商，母亲玛丽是地主的女儿。莎士比亚 18 岁时与安·哈瑟维结婚并育有三个孩子：苏珊娜，以及双胞胎哈姆奈特和珠迪丝。他们唯一的儿子哈姆奈特 11 岁夭折。在 1585 年到 1592 年之间，莎士比亚在伦敦当过演员、作家，后来还成为张伯伦勋爵剧团的合伙人之一。49 岁时莎士比亚隐退回归故里斯特拉福并在 3 年后去世。

1590 年到 1613 年是莎士比亚的创作高峰期。他的早期剧本主要是喜剧（如《无事生非》、《仲夏夜之梦》）和历史剧（如《亨利五世》）。接下来到 1608 年，他的创作主要是悲剧，包括《哈姆雷特》、《奥赛罗》、《李尔王》和《麦克白》等。莎士比亚的悲剧是人物命运的悲剧或性格的悲剧，它们探索了人类灵魂的黑暗面。这些悲剧被认为是莎士比亚最杰出的成就。在他人生的最后阶段，莎士比亚开始创作悲喜剧，又称为传奇剧，并与其他剧作家合作。除了这些著名的戏剧，莎士比亚的诗歌也非常有名，尤其是他的十四行诗。一般认为他的十四行诗大多完成于

16 世纪 90 年代。

有关莎士比亚私人生活的记录流传下来的很少，关于他的外貌、性取向、宗教信仰，以及他的著作是否出自他人之手都依然是谜。人们对于目前的这些知名作品到底是出自莎士比亚一人之手还是群体智慧的结晶至今意见不一，甚至有人还怀疑莎士比亚此人是否真的存在。学术界只有少数人在质疑这些作品的出处，但关于这个课题的研究一直持续至今。

《哈姆雷特》

这部戏开始于一个寒冷的夜晚。神秘鬼魂告诉丹麦王子哈姆雷特，他的父王是被皇叔克劳狄斯所杀。克劳狄斯继承了王位并娶了哈姆雷特的母亲乔特鲁德。鬼魂鼓励哈姆雷特为父报仇，杀死克劳迪斯。

随后哈姆雷特利用装疯掩护自己，并通过重演父王遇害的一部戏证实了克劳狄斯的罪行。他就此事质问母亲时误以为克劳狄斯躲在挂毯后便用剑将其刺死，最后却发现自己误杀了爱人奥菲利娅的父亲波洛涅斯。奥菲利娅在父亲被爱人杀死后悲伤过度精神失常，最后不幸溺水身亡。

克劳狄斯发现了哈姆雷特的复仇计划，他派遣哈姆雷特到英国，并计划将其杀害。哈姆雷特逃回丹麦时看到奥菲利娅的葬礼。奥菲利娅的死让他思考生命、死亡和人性的脆弱。

奥菲利娅的哥哥莱尔提斯要替父亲和妹妹报仇。克劳迪斯让他用毒剑和毒酒杀死哈姆雷特。在决斗中，两人的剑被交换，莱尔提斯被毒剑刺死。乔特鲁德也因误喝毒药死去。哈姆雷特刺死克劳狄斯，而自己也中毒剑身亡。在临死前，他将王位传给挪威王子福丁布拉斯。

《哈姆雷特》的主题

《哈姆雷特》之所以与其他的复仇剧有所区别，主要在于当哈姆雷特不断对自己的行为进行思考时，观众期待看到的情节却迟迟没有出现。在别的剧中一些理所当然的情节在这里都成了值得思考的问题。在许多人看来，《哈姆雷特》就是一部关于主人翁犹豫不定、无所作为的戏剧。然而有意思的是，这部戏剧也向我们展示了生活中其实是有太多的不确定因素。

《哈姆雷特》反映了很多主题，包括复仇、死亡、主人翁的无所作为、乱伦和丹麦的局势等。

复仇　《哈姆雷特》是一部复仇悲剧，一个无法动手复仇的人却要背负复仇的责任。正是哈姆雷特的犹豫推动着剧情的发展。每一次他决定采取行动时都会拖延放弃，直到剧尾。为了突显出哈姆雷特的无所作为，莎士比亚设置了福丁布拉斯和莱尔提斯这些能够采取果决复仇行动的角色。然而《哈姆雷特》的独特之处正是在于莎士比亚巧妙地运用主人翁的犹豫来反映其复杂的情感和心理过程。尽管最终哈姆雷特还是杀死了克劳狄斯，人们也不能确定这是哈姆雷特的计划内行动，还是受到克劳狄斯攻击的反抗。人们也不禁会想，如果哈姆雷特能早点采取行动，是否就能挽救许多人的生命呢？

死亡 在整部剧中，哈姆雷特都沉浸在关于死亡的思考中，他想到了死亡的各个方面。哈姆雷特的悲哀和可怜之处就在于他多次想用死亡来结束自己遭受的折磨，但出于对基督教的信仰，又害怕自杀会让自己死后在地狱里承受无尽的痛苦。

乱伦 相比较父亲的去世，母亲乔特鲁德与叔叔的乱伦关系更让哈姆雷特感到痛苦。他甚至没有那么痛恨克劳狄斯，因为他认为一切都是母亲的错。乔特鲁德毁掉了哈姆雷特对女性的信任，这也许就是为什么他对奥菲利娅会有矛盾的情绪。

丹麦局势 剧中对丹麦的政治社会局势有所介绍，剧首那个神秘的鬼魂就是丹麦社会动乱的象征，因为此时皇室的血统已经被卑鄙又野心勃勃的克劳狄斯扰乱。而剧尾哈姆雷特将王位传给了鲁莽又残暴的福丁布拉斯更是让丹麦的未来飘摇不定。

这部悲剧在创作时伊丽莎白女王已经60岁，王位继承人问题悬而未决，剧中丹麦的局势正是英国社会不稳定的写照。

12.2.2 威廉·华兹华斯和《我好似一朵流云独自漫游》（又名《水仙花》）

威廉·华兹华斯（1770—1850）是19世纪英国最伟大的浪漫主义诗人之一。他与塞缪尔·泰勒·柯勒律治合著出版的《抒情歌谣集》标志着诗歌风格的转变，宣告了浪漫主义新诗的诞生。

华兹华斯曾在剑桥大学就读，毕业后去了法国，见证了法国大革命，这段经历对他的政治思想影响极大。回到英国后，他遇到柯勒律治，两人在1798年合作出版了《抒情歌谣集》，其中收录了柯勒律治的《古舟子咏》和华兹华斯的《丁登寺》。在《丁登寺》一诗中，诗人描绘了古寺石墙残垣旁“陡峭挺拔的山峰”和“绿色田园”，表达了自己对人与自然关系的思考。尽管早期华兹华斯的诗歌和政治思想备受批评，但后期他仍然成为浪漫主义运动的代表人物。华兹华斯的其他作品还包括《诗，两卷》（1807）和《远行》（1814）。从1843年直到他1850年去世，华兹华斯享有桂冠诗人的称号。他的自传体长诗《序曲》是在他去世之后由他的妻子出版，这是华兹华斯最著名的一部作品，被很多人奉为英国浪漫主义文学的最高成就。

华兹华斯是“湖畔诗人”之一，也是一位崇尚“自然”的诗人。一方面，他对（植物、动物、地理、天气等）自然环境观察细致。另一方面，他又是一个具有自我意识的文学艺术家，在他看来，“所有的好诗都是强烈情感的自然流露”。

他的诗歌用简单平实的语言歌颂了大自然和人类精神的美好，这在当时那个时代是一种全新的观念。

《我好似一朵流云独自漫游》（又名《水仙花》）

威廉·华兹华斯　著　　飞白　译

我是一朵独自漫游的云。
在山丘和谷地上飘荡，
忽然间我看见一簇
金色的水仙花迎春开放，
在树荫下，在湖水边，
迎着微风起舞翩翩。

连绵不绝，如繁星灿烂，
在银河里闪闪发光，
它们沿着湖湾的边缘
延伸成无穷无尽的一行；
我一眼看见了一万朵，
在欢舞之中起伏颠簸。

粼粼波光也跳着舞，
水仙的欢欣却胜过水波；
与这样快活的伴侣为伍，
诗人怎能不满心快乐！
我久久凝望，却想象不到
这奇景赋予我多少财宝。

每当我躺在床上不眠，
或心神空茫，或默默沉思，
它们常在心灵中闪现，
那是孤独之中的福；
于是我的心便涨满幸福，
和水仙一同翩翩起舞。

《我好似一朵流云独自漫游》分析

《我好似一朵流云独自漫游》(又名《水仙花》)是一首抒情诗。诗人华兹华斯与妹妹多萝茜途经湖区的乌斯瓦特湖畔格林可因湾时，看见“长长的一片”水仙花，并于1804年创作了这首诗。这首诗简单易懂，节奏感强、韵律整齐，整首诗中萦绕着一股伤感的氛围，一直颇受读者欢迎。诗歌共有四节，每节六行，使用ababcc韵脚，节奏为抑扬格四音步，朗诵时朗朗上口，让人联想到摇曳的水仙花。

总结

在第一节中，诗人交代了自己“好似一朵孤独的流云”在山谷中徘徊，突然偶遇一片似乎无边无际的水仙花，花儿“迎着微风，起舞翩翩”。诗人将自己比做流云，又多次将水仙比做人，使人与自然融为一体。第二节中，诗人更加细致地描绘了水仙之美。这一片水仙漫无边际，如此之多，让人联想到银河。诗人甚至禁不住猜测这里恐怕有一万朵之多，“在欢舞之中起伏颠簸”。第三节中，诗人将水波比作水仙随风摇曳时的波纹，甚至感到“波光粼粼”的湖水比不上水仙之美，因为花儿们有更多的“欢欣快乐”。然后他点评说，此刻任何一位诗人站在这里，都会像他一样，“与这些快活的伴侣为伍，感到满心快乐”。他久久看着这些美景，当时却根本没有发现这景致已经赋予他那么多宝贵的财富。在最后一节中，诗人总结了他的收获。从那之后，每当他感到孤独或“忧郁”时，他总是会想起这一片水仙花，它们在诗人的“心灵中闪现”，让他心中涨满幸福。

主题

这首诗的主题包括：首先，如果想更好地了解自己，以及自己在宇宙中的位置，就一定要亲近大自然（如第15、第23、第24行所示）。大自然之美使人的心灵更美。其次，人们终日忙于日常琐事，错过了大自然的种种神奇（如第17、18行所示）。最后，大自然中植物悄无声息地茁壮成长，水仙花在湖畔怒放，绚丽多彩，丝毫不在意人类是否关注。

修辞手法

头韵：本诗中多处出现头韵法。例如，“cloudless climes”（第2行）中/cl/音重复；“Beside the Lake, beneath the trees”（第5行）中/b/和/ð/音重复。

明喻：第1行中，诗人将自己比做流云，与大自然融为一体，通过比喻说明自己自由自在和慵懒的状态。此刻诗人是轻松自在的，这一片“金色的水仙花”吸引了他的注意。

夸张：第9行中，诗人用“它们延伸成无穷无尽的一行”来表达水仙之多，给人视觉上的浩瀚感。

拟人和比较：第13行中，诗人描述水中波纹也在起舞，但它们缺少了一份水仙花独有的欢乐。

12.2.3　戈登·拜伦和《她走在美的光影里》

戈登·拜伦（1788—1824）常被称为拜伦勋爵，是英国 19 世纪初期伟大的浪漫主义诗人，浪漫主义运动的领军人物。拜伦最著名的作品有长篇叙事诗《唐璜》、《恰尔德·哈洛尔德游记》，以及短篇抒情诗《她走在美的光影里》。拜伦被誉为英国最伟大的诗人之一，他的作品至今仍然被广泛阅读，并对后世有着深远的影响。

拜伦出生时就有一只脚残疾，他对此非常敏感。年幼时他在阿伯丁生活窘困，直到十岁才上学。1798 年世袭了伯父的爵位和产业，之后到哈罗公学和剑桥大学学习。拜伦年轻时游历欧洲诸国，尤其在意大利生活了七年。他还投身希腊民族解放运动，对抗奥斯曼帝国，至今被许多希腊人尊为民族英雄。

拜伦经常被描述为浪漫主义时期最耀眼，也最声名狼藉的诗人。他的恶名一方面源于人们对他作品的批判，一方面来自于他的贵族习气、巨额债务，以及无数的风流韵事和自我放逐的随性。尽管拜伦经常沦为同时代人道德批判的对象，但他对欧洲诗歌、音乐、小说、戏曲、绘画的影响却是毋庸置疑的。他塑造了一批“拜伦式英雄”的形象，这些形象不仅出现在他的多部作品中，他本人被认为极具这种文学形象的特点。“拜伦式英雄”代表了一批思想理想化、性格有缺陷的人物，他们极具才情和激情、对社会和社会制度嗤之以鼻，对等级和特权缺乏尊重（尽管本身两者兼具），因社会禁锢或死亡阻隔而失去爱情，富有反抗精神，不得不放逐自己，有一段隐秘不能为人所知的黑暗过往、傲慢自大、缺乏远见，最后不得不自我毁灭。这种人物类型在文学和政治领域随处可见。

她走在美的光影里

戈登·拜伦　著　　杨德豫　译

她走在美的光影里，好像
无云的夜空，繁星闪烁；
明与暗的最美的形象
交会于她的容颜和眼波，
融成一片恬淡的清光——
浓艳的白天得不到的恩泽。
多一道阴影，少一缕光芒，
都会损害那难言的优美：
美在她绺绺黑发上飘荡，
在她的腮颊上洒布柔辉；

愉悦的思想在那儿颂扬，
这神圣寓所的纯洁、高贵。
那脸颊，那眉宇，幽娴、沉静，
情意却胜似万语千言；
迷人的笑容，灼人的红晕，
显示温情伴送着芳年；
和平的、涵容一切的灵魂！
蕴蓄着真纯爱情的心田！

《她走在美的光影里》分析

《她走在美的光影里》是戈登·拜伦写的一首浪漫主义诗歌，诗歌创作于1814年，发表于1815年。据说这首诗描绘的是拜伦表弟的妻子霍顿夫人。拜伦在舞会上与她相遇，当时她穿着一件金箔闪烁的黑色晨服，她的美让拜伦怦然心动，于是写下了这首脍炙人口的诗歌。

诗中并没有具体描绘霍顿夫人的容貌，也没有明确说明她的着装、衣裙颜色、身高或眼睛的颜色，直到诗歌的最后读者才得知她有一头黑发。但毋庸置疑的是，这位夫人已经给作者和读者留下了深刻的印象。对于作者来说她和“夜色”一样美，尤其作者还补充——这是一个特别的夜晚——“夜空无云，繁星闪烁”。在这个尽情想象的景致中没有暴风雨的威胁，也没有云层的遮蔽。这个夜晚并不是一片漆黑，因为天空繁星闪烁，光线柔和静默，正如夜色中夫人眼中“恬淡的清光”，作者将“浓艳的白天”与“星光闪烁”的夜晚相对比，衬托夫人的娴静典雅。读者还可以从诗中感受到夫人迷人的微笑、平和的心境和纯洁的心灵。她是那么纯净，正如最后一节所描述的，正是这些美好的品质让她“走在美的光影里”。她的外表无疑是美好的，然而真正令读者感受到她无与伦比的美的正是她美好的品格。

这首诗短小且容易理解，并没有使用很多象征手段，但还是有一些明喻、隐喻、拟人、头韵和尾韵的手法。

明喻：诗中的明喻是将夫人的美明白地比喻成夜空。

隐喻：第11、第12行（愉悦的思想在那儿颂扬，这神圣寓所的纯洁、高贵。）隐喻夫人思想的纯洁。

拟人：第6行（浓艳的白天得不到的恩泽）运用拟人的手法，作者赋予“白天”以情绪和品性。

头韵和尾韵：本诗中多处出现头韵和尾韵法。例如，“cloudless climes”中重复/cl/音，富有音律美；重复的/s/音，或称齿擦音，读起来舒缓动听。

12.2.4　简·奥斯汀和《傲慢与偏见》

简·奥斯汀（1775—1817）是英国文学史上第一位重要的女性小说家，也是作品最受欢迎的作家之一。虽然生于浪漫主义文学时期，奥斯汀却是一位现实主义作家。她的现实主义风格、嘲讽的基调、对社会问题的评论，以及引人入胜的故事情节已经征服了众多的学者和批评家，在文学史上赢得了重要的历史地位。

奥斯汀出生在英国西南部汉普郡的小城镇斯蒂文顿镇。她从小受到父亲和哥哥的教导，阅读了大量的书籍，家人的全力支持为她的作家之路奠定了基础。1811—1816 年间，奥斯汀陆续发表了《理智与伤感》（1811）、《傲慢与偏见》（1813）、《曼斯菲尔德庄园》（1814）和《艾玛》（1815），成为一位成功的作家。尤其特别的是，由于当时社会并不认可女性作家，所以她的主要作品都是匿名发表，直到去世后作品才开始署名简·奥斯汀。1869 年，她的侄子出版了《简·奥斯汀回忆录》，让更多的人认识了她，到 20 世纪 40 年代，学术界广泛认可奥斯汀是一位伟大的英国作家。

奥斯汀的小说以诙谐、温和又具讽刺的笔触描绘了 18、19 世纪英国中产阶级的生活风貌，通过喜剧的形式反映出女性依靠婚姻来保障社会和经济地位的现状。在她最著名的小说《傲慢与偏见》中，聪慧、机敏又独立的女主人翁伊丽莎白与她英俊睿智的追求者达西先生已经成为英国小说中最著名的情侣之一。

她的小说也一直受到好莱坞的青睐，多部作品已经被改编后搬上屏幕，包括《傲慢与偏见》（1995 年 BBC 电视制作版由科林·费尔斯饰演达西；2005 年的剧情片由凯拉·奈特莉饰演伊丽莎白）、《艾玛》（1996 年由格温妮丝·帕特洛主演）、《理智与伤感》（1995 年由艾玛·汤普森和凯特·温斯莱特主演）。1995 年由艾丽西亚·希尔维斯通饰演的《独领风骚》就是改编自《艾玛》。2007 年由安妮·海瑟薇主演的《成为简·奥斯汀》还将简·奥斯汀本人的生活搬上了银幕。2013 年英国央行英格兰银行宣布新版 10 英镑纸币将使用简·奥斯汀的头像，这一版纸币将在 2017 年发行。

《傲慢与偏见》

《傲慢与偏见》讲述了班纳特夫妇和他们五个待字闺中的女儿的故事。班纳特一家生活在距伦敦 30 英里赫特福德郡里的浪博恩庄园。由于没有男性继承人，班纳特先生的家产将由远亲柯林斯先生继承。所以班纳特太太整天操心着为五个女儿——简、伊丽莎白、玛丽、基蒂和莉迪亚——物色称心如意的丈夫。当有钱的单身汉查尔斯·宾利先生从城里搬到附近的尼日斐庄园时，班纳特太太发现大女儿的机会来了。

宾利先生在舞会上遇到了简，并对她一见钟情。他的朋友达西先生却对伊丽莎白傲慢无礼。在接下来的几次聚会中，简和宾利对彼此越来越有好感，达西也发现自己已经被伊丽莎白的美丽和智慧所吸引。但伊丽莎白仍然对达西抱有偏见，认为他是一个傲慢势利的人。当一位让她颇有好感的青年军官威克汉姆对达西横加指责时，伊丽莎白对达西的偏见越来越深。在之后不久的一场尼日斐庄园的舞会上，达西先生听到班纳特太太宣称简和宾利先生将很快举行婚礼，这让他很不满。

之后，宾利先生突然不辞而别，简听说宾利将迎娶达西的妹妹后非常伤心。伊丽莎白断定是达西从中作梗，促使宾利和简分开。伊丽莎白与达西碰面后证实的确是达西劝说宾利放弃了简，她非常生气。此时的达西对她尽述衷肠，并向她求婚，伊丽莎白当场拒绝，并指责他破坏了简的婚姻，还坑害过威克汉姆。此后达西给伊丽莎白写了一封信，解释道，他阻拦宾利是因为他认为简并没有真正爱上宾利，威克汉姆之名则根本是个骗子加无赖。伊丽莎白开始意识到自己可能错怪了达西，她的拒绝也似乎过于鲁莽。

第二年，伊丽莎白随舅父母出游时经过达西的庄园彭伯里，达西突然出现并将伊丽莎白介绍给自己的妹妹。这时宾利也出现了，他表明自己依然爱着简。一封简的家书中断了伊丽莎白的旅行，简在信中说莉迪亚随威克汉姆私奔了。班纳特夫妇害怕丑闻会毁掉女儿们的未来，赶到伦敦寻找莉迪亚。达西找到了这对出逃的小情侣，并以替威克汉姆还清大笔欠款来换取两人完婚。达西挽回了班纳特家的声誉。伊丽莎白发现是达西伸出援手后，为他的善良深深感动。

宾利和达西回到尼日斐庄园，宾利向简求婚，这让简喜出望外。达西也再次向伊丽莎白求婚，这一次伊丽莎白欣然接受，并告诉达西，是偏见令她蒙蔽了自己的双眼。达西也承认是自己的傲慢让他看起来粗鲁无礼。

《傲慢与偏见》主题

《傲慢与偏见》围绕傲慢和偏见进行思考，描述了这些道德品质对爱情、家庭、婚姻和社会的影响。在故事中，每个人物都有某种程度的傲慢和偏见。奥斯丁细细分析了每个角色傲慢和偏见的程度，将每个人进行对比，揭示其程度差异对爱情、家庭和婚姻的不同影响。故事的最后，几位主要人物已经成长为正确道德品质的代表，他们的爱情、家庭和婚姻都从中获益。

骄傲

达西：故事开头，达西看起来对自己的社会地位颇为骄傲，他看不起别人，尤其是班纳特一家，他内敛的个性也使他看起来更加冷漠。

伊丽莎白：伊丽莎白的本性并没有达西那样骄傲，但当她在第一次舞会上察觉到达西的轻视后，自尊心受到伤害，所以她用骄傲武装自己，保护家人。

凯瑟琳夫人：凯瑟琳夫人的本性傲慢无比，在她眼中别人理应对她赞扬和顺从。

柯林斯：柯林斯的傲慢取决于与他交谈的对象。当他与自认为社会地位低于他的人相处时，他喜欢站在道德高处标榜自己。而与地位高于他的人相处时，他又会变得谦逊有礼，一丝傲慢也没有。

偏见

达西：在根本不了解班纳特一家，或其他任何人的情况下就草率地对人抱有偏见，甚至没想过要费心去了解这些人。

伊丽莎白：伊丽莎白并不是天生对人有偏见，只是当察觉到达西的无礼后，她放任自己的偏见，并愿意相信一切对达西不好的传言，来印证和加深自己对他的坏印象（这一点尤其体现在威克汉姆一事中）。

班纳特太太：当班纳特太太发现了达西在舞会上的举动后，开始对达西有着明显的偏见。班纳特太太丝毫没有在行为上掩饰这一点，甚至当众侮辱达西。而当达西向伊丽莎白求婚时，她的偏见也不翼而飞，这也体现出她个性的浅薄。

凯瑟琳夫人：凯瑟琳夫人对所有社会地位低于她的人抱有偏见，（如她自己所言）除非这些人遵守她的规则。所以她愿意忍受柯林斯，但鄙视伊丽莎白。

宾利姐妹：赫斯特太太和宾利小姐对简和伊丽莎白抱有偏见，这主要是出于私利。她们不喜欢简是因为觉得简配不上自己的哥哥；而不喜欢伊丽莎白则是因为达西喜欢伊丽莎白，而宾利小姐却想嫁给达西。

12.2.5　查尔斯·狄更斯和《双城记》

查尔斯·狄更斯（1812—1870）是英国作家、社会批评家，英国批判现实主义最伟大的代表。他创造了诸多世界著名的小说人物，被誉为维多利亚时代最伟大的小说家。在他的时代，他的作品畅销量是前所未有的，到了 20 世纪，评论家和学者们都奉他为文学天才。他的长、短篇小说一直受到读者的欢迎。

狄更斯出生于英国朴茨茅斯的波特西地区，孩童时他曾经历了许多痛苦和波折。在他十岁时，父亲因欠债入狱，他也辍学进入当地的皮鞋油作坊做童工，每天工作长达 10 小时。这段艰苦、危险的工作经历给狄更斯留下了永久的伤痕，所以，在后来他的作品中常常会反映维多利亚时代英国社会的黑暗不公。

狄更斯虽然没有接受过系统教育，但他独自花了大量的时间阅读，尤其是 18 世纪的小说。狄更斯一生写了 15 部长篇小说、5 部中长篇小说，以及数百篇短篇小说和文章。在他笔下，人物性格常常被刻画得丰富多样，且常常出现性格怪异的人物，他通过自己记忆中形形色色的人物原型，加上一些幻想和夸张的手法，将人物描绘得惟妙惟肖，给读者留下了深刻的印象。至今他的《圣诞颂歌》仍然很受欢迎，不断被改编成各种艺术形式展现出来。他的小说《雾都孤儿》和《远大前程》反映了维多利亚早期的伦敦风貌。《双城记》的故事发生在伦敦和巴黎，这是狄更斯最著名的历史小说。《大卫·科波菲尔》给人幽默、宽容和趣味，让人感觉世界充满希望和阳光，据说这是狄更斯最喜欢的一部作品。

狄更斯被奉为他那个时代的文学巨人。从列夫·托尔斯泰到乔治·奥威尔和G. K. 切斯特顿，后来的许多作家对狄更斯的创作才华赞誉有加，他的写实风格、喜剧手法、散文风格以及独特的个性特征和对社会的批判都让人称道。当然狄更斯也收到一些负面评价，奥斯卡·王尔德、亨利·詹姆斯和弗吉尼亚·伍尔芙也批评过他的小说结构松散，缺乏心理深度。

《双城记》

1775年，伦敦台尔森银行的罗瑞先生得知失踪了18年的朋友马奈特医生还活着的消息，于是带着马奈特的女儿露西赶去巴黎。原来马奈特医生当年被误判在巴士底监狱终身监禁，他获释后被旧日的仆人，巴黎一家酒店的老板德法尔热先生收留。这时马奈特医生已经非常苍老，不仅失忆而且还精神失常。露西把父亲接回伦敦悉心照料，希望父亲恢复健康和神志。

几年过去，露西嫁给了查尔斯·达尔奈。达尔奈曾经是一名法国贵族，但现在放弃继承权，隐姓埋名，在伦敦当了一名教师。他的叔叔就是残忍无情、臭名昭著的马奎斯·厄弗里蒙得侯爵。

1789年，法国大革命爆发，巴黎人民攻占巴士底狱。这时远在伦敦的达尔奈已经与露西成婚11年并育有一女。在得知以前的仆人有难后，达尔奈秘密赶回巴黎却被捕入狱。在得知消息后露西和父亲赶往巴黎去营救达尔奈。马奈特医生因为曾经受过迫害而备受尊重，他证明女婿无罪，并将达尔奈救出。可是达尔奈很快又被逮捕并判死刑。原来达尔奈的叔叔曾经残忍地杀害了德法尔热太太的姐姐和弟弟，德法尔热太太出于对厄弗里蒙得家族的痛恨，促使达尔奈被判刑。此时不仅无法拯救达尔奈，就连露西和她的女儿也很危险，因为包括德法尔热夫妇在内的革命主力想要消灭与贵族有牵连的每一个人。

这时，与达尔奈面貌相似的悉尼·卡顿混进监狱顶替了达尔奈。达尔奈一家逃回英国时，卡顿代替他被判决。为了心爱的露西，卡顿履行了他为爱人牺牲一切的承诺，虽然牺牲了自己，但卡顿为自己的行为感到自豪，他知道他将永远活在达尔奈一家人心中。

《双城记》主题

拯救　小说的主题是拯救，让人从看似无法挽回的死局中逃离。马奈特医生原本被判长期监禁，注定将悄然死去，但他最终被拯救出狱，在女儿露西的关爱与悉心照料下恢复健康。达尔奈因为卡顿的怜悯之心两次被救。这些被挽回的生命成为故事情节中不可缺少的部分，它们使整个故事成为一体。

战争的残酷　小说的次主题是法国大革命所反映出来的战争的残酷。尽管法国的暴乱完全可以理解，而且法国大革命因其所宣扬的“自由、平等、博爱”口号而受到肯定，但狄更斯对此是持一种很消极的态度。在《双城记》中狄更斯所描绘的革命者们用压迫和杀戮去满足自己自私嗜血的目的，在他看来，无论是贵族还是平民，掌权的一方都会充分行使特权。换言之，在狄更斯眼中，正如暴政会导致革命，革命也会走向暴政。要想打破这种局面唯有通过公正和宽容。

12.2.6　托马斯·哈代和《无名的裘德》

托马斯·哈代（1840—1928）是英国小说家和诗人，作为一名维多利亚时代的现实主义作家，哈代延续了乔治·艾略特的风格，他的小说和诗歌也深受浪漫主义风格的影响，其中尤以华兹华斯为甚。哈代最著名的小说当属《还乡》（1874）、《德伯家的苔丝》（1891）以及《无名的裘德》（1896）。

哈代的大部分时光是在多塞特郡的乡村度过的，他的小说也多以此为背景。因为学过建筑，哈代在伦敦花了 5 年时间从事建筑业，19 世纪 70 年代成为知名小说家。此后 20 年中，哈代出版了多本畅销小说，但《德伯家的苔丝》和《无名的裘德》出版后被指有违道德且过于悲观而受到尖锐的批评。这些争议也让人们更加关注他的作品，他的小说很快在欧洲和北美流传起来。然而哈代却放弃了写小说，开始转向戏剧和诗歌创作。哈代一生中虽然创作了大量诗歌，在他有生之年却没有获得比较大的反响。反而在 20 世纪 50 年代被人们重新发现，并对 20 世纪 50—60 年代的运动诗人产生了极大的影响，其中包括菲利普·拉金。

哈代的梦想是成为一名诗人，他以敏锐的观察力和细致的感悟力在情感上与环境融为一体，同时他务实的建筑师职业，以及在外从事修造工程的经历又让他得以拿起笔来为 20 世纪的文学做出杰出贡献。他的作品影响了包括伍尔夫和劳伦斯在内的许多作家，许多作品也在被广泛阅读，其中一些被改编为舞台剧或被搬上银幕。

《无名的裘德》

裘德一直以来的梦想就是能在基督寺上大学，但身为一名孤儿，从小由工人阶级的婶婶养大，他只能做一名石匠。为了有一天能上大学，裘德自年少时就开始在业余时间自学古希腊文和拉丁文。但梦想还没来得及实现，单纯的裘德就被粗俗肤浅的阿拉贝娜引诱，最终陷入假怀孕的骗局而与她结婚。他们的婚姻是一场悲剧，两人最终和平分手。阿拉贝娜移居澳大利亚，并在那里与人结婚。

阿拉贝娜离开后，裘德搬到基督寺，一边做石匠维持生计，一边自学。在那里，他遇到并爱上了具有独立人格和思想的表妹苏。为了帮助苏留在基督寺，裘德介绍她与镇上的小学教师菲洛特桑共事，最后却发现这两人订了婚。两人结婚后，苏开始后悔，很快便离开菲洛特桑，与裘德一起生活。尽管裘德和苏都已离婚，但苏不愿再婚。此时阿拉贝娜告诉裘德他们俩还有一个儿子在澳大利亚，裘德接纳了孩子，与苏一起抚养这个孩子，以及他们自己的两个孩子。

裘德和苏未婚同居为社会所不容。裘德的雇主不齿他这种不当行为而解雇了他，一家人过着居无定所的生活，从威塞克斯的一个城镇搬到另一个城镇，寻找工作和住房。最后他们决定回到基督寺。裘德的儿子认为全家人的困境都来自三个孩子的拖累，于是在到达基督寺的当天早晨吊死了苏的两个孩子，自己也上吊自杀。

苏认为这一切都是上帝在惩罚她与裘德的不当关系，于是再次离开裘德，回到菲洛特桑身边。此时的裘德已经悲伤到绝望。阿拉贝娜用酒精再次骗得裘德与她结婚。在寒冷的一天最后一次不顾一切地探望过苏后，裘德大病一场，不久便离开人世。

《无名的裘德》主题及分析

《无名的裘德》讲述了乡村石匠裘德的一生，以及他对表妹苏的爱情。裘德从一开始就认为自己的家族像被诅咒了一样，每个人都无法逃脱婚姻的不幸。他和苏都是这个家族的一员，他们的爱情只会更不幸。这部小说虽然是讲述爱情，但婚姻制度才是它的主题。裘德和苏各自与他人结婚，却逃脱不了彼此的牵绊，而他们在一起也注定是一场悲剧，这不仅源于家族的诅咒，更是因为他们的关系无法容于当时的社会。

整本书的高潮当属裘德的儿子杀人又自杀的一幕，之前的种种磨难逐渐加剧，再加上这重重一击。而这一击让他们再无所盼，只能各自回到原来不幸的婚姻，余生为年轻时犯下的错误而自我禁锢。他们陷入了一个又一个苦痛的恶性循环，无法挣脱。他们对世俗的蔑视和挑战为社会所不容，最后只能沦为牺牲品。裘德的儿子对这些磨难有着自己的理解，他想以自认为正确的方式挽救父母和弟妹，这些孩子都是牺牲品，他们的死是社会的不容所造成的，也是苏对离婚的羞耻感所造成的。

随着故事情节的发展，裘德上不上得了大学已经变得无足轻重，只是他对基督寺的执念一直不曾消失。基督寺是裘德与苏最初相遇的地方，也是裘德度过余生并走向死亡的地方，而且也是整本书悲剧的所在。对于裘德、苏，甚至他们一家来说，基督寺就是裘德一生向往，却又无法企及、充满危险的地方。

* * * * *

第 13 章　大众传媒

英国大众传媒的作用有以下几个方面：为大众了解政治和社会事件提供信息，为人们了解天气情况提供平台，为大众提供一个可以通过写信或来电方式表达意见或寻求咨询的互动渠道。此外，大众媒体还可以进行广告宣传，从事娱乐和教育活动，从而形成自身的民族文化。

13.1　出版业（报纸和杂志）

英国的报纸文化

英国是当代报业的发祥地。从 18 世纪末到 19 世纪初，英国的工业革命使其成为世界领先的经济强国，越来越多的人有机会阅读更多的报纸。大多数英国人习惯把阅读报纸作为一天的开始，从全国性报纸到地方性报纸，从日报到周报，从晨报到晚报，他们的阅读范围非常广泛。不同的读报习惯也反映了英国读者的不同阶层和教育背景。中产阶级是读报的最大群体，下层阶级在整个读者群体中也占有很大的比例。不同社会阶层的人会根据个人的喜好来购买报纸。因此，英国的报纸普及率排名世界第三，仅次于瑞典和日本。

起初，英国议会候选人想表达他们观点时，必须通过长时间地演讲和分发小册子来向选民宣传。后来，报纸成为向英国选民提供政治信息的一个重要途径。所以，不仅政客们非常重视报纸的影响力，英国的商人们也开始把产品信息和广告投放在报纸上，当然，他们必须遵守《广告法》。在英国，报纸不受政府的管制，也不用政府审查，它们可以出版发行自己想刊登的内容。

全国性报纸和地方报纸的区别

全国范围内发行的报纸被称为全国性报纸。在英国，主要有三类国家级报纸，分别为严肃报纸、大众报纸及中间市场类报纸，他们的风格和内容有所差异。

英国有十家全国性日报报道全国的重要新闻，其中近一半属于严肃报纸或大报（大张报纸）。严肃报纸是全国发行的一种报纸，以其内容的严肃性区别于其他报纸。严肃报纸中反映政治和社会重要事件的文章往往用词朴素、内容深刻，并且新闻的覆盖面也更加的宽广。此外，严肃报纸会对有深度的文化内容发表评论，或是进行文化特写，其受众大多为受过良好教育的中产阶级。在英国，根据报纸的发行频率，主要分为日报和星期日报。日报每天发行，而星期日报只在周日发行。星期日报通常刊载日报的一部分内容，在厚度和重量方面与日报不同，并且包含日报编辑所没有的特别部分。另外，广告类型和数量方面也各不相同。在英国的严肃报纸中，有 6 家日报和 4 家星期日报。根据其创建时间，日报分别为：《泰晤士报》（创办于 1785 年），《卫报》（创办于 1821 年），《每日电讯报》（创办于 1855 年），《金融时报》（创办于 1888 年），《独立日报》（创办于 1986 年）和《i 报》（创办于 2010 年）；严肃星期日报纸分别为《观察者》（创办于 1791 年），《星期日时报》（创办于 1822 年），《独立星期日报》（创办于 1990 年）和《星期日电讯报》（创办于 1961 年)。

不同于严肃报纸的严肃性，英国的大众报纸（小报）更侧重于报道名人的丑闻以及八卦新闻。他们还发布政治、体育和娱乐等方面的亮点新闻。这种报纸的篇幅较小，并配有彩色照片和醒目的标题。报纸上的文章多为易读的短篇小故事，给读者呈现的更多是观点，而不是事实。根据其创建时间，主要有四家大众日报：《每日镜报》(创办于 1903 年)、《晨星》(创办于 1930 年)、《太阳日报》(创办于 1964 年）和《每日星报》（创办于 1978 年)。此外还有四个星期日报：《星期日报》(创办于 1881 年)、《星期日镜报》(创办于 1915 年)、《每日星报星期日刊》(创办于 2002 年）和《太阳星期日报》(创办于 2012 年)。

中间市场类报纸面向中间市场，英国主要有四家中间市场类小报：《每日邮报》(创办于 1896 年)、《每日快报》(创办于 1900 年)、《星期日快报》(创办于 1918 年)，以及《星期日邮报》(创办于 1982 年)。

地方性报纸经常在地方区域内发行，他们主要涉及本地新闻及广告。分为晨报、晚报、星期日报和日报。在英国，包括英格兰、北爱尔兰、苏格兰和威尔士在内，有很多地方性报纸。比较著名的是：《格拉斯哥先驱报》、《晚间旗报》和《晚间新闻报》。

英国报纸及杂志介绍

报纸类：

《泰晤士报》

《泰晤士报》是英国全国性日报，1785 年创建时命名为《每日环球记录报》，后在 1788 年 1 月改名为《泰晤士报》，它的姊妹报为《星期日时报》，由新闻国际子公司发行，新闻集团老板鲁伯特·默克多拥有该报。

《金融时报》

《金融时报》是以国际商业为主的英文报纸，使用浅橙色宽幅纸张印刷。创建于 1888 年，注重商业及金融新闻报道。

《卫报》

《卫报》为英国全国性日报，创建于 1821 年，属于卫报传媒集团所有。

《每日电讯》

《每日电讯》为每日晨报，创建于 1855 年，在全英国及全世界范围发行。

杂志类：

《经济学家》

创建于 1843 年，为国际新闻及商业出版类周刊，内容涉及当今世界时事、商业、金融、科技、文化、社会、媒体及艺术等方面，以报道准确、注重新闻事实、分析客观理性著称。

《旁观者》

《旁观者》是保守派周刊，创建于1828年，是英国全国性周刊中历史最悠久的杂志。

《新政治家》

《新政治家》是政治文化类杂志周刊，1913年2月在伦敦发行。主要发表政治类、文学类评论。

13.2　电视与广播

英国广播业的背景

当谈到大众媒体在英国的普及程度时，在英国人心中，电视排在首位，紧随其后的是报纸和广播。广播媒体是英国人日常生活的重要组成部分。据统计，全国大约有97%的家庭拥有一台电视机和一台收音机，接收电台的电波和信号，欣赏自己想看或想听的节目。约有70%的英国人每天都会听收音机。英国人每天大约会花3.5个小时观看电视，许多人会通过报纸了解电视节目的播放情况和具体节目的信息，他们在谈话时最常见的话题也是电视节目。

起初，英国广播业是一项公共服务，成立于1926年的英国国家广播公司（通常被称为英国广播公司，即BBC）是提供这一服务的唯一机构。那时，英国广播公司是英国最大的广播媒体，也是世界上最大的广播媒体之一。1955年之后，私人广播公司获准开始为大众提供电视和广播服务。现在能向公众提供服务的私营广播机构有独立电视网络有限公司、4频道电视公司、5频道电视公司和英国天空广播集团。

所有的广播公司必须遵循广播业的相关规定和基本原则。说到广播业的规定，独立电视委员会（ITC）和广播标准委员会是英国两个重要的管理机构。从1991年1月28日到2003年12月1日，是由独立电视委员会为商业电视服务提供许可和管制，该委员会是依据1990年的《广播法》而成立的（1990年通过的广播法案旨在确保广播业规则的标准性和新闻报道的准确性，以及平衡有争议的内容，鼓励电视和广播业的竞争）。广播标准委员会是监管广播业标准性和公平性的法定机构，这是英国广播业中唯一一个全面监管地面和卫星通讯的所有电视和广播的机构，包括监管文本、电缆和数字服务。1996年颁布的《广播法》规定它有3个主要任务：制定有关标准和公平性的行为准则；受理并处理投诉；监管、调查和公布广播业中的标准和公平性问题。广播标准委员会成立于1997年，旨在确定标准、监管暴力及色情内容，并处理业内投诉问题。至于广播业的基本原则，公共广播应该集娱乐性、信息化和教育性于一体，电视上不得播出抱有政治偏见，或含暴力和色情的内容。

英国广播公司（BBC）简介及主要频道介绍

BBC（英国广播公司）成立于1926年，是英国的主要公共广播服务机构。1936年，BBC转变为电视台，一直是世界上广受赞誉的媒体之一。在1955年英国独立电视台成立之前，BBC是英国唯一的电台和电视台，它还经营图书出版、报纸、英语教学、交响乐团和互联网新闻服务等业务。

BBC有BBC1台和BBC2台两个电视频道，以及一些区域性电台。它用英语及其他43种语言向全球播出节目。BBC1台（于1936年建立）负责播放一些观众喜爱的节目，BBC2台播放少数人及专业人士感兴趣的节目，这两个台都没有商业广告。独立电视台（1955年起称为3频道）播放的节目中约33%为资讯类节目，66%为轻娱乐节目。4频道（1982年建立）播放的节目中15%为教育类节目，注重鼓励创新与实验。5频道（于1997年建立）是一个综合娱乐频道，播放国内外的娱乐节目。

频道的资金渠道与电视收看许可证

BBC1台和BBC2台的资金来源包括观众缴纳的电视收看许可费和一些节目的播出费。因此，它们并不依赖于商业广告收入。BBC全球新闻服务电视频道通过广告盈利提供资金，这个台24小时报道世界新闻、消息和分析报道。独立电视台、4频道和5频道都是盈利性频道，通过商业广告收入来维持。

在英国，想要观看电视直播的家庭每年需要购买电视牌照（即电视收看许可证），黑白电视机的费用为50英镑，彩色电视机费用为145英镑。

流行节目和英国人喜欢看的电视节目

观众最喜爱的节目有《东区人》和《加冕街》。《东区人》是一部在BBC 1台播放的肥皂剧。它讲述了生活在伦敦东区艾伯特广场的几个工人家庭的故事，大部分故事情节发生在当地一家名为“维多利亚女王”的酒吧附近。整部剧的剧情节奏快，比另一电视剧《加冕街》更富戏剧性。

英国独立电视台播出的《加冕街》是全球电视史上播出时间最久的晚间电视剧，讲述了英格兰北部小镇里，居住在加冕街上的一群工人们的生活。作为一部典型的肥皂剧，《加冕街》剧情生动，讲述了人们生活中的悲喜。

英国还有一些节目也颇受观众的欢迎，如《流行偶像》（原来的“美国偶像”）、《老大哥》和《幸存者》等真人秀节目，以及电视游戏节目《智者为王》等。

广播电台和最受欢迎的电台

至于广播服务，英国一共有 5 个 BBC 广播电台、3 个独立的国家广播台和大约 200 个独立的地方广播台。独立电台从无线电管理局获得许可证。英国最受欢迎的广播电台有克莱尔调频广播、安娜丽维亚调频、LIVE 95、威尔士国际广播电台、帝国学院广播、首都调频广播以及 BBC 2 台。

References

Books

1. 常俊跃，夏洋．英国历史文化［M］．北京：北京大学出版社，2010.
2. 董晓波．英国历史文化概况［M］．北京：对外经济贸易大学出版社，2012.
3. 郭群英．英国文学新编［M］．北京：外语教学与研究出版社，2011.
4. 刘芬．英国文学地图［M］．武汉：武汉大学出版社，2010.
5. 王俊生，刘沛富．最新英美概况［M］．北京：外语教学与研究出版社，2012.
6. 王泉．每天读点世界文化——这里是英国［M］．北京：中国水利水电出版社，2013.
7. 王守仁．英国文学选读［M］．北京：高等教育出版社，2004.
8. 张伯香．英国文学教程学习指南［M］．武汉：武汉大学出版社，2006.
9. 赵红英．英国文学简史学习指南［M］．北京：中国传媒大学出版社，2006.
10. 郑春荣．英国社会保障制度［M］．上海：上海人民出版社，2011.
11. Clemen Gina D B. *Great English Monarchs and their Times*.［M］. Hong Kong：The Commercial Press，2003.
12. Evans E. *British History*：*An Illustrated Guide*［M］. London：Star Fire Publishing Ltd. 2007.
13. Kearney Hugh. *The British Isles*：*A History of Four Nations*［M］. Cambridge：Cambridge University Press，2006.
14. McCaughrean Geraldine. *Britannia*：*100 Great Stories from British History*［M］. London：Orion Children，2004.
15. Pimlott Ben. *The Queen*：*Elizabeth II and the Monarchy*［M］. London：HarperCollins. 2001.
16. Rebecca Fraser. *A People's History of Britain*.［M］. London：Pimlica，2004.
17. Somerset Anne. *Elizabeth I*.（*1st Anchor Books ed.*）［M］. London：Anchor Books，2003.

Websites

1. http：//www. bbc. co. uk/history/british/normans/

2. http: //www. biographyonline. net/people/famous/english. html
3. http: //www. britainexpress. com/History/index. htm
4. http: //www. british-history. ac. uk/
5. https: //www. churchofengland. org/about-us/history/detailed-history. aspx
6. http: //www. englishmonarchs. co. uk/index. htm
7. http: //www. guardian. co. uk/politics/2003/oct/21/uk. freedomofinformation
8. http: //www. geography. about. com/od/unitedkingdommaps/a/united-kingdom-geography-overview. htm
9. http: //www. royal. gov. uk/
10. http: //www. thinkinghistory. co. uk/Index. html
11. http: //www. touropia. com/tourist-attractions-in-england/
12. http: //www. visitbritain. com/en/Destinations-and-Maps/Countries/England. html
13. http: //www. who2. com/
14. http: //www. woodlands-junior. kent. sch. uk/customs/behaviour. html